I0213797

Kentucky's Last Cavalier

Courtesy Filson Historical Society

General William Preston, portrait by H. Niemeier.

Kentucky's Last Cavalier
General William Preston, 1816-1887

Peter J. Sehlinger

The Kentucky Historical Society

Distributed for the Kentucky Historical Society by the
University Press of Kentucky

Sales office: 663 South Limestone, Lexington, KY 40508

Copyright © 2004

Library of Congress Cataloging-in-Publication Data

Sehlinger, Peter J.
    Kentucky's last cavalier : General William Preston, 1816-1887 / Peter
J. Sehlinger.
        p. cm.
Includes bibliographical references (p.) and index.
    ISBN 0-916968-33-2 (hardback : alk. paper)
    1. Preston, William, 1816-1887. 2. Generals—Confederate States of
America—Biography. 3. Confederate States of America. Army—Biography.
4. Kentucky—History—1792-1865. I. Title.
    E467.1.P86S44 2004
    973.7'3'092—dc21

                                                             2003022252

To

Sabine Jessner

Historian, Researcher, and My Beloved Wife

Contents

Foreword

Historians of the American experience, early on, focused their attentions chiefly on the most prominent leaders, chiefly male, usually white. More recent generations have stressed the need for history "from the bottom up," a chronicle that stresses the life histories of everyday people, the bulk of the population. Those stories bring the spotlight on the once-forgotten figures of that earlier writing, specifically women and people of color. While both approaches have value, both also threaten to overlook key elements of the story. The middle class may not receive deserved attention, nor might those who led but never achieved the level of prominence of major leaders. One of those in that last category was William Preston.

Preston probably never would have admitted that he had not reached the pinnacles of power. With much justification, he considered himself one of the elite, and his background certainly showed that. From his birth in 1816, he came into wealth as part of the landed gentry of Kentucky. The considerable social standing he achieved simply by being a member of the very well-connected Preston family, he solidified through his 1840 marriage to his cousin, Margaret Preston Wickliffe. Nor was William Preston an aristocrat of limited background and learning. He went north for schooling at Yale and then Harvard and throughout his life traveled widely—to Canada and the Caribbean in the Western Hemisphere and to Europe in the Old World. The tall, handsome, well-read attorney who entered public life seemed a man of high promise, likely to rise. And rise he did, though perhaps never to the heights he expected or wanted. That trek toward greatness forms the core of the Preston story, one that explains much about those who led the nation before and during the Civil War. Preston's life tells us more than just the experiences of one individual, if we but listen. It reveals much about his entire generation and his world.

Historian Peter Sehlinger portrays Preston as "Kentucky's Last Cavalier." Whether the last or not, Preston certainly represented that part of southern society and the elements that composed it—family and honor, gender and economics, public service and noblesse oblige, militarism and war, slavery and race.

Many of Preston's successes resulted from family ties. To recount only some of the connections seems almost numbing in the genea-logical aspect of the listings, but those connections not only formed a web of allies, but also a supportive network of caring members. Preston, for example, had an uncle who served as governor of Vir-ginia, another who represented the Old Dominion in Congress, and an aunt who had married a Missouri governor. Preston called as cousin presidential candidate John C. Breckinridge, the wife of Mis-souri senator Thomas Hart Benton, South Carolina senator William Campbell Preston, and another Virginia chief executive. Through marriage, Preston became a brother-in-law to later Confederate gen-eral Albert Sidney Johnston and son-in-law to the largest slaveholder in the state. His wife's uncle had been a Kentucky governor and congressman; his own grandfather had served as congressman from the Mother State. While these connections could, overall, cause con-cerns and problems, family generally made a great difference in his life, and he honored those ties of hearth and home.

Preston's career and family letters provide detailed information about gender roles in an upper-class antebellum southern family. A subject of continued study and much discussion, the place of women in that society becomes clearer through the Preston family example. Wife Margaret Preston brought considerable wealth into the mar-riage and showed her desire to safeguard that from a husband not always wise in such matters. She also showed her own desire for her husband to achieve and sought to share in that acclaim. At the same time, William Preston's resistance to his wife on economic matters reveals much, as does, at the same time, his desire to be worthy of her hopes and bring honor to her name. Later marital difficulties indicate the hidden pressures in that Old South union, as it operated in a different postwar atmosphere.

A crucial element of Cavalier leadership focused on public ser-vice. Noblesse oblige required that, and Preston eagerly took up the banner. It should be noted that such an attitude, such a way of life even, did influence and did motivate toward worthy effort. But other parts also mixed with that and came into play as well, including a personal ambition that could be separate from those ideals. Preston's firm belief in leadership by the best (male) people, as part of a natu-ral aristocracy, contrasted with an America that increasingly stressed the worth of the individual. Yet his tenets drew him to seek to influ-ence public life and make it—as he saw it—better. His time as delegate to a state constitutional convention, as legislator, and as congressman did not take huge parts of his life. Yet these experiences confirmed to him that he, indeed, was the peer of presidents and could achieve more. Such beliefs brought his acceptance of posts as minister to Spain and, under the Confederacy, to Mexico. Sehlinger has delved deeply into foreign archives to find out more about that part of Preston's life, and to good effect. After all, Preston in Spain tried to achieve the annexation of Cuba, dealt with the lingering *Amistad* claims, and voiced a key warning regarding the Monroe Doctrine. In his Mexican assignment, he tried to ally that country to the South. Great success did not result in either situation, but Preston served well in difficult times.

His life also displayed the martial spirit so prevalent in the South. In the Mexican-American conflict, he saw little bloodshed but did learn of a foreign culture and made important contacts. During the Civil War the eventual General Preston fought at Shiloh, Stones River, Chickamauga, and other places from 1861 until 1864, when he went on his foreign mission. To the end, he defended the Confederate course of action and was among the last to surrender. Formally, he was among the Last Rebels.

Part of Preston's deep support for the southern cause resulted from his views on slavery and race. A large slave owner himself (and a millionaire several times over at present-day levels), he represented the paradoxes of his region. On a one-on-one basis, he could be kind—in a way—to his bondsmen and servants; yet, in a general sense he could never recognize the humanity of the enslaved. Quite simply, he believed whites the superior, "pure" race and strongly defended the right to hold slaves as property. Even war's end and the demise of the "Peculiar Institution" could not remove his moral blinders—which he wore with millions of his race and time.

For the Prestons, the end of the war reduced their wealth but did not eliminate it. They continued to live in luxury, even if often in debt to keep that lifestyle. In that way, William Preston tried to keep parts of the Old Order in the postwar world. A contemporary of his, Kentucky novelist James Lane Allen, wrote of a character named Colonel Romulus Fields, who could never recover from the war: "The very basic virtues on which had rested his once spacious and stately character were now but the mouldy corner-stones of a crumbling ruin"; he had no place in the present, and "his mind turned from the cracked and smokey [*sic*] mirror of the times and dwelt fondly upon the scenes of the past."

Preston did not go as far as the fictional Colonel Fields, for he tried to reconcile his Cavalier ideas and ideals with those of the emerging nation. In one sense, the family's ties both to the commercial, New South city of Louisville and to the more traditional town of Lexington symbolized that attempt. But Preston never could make the same mark on society as before the war and lived until his 1887 death in the frustration of a faded glory and of a life that never met many of his high expectations.

His is a case study of a part of the leadership generation of the South, one that goes below the surface to reveal much about beliefs on matters of family, gender, race, and more. Like many human stories, it is one of successes and failures, of vision and narrowness, of happiness and sorrow. It is a story that needs to be told.

James C. Klotter
Kentucky State Historian
and Professor of History at
Georgetown College

Acknowledgments

This volume traces its genesis to an article on William Preston I contributed more than twenty years ago to a *Festschrift* in honor of Professor Holman Hamilton of the University of Kentucky. My interest in Preston led to more and more research, until I decided to write this biography. The quest for sources has taken me to five countries, and en route many archivists, librarians, and historians have offered their assistance.

Historians and archivists in Kentucky, Louisiana, and Spain helped me during my first years of research. I owe a special debt of gratitude to Charles C. Hay, then archivist at Eastern Kentucky University, Richmond, who generously shared his Preston sources with me. I also wish to thank James R. Bentley, former director of the Filson Club (now Filson Historical Society), Louisville, who guided me through the several relevant collections there. Wilbur E. Meneray, manuscripts librarian at the Howard-Tilton Library of Tulane University in New Orleans, and María José Lazano Rincón at the archive of the Ministry of Foreign Affairs in Madrid also were of great assistance.

Many others have aided me during the past decade. Randolph Hollingsworth, the author of a fine dissertation on Margaret Wickliffe Preston, William's wife, shared both her enthusiasm for and knowledge of the Preston family with me, as well as suggesting additional sources. William J. Marshall, director of the archives at the Margaret I. King Library of the University of Kentucky, and his able assistants, James D. Birchfield, Frank Stanger, and Claire McCann, found documents and offered valuable counsel during visits to Lexington. James J. Holmberg and Craig M. Heuser in special collections at the Filson Historical Society and Conrad F. Weitzel at the Ohio Historical Society, Columbus, identified important letters. Frances Keller Barr, longtime historiographer for the Diocese of Lexington, and William C. Simpson at the Preston Masonic Lodge # 281 in Louisville provided me with useful materials. At the Shiloh National Military Park in Tennessee, George A. Reaves carefully explained the complex maneuvers of this Civil War battle to me.

Several archivists abroad assisted me in locating documents on the Confederacy's relations with Mexico. The archivist at the Mexican Embassy in Paris, Ricardo Cámara, and Elisabeth Springer and Christiane Thomas of the Haus-, Hof-, und Staatsarchiv in Vienna

Acknowledgments

showed me collections that had not been consulted for decades. In Mexico City José María Muría, director of the Archivo Diplomático Histórico, and Juan Manuel Herrera Huerta at the Archivo General de la Nación pointed out several sources that allowed me to unravel some of the mysteries of Civil War diplomacy.

Historian friends have given generously of their time to improve my manuscript. My colleagues at Indiana University, Indianapolis, emeritus professors Ralph D. Gray and Bernard Friedman, Robert E. May of Purdue University, and Alan Nolan of Indianapolis read chapters of the work and offered insightful comments. Likewise, I am indebted to three historians who read the entire text and made corrections and suggestions: Thomas H. Appleton Jr., professor of history at Eastern Kentucky University, Richmond; Nelson L. Dawson, former publications editor at the Filson Historical Society, now an editor at the Kentucky Historical Society; and James C. Klotter, state historian of Kentucky and professor of history at Georgetown College.

In preparing the manuscript for publication, I have had the good fortune of working with several competent and helpful members at the Kentucky Historical Society. For the illustrations, I am indebted to photographer James Nathan Pritchard and to Mary E. Winter, who located materials in the Society's archives. Daniel Bundy took care of the design and desktop publishing of the biography, while Gretchen M. Haney prepared the dust jacket. I particularly appreciate the dedication and editorial skills of Melba Porter Hay, division manager for Research and Publications at the Society. Her suggestions, corrections, and diligence brought many improvements to the manuscript.

My greatest debt of gratitude is owed to my wife Sabine Jessner, who also was my history colleague for two decades at Indiana University, Indianapolis. On research trips she helped me ferret out documents and took excellent notes, and in preparing the manuscript she assisted me in organizing my notes, checking many statements, editing my prose, and entering the text on the computer. Because of her appreciated labors and her encouragement while I was working on this biography, I am pleased to dedicate the work to her.

Introduction

"Of the five major-generals commissioned from Kentucky in the Confederate army, that one, next to John C. Breckinridge, who had achieved most distinction before the war, and who performed a greater share of gallant and intrepid service during the war, was Gen. William Preston," asserted General Basil W. Duke, a fellow Louisvillian, friend, and southern officer. "He will appear in the history of his day and time as one of its most attractive . . . figures."[1]

William Preston's accomplishments were impressive and are worthy of the telling. For three decades he defended the interests of the antebellum South, both in Kentucky and in Washington. Because of his close identification with regional causes, Preston's ultimate successes and failures as a public figure inextricably linked him to the fortunes of the South. He helped draft the commonwealth's proslavery constitution of 1850 and became a leader first among the Whigs and then the Democrats in state and national politics. As a delegate to the 1839 Whig National Convention in Harrisburg, Pennsylvania, the Kentuckian spoke in support of William Henry Harrison's presidential candidacy. In Congress Preston championed passage of the Kansas-Nebraska Act, which removed the barrier to the extension of slavery, played a role in James Buchanan's nomination for the presidency at the Democratic convention in 1856, and then campaigned for him in Pennsylvania, New York, Illinois, Indiana, and Kentucky. After the Civil War, Preston served as a state legislator and a delegate to the Democratic National Conventions of 1868, 1876, and 1880. Though a personal friend of New York governor Samuel J. Tilden, the Democratic presidential nominee, Preston influenced the compromise in 1877 that gave the presidency to Republican Rutherford B. Hayes.

As a diplomat, the Kentucky politician represented southern interests as President Buchanan's minister to Madrid and as the Confederacy's representative to the Court of Maximilian in Mexico City. Preston's attempts to purchase Cuba from Spain to create additional slave states were frustrated by vigorous Republican opposition in Congress on the eve of the Civil War and by Madrid's determination to retain its most important colonial possession. Despite this failure, Preston is remembered for his role in the evolution of the Monroe Doctrine into a tenet of foreign policy. At the start of the American Civil War, Spain annexed the Dominican Republic. Without waiting for instructions from Washington, Preston forcefully expressed his country's opposition to European recolonization in the Western Hemisphere. He based his warning to Spain's Ministry of Foreign Affairs squarely on President James Monroe's statement of 1823 and in so doing played a part in making this declaration a dogma of American foreign policy. Although constantly invoked at home, the Monroe Doctrine seldom had been alluded to by United States diplomats abroad. During the Civil War, Preston's efforts as Confederate minister to Maximilian met with failure. Union victories encouraged British and French neutrality, thus dooming southern hopes to persuade Mexico to recognize the Confederacy.

As a soldier, Preston served in the Mexican War and for the South in the Civil War. Arriving in Veracruz in 1847 following General Winfield Scott's victories, the Kentuckian missed the fighting, but he helped oversee the transport of supplies as an army lieutenant colonel. His military service to the Confederacy as a colonel and general proved more significant. As aide-de-camp to his brother-in-law, General Albert Sidney Johnston, and as commander of troops defending valuable salt mines in southwestern Virginia, Preston skillfully handled logistics and organized his men. But people most remembered his heroic leadership on the battlefields at Stones River and Chickamauga. In the latter conflict, his troops overcame an entrenched Union bastion and foreign observers lauded his valor.

The South unsuccessfully defended slavery and states' rights, and the efforts of southerners like Preston to safeguard sectional interests ended in failure. Political victories such as passage of the Kansas-Nebraska Act in 1854 proved of short duration. The Kentuckian's attempts as a United States minister to purchase Cuba and as a Confederate envoy to gain Mexican recognition made him a diplomat of lost causes. Likewise, his military leadership and exploits on the battlefield–like those of so many other Confederates–while valiant efforts, ultimately proved in vain.

Despite Preston's failures, his actions and ardor for his cause illuminate the vitality of Kentucky's antebellum aristocracy. Wealthy as an inheritor of valuable lands, he represented the second generation of settlers who controlled the political, economic, and social life in the state. They created a society that suited their interests. Preston and others of his class constituted an elite group in which kinship, friendship, and education reinforced their dominance. The prominence of his forebears and that of his relatives in Kentucky, Virginia, South Carolina, and Missouri gave him a sense of entitlement and predisposed him to exercise leadership. Taking advantage of his inheritance, he had the abilities and the resolve to serve his state and region as a politician, diplomat, and soldier.

In one significant way, Preston was different from the vast majority of southern aristocrats. Like other slaveholders, he was convinced that blacks were inferior and should be controlled and protected by their white masters. But, unlike most elite southerners, Preston recognized the contributions that recent European immigrants were making to United States development and became a champion of the rights of German and Irish Americans. In so doing, he also respected Roman Catholics, an uncommon view among many leading southerners. Preston's different attitudes toward foreigners and Roman Catholics came from his Louisville origins. With the notable exception of New Orleans, Louisville was unlike other southern cities in its ethnic and religious make-up. In the decades before the Civil War, thousands of German and Irish settlers came to work in the emerging metropolis on the banks of the Ohio River. The Preston land grant, adjacent to the city, meant that the family owed much of its economic fortune to selling parcels of that property to these industrious foreigners, many of them Roman Catholics. Nor did pecuniary gain alone determine Preston's respect for Catholicism. The area south of Louisville around Bardstown was one of the notable centers of Catholic settlement in the South. For two years William attended a Jesuit school there–an educational experience he appreciated.

But if Preston differed from his white southern brethren concerning immigrants and Roman Catholics, his other convictions and assumptions reflected the values of the South's antebellum gentry. Outspoken in his defense of states' rights, slavery, and expansionism, he believed that the upper classes should direct national life. For him, the hierarchical society of the South accorded with a Divine plan. Only after the Civil War did Preston come to recognize that the growing might of the country was based on the industry and skills of the growing urban middle classes. Nevertheless, his own social status, family connections, and long-established friendships isolated him from these important citizens, a fact he later noted and rued.

In the larger sense, William Preston's life was a tragic one. He had impressive talents, intelligence, and leadership abilities, but spent his energies as a politician, diplomat, and soldier in defense of a social and economic system that would perish. Like so many other southerners of his background, he devoted much of his life to a lost cause. Before his death in 1887, Preston was affectionately referred to by his friends as "Kentucky's Last Cavalier."

---

[1] Basil W. Duke, *Reminiscences of General Basil W. Duke* (New York, 1911), 195.

Kentucky's Last Cavalier

Chapter I: Boyhood

∼

Amid the yellow and russet hues of the tulip poplars and oaks surrounding their log home, Major William and Caroline Hancock Preston gave thanks for the birth of a son on 16 October 1816.[1] The place was Preston's Lodge just to the east of Louisville, a rapidly growing town at the Falls of the Ohio River. William was their fifth child, the first born in Kentucky. He would be their sole male heir, a matter of utmost importance to his parents, both of whom descended from Virginia's first families. For seven decades their son would strive to uphold his forebears' illustrious name as a soldier, politician, and diplomat.

William Preston's ancestors had acquired a definite measure of landed wealth and status that would exert a profound influence on every aspect of his life. Four generations earlier, his paternal great-great-grandfather Archibald Preston, an Englishman, had served in William of Orange's army in Ireland and helped withstand a five-day siege of Londonderry by the Roman Catholic forces of King James II in 1689. Preston established his home in Ulster following the Protestant victory. His son John, William's great-grandfather, was a ship's carpenter who wed Elizabeth Patton of nearby County Donegal. According to family tradition, they met each other in a boat while crossing the Shannon River. Against parental advice, she insisted on marrying the humble youth and eloped with him. Her family was socially and financially more important than the Prestons and would furnish her husband with connections to gain lands in the New World. Elizabeth's father also had fought with the Protestant forces. He presided over Springfield Manor, a massive house built on an extensive grant awarded by King William.[2]

John and Elizabeth Preston probably lived in Newton-Limavady, a market town thirteen miles from Londonderry, where four of their six children were born. Elizabeth's brother, Colonel James Patton, owned a ship and had mercantile interests in Virginia. In 1737 he entered into an agreement to establish families on western lands granted by the Virginia County Council. Patton asked his brother-in-law to join him in America, promising him 4,000 acres. Not possessing lands or wealth, the Prestons decided to sail to Virginia, and in 1738 they settled this "valuable tract of land" in the Shenandoah Valley near the present city of Staunton. In the upper valley of western Virginia, the family joined others from Ulster in establishing homesteads on the frontier, and they were faithful members of the local Presbyterian church. A man noted for his "great industry," John Preston worked as a cabinetmaker and purchased additional property in 1742 near his original grant.[3]

Born in Ireland in 1729, William was John and Elizabeth Preston's only son. Following his father's death in 1748, the young man became his uncle's favorite. James Patton was perhaps the most influential man in Augusta County. A prominent land speculator, militia colonel, the county lieutenant, and often a negotiator with the Indians, he made his nephew Billy his secretary. When the clerkship of the vestry of the Anglican Augusta Parish became vacant in 1750, Patton saw to it that William assumed the office. Although a Presbyterian, Preston served as clerk for sixteen years, a useful position as the established Church of England vestry controlled taxation. Two years later the nephew accompanied his uncle to Log Town on the upper Ohio River to negotiate a treaty with the Iroquois Indians on settlement of the Ohio country. In 1755 Preston became a county justice of the peace and was commissioned captain of a company of rangers. During the next four years he led volunteers in a Virginia regiment fighting the Shawnee Indians during the French and Indian War. He was in charge of a company of men under Colonel George Washington's command during his 1756 survey of frontier fortifications and was commissioned lieutenant colonel in 1759. That year Preston became county sheriff, coroner, and escheator.[4] From 1766 to 1771, he was elected to serve in the House of Burgesses, where he was an outspoken Whig and defender of western land rights.

The main source of William Preston's wealth came from his position as county surveyor. These officials in eighteenth-century Virginia enjoyed considerable power over the disposition of public grants, and their services were required to determine the legal ownership of newly claimed tracts. While looking after the public good as government officials, they also were tending their own personal interests. County surveyors on the Virginia frontier were awarded land from the Crown for their work, and often they received land in payment for their expensive surveying fees. Their knowledge of the

2

terrain also made them astute purchasers of prime real estate. With this landed wealth came social and political importance. George Washington and George Rogers Clark were surveyors, and four sons of surveyors became governors of the Old Dominion in the quarter-century following independence, including Patrick Henry and Thomas Jefferson.[5] William Preston's son, James Patton Preston, would serve as governor from 1816 to 1819.

For more than three decades William Preston held a number of surveying positions. He became assistant surveyor of Augusta County in 1751 and continued in this position for eighteen years. With the help of his friend John Madison, an Augusta County clerk and a second cousin of future president James Madison, Preston in 1769 was named surveyor of the newly created Botetourt County. Three years later he moved to another new county, Fincastle, where he remained surveyor until this county was subdivided in 1776 into Kentucky, Montgomery, and Washington Counties. Preston then became the surveyor for Montgomery County. While surveyor in four counties, he also held a variety of other posts, including coroner, sheriff, county lieutenant, and chief militia officer. During his years as surveyor, Preston amassed considerable landholdings. By 1770 he held forty-two tracts, ranging in size from 32 to 650 acres. On his death in 1783, the longtime surveyor owned between eight and nine thousand acres in Virginia.[6]

Like many other upcountry Virginians, Preston was eager to own property west of the Alleghenies. The land around the Falls of the Ohio had remained uninhabited by Europeans in the century following discovery of the site by the French in the 1670s and had obvious appeal to land-hungry Virginians. These limestone-strewn rapids offered the only impediment to navigation along the almost one-thousand-mile course of the waterway as it flowed from Pennsylvania to the Mississippi River. Settlement along La Belle Rivière–as the French called the broad stream–would make the falls area a transportation and commercial center. On the eve of the American Revolution, colonists east of the Alleghenies were determined to cross over the blue ramparts into "the land on the Western Waters." In the mid-1770s the first permanent fortifications were established at Harrodsburg and Boonesborough.[7]

In addition to his substantial holdings in Virginia, Preston also claimed several thousand acres in Kentucky. Much of this terrain was inherited from his uncle James Patton, but some of Preston's acreage was acquired in his own right. In April 1774 he had sent an expedition to Kentucky, led by his assistant surveyor John Floyd, to use the compass and chain to delineate lands granted by the Crown to Preston and other veterans of the French and Indian War. En route the assistant surveyor set aside two thousand acres on the Kanawha River for George Washington. With rifles and notebooks in hand, Floyd's party of twenty-two men reached the Falls of the Ohio in late May. There they laid out thirty tracts of land for prominent Virginians such as Preston, William Christian, and William Byrd. On 31 May Floyd's assistants, Hancock Taylor–the uncle of future president Zachary Taylor–and James Douglas, completed a survey of one thousand acres from the river southward along Beargrass Creek for Colonel Preston.[8] Four decades later, this plot would become the plantation of his son William Preston. Meanwhile, Floyd was staking out another one thousand acres a few miles to the southwest–today the site of Audubon Park and a portion of the state fairgrounds in Jefferson County–for his Virginia employer. By 8 July the party had surveyed approximately forty thousand acres in the vicinity of the falls. From the Ohio River the party moved to Elkhorn Creek, where the head of the expedition marked off two more tracts of one thousand acres each for Preston near the soon-to-be-founded settlement of Lexington.[9] Preston's lands and another eighty-some surveys made in Kentucky under Floyd were recorded in the Fincastle County Survey Book in 1774.

The year 1775 marked the end of effective British rule in Virginia. The colonial legislature met for the last time and the royal governor fled the capital at Williamsburg. Following the American Revolution, the Commonwealth of Virginia would recognize title to the lands granted by the Crown and surveyed by Floyd's expedition.

The Scotch-Irish colonists in western Virginia proved strong supporters of American independence. Despite the advances of age and his poor health, Preston played an active role in planning military affairs on the frontier throughout the Revolution. When Fincastle County set up a Committee of Safety in 1775, Colonel Preston was named a member, and he was commissioned commander-in-chief of the county militia. The colonel ordered his men to collect funds to cover expenses of Virginia's delegates to the Continental Congress and arranged for supplies in 1776 to permit the colonists to thwart

British-sponsored raids by the Cherokee Indians. Governor Thomas Jefferson in 1779 asked him to organize a company to defend the frontier, and the following year Jefferson commended him for suppressing the threat of a Tory revolt in Montgomery County. When British troops in North Carolina were preparing to invade western Virginia in February 1781, Preston marched his men to join General Nathanael Greene's army at Guilford in North Carolina, without waiting for orders from the governor, an action Jefferson lauded. But not all of Preston's military actions were exemplary. When the British attacked his company in March 1781, Preston was thrown from his frightened horse into a pond. Fortunately, another officer helped the obese colonel remount his steed and avoid capture.[10]

"In consideration of military service performed by William Preston in the late war between Great Britain and France," Jefferson in 1780 recognized Preston's title to the thousand acres of land near the Falls of the Ohio that had been surveyed for him six years earlier. This original conveyance delineated his property by citing such natural boundaries as "three Ash Trees by a Meadow," "two large white oaks, a poplar and Sweet Gum," and "a Cherry Tree and four Sugar Trees." Today this land is located in eastern Louisville and runs approximately from the river, between the George Rogers Clark and the John F. Kennedy Bridges on the north, south to Eastern Parkway. Its eastern and western boundaries would be Baxter Avenue and Preston Street, respectively. The eastern portions of today's Main, Market, Jefferson, Liberty, Muhammad Ali, and Chestnut Streets, as well as Broadway, were included in this land grant, as were Shelby and Campbell Streets, the northern ends of Preston and Jackson Streets, and the area of the Highlands northwest of Baxter Avenue and Eastern Parkway.[11]

Throughout his years as a successful land speculator, public official, and militia commander, Preston also was a devoted husband and father. His fair hair, hazel eyes, and ruddy complexion made him a "reasonably handsome man," but by adulthood he was much too heavy even for his almost-six-foot frame. In 1761 he married Susannah Smith, whose father–like his own–was a carpenter as well as a prosperous farmer and tavern keeper. The couple had twelve children. The family's first residence was Greenfield on the "Great Road" to the Alleghenies. There they lived for eleven years in a log-walled structure, before moving fifty miles westward to Smithfield, where they resided in a two-story, clapboard house with dormer windows, near present-day Blacksburg. On their plantations the Prestons raised flax, wheat, corn, hemp, horses, and cattle and owned as many as fifty-one slaves–an unusually large number for a frontier farm.[12]

As expected in the homes of wealthy families of his day, Smithfield included touches of elegance–carved mantles, a Chippendale staircase, glass windows, ample supplies of linen, and expensive china and silver–and William Preston took pride in the food and drink offered at his table. Unlike most of his prosperous frontier neighbors, he was interested in learning and boasted a library of 273 volumes, including Latin classics, histories, theological works, Shakespeare's plays, and manuals on medicine and farming. He also wrote poetry. Determined that his children would receive a good education, Preston hired tutors. John Floyd, his assistant surveyor, was "tall, and rather spare, his figure genteel, his complexion dark," with "the manners of a well bred gentleman." Preston had Floyd serve as instructor for his children the year before he was sent on his first surveying expedition to Kentucky. Floyd became a friend and confidant of his employer and would name his son William Preston Floyd.[13]

On Preston's death in 1783, his complex will bequeathed his thousand acres near the Falls of the Ohio to his two older sons, John and Francis, provided they would settle at Horse Shoe Bottom along the New River in Montgomery County. There they were to care for their mother and their two younger brothers, William and James. But it was Preston's third son William who eventually would gain ownership of this land in Kentucky and settle there.

Son William made his mark in the military. In 1788, at eighteen years of age, he became a member of a cavalry company in the Montgomery County militia. Three years later he served as an ensign under his brother, Captain John Preston, in a company protecting western Virginia and was a captain in the United States Army in 1791. After organizing a group of Virginia recruits in 1793 to join General Anthony Wayne's expeditionary force in the Northwest Territory, William Preston served in Ohio and Indiana for three years. He fought at the Battle of Fallen Timbers on the Miami River, where the Americans defeated the Indians and their British allies in 1794, and devoted his spare time to learning Indian languages. Following a year's assignment in Virginia, he next spent almost two years in Tennessee maintaining order in the Cherokee lands. He resigned from

Chapter I: Boyhood

Courtesy Filson Historical Society

Major William Preston (1770–1821), portrait by Aurelius O. Revenaugh from a miniature by Charles W. Peale.

the army in July 1798 with the rank of major. While in the military, he also served as an assistant enumerator for the county in the first national census in 1790 and held the post of county surveyor for two years.

Virginia would be Preston's home for the next fifteen years. He settled in Wythe County on a plantation he had inherited from his father. By this time William was a young man whose appearance seemed to indicate a sense of satisfaction with his status: his round face with its firm mouth, hazel eyes, and pleasant smile, complemented by his brown hair, and the splendor of his military attire combined to make him the portrait of a distinguished gentleman. In 1802 he wed Caroline Hancock, the daughter of a Revolutionary War colonel from Virginia and member of Congress. This practical and firm-willed woman proved an invaluable mate when her husband later decided to move to Kentucky and carve a plantation out of the wilderness. The couple became the parents of eight children–six daughters and two sons–but only five of the girls and one boy would survive childhood. After he had been married for ten years, Preston applied to President James Madison for a commission to fight in the War of 1812, and he assisted in the defense of Norfolk when the British fleet was at Hampton Roads, Virginia.[14]

Despite his comfortable life as the owner of a 2,175-acre plantation in Wythe County, Preston was interested in moving westward to enjoy an even more prosperous life on the new frontier. His military service originally had familiarized him with the territory west of the Alleghenies, and he traveled to Tennessee and Kentucky in the summer of 1808 to look after lands he and his siblings had inherited. Much of his correspondence dealt with the possibility of establishing his family in the west. Among William's army friends in the 1790s was fellow Virginian Meriwether Lewis, later a leader of the Lewis and Clark Expedition to the Pacific Northwest. He owned land in Kentucky but was governor in St. Louis of the Louisiana Territory. In 1808 Lewis wrote Preston urging him to take up residence in Missouri. "Were I to dwell on the advantages of this country I might fill a volume," his friend assured him, predicting that "if you do not celect [sic] Louisiana as your place of residence I will wrisk [sic] my existence that you will at some future period regret having chosen any other."[15] Preston did move westward, but not to Missouri.

Major William Preston in 1811 claimed a portion of his father's one thousand acres near the Falls of the Ohio. Brother John had sold his interest in this property to Francis in 1793, but William challenged Francis's ownership. He argued that his older brother had forfeited his sole right to this tract by not settling at Horse Shoe Bottom as stipulated in their father's will. Arbitrators upheld William's contention, forcing Francis to share ownership of the property on the Ohio with William and his younger brother James, who conveyed his interest in the tract to William in 1814. That year William and Caroline settled on this land with their four Virginia daughters, Henrietta, Maria, Caroline Letitia, and Josephine, and their one-year-old son Hancock. Another child, Julia Clark, had died soon after birth three years earlier. Their new lands became known as the Preston Plantation.

When William and Caroline Preston moved to Kentucky in 1814,

Louisville was already a prosperous town. During the American Revolution, General George Rogers Clark had established a military outpost at the Falls of the Ohio in 1778, and a settlement began to form. The Virginia Assembly in 1780 formally established the town of Louisville, named for Louis XVI of France, an ally of the patriotic cause. Portaging cargoes around the river's rapids demanded a labor force and created a commercial center. Above the falls "the mouth of Bear Grass [Creek]," according to an early historian, provided "a safe and commodious harbor for the labouring barge" and became the port.[16] When Kentucky was admitted as the fifteenth state in 1792, more than seventy thousand immigrants already had made the commonwealth their home. The defeat of the Indians two years later at the Battle of Fallen Timbers in Ohio encouraged more settlers to venture westward. Pinckney's Treaty with Spain in 1795 and the Louisiana Purchase in 1803 guaranteed a river outlet to world markets through New Orleans for the flour, hemp, pork, tobacco, and other staples produced in the region.

Louisville's future as a busy port city was certain. By 1810 the town counted 1,300 inhabitants and enjoyed such urban amenities as a theater, newspapers, a market house, churches, warehouses, and mercantile establishments. During the next decade the population more than tripled, the first steamboats appeared on the waterfront at the mouth of Beargrass Creek, commerce increased several fold, stores multiplied, and an iron foundry, flour and sawmills, a distillery, rope walks, and soap factories were established. The citizens noted that the city counted among its amenities a hospital, a police force, paved streets, and many brick houses.[17]

The Preston family's residence east of town was a two-story dwelling constructed in 1815 with birch logs that had been hewn to align on the outer and inner sides. There son William joined the family the following year and his sister Susan in 1819. The house sat atop a wooded hill and looked out on a stream that flowed into the south fork of Beargrass Creek. It was close to the Bardstown Road, a thoroughfare filled with travelers on horseback and on foot, wagons laden with goods, and the "marvel of the day," the stagecoach, rumbled along with its passengers and mail. Slaves felled much of the virgin forest for farmland and pasture, using the logs to construct Preston's Lodge, slave quarters, and storage buildings. The rapid growth of blackberry bushes around the house in the openings cut out of the woods gave the plantation its popular name, the "Briar Patch." The two-story, clapboard-framed portion of the building that occupies this site today on the southwest corner of Baxter Avenue and Grinstead Drive in Louisville's Highlands may have been constructed around the log walls of Preston's Lodge.[18]

Major Preston was but one of several Revolutionary stalwarts who came out from the Old Dominion to settle the fertile lands on Louisville's eastern periphery. In 1779 the surveyor John Floyd began constructing a cabin for his family east of the falls where today St. Matthews is located, and William Johnson in 1785 established his Cave Hill Farm in the highlands bordering the Preston Plantation. Two years later Alexander Scott Bullitt became master of Oxmoor, then the easternmost settlement in the area. On a bluff overlooking the Ohio upstream from Louisville, George Rogers Clark spent his last years at Locust Grove with his sister Lucy and brother-in-law William Croghan in their imposing, symmetrical brick residence constructed in 1790. On the road to Bardstown several miles beyond Preston's Lodge, John Speed in 1810 built Farmington, a Federal plantation house incorporating architectural designs favored by Thomas Jefferson. Another Virginian, Lieutenant Colonel Richard Taylor, established his family estate called Springfield along Beargrass Creek, five miles east of town. He gave Zachary, his son and future president of the United States, a homestead at the mouth of the stream in 1811.

In the rich Bluegrass region around Lexington, other upcountry Virginians were making their new homes. There, families such as the Todds, the Breckinridges, and the McDowells took possession of large estates. The Kentucky frontier was never a democratic one, as the early landowners occupied large tracts of the most valuable land. Their real estate and slaves became the basis of their wealth. Together the transplanted Virginians living around the Falls of the Ohio and in the Bluegrass country created a ruling elite or squirearchy that would dominate the political, economic, and social life of their new commonwealth until the Civil War.[19]

The Prestons were among the largest landowners in the rapidly growing area around the Falls of the Ohio. In addition to the Briar Patch, William owned a large tract of land near Middletown to the east of Louisville. While overseeing the development of the plantation with its fields of tobacco, corn, hemp, and other crops for market, as well as its hogs and cows, he also began to divide some of his property adjacent to Louisville into lots for sale. He acquired influence in the community, was elected a director of the Louisville branch of the Bank of Kentucky in 1815, and was made an artillery captain in the state militia two years later.

By 1818 Preston's health was declining. He went to Virginia several times to "take the waters," but to no effect. When he died in January 1821, he left detailed instructions concerning his family's future. After selling lots to take care of certain expenses and granting some property to his brother Francis as previously agreed to, his will gave the bulk of his considerable landholdings to his wife Caroline and their children. He also emancipated Nassau, a slave who had served his wife for five years. Like his father, Preston was concerned with his children's education. In his will he directed his executors to sell $6,000 worth of property to pay for their schooling, and he asked his wife to entrust his two sons' instruction to "a man who himself had been liberally educated," so that they would be given "every advantage for the cultivation of sound morals and solid learning."[20]

Son William Preston's childhood was shaped by a sense of family pride and entitlement that he shared with his six siblings. His older brother's death in 1827 made William the only remaining male in the family, and his mother and sisters impressed on him the responsibility he owed to his fatherless household. Caroline Hancock Preston and her children were proud of their patriotic antecedents, and throughout their lives they enjoyed the social connections and status they had inherited. In addition to a history of four generations of soldiers on their father's side of the family and a maternal grandfather who had fought in the American Revolution and had been a congressman, the children counted many other relatives of importance. Their Preston uncles in Virginia were men of political and military prominence: John served as a member of the Virginia senate and was a major general; James Patton was governor and Preston County, created in 1818, was named in his honor; and Francis was a United States congressman and major general. Their Preston aunt Letitia was wed to Governor John Floyd, whose son John Buchanan also became governor. Through correspondence and frequent visits, the Kentucky Prestons continued their close connections with their Virginia kin. The senior William Preston died in Virginia while at his brother's home, and wife Caroline–often accompanied by her children–returned regularly to the Old Dominion to stay with relatives.

Following the custom of Virginia's elite families, the Prestons underscored the links with their ancestors by naming family members after close relatives. Twenty of the twenty-eight grandchildren of John and Elizabeth Preston called their first child after one of their parents or one of their spouses' parents. The Kentucky-born William Preston carried not only his father's appellation, but that of his grandfather. Five of the six offspring of this William, in turn, would be named for his mother, his favorite sister, and his wife's stepmother, mother, and father.

The Louisville Prestons also enjoyed close ties with other Virginia families that would be of help to them throughout their lives. The Breckinridges, Browns, Clarks, McDowells, Christians, Howards, Hancocks, and Prestons were among the Old Dominion's most prominent clans. By the late eighteenth century, these families were related through marriage, often supported each other in economic ventures and politics, and were part of a ruling elite. Many of their number moved across the Alleghenies, where they continued their family friendships and often intermarried. William's maternal aunt was the wife of William Clark, Meriwether Lewis's associate on the famous expedition to the Pacific and later governor of Missouri (George Rogers Clark, the Revolutionary War hero and Kentucky settler, was the older brother of William Clark). When Kentucky was admitted to the Union in 1792, one of the state's first United States senators was John Brown, whose mother Margaret was the sister of Colonel William Preston, the grandfather of the Louisville Prestons. Another sister of the colonel, Letitia Preston, had married Robert Breckinridge in Virginia. As a widow she moved to Fayette County with four of her five children, establishing the Breckinridge line in Kentucky.

By the time the Preston children reached adulthood, both they and their relatives in their generation would continue the family legacy, occupying positions of prominence. Their cousins followed in the footsteps of the previous generation. James McDowell became governor of Virginia, William Campbell Preston was elected senator from South Carolina, and William Ballard Preston served in Congress and as secretary of the navy under President Zachary Taylor. Another cousin, Elizabeth Preston McDowell, was the wife of Senator Thomas Hart Benton of Missouri, and their Lexington cousin John C. Breckinridge would become vice president of the United

States. William and Caroline Preston's daughters–as expected–married men who gained prominence. Albert Sidney Johnston, an army officer for Texas, the United States, and the Confederacy, became Henrietta's husband, while Josephine wed Jason Rogers, commander of the Louisville Legion at the outbreak of the Mexican War. Caroline, Maria, and Susan also took as partners men of means and social rank.[21] These ties of kinship would be of paramount importance to the Preston children as they grew older.

The young Prestons were very aware of their family's privileged economic position. Mother Caroline oversaw the finances of her properties with the assistance of several trusted advisors and lawyers. She often reminded her son and daughters that her resources were not limitless–and on many occasions she complained that she lacked funds to cover her obligations. But the members of the family were secure in the knowledge that their landholdings placed them in a fortunate–even enviable–position. On Caroline's death in 1847, her will stipulated that, except for a house in Louisville that went in trust to daughter Henrietta, her six surviving children would divide her property equally.[22] This inheritance provided Mrs. Preston's heirs with ample wealth throughout their lives.

William was but a lad of four when his father died in 1821, and his mother moved the children from Preston's Lodge to the city. There Mrs. Preston lived for the remainder of her life. She first resided with her children in a brick house on the north side of Market Street between Brook and Floyd—to the east of the business district—and later she made her home on the south side of Jefferson Street between Fourth and Fifth.[23] In addition to her children, she oversaw several domestic slaves who took care of the cleaning and cooking and looked after her children, as well as tending to the carriage and horses.

Louisville was a town of four thousand inhabitants when the Prestons moved there in 1821. The landscape retained its swampy appearance, with marshes and ponds surrounding the settlement, and yellow fever epidemics threatened the citizens. But the community was witnessing constant changes. The original log cabins were giving way to clapboard and brick houses, and glass windows were no longer a novelty. There were newspapers and a public library, as well as physicians and lawyers. Houses of worship existed for Baptists, Presbyterians, Episcopalians, Methodists, and Roman Catholics. Hotels and bars served both visitors and residents. A police force and fire-fighting companies had been established, and the tobacco warehouses were examined by inspectors appointed by law. Shops were offering better goods, ranging from calico dresses and bonnets for the belles to silverware that was replacing the wooden spoons and forks.

The river metropolis by 1830 had become one of the major cities west of the Alleghenies and the nation's seventeenth largest. The city's 10,336 inhabitants for the first time surpassed the population of Lexington, its instate rival. Several reasons accounted for such rapid growth. As contemporaries recognized, "The population of Louisville depends almost entirely upon her commerce."[24] From earliest times, the city's location at the Falls of the Ohio made it a natural stopping place for travelers and boatmen, and craft continued in greater numbers to be guided over the rapids by pilots, or their cargoes were transported around the falls throughout the 1820s. Growing communities upriver such as Cincinnati and Pittsburgh were shipping larger and larger quantities of pelts, flour, and salted meat destined for New Orleans and points in between. Begun in 1826, the Louisville and Portland Canal employed as many as a thousand workers to construct the two-mile-long waterway. It was opened four years later, permitting vessels year-round to navigate the twenty-four-foot descent in the Ohio.

In addition to river traffic, Louisville profited from the natural resources surrounding the town–especially the forests–the development of new farms, and the establishment of new commercial ventures. Foreign visitors in the 1820s were quick to note that "the crops are gloriously abundant," and an Englishwoman even admitted that the woodlands contained specimens that "would be considered really fine trees in England." "Behind Louisville," another English traveler asserted, "the country is delightful."[25] Tobacco, hemp, corn, whiskey, livestock, timber, and pelts were among the goods brought to the city for sale, creating jobs for laborers and tradesmen. In 1828 the state gave Louisville a city charter, granting broad powers to the mayor and municipal council.

More inhabitants, in turn, brought a demand for more stores and services. The slave market was flourishing, lawyers prospered, and public houses relieved the thirst of many. A construction boom was transforming the city's appearance, particularly in the business district concentrated along the four thoroughfares parallel to the river,

Kentucky Historical Society Special Collections

View of Louisville from the Indiana shore in the late 1830s.

Water, Main, Market, and Jefferson Streets. Educational and cultural organizations also were founded. The first municipal school system west of the Alleghenies was established in 1829, and the next year four hundred youngsters were studying in the new, three-story, brick Center School House at Fifth and Walnut Streets. The Louisville Lyceum was "formed professedly for literary improvement," and the City Theater was constructed on Jefferson Street in 1828.[26]

Against this background of rapid change, the widow Caroline Preston oversaw the fortunes of her family. Although she employed attorneys and advisors to help with her affairs, she decided which properties to sell and when, how much rent to charge, and how to invest her funds. But such responsibilities proved a burden. In 1827 her financial problems were so acute that she believed that "our distress is well known here." During an economic downturn in 1832, she feared she would be forced to cut back on spending, and eight years later she was lamenting that lots could not be sold at any price or property rented.[27]

Despite intermittent difficulties, Caroline Preston's wealth in real estate provided ample funds to cover her family's many expenses. As the urban population west of the Alleghenies increased, municipal land prices rose and cities began to expand beyond their original borders. By the late 1820s pressure for housing sites in Louisville permitted Mrs. Preston to subdivide some of her property adjacent to the city limits and sell lots. This land north of Prather Street—today Broadway—was known as the Preston Enlargement, and in 1827 it was annexed to Louisville, becoming its first suburb. In the next decades much of the family's land to the south was developed, furnishing Caroline and her heirs a handsome income for the rest of the century.

Mrs. Preston was a strong-willed woman who proved able to rear her children as might be expected of the scions of Virginia gentry. A carefully dressed woman of average height, her appearance indicated her serious nature. She was intent on inculcating in her only surviving son a sense of responsibility for safeguarding the well-being of his family. Throughout William's adolescence his mother and older sisters reminded him of the great expectations they held for him. "The eyes of many are on you," his mother often wrote him. Even his younger sister Susan admonished him in her letters to "do credit to our family."[28]

William took his responsibility seriously. In his correspondence he declared his determination "to sustain if I do not advance the name my father bequeathed." Throughout his adult years, this expectation would weigh on his consciousness and influence his every endeavor.

But Mrs. Preston was more than a stern widow; she also was a caring mother whose kindness and concern for her son and daughters brought them a sense of confidence that complemented their feeling of entitlement. Throughout her life she demonstrated her dedication to William's happiness and health, as well as his educational and professional advancement. As his sisters often reminded William, he was such a favorite of his mother that they considered this affection "Mama's weakness." When the lad was away at boarding school and at university she wrote often. On countless occasions she warned him to look after his health, urging him to take such precautions as avoiding the night air or wearing a flannel vest "next to your skin."[29]

Mother Caroline provided a careful domestic surrounding for her children. While church activities were not important in the family's affairs, Mrs. Preston had inherited the Presbyterian beliefs of her upcountry Virginia ancestors and impressed on her son and daughters the importance of religious faith. She prayed regularly and saw that the Bible was read at home. The attentive mother also read to her children. William later remembered this with fondness, but he recalled, "When a boy I was alarmed at ghost stories." She also oversaw their dress and household chores, often taking part in the latter, particularly kitchen tasks such as pickling cucumbers and making preserves. Mrs. Preston took pride in her table, and her recipe book included instructions on how to prepare such items as beef flank steak rolled around a bread-and-herb stuffing and fried brains dipped in egg yolks, as well as currant and raspberry wine and ginger beer. In the summer she moved her family to Middletown Farm, a property east of Louisville that belonged to her husband, to avoid the mosquitos and the threat of "approaching diseases"—yellow fever and cholera—that on occasion visited the city.[30]

Slaves also played a major role in the Preston household, taking charge of such tasks as cleaning, purchasing food, cooking, making clothing, and serving the adults, as well as looking after the children. While the family unquestionably accepted slavery as a necessary part of life, Mrs. Preston was careful to make the servants appear as members of the family. She and her children often referred to "the family . . . black and white" in their correspondence. When she moved to Middletown Farm in the summer, Caroline Preston also tried "to get a place for my white as well as black family." The reference to "the family, white and black," was ubiquitous among southern slaveholders. While the phrase was redolent with justification of servitude, the sentiment expressed certainly reflected the paternalism of many owners.[31]

The Preston son enjoyed a happy home life. The family's social calendar revolved around the visits of relatives and friends—who returned their hospitality. Trips by steamboat up the Ohio and Kentucky Rivers and then overland by coach to Lexington, to visit their Wickliffe and Breckinridge kin, were highlights in the children's lives. Time together with relatives led to friendships that lasted for life and helped to inculcate a sense of identity and pride in their origins. Family marriages provided other happy occasions. The Louisville nuptials of sisters Caroline Letitia to Captain Abram R. Woolley in September 1827 and Josephine to Jason Rogers, a West Point graduate, in October 1831 were elaborate and joyous affairs. But it was the wedding of the oldest sister, Henrietta, to Albert Sidney Johnston at the Preston home in June 1829 that proved the most important for

William's future. Johnston had studied at Transylvania College in Lexington and was a graduate of West Point. William became a friend and confidant of this older brother-in-law, who would die in his arms during the Civil War.

The Preston family also faced its share of tragedy. John Pope died in 1825, a year after his marriage to William's second-oldest sister Maria. Two years later Hancock, William's fourteen-year-old brother, was killed when thrown from a horse. For the remainder of her life Caroline Preston grieved his death and reminded William that he was her "hope."[32]

Holidays and community events entertained William and his sisters. Reflecting the strong patriotic and civic feelings of the era, national holidays, election campaigns, and visits of eminent guests to the community provided occasions for public celebrations. Accompanied by their mother and friends, the Preston children looked on as speakers espoused patriotic virtues at Fourth of July celebrations and when the famous came to Louisville. The whole city turned out in May 1825 to greet General Lafayette, who was received with speeches and a procession where "bevies of young girls strewed his pathway with flowers."[33]

In addition to his fondness for his mother, William was close to his sisters, and they helped him. On occasion the youth would write to ask for money from his widowed sister Maria Preston Pope—twelve years his senior. He claimed he did not wish to "inconvenience" his mother by making such a request and asked Maria to burn his letters. Perhaps because they were born only three years apart, William and his younger sister Susan enjoyed a close friendship that would remain throughout their adult years. The two played together as children and corresponded frequently when separated as adults. Her brother remarked years later to Susan that the two shared "a love more imperishable than that ordinarily exists between brother and sister."[34]

William's favorite playmate was not one of his siblings, but Samuel Giles, a young slave his own age owned by the family. As was common among slaveholders, a "play boy" slave was selected for the young "marster." This child and William enjoyed games and childhood adventures together.[35] The activity of bearded boatmen and busy tradesmen along the riverfront fascinated boys like William and Sam, making visits to the wharf an enjoyable pastime. As they grew older, more serious matters attracted their attention, but their lives would remain intertwined for seven decades.

The Preston son's formative years were occupied in large measure by his determination to excel in learning. Whether from his nature or from his educational experiences, he became a serious student as an adolescent and remained one throughout his adult years. But William enjoyed other pleasures as well, and on several occasions his excesses caused problems. Despite characterizations of the youth as "headstrong and wayward," he did display what a relative insisted were "natural gifts and a certain fire and concentration in study, which marked all his mentality and action." William received his elementary schooling in Louisville from his mother and tutors and at private establishments.[36]

At the age of fourteen, William was sent to Augusta College in 1830. Founded eight years earlier, this was the first Methodist school established in Kentucky, and some contemporaries considered it "one of the best literary institutions of the west." There in Augusta, on the Ohio River in Bracken County forty-five miles upriver from Cincinnati, he attended classes for a year with 150 other students in the college's neoclassical, three-story brick main building. This "spacious and elegant edifice" contained classrooms, laboratories, and a chapel, but the students lived in Echo Hall, a dormitory a block away. The institution attracted the sons of many leading families in the commonwealth and elsewhere in the South. During the college's twenty-four-year history, its faculty and alumni included future presidents of Transylvania, Northwestern, and Miami Universities and Washington College (later Washington and Lee University). Augusta College had active debating societies, and while there is no record of William's participation in them, no doubt he went to some of their programs.[37]

After Augusta College, young Preston attended St. Joseph's College in Bardstown for almost two years. In early 1831 he traveled for two days in a snowstorm from Louisville to the Nelson County town with "old Jo, a colored companion du voyage," and Ben Hardin, a lawyer for the Preston family and a partisan Whig orator and statesman. There William stayed with the Hardins at Edgewood, their large, two-story brick home surrounded by trees. He lived on the second floor, and on 1 July 1831, he carved his name and the date on the inside of a cupboard door in his room–a souvenir that remained there for more than a century. The youth came from a fatherless home

AUGUSTA COLLEGE, AUGUSTA, KY.

Published in Lewis Collins, Historical Sketches of Kentucky *(Maysville, Ky., 1847)*

and quickly became an admirer of his humorous host, who took an instant liking to him. "Mr. Hardin had a striking presence," Preston later recalled, and "a hearty appreciation of all that was refined in sentiment and manners." "His house proved a happy home for me for nearly two years." A lifelong friendship developed between the boarding student and his host, and in 1849 Preston and Hardin would serve together at the state constitutional convention. William developed a fondness for the Hardins' daughter Kate, whom he referred to in correspondence to his younger sister Susan as his "cher [*sic*] amie" and "flame." He later wrote that "my penchant for her at one time was even suicidal."[38] The youth survived this brush with teenage love and managed to complete his secondary education.

As a relative remarked, Preston "learned a great deal in a rather desultory manner." In Louisville and Augusta, he had studied grammar, arithmetic, the basic sciences, and religion; read many of the English classics; and begun to learn French and Latin. By the time he left St. Joseph's College in 1834, he had acquired a background in history, literature, and philosophy and studied Latin, Greek, and French. Among Roman writers, William particularly admired Virgil. He also read works by leading eighteenth- and nineteenth-century American and British authors such as Burke, Hamilton, Wordsworth, and Byron.[39] The Kentuckian would remain an avid reader of history, the classics, and English and French literature during his university years.

William's life in Bardstown was not without problems. Despite innumerable missives from his family imploring him to dedicate himself to his studies, the youth soon was wagering on card games with friends at a tavern and losing money. "I owe about 500 dollars in this place mostly from gaming," he wrote his mother during his first year at St. Joseph's. He asked for money, assuring her, "You are aware of the humiliating nature of the debt and how unpleasant it must be for your son to be pressed and dinned by gamesters." He also ran up large bills for "breakage" at the school, paying for a "venison supper for 6 and Bar" and the purchase of cigars, Port wine, and four bottles of whiskey. Such "juvenile follies"—as his sister Henrietta called them—led school authorities to threaten him with expulsion. Predictably, his mother viewed the matter more seriously and asked him, "Do you think your tavern companions will add to your future advancement?" She noted he had caused the family "deep affliction" and prayed to God to guide him. William's disciplinary problems produced a positive effect. By the summer of 1833 his family was commending him for his changed behavior and academic record.[40]

The years Preston spent at St. Joseph's College were important in influencing the Protestant youth's attitudes toward Roman Catholics. The area around Bardstown was an early center of Catholic missionary activity and settled by many of the faithful who had emigrated from Maryland. Bardstown was made the see of a new diocese in 1808, and Benedict Joseph Flaget, a priest who had fled the French Revolution, was made its bishop. St. Joseph's Cathedral, with its classical brick façade and tall spire, was completed in 1819, and the next year St. Joseph's College opened on the cathedral grounds. Soon students were attending classes in a spacious, four-

"Edgewood," Ben Hardin's home in Bardstown. Published in Lucius P. Little, Ben Hardin: His Times and Contemporaries, with Selections from His Speeches *(Louisville, 1887).*

story brick building.[41] The college was a favorite institution of Bishop Flaget and gained a reputation for its fine academic program. By the 1830s two hundred students from throughout the South–most came from Kentucky and Louisiana–attended the college. Many were not Roman Catholics, but they attended religious services. Three of the college's early students became governors of Kentucky and Louisiana, and two became congressmen from Mississippi.[42]

Preston's exposure to Roman Catholicism as a student was not an experience shared by most southern leaders and brought him a respect for Catholics. Except for the concentrations of Catholics in Kentucky, Maryland, and southern Louisiana, the antebellum South was a Protestant bastion, and many southerners were hostile toward Catholics. While throughout his life Preston showed disdain for the theology and practices of the Church of Rome, he defended religious freedom. As an adult he would champion the rights of the thousands of Irish and German Catholic immigrants who made Louisville their home by the 1850s. The religious tolerance of other Protestant Kentuckians who attended St. Joseph's likewise has been credited in part to their schooling there.[43]

Young Preston's determination to excel in every endeavor was also seen in his nonacademic pursuits. His father had been a man of "extraordinary size and strength," and son William inherited his father's stature. He early became "a splendid horseman and famous swimmer," often swimming across the broad Ohio River not far above the falls. Like most male Kentuckians, William learned to use firearms and enjoyed hunting. In undertaking these endeavors, he was living up to the expectations of his family and his contemporaries who considered such skills and activities the natural attributes of his gender. As his older sister Henrietta reminded him when he was sixteen years old, "You have received a rich inheritance of all the manly virtues from your honorable father."[44]

With his primary and secondary studies completed, Preston commenced his university studies. This time, New England would be his venue.

Chapter II: Youth

~

Wﬁlliam Preston's next eight years saw him pursue a university education, begin the practice of law, and marry a distant cousin. He divided his time from September 1833 until December 1837 between Yale, where he studied literature, and Harvard, where he received a legal education. In his letters from New England he presented himself as a serious student, often informing his family that he seldom missed classroom recitations. From New Haven he reported that he often remained at his studies beyond midnight until the candle was almost consumed. At Harvard the Kentuckian claimed he spent "five hours in the lecture-room alone" and wrote that he was "hard at work filling reservoirs of my brain with as copious a supply of the principles of law as I could get into it." To Albert Sidney Johnston, who by 1837 had become commander of the army of the new Texas Republic, William told how his academic year had been one of "steady uniformity." He added with a tinge of envy, "How different the same time must appear to you."[1]

Preston sought to give the impression that he was devoting his full efforts to academic pursuits, but this was not so. At Yale and Harvard he continued to gamble, and this led to debts, forcing him to seek money from his brother-in-law Albert Sidney Johnston and his uncle George Hancock. His uncle told him that his "appetite for gambling" was "inherited from both sides of your House," but he warned him that continued wagering would leave him "bankrupt in property and in reputation which is worse." William lied to his mother, claiming that he was abstaining from "that vice which was once almost a passion with me," but her son's lavish spending habits caused Mrs. Preston concern. When he spent twice as much money at Yale as his allowance provided, he explained to her that his expenses were what "a student incurs here who mingles in good society." Even discarding his gambling debts, his expenditures on clothing, travel, physicians, tuition, and books amounted to the princely sum of $1,250 a year in New Haven.[2]

A continuing need for additional funds and ill health threatened to cut short Preston's university years. Despite his difficulties, William was "determined to 'stick it out'" and finish his education. In this resolve he enjoyed the support of his mother and sisters, who implored him to continue his studies, thereby enhancing his own and the family's reputation. In many of his letters to Louisville he continued to mention his need of money. Aware that his requests might cause problems, he offered to return home if his mother "should find any difficulty" in providing funds. Once, during his last year at Harvard, the worried student wrote, "If I don't receive a remittance soon, I'll have to give up my studies and leave this place." Although the requested aid sometimes was not promptly provided, his land-rich but cash-poor mother always managed to find the money required. William's determination to continue his studies stood in sharp contrast to the decision taken by his relative and classmate, Robert Wickliffe Jr. When asked by his father to leave Harvard in 1836 and return to Lexington, Kentucky, where Robert was needed "to go to parties with his sisters," the dutiful son did so.[3]

Often William complained of the "long, long winter" in New England, and in his second year at Yale he confided to his sister Susan that he was suffering from influenza that threatened to turn "into some pulmonary complaint." Although he asked Susan not to mention this to "Mama," she was informed. When sister Maria suggested that her brother return to Louisville until his health improved, his mother urged him to persevere with his studies.[4] He did so.

At Yale Preston studied history, politics, and especially literature, with emphasis on the classics. With the class valedictorian, Sidney Johnston, William spent his first four months in New Haven reading Herodotus and "the whole of the 24 Books of Homer's Iliad." He also translated the first book into English blank verse. This opened "a new world to me at eighteen which was so beautiful that I looked down with pity on my favorite Virgil as a servile Latin imitator." While admitting that "both Virgil and Ovid are great, very great poets," the Kentuckian claimed "both are immensely below the Greek, as are the moderns Dante, Tasso, Ariosto, Milton and Voltaire." He argued that Hellenic literature was superior because it "inspires a lofty sense of individual and national independence." "From my observations, the great use of classical studies is to give that spirit of freedom and that heroism in action which disdains adversity, or even death when duty is to be obeyed." [5] But the Yale student also appreciated Latin literature and praised the works of Lucretius and Horace.

Interest in Greek and Latin authors remained a hallmark of William Preston for the rest of his life. He even read their works in the evenings at camp in military campaigns. As he remarked in his old age, "To work 6 months of 3-4 hours a day will enable you to read Homer, etc. understandingly–but a lifetime to unravel the questions their works suggest." Preston's nephew, William Preston Johnston, became a university professor and the first president of Tulane University in New Orleans. The latter remarked of his uncle, "It was always rather a marvel to the writer how he got a scholarship in the classics, as easy, as gentlemanly and as critically correct as need be for a professorial chair." Preston's love of classical literature was a preference he held in common with many other educated southerners of that day, who saw the ancient authors as models for oratory and character building.[6]

Nor did Preston confine his education to the classics. He believed that a cultivated person should "study French thoroughly so as to be able to speak, read and write it." Among the French authors he read were Voltaire and the historian François Guizot. In English he pursued works of history and politics by such writers as John Locke, Edward Gibbon, and George Bancroft.

In Cambridge, Massachusetts, the Kentuckian attended law classes for two years at Harvard. His social rank and sense of family responsibility at first determined his attitude toward a legal education. Like many well-to-do gentry sons, William originally viewed the law as a fitting subject of inquiry, but he eschewed becoming an attorney. For him, legal training was only "supplementary to my education," a constructive pastime, not an economic necessity. In 1837 William admitted that he had decided to study law "even though I should never practice it. I thought it was necessary for every well educated man, to understand the principles upon which the theory of government is based." He wrote his sister Susan that he would pursue the attainment of "the new trifle of a piece of Latin scribbled on parchment," but he assured her, "I look upon it as a kind of certificate of proficiency of my profession, which may be a source of gratification to my mother."[7]

Preston's attitude toward a legal education and the practice of law changed during his last year at Harvard. "I am extremely glad I determined to study law," he wrote his Texas brother-in-law in June 1837. "If any money is to be made in Kentucky by the practice of my profession, I'll try and make it. If not, I shall set into farming <u>immediately</u>." He also assured his sister Susan he was "anxious" to practice law. When he finished his studies at Harvard, Simon Greenleaf, the Royall Professor of Law, gave Preston a form letter recommending him "to the Profession, as entitled to their respect and confidence," and stating that he had been "diligent in his studies and exemplary in his conduct and demeanor." Greenleaf described this letter as Preston's "diploma," which he hoped would "serve as a memorial of the months passed in our Institution as profitably to yourself, as they certainly were to us whose privilege it was to direct your studies." In 1838 the Harvard Law School awarded him an LL.B. degree.[8]

One event in Preston's life while at Harvard remains shrouded in mystery. In March 1837 he was involved in a dispute with a navy lieutenant, Dr. Charles H. McBlair, which was to be settled on the field of honor. The nature of their confrontation is unknown, but it might have been related to a social offense or originated in a gambling altercation. Like most dueling challenges, their differences were resolved without resort to pistols. According to a notice issued by a representative of the two potential combatants, they found that their problem was "susceptible of mutual explanation," and the affront was "adjusted in a manner honorable alike to both parties." Perhaps, as was often the case, the affair was averted by the intervention of the opponents' seconds or mutual friends who managed to negotiate an agreeable settlement.[9] Even though the duel did not take place, in the eyes of his contemporaries Preston had demonstrated his valor by agreeing to one. He realized that a willingness to defend one's honor by dueling was considered a display of character and manliness expected of a southern gentleman. Eight years earlier Charles Wickliffe, William's distant cousin and the brother of his future wife, had been killed on the field of honor defending his family's reputation. Preston would continue to show respect for dueling. In the course of the next seven years he would serve his brother-in-law at a duel and negotiate plans for a duel between two childhood friends.[10]

William also found time for social activities while in New England, going to dances and dinner parties. While her brother was at Yale, his sister Susan attended Madame Sigoigne's fashionable girls' school in Philadelphia. Their Wickliffe cousins, Mary and her younger sister Margaret Preston, also were students there. The

Preston children and the Wickliffe children, including Mary, Margaret, and Robert Jr., considered each other cousins. They were rather distant cousins, for they shared common great-grandparents, John and Elizabeth Preston, who had come to Virginia from Ireland in 1738. William invited Mary Wickliffe to a ball in New Haven, much to the expressed jealousy of her sister.

Boston offered William more entertainment than the environs of New Haven. Soon after arriving at Harvard in 1836, he wrote his mother, "I have been at two or three parties and seen a good deal of the gay society of Boston." In a letter to sister Susan he described his extracurricular life in all but idyllic terms: "Boston is at present exceedingly gay, and I have it in my power if I wished it to attend a party almost every evening in the week. Thank God! The scarcity of beaux here is so great . . . [they] have acquired something of a fair marketable value." One of William's most memorable activities was his visit to Washington City, where he spent the Christmas recess in 1836. There he attended numerous social functions and concluded that the capital's society was composed of "the collective talent of the country."[11]

With his university studies behind him, Preston undertook the eight-day trip back to Louisville in December 1837. He traveled south from Boston by train, then set out by coach from Washington to Wheeling, Virginia, along the National Road, and finally journeyed down the Ohio River. The city he returned to was in the throes of tremendous changes. During the 1830s its population more than doubled to 21,305 inhabitants in 1840–including 600 freed blacks and 3,400 slaves–ranking it number eleven among the cities in the Union. Much of this growth came from a quickening of commerce. After its opening in 1830, more than nine hundred boats a year were traversing the new Louisville and Portland Canal.[12] This meant that more warehouses and shops opened, as did financial institutions. The Bank of Louisville was chartered in 1833, and its elegant headquarters, a Greek Revival structure still standing, was erected on Main Street.

The changes in the Falls City went beyond increased population and business activity. Education prospered, and public and private construction boomed. A medical institute, intended to be the first part of a university, was established, and by 1840 the city counted seven primary schools. During the decade two splendid hotels were inaugurated on Main Street, the Louisville Hotel and the Galt House.

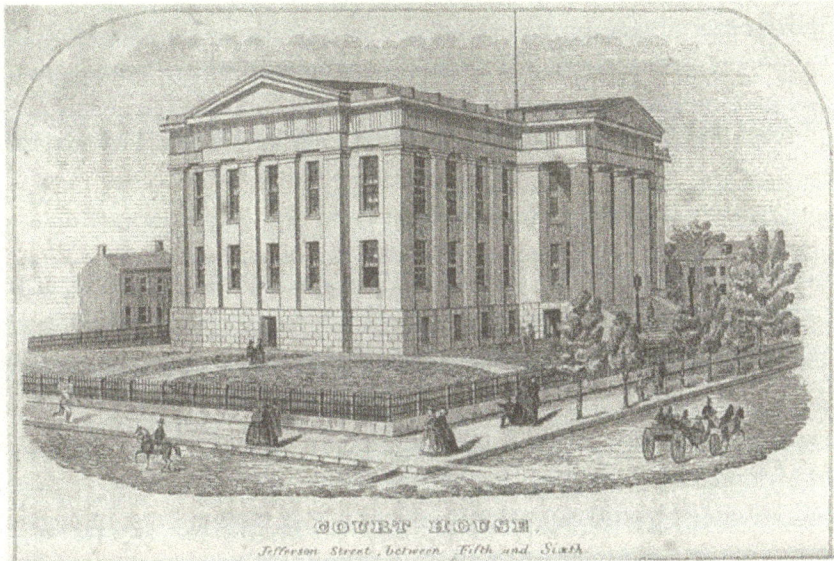

Jefferson County Courthouse. Lithograph from Williamson's Annual Directory of the City of Louisville, 1865 & 1866 *(Louisville, 1865).*

Church steeples pierced the horizon and hundreds of new houses were built annually. The cornerstone was laid in 1837 for what would become the county courthouse, but it would not be completed until thirteen years later.

Foreigners continued to be impressed by the city in the 1830s. Alexis de Tocqueville, one of America's most famous visitors, considered Louisville's prosperity "immense" in the 1830s and predicted that it "is destined to become a very large city." However, the Frenchman noted the deleterious effects of slavery on the state's economy. He claimed that a traveler descending the Ohio River "may be said to sail between liberty and servitude." On the north bank one viewed "fields covered by abundant harvests," while on the Kentucky shore he saw "slaves loitering in the half-desert fields."[13]

Amid these many changes, Preston was admitted to the bar in 1839 and opened a law office across from the Jefferson County Courthouse with his friend William J. Graves. The tall, athletic partner had a commanding presence that did not hinder his appeal to juries. Although he enjoyed playing cards and could be a warm friend, Graves had a reputation for being arrogant and was held in low esteem by several influential Kentuckians.[14] Preston enjoyed his association with Graves, however, and they remained close until his partner died in 1848.

Preston's prominence and social connections brought distinguished clients to his office. In addition, the litigious problems his family encountered as large landowners helped fill his agenda. Real estate law became his specialty, and when he became interested in a case, he was known to "pursue its analysis for days and nights of unremitting assiduity." But more often his legal practice involved monotonous work of slight interest to him. Soon the law was failing to engage his full attention. "My fortune is sufficiently large to supersed [sic] the necessity of severe professional exertion at the present time," he noted in early 1839. Although he later would give up law as a profession, he continued throughout his life to handle legal matters for both his family and friends and to argue cases before the Kentucky bar.[15]

Convinced he did not want to follow a legal career, Preston began to investigate the possibility of a diplomatic position. After only a year as an attorney, he lamented, "I am at work here and will be so for 20 years to come, unless some opening offers by which I can probably benefit myself more." To his brother-in-law Johnston, then secretary of war for the Texas Republic, the Louisvillian wrote in early 1839 asking to be named to a diplomatic mission he understood Texas was planning to send to Paris. So serious was the young lawyer in this proposal that he declared he would become a citizen of Texas if necessary, for "in this life I never intend if I have an opportunity, to let an unvalued adherence to my own country interfere with my prosperity in another." Despite his brother-in-law's efforts, Preston was not offered a foreign post by Texas, but he assured Johnston that "I have sense enough to push my fortune here or elsewhere."[16] Later, he would have the opportunity to serve as a diplomat, representing his country of birth as well as another nation to which he would pledge his allegiance.

It is hardly surprising that Preston became active in politics. Following the party loyalty of his family, he was an ardent Whig and admired "Henry Clay's Whig principles." Like many proponents of states' rights and members of the South's planting class, Preston believed this party best represented the conservative interests he espoused. Although the leadership of both the Whig and Democratic parties in the South came from the elite property- and slave-owning class, the Whigs drew heavily from the slaveholding aristocracy, "the elements in the community which, by virtue of wealth and social position, were separated from the 'common people.'"[17] Clay's American System, with its concern for transportation improvement with government subsidies, also had a great appeal to urban southerners like Preston, who was interested in the construction of a canal around the falls at Louisville and a highway between Lexington and Maysville on the Ohio.[18]

Soon Preston found himself involved in party affairs. He attended the Whig National Convention in Harrisburg, Pennsylvania, as the delegate from his congressional district in December 1839. Although he believed he was "the youngest man in the convention," he made a speech for the Kentuckians supporting William Henry Harrison for the presidency. That year Preston also was "unanimously elected a member of the Louisville Guards" and paraded with them. This new dimension brought additional respect in a society that revered military service—and did no harm to the political ambitions he was beginning to consider. In February 1840 Preston attended the caucus of Whig legislators in Frankfort and noted that some friends wanted him to run for the Kentucky house in August–but he was ineligible since he was not then twenty-four years old, the minimum age required for a legislator. Although admitting he was "inclined" to politics, Preston that month declined appointment by the Kentucky Whigs as a delegate to the Whig Young Men's National Convention to be held in Baltimore in May.[19]

Both national and state elections were of great interest to Preston in 1840. In the "rip-roaring" presidential contest that year, the Whigs promoted General William Henry Harrison, the hero of the Battle of Tippecanoe, as a common man of log-cabin and hard-cider origins, while claiming that the Democratic nominee, President Martin Van Buren, was an effete, "silver-spoon" man. Harrison's Virginia origins and his advocacy of the extension of slavery to the Northwest Territory made him a favorite of many southerners, Preston included. "I am not governed by party or prejudiced feelings," he correctly predicted in February, "when I state that he [Harrison] will beat Van Buren." William had mixed feelings about electioneering. In 1840 he found the bands, songs, processions, and political flags at rallies "pleasing and picturesque," but he feared that campaigning "seems to have a tendency to deprave the public." While some candidates tried to lift "the tastes of the People," others descended to their low level. The result of the presidential canvass pleased him, but the young Whig was disappointed when Cassius M. Clay, an outspoken emancipationist, won "a very excited contest" in the Lexington legislative district against Robert Wickliffe Jr., Preston's relative.[20]

A bon vivant, Preston enjoyed Louisville's social life and was the suitor of several local belles. He relished "brilliant" evening festivities with good music and "superb" food and took pleasure in listening to gossip about ladies' hairstyles and men's dress. Weddings offered him the opportunity to mingle in "scenes of pleasure and dissipation," and Robert Wickliffe Jr. insisted that for an elaborate nuptial celebration in late 1838, his presence would be indispensable. To tease him, Robert claimed to have told a "gay prancing waltzing" girlfriend of William's that he also wished "to walk home with you and squeeze your hand and throw my arms around your slender waist and plait your raven locks as Preston does!" Wickliffe assured his cousin in 1839 that another young lady "spoke of you as being one of the most agreeable beaux in Louisville," adding, "Is that a sufficient compliment to satisfy your ambition[?]"[21]

Preston also spent a great deal of time away from Louisville. The nation's capital continued to be a favorite destination, and while there he stayed at the home of his widowed sister, Maria Preston Pope. In December and January 1838-39, he was in Washington for three weeks, going to a "succession" of parties and dinners. Although a partisan Whig, Preston was invited to dinner by Democratic president Van Buren. Clearly social position counted more than party affiliation in receiving an invitation to the White House. There the guest was impressed by the beautiful women and the gold plate. After attending the Harrisburg Whig convention in December 1839, the young Kentuckian again spent the Christmas holidays in Washington and was among twenty guests at the White House in late December. "I had the honour of taking soup with the prince of Democracy, the president," he informed his sister Susan. "We sat down at 7 o'cl[oc]k and rose about ten." Preston found Van Buren a gracious host, but he was taken by a "very pretty belle," the daughter of Francis Granger, a prominent New York Whig. William noted that she was "worth some $250,000. Can she be otherwise than irresistible?"[22]

But Preston's favorite destination by 1840 was Lexington, where he was courting his distant cousin, Margaret Preston Wickliffe. He had known Mag and her brother Robert since childhood. In the Bluegrass city he stayed at the fashionable Phoenix Hotel at the corner of

Main and Limestone Streets. "Behold the rosy hours float by," the suitor remarked in 1840 after one of his frequent calls at the Wickliffe home. When apart that year, William sent her a series of love letters and assured her that she should not "even fear that you would be guilty of the slightest, even the shadow of impropriety in writing to me." When she did answer him, her suitor complained that her two-and-a-half-page letters were too brief, imploring her not to "attempt further to cultivate your already singular power of condensation." As demanded by their contemporaries and Victorian mores, the courtship obeyed the expected proprieties and received the blessing of both families. William and Margaret were engaged on 23 August 1840, and a month later he wrote to her father, Robert Wickliffe Sr., asking permission to marry her. Wickliffe was pleased with his daughter's marriage and gave her husband three hundred acres of land in Jefferson County, called Mann's Lick, at the time of the wedding.[23]

Following days of parties, William Preston and Margaret Preston Wickliffe were married on 9 December 1840, in an elaborate ceremony at Christ Church in Lexington, where her father was a vestryman. Although hyperbole was a part of nineteenth-century descriptions of women, so many observers described Margaret as a "reigning beauty" and "brilliant conversationalist" that there must have been a good foundation for these claims. One contemporary described her as "nearly as tall" as her husband and having "an Eagle nose and mouth." William was enchanted with his wife, finding Margaret "the most charming en bon point imaginable, the freshest and most delicate complexion, the fullest and finest development of a person."[24]

Margaret Wickliffe's pulchritude was but one of her virtues. She was well educated. Her parents saw to her schooling first at home and then at private Lexington academies, where she studied literature, history, the natural sciences, religion, music, and French. One classmate was Mary Todd, the future wife of Abraham Lincoln, who considered Mag "the best friend of my earlier days." Next Margaret attended Madame Sigoigne's school for young ladies in Philadelphia, where she followed a demanding schedule and was a schoolmate of William's sister Susan.[25] The books Margaret later purchased–biographies, Roman histories, and Latin grammars–demonstrate that by the time she left Madame Sigoigne's she was a well-educated woman.

In addition to her formal schooling, Margaret was reared to be the wife of an elite husband who shared her family's social standing. Her home life and schooling trained her in etiquette and the social graces. Visits to the capital, where one winter she spent the social season at the home of her mother's cousin, South Carolina senator William C. Preston, and stays in Charleston, South Carolina, where she made her debut at eighteen, complemented her schooling in Philadelphia and introduced Margaret to her social equals outside Kentucky. Her stepmother saw to it that she would be able to manage a house staffed with maids, butlers, and cooks. The fulsome hospitality Margaret customarily dispensed as a wife would be the subject of much comment and proved a virtue to her husband's career in an age that valued ostentatious display.[26] Later, particularly during his diplomatic service and in matters of religion, she would exert a strong influence on her husband's decisions. Spanish ministers were quick to note this during Preston's Madrid years.

Margaret Wickliffe would prove to be a very independent wife. Her family's wealth and social and political prominence–together with her determination to exercise control over her inherited properties–gave her a considerable degree of freedom. Her father, Robert Wickliffe Sr., was "one of the shrewdest and ablest land lawyers in Kentucky" and a Democratic party chieftain. Earlier he had been a leader in both houses of the state legislature and United States attorney for Kentucky, while Margaret's mother, Margaretta Preston Howard, was the daughter of a large landowner. She died when Mag was five years old, and her father soon married another Lexington heiress, Mary Owen Todd Russell. A special affection linked Margaret and her stepmother, whom Mag often referred to as "my best friend in the world." After receiving property from her parents, she was able–despite legislation that gave husbands economic control–to use her status and influence to administer her inheritance and later to keep her husband from selling her lands. Though the wife of an active Whig, in politics she favored the Democratic party and shared her father's animosity toward Henry Clay.[27]

The marriage of William Preston and Margaret Wickliffe was an excellent match in social and economic terms. In Kentucky, as in Virginia and elsewhere in the South, intermarriage among upper-class families was commonplace. This close kinship pattern reinforced bonds of friendship and helped to perpetuate the dominance of their class–which they believed represented a natural aristocracy of talent and leadership. Both families belonged to the state's original aristocracy, and the Preston-Wickliffe marriage solidified the ties between the two families.[28] The advantages of this union would prove to be of importance to William as a soldier, politician, and diplomat. Like her husband, Margaret Wickliffe had relatives who occupied positions of power and prestige. Her uncle Charles A. Wicklilffe was a Kentucky congressman and later governor, and in South Carolina, Senator William C. Preston and General John S. Preston were her mother's cousins. Margaret's stepmother, Mary Owen Todd Russell, also was from one of the first families of the Bluegrass.

Like the Prestons, the Wickliffes owned tremendous amounts of property and considered landed wealth the basis of economic prosperity and social station. As in Virginia, in Kentucky the status of "gentleman" was associated with landed estates. Robert Wickliffe Sr., known as the "Old Duke," possessed perhaps the greatest fortune in antebellum Kentucky. As the state's largest slaveholder, he owned 180 slaves valued at $73,000 in 1839.[29]

By the time of his marriage in 1840, William Preston displayed both the physical and ideological traits that would characterize him for the remainder of his life. Contemporaries considered him an extraordinarily handsome man of "magnificent personal appearance" and described him as "a powerfully built man," "deep chested, rather pale faced, with perfect Bourbon features." His "well proportioned," "vigorous physique" was often commented on. Preston's sharp features endowed him with a striking countenance. His prominent nose was circled by his rather small mouth and delicate lips, and stern, light-brown eyes that imparted a pleasant countenance when he smiled. His long, dark-brown hair was parted to his right and complemented his often-serious mien.[30] Preston's stature of six feet and his erect carriage projected a commanding air. In fact, his decisive bearing connoted a measure of hauteur which betrayed his aristocratic station. Later he would have a well-trimmed mustache and small v-shaped beard under his lower lip, features he would continue to cultivate the rest of his life.[31] While his correct appearance betrayed his concern for detail and precision, it belied the sense of humor he often displayed among friends. In his later years, Preston became increasingly bald and parted his hair carefully to obscure this as much as possible. His high forehead was marred by furrows, while he read and imparted the certain impression of a dignified intellectual.

Not surprisingly, as an adult Preston was devoted to both his immediate and extended family. He displayed a respect for and an obligation to family that was inculcated in him throughout his childhood. The many terms of endearment found in his letters to his mother and sisters and in his correspondence with his kinsfolk represented more than the expected literary conventions of his era. For Preston they also demonstrated his affection for his relatives and connoted his willingness to be of service. Throughout his adult years he would help many of them with legal and financial matters, as well as offering counsel and friendship.

Preston's social beliefs and political attitudes were fully developed by 1840. His genteel background and economic interests combined to reinforce his conservative outlook. He believed in the correctness of slavery and was an outspoken defender of this institution. Like many white southerners and northerners, he was convinced of the inferiority of blacks and of the need to hold Africans "in bondage because we are unwilling to amalgamate with them, and desire to keep our Teutonic blood pure and uncorrupted by any baser admixture, because we prefer that their untutored labor should be directed by the superior intelligence of our race to useful industry." Preston owned fourteen slaves in 1850 and insisted that "the zeal and bigotry of the abolitionists would not soften the bondage of the slave but would overwhelm the white race with ruin."[32]

Belief in the superiority of whites led Preston–like many other slaveholders–to advocate territorial expansion of the Union into Mexico and the Caribbean. He was convinced that the inferior, racially mixed populations in these lands would benefit from the blessings of the United States's superior republican institutions and society. His advocacy of Texas annexation and the Mexican War, as well as American ownership of Cuba, came from this conviction.

Later Preston would claim that toward slavery he felt "the same perplexity and the same difficulties that troubled Washington and the great and wise men of his time." He therefore refused to advise his children either "to manumit or hold your slaves in bondage. You must be controlled by your sense of right, being governed only by a sense of benevolence and justice to them, instead of cupidity in yourselves, and trying by wisdom, forethought and kindness to make them happy and even to liberate them, if that in your conscience will most conduce to their moral and physical improvement."[33]

Toward the end of the Civil War, when the defeat of the South and the abolition of slavery appeared probable, the Kentucky squire reflected that his proslavery views were moderate when compared with the more extremist defenders of this institution. He even claimed to his son in February 1865, "I was never a strong advocate for slavery." This statement was hardly in keeping with his vigorous efforts in Kentucky and in national politics for thirty years to defend involuntary servitude. In self-defense Preston correctly noted that he never bought a slave, except to free him, and that he never sold a servant of his "except for crime." But he admitted, "I did not consider it wrong to inherit them, thought it was right for me to hold, govern, protect and direct them according to the best of my ability, as it was better for them, and indispensable to the harmony and well being of my country."[34]

Certainly slavery was a heinous evil that degraded both master and slave, but within this institution there were gradations in the form of servitude. Despite his racist views and belief that slaves were property, Preston's own confident sense of superiority and upper-class feeling of paternalism tempered his treatment of his slaves. On the eve of the Civil War, Preston manumitted his favorite bondsman, Samuel Giles, his childhood playmate and loyal servant for three decades. According to Preston, Giles "burst into tears and begged to follow me," when his master was leaving for the Confederacy. The former slave served him faithfully during his years in the southern army–as he had earlier during the Mexican War. Before the Battle of Shiloh in 1862, Preston urged his children in the event of his death to look after Giles. But the master's affection for and trust in his friend never overcame his racist beliefs. "I trust you will not let him suffer, if he is idle or poor," he wrote his son and daughters, "but will shelter him against the thriftlessness and evils that are usual among his race."[35]

Many of his class in Kentucky shared William Preston's views as a slave owner. The plantations in the commonwealth were not so large as those in the "cotton states," so the number of slaves possessed by each owner tended to be smaller. In the decade before the Civil War, fewer than sixty Kentuckians owned more than fifty slaves. This sometimes led to a different relationship between owner and slave, as often the master himself directed the several slaves who worked his farm. Some large slaveholders in Kentucky shared certain paternalistic attitudes with Preston. Robert Wickliffe Sr. spoke against dividing slave families if the owners needed to sell their bondsmen, but he approved of beating even female slaves for disobedience—a common practice among the state's slave masters. As a legislator in Frankfort in 1840, he denounced the growing Kentucky slave trade with the cotton states and later opposed the 1850 Kentucky Constitution for "restricting emancipation and authorising [sic] the Legislature to make it felony for a free negroe to come into the state." However, regardless of the degree of benevolence of the owner, slaves had little chance to escape their primitive living conditions. Kentucky's bondsmen were subject to onerous regulations through the state slave codes. A Louisville ordinance prohibited more than three African Americans from assembling at the market or other public place, and at 10:00 p.m. a bell tolled to warn those without a pass that they had a half-hour to return home.[36]

Not all whites in Kentucky willingly accepted slavery. For moral reasons many were repelled by human bondage, but they remained a minority. Opposition to the peculiar institution was expressed at the state constitutional conventions of 1792 and 1799, and in 1806 the Kentucky Abolition Society was founded. However, two decades later the abolitionist groups counted only two hundred members. More popular in Kentucky was the colonization movement that advocated removing freed blacks and slaves to Africa. It disclaimed any intention of abolition. Henry Clay was a president of the American Colonization Society, and by 1832 the Kentucky Colonization Society counted thirty-one branches. But these groups had little success. Only a few hundred liberated Kentucky blacks managed to reach Africa.[37]

Margaret Preston's stepmother, Mary, opposed slavery out of religious conviction and supported the American Colonization Society. She freed ten slaves, sending seven of them to Liberia in 1833.[38] However, while her husband and stepdaughter respected her antislavery beliefs, she never converted them to her views.

The abolition movement gained strength nationally in the 1830s, and arguments about slavery became a prominent feature of debates in Congress. Although legislators since the first Congress sporadically had reviewed petitions to end slavery, debate on the subject became increasingly intense and frequent in the 1830s. William Lloyd Garrison's militant campaign to abolish slavery gained many adherents in the North, and even in the South a small group of more moderate antislavery spokesmen came forward. In Kentucky their cause enlisted important proponents. Dr. Robert J. Breckinridge, a Presbyterian divine in Lexington, wrote and preached against slavery, while James G. Birney of Danville, a slaveholder and former agent of the American Colonization Society, denounced slavery and freed his own bondsmen.[39] While at Yale University in 1831, Cassius Marcellus Clay heard Garrison inveigh against slavery. The Kentuckian disagreed with the northerner's call for immediate abolition but became an advocate of emancipation. Clay based his antislavery creed on economic rather than moral grounds, believing that the institution hindered commercial development and prosperity.[40]

The moral fervor of the abolitionists' unprecedented onslaught against slavery brought a furious counterattack from the South. In the eyes of most slaveholders, Garrison's insistence that the institution was immoral was insult enough, but his contention that slavery had turned the South into "one great Sodom" was anathema. In the Senate John C. Calhoun of South Carolina defiantly asserted in 1837 that "the South will not, cannot, surrender our institutions," and instead of an evil, he declared slavery "a good–a positive good." Throughout the South strident authors in the 1830s created a literature justifying the peculiar institution. Their defenses of slavery appealed to history (the Haitian Revolution was much cited as evidence of what would happen if slavery were abolished), the Bible (noting the existence of slavery in both the Old and New Testaments), natural law (contending that certain races were inherently inferior to others), and morality (often mentioning the Christian duty of the owner to uplift and protect his servants).[41]

Slavery became the "cornerstone" of the South's social order and essential to the southern way of life. Slaveholding defined wealth, class, and prestige in the region, as well as providing whites with a mechanism to control blacks.[42] As slave owners like Preston viewed the matter, the abolitionists were threatening their liberty–the right to control their own affairs–and besmirched their honor as upright Christians and good Americans. Even southerners like Henry Clay who were aware of the evils of slavery were frightened by the abolitionists' vehemence and considered them dangerous.[43]

Southern apologists for slavery were heartened by prominent proslavery advocates in the North. Some conservative politicians and clerics concerned with authority and order saw the peculiar institution as a valuable conservator of America's social organism. Their backing demonstrated–to southern eyes–that defense of slavery was not a selfish regional argument, but one that brought southerners and northerners together in defense of property rights, the Constitution, and the Union.

Despite the occasionally benevolent sentiments of some masters like Preston toward their slaves, these owners remained staunch defenders of the peculiar institution. Economic interest, combined with their belief in black inferiority, made them determined to oppose abolition. They feared a world without slavery and its racial controls.

The explosive issue of slavery turned many of its defenders and its detractors into bitter enemies. The "Old Duke" and his son Robert Wickliffe were "arch-foes" of Cassius Clay, the commonwealth's champion of emancipation. Following Robert Jr.'s defeat by Clay in the 1840 legislative campaign, the animosity between the two grew. The next spring both became involved in an affair of honor, when again they were running for the statehouse. Clay demanded redress for alleged insults made against him and his wife by Wickliffe. Preston, of course, sided with his brother-in-law, and Albert Sidney Johnston served as Robert's second. The duel took place on 13 May 1841 at Locust Grove in Jefferson County, where both contestants exchanged one shot without effect. At their seconds' recommendation, both principals then agreed to drop the affair, but their animosity continued.[44] Later that year, Robert Wickliffe avenged his electoral defeat of 1840 by vanquishing his adversary at the ballot box.

Despite the prominence of the Kentuckians who attacked slavery, they gained few adherents. The Rev. Robert Breckinridge was defeated for election to the Kentucky legislature in 1831, after serving several terms, and in 1838 voters by a ratio of nearly four to one turned down a call to convene a constitutional convention to reconsider slavery. In 1830 the value of Kentucky's 165,213 slaves–almost a quarter of the state's population–was enormous and guaranteed a strong proslavery vote.[45] While most white families did not own bondsmen, many of them approved of slavery. Whites without slaves also had an economic interest in the institution, for farmers and urban businessmen used bondsmen hired out by their owners.[46] Fear of blacks and pervasive racism also helped to explain the willingness of the white majority to support slavery. The adamant defense of the peculiar institution by most of the leading–and therefore wealthy–Kentucky families also helped to predispose others to accept slavery as a normal aspect of their society and made slaveholding the goal of many ambitious whites.[47] Although Preston's views on servitude and race remained dominant in his home state and elsewhere in the South, challenges to those beliefs by more and more citizens elsewhere in the Union warned that words of anger might evolve into words of war.

William Preston's aristocratic upbringing inculcated in him a conviction that the upper class should bear the burden of noblesse oblige and provide direction for their social and economic inferiors. A staunch supporter of universal male suffrage for whites, Preston was outspoken in defending the immigrants' right to vote. Nevertheless, he believed that political leadership should rest with the better-educated and socially prominent sectors.

Given the political success of his own family members and his upper-class friends, Preston assumed that such elite direction was natural and preferable. The many civil and military leaders among his ancestors and in his own generation reinforced this belief, as did the numerous state and national leaders among his wife's relatives. In addition, Preston's aristocratic friends, such as Basil W. Duke, Simon Bolivar Buckner, Joshua F. Bullitt, Reuben T. Durrett, and James Speed, also shared political leadership with other Kentuckians from their social station.

At a time when United States political and economic life was becoming more broadly based and business oriented, Preston's assumed views on the nature of governmental and social leadership were at variance with a changing reality. Like many contemporary Kentucky gentry, he believed that the upper-class domination of southern society accorded with Divine will. This attitude stood in marked contrast to the increasingly more socially democratic leadership in the North. Preston's belief in southern superiority was clearly expressed by his nephew William Preston Johnston, who credited his namesake with "moulding" his views on the subject. Johnston wrote in 1862 that through warfare the North was "trying to assert the domination of a base democracy over a proud and fierce aristocracy, who were born and bred their betters." Preston displayed his adhesion to this view when during the Civil War he remarked, "I entered the service of the Confederacy to which I was allied by my birth, my education, and my convictions of justice." In his political campaigns, the Kentuckian would receive the electoral support of many hard-working immigrants and middle-class merchants, but his circle of friends was confined to members of the socially prominent upper class.[48]

Preston's political credo likewise was the product of his family background and economic station. Like many others of his class, he insisted that the right of property was a necessary principle of law and asserted it "is not coeval with, but antecedent to, government." Ignoring the human side of the peculiar institution, he argued that slaves were property and thus the government could not legally deprive their owners of their belongings under any circumstances. Such thinking allowed slave owners to couch their defense in legal, rather than in moral, terms. In 1849 Preston maintained, "If a difference exist [sic] between slaves and other property, I defy any man to show the difference."[49]

His belief in limited governmental authority also made Preston a defender of states' rights. He recognized the duty of the civil authority to restrain arbitrary power and to curtail "the unlimited will of an individual," but he affirmed that certain rights were so fundamental that they could not be violated even by the will of the majority. "The great principles of life, liberty and property," he insisted, "cannot be interfered with"–though he ignored the liberty of slaves in that balance. Even if three-fourths of the states would agree to amend the Constitution to outlaw slavery or any right guaranteed by solemn compact, Preston believed the minority would have the legal obligation to resist. In such cases the majority would have "stricken down the fundamental right which society was made to guard."[50] Such views would make compromise difficult for those of his generation as the war drums grew louder.

In the quarter-century following his marriage, William Preston would dedicate his energies to promoting his beliefs and the interests of the South's slaveholding aristocracy. He would do so as a soldier, politician, and diplomat.

Chapter III: Husband and Soldier

～

D uring the Prestons' first decade of married life in Louisville, William began to fulfill his ambitions. He continued his legal practice, became prominent in civic affairs, and retained his interest in politics. But more significant for his political future was the Mexican War, which allowed him the opportunity to serve as an army officer. These years also were important in family terms, for by 1855 the couple had become the proud parents of six healthy children.

In the 1840s the Prestons saw Louisville grow into one of the leading cities in the Union. By 1850 its population had surged to 43,000, more than twice the number of inhabitants a decade earlier. This made Louisville the nation's tenth most populous city. While commerce earlier had been the major factor in Louisville's growth, during the 1840s an impressive increase in manufacturing also contributed to its expansion. William B. Belknap opened an iron store on Main Street in 1840 that he soon converted into the largest wholesale hardware business in the South. By 1850 Louisville could count ten foundries making iron, ploughs, and machinery for grist and lumber mills, nine bagging and rope factories, nine brickyards, eight establishments producing candles and soap, and a plant that turned out twelve thousand hats a year.[1]

Commerce remained an essential pillar of the city's economy, and agriculture, livestock, and natural resources in the surrounding region fueled exports. Louisville's slaughterhouses increased their output and the tobacco trade remained a staple. Though railroads soon would rival the influence of river trade, steamboats continued to be the backbone of transportation throughout the 1840s.

The increase in the city's institutions, cultural offerings, and public buildings paralleled its booming economy and brought a sense of pride to its citizens. In 1846 a charter was granted to establish the University of Louisville, and its medical college gained a national reputation. The community attracted prominent lecturers, such as the poet Walt Whitman in 1848, and was home to three "highly professional newspapers." But the pride of local denizens was the new county courthouse begun in 1837 and designed by

Gideon Shryock, a Lexington architect trained in Philadelphia. When completed in 1850, this impressive Greek Revival building was fronted by four Doric columns supporting its pediment, while beneath its rotunda a cast-iron stairway ushered visitors to the second floor. Another building designed by Shryock, the nearby Bank of Louisville, with its Ionic columns and elaborate ornamentation, gave the city another classical structure that helped set a precedent for elegance and dignity in public buildings.[2]

Louisville had developed a fashionable social set by the 1840s. For the local aristocracy, servants, expensive clothing, frequent entertaining, and attendance at social gatherings comprised essential parts of their identity. The elite amused each other with elaborate receptions, sumptuous dinners with refined tableware, and dances in their homes. Shops and dry-goods stores catered to their demand for stylish dress and ostentatious household decoration. They drove expensive carriages through the crowded streets and attended soirées at the elegant Galt House. This hotel also was the site of lavish banquets and balls to celebrate national holidays and the visits of celebrated guests. In 1848 the city's fashionable cemetery, Cave Hill, was inaugurated on land adjacent to the Preston Plantation.

Despite Louisville's economic, cultural, and social advances, many aspects of life at mid-century remained reminiscent of the city's frontier origins. During his 1842 visit to the Falls City, Charles Dickens believed that at the Galt House he was "as handsomely lodged as though we had been in Paris," but he noted that "the [city's] buildings are smoky and blackened, from the use of bituminous coal." Furthermore, he observed that the roads "were perfectly alive with pigs of all ages; lying about in every direction, fast asleep; or grunting."[3]

The prosperity, political importance, and lifestyle of the Preston family in the decades before the Civil War depended on all the various trends affecting the city. Population growth raised the value of the Preston lands. Increasing affluence and more inhabitants permitted additional services and a more cultivated social atmosphere. By the 1840s the lives of the Prestons and other upper-class Louisville families closely resembled those of their peers on the east coast.

Following their wedding in 1840, William and Margaret Preston had spent three months of their honeymoon in Louisville with his family. Margaret returned to Lexington to live with her parents until their new house was ready, while her husband practiced law and lived at his mother's. "This shall be the last time that I will ever be separated from you," Margaret wrote William, and she constantly urged him to come to Lexington to be with her and to attend social events. She also feared that their separation might be interpreted by some as a marital blemish.[4]

It was not until two years after their wedding that the Prestons' new Louisville home was ready for occupancy. "No residential property was more desirable than that on Walnut between Third and Fourth Streets," and it was on the north side of this tree-lined avenue that the Prestons had built their new house. George Keats, the brother of the English poet John Keats, had amassed wealth in Louisville from flour and lumber mills and already lived across the street in a gray stone-fronted dwelling, one of the first in the city. The Democratic legislator James Guthrie, a promoter of the Portland Canal and later president of the Louisville and Nashville Railroad, resided in a three-story brick mansion at Walnut on the corner of Second Street, and wealthy William Belknap would move into a stone mansion on the south side of Walnut between Second and Third.[5]

William and Mag's new residence fit into its elegant location. The stone façade of the three-story dwelling demonstrated the couple's affluence and fashionable taste. The ground floor featured a parlor, furnished with a pianoforte, lounges, and rocking chairs, and a dining room, with its six mahogany chairs, table, and sideboard, suitable for lavish entertaining. The couple's bedroom on the first floor had a bath and a large dressing room. An armchair for reading, six other chairs, bookcases, a secretary, and a table were found in the library. The second and third floors contained a bedroom for guests–with a mahogany bed, wardrobe, washstand, and six chairs–and three bedrooms, with walnut furniture, for the family. The piano and a mahogany bed were brought from Lexington, but the other furnishings were purchased new. The basement served as a storage area, and behind the residence stood slave quarters, a coal shed and smokehouse, and a stable for horses, milch cows, and the family's coach. The land-rich husband elected to borrow $3,500 from his father-in-law to pay for part of the expensive house. Complaining about its cost, he wrote his sister Susan, "It has been the Delilah which has shorn me of my strength and delivered me over into the hands of the Philistines. This however is between us, for I never publicly regret what I cannot remedy."[6]

In 1857 the Prestons would purchase the large house of Joseph and Margaret Wickliffe Holt. Two years later Holt would become postmaster general under President James Buchanan; his wife was a Bardstown cousin of Mrs. Preston. The new residence also was on the north side of Walnut Street, this time between Floyd and East Streets. However, the Prestons only lived at this new address for a year, for in late 1858 they left Louisville.

Margaret took satisfaction in running the Louisville household. William gave her $50 a month to cover expenses, and she found the family could live "sumptuously" on this. Food–including "every luxury the market afforded"–cost only $10 a month. Margaret estimated in 1843 that her yearly budget of $600 would cover everything, "wines included, servants clothes, horse and cow feed, traveling expenses, everything except William's personal expenditures." The managerial wife reported to her father that the overseer of Liberia, the Old Duke's farm in Bath County, was sending her food shipments, including such staples as turkeys, ducks, roast pigs, chickens, barrels of apples, and butter. These supplies meant less expenditures and allowed the businesswoman in Margaret to exclaim with glee, "I expect to make quite a fortune out of my month's allowance." To help her with domestic chores, her father sometimes traded a household slave in Lexington for one of hers. Complaining about the expense of keeping slaves in Louisville, Margaret asked to receive only slaves without children.[7]

Her husband was delighted with Mag's attention to household affairs, remarking to her father in 1845 that she was "busily engaged in fixing her household, planting shrubbery, varnishing furniture etc. preparatory for the summer. Our acquisition of the few feet adjoining us seems to be regarded by her as quite an extensive domain and she is laying various plans for ornamenting it." Margaret was concerned with even such minor household needs as seeing that the porch received another coat of paint and making certain there were enough cats to devour mice.[8]

However, Mrs. Preston also spent a great part of her early married years pregnant and nursing her children. Her first offspring were three daughters. Mary ("Polly") Owen, born in October 1841, was named for her beloved stepmother, while Caroline (Carrie) Hancock and Margaret ("Poogie") Howard, named after William's mother and Mag's mother, respectively, entered the family in 1843 and 1845. Margaret gave birth to the first two girls in Lexington at her father's home, but a family marriage perhaps accounts for her remaining in Louisville for Poogie's birthing. The children had common illnesses–scarlet fever, whooping cough, and diarrhea. William urged Mag not to give them "medicine without advice of a physician," but he also worried that their sicknesses "imposed a great deal of care and trouble on Margaret." Despite childhood maladies, "Mary and Caroline are in the most robust health," William reported in 1845. Although the evidence is not conclusive, Margaret may have had miscarriages in 1847 and 1849.[9]

Margaret's doting father, the Old Duke, was overjoyed with his Preston grandchildren and was solicitous of their well-being. He told his son-in-law that Mary Owen's birth signaled William's "beginning of life" as a male, reminding him to "take great pleasure in earning bread for such a family I can but hope you may be blest with." In 1846 Wickliffe sent two cows to Louisville for milk for his granddaughters, and two years later gave each of them land in their names in Carrollton, Kentucky.[10]

Both parents were delighted in December 1850 with the birth of a male heir, Robert Wickliffe (Wick), named for the Old Duke. The proud father reported to sister Susan that the child "is one of the handsomest and sturdiest little imps you ever saw." "You cannot imagine . . . the satisfaction of having my wishes gratified in the birth of a son," William confessed. Wick's pleased mother would refer to him as "the sole hope of our house," while his Lexington grandfather stated that his namesake was "great in stature, great in voice and of unparallell [sic] beauty." Aware of the family's joy, a Lexington friend and writer, Rosa Vertner Johnson, wrote verses in honor of Wick's birth that lauded his parents and spoke of their ambitious hopes:

> In short, may he live to be *all* you desire,
> With the beauty, and genius, of Mother and Sire;
> For a richer inheritance where may we find
> Than fairness of person and talent combined.[11]

Three years later, Margaret gave birth to her fifth child, Susan (Sunie) Christy, named for William's sister Susan and her husband Howard Christy, and in 1855 came another daughter, Jessie Fremont.

By 1850 Margaret was a woman of considerable size, and she was enfeebled by the birth of Sunie. But her new babies were healthy—especially Sunie, whom her father described as "wonderfully stout" and "rosy." After Jessie's birth, Margaret's father gave his daughter Liberia Farm and the income from the winter's hog sale.[12] The last Preston child was born prematurely in March 1857 and died the next year from the croup.

The couple proved to be concerned and loving parents, and the rearing of their children followed a similar pattern. Margaret participated actively in many aspects of their upbringing, and William assisted in some of her efforts. She breast-fed the babies, cared for their health, and played games with them as adolescents—racing them on the porch and around the grape arbor. A small grass plot was converted into the children's playground. With her husband Margaret did other things expected of parents: she chided the youths to keep their rooms neat, disciplined them, rewarded them with gifts, and took them in fancy dress to numerous social and family affairs. When the oldest child Mary was but six years old, she attended a party where "all the little boys ran up and asked her to dance," including, to her mother's approval, Henry Clay [III], grandson of the senator, who paid her "particular attention."[13]

Margaret carefully oversaw the children's formal education. She personally gave their first lessons at home, teaching them songs and tutoring the children in reading, arithmetic, history, geography, and French. Like typical parents, the Prestons were proud of their offspring's progress. "Little Mary has learned her A B C–and is trying very hard to learn to read," her mother reported in 1846. That same year William bragged that three-year-old Carrie "has learned with the utmost accuracy the charming rhymes of Mother Goose." Margaret enjoyed her classes so much that her father jokingly accused her of "playing at teaching." On at least one occasion, she hired a French "master" for her older girls. The daughters proved good students. Margaret was pleased that her oldest child Mary "is learning very rapidly french and reviewing her geography."[14]

Yet Mrs. Preston often tired of her maternal responsibilities and did not want a life centered on her children. Fortunately, the Prestons always had a nurse to care for them, and several house slaves attended to details of cleaning, cooking, and laundry. But for Margaret, this help did not offer enough relief, so she arranged for all of her children from an early age to spend weeks with their kinsfolk. When only two years old, Mary was sent to Lexington for several weeks to stay with Margaret's sister Sally Woolley. Margaret's father also obliged on many occasions. In 1849 he urged her to send the three oldest girls to stay with him and her older sister Mary Howard in Lexington. Four years later the daughters again were at Wickliffe Place, where they studied needlework, reading, and arithmetic with the slave children at classes organized by Aunt Mary Howard. Aunt Susan Preston Christy also assisted Mag with her brood, serving in William's words as a "mother to my dear children."[15] When the young Prestons grew older, they were sent away from home to boarding school, just as their mother and father had been.

In addition to their own family, the Prestons reared William Preston Johnston. Named for his uncle, the lad was the son of William's sister Henrietta and Albert Sidney Johnston. The boy and his younger sister Henrietta Preston would spend their childhood years separated from their father. Johnston's military career in the United States army, his residence in far-away Texas where proper schooling was not available, and his continuing financial difficulties caused him to leave his wife and children with relatives in Kentucky. Following their mother's death in 1835, four-year-old Will and sister Hennie lived with their grandmother, Caroline Hancock Preston, and then with their aunt, Josephine Preston Rogers. During these years his Uncle William developed an affection for the lad. As Preston confessed to his brother-in-law in 1840, "I have always regarded him as 'my own peculiar.'" When Aunt Josephine died in 1842, Will went to live with William and Margaret for the next eight years.[16]

The loving relationship between uncle and nephew strengthened with the passing years. Both shared similar characteristics. The boy possessed "a serious and studious nature" and was a hard worker. In addition to helping with his schooling, his namesake enjoyed taking him to public events and teaching him to play chess–a pastime the two would continue to share for more than forty years. By 1843 Preston was proudly writing to Albert Sidney that his son "is everything either you or I could wish." "Will is learning finely and I have become so attached to him that I do not think I can spare him from me til he goes to college. I think he is going to make a bold fine fellow, with a mind highly cultivated, and a character of the brightest sort." Five years later the Louisville uncle confessed to Will's father, "He is already to me a companion and a friend, and seems a younger brother."[17]

Preston had a strong influence on his nephew's development. Will later credited his belief in the "moderate Southern idea" on slavery to conversations with his surrogate father. Johnston studied in Louisville schools, at an academy in Shelbyville, and at the Kentucky Military Institute before attending Centre College in Danville and the Western Military Institute in Georgetown. In 1850 the youth went off to Yale University, as his uncle had done, and then returned to study law at the University of Louisville.[18] Certainly Preston would be more pleased with the diligence and intellectual qualities of his nephew than he would be with his own son, whose academic failures and disregard for his parents' counsel would cause them grief.

Throughout their married life William and Margaret lived in the ostentatious manner expected of the first families of Kentucky, for lavish display was a component of gentry life in the South. Elegance in dress was important, and both William and Margaret purchased their wardrobes from shops on the east coast. He bought most of his clothing from a Boston haberdasher, while her dresses and gowns often came from Philadelphia and New York.

Entertaining was another essential element of life for the elite–and an expected ingredient in advancing one's political ambitions. Determined to make their home a center of social activity, the Prestons employed expensive china and silver settings and costly piles of food to impress their guests. Parmesan cheese, smoked Scotch salmon, sardines, and oranges were among the delicacies of the day that Margaret purchased from the boats steaming up the river. In addition to a cook who oversaw food preparation, she employed a pastry chef renowned for his pies.[19]

Soon the Prestons' hospitality became famous throughout Louisville. Dr. Samuel D. Gross, a professor of surgery, was a next-door neighbor to the east of the Prestons and a frequent guest. He later recalled a dinner party the recently married couple gave: "The entertainment was a very agreeable one, and I recollect how every one was struck by the appearance of the groom and his bride–two noble specimens of a man and a woman." "No one ever arranged more elegantly for a dinner party, or presided with more grace than Mrs. Preston." On the other side of the Prestons lived his law partner William J. Graves and his wife, who often dined with them, as did a Democratic neighbor, James Guthrie, and his spouse. The lawyer Reuben T. Durrett was another prominent friend. "Among my most pleasing recollections of Louisville society," he later recalled, "are the entertainments by the Prestons." "Her menus always displayed exquisite taste in the midst of smiling abundance," Durrett affirmed, noting that "her husband owed no little of his political success to the entertainments graced by his accomplished wife at their own home." But more than culinary triumphs accounted for the Prestons' reputation as hosts. As many guests remarked, Margaret was an excellent conversationalist, and William was renowned for his "courtly manners."[20]

Extending hospitality to "acquaintances passing through" and to kinsfolk was expected of the Prestons. Mag's parents and sister Mary came several times each year. When back in Louisville, Albert Sidney Johnston stayed with the Prestons, as did members of the Hancock family and visiting Prestons from Virginia, South Carolina, and Louisiana. On their honeymoon, Margaret's brother Robert and bride spent several days with the couple. "Have all my rooms filled" was a refrain often found in Margaret's correspondence.[21]

Attending the elegant affairs of their social and political peers was another expected duty of the Prestons. Their prominence involved them in countless receptions, teas, and soirées. When former president Martin Van Buren visited Louisville in May 1842, Judge John Rowan chose the Prestons to dine at his house with the New York Democrat. Both husband and wife enjoyed the social whirl, and in 1848 Mag's sister insisted that the domineering Mrs. Preston still loved playing the role of "Madame La Flirt."[22]

William Preston considered his life in Louisville during the 1840s "bright and beautiful," and he described his marriage and family relations as "cloudless." He was a caring husband. When his wife was fatigued after birthing or depressed, he proved attentive to her health, making her "take as much exercise as possible" and walking "a mile or two every favourable night with her." While William was away on business or she in Lexington, both wrote the other tender missives. In their first decade together, Mag was pleased with her situation. "I am more than ever in love with Louisville," she admitted in 1843, and she was clearly in love with her husband. On occasion Mag addressed passionate letters to him in French. She insisted she was "impatient to be together again" and eager to put on her finery for his return, adding that she had "much to say to you, but I am afraid to put it on paper." Although loving, Mag also was a possessive wife, and she did not hesitate to remind her spouse of his promise never to marry again if she were to die before him.[23]

Despite Margaret's contentment as Mrs. William Preston, she remained a very independent woman. Although married to a prominent Whig, she privately followed her father's politics and remained a loyal Democrat throughout the 1840s. "Don't let anyone see this letter," Mag confided to her father, and then she proceeded to attack her husband's law partner, a strong backer of Henry Clay: "I pretend to think Graves as great a man as he tries to be–but I am tired of him and his politicks [sic] too." "It is almost the wish of my heart to see Mr. Clay beaten," she wrote of the 1844 Whig presidential nominee, and later she celebrated the victory of his opponent. "[James K.] Polk is elected, the country saved. . . . Democracy had triumphed and that old Clay was a dead coon." By winning, Polk allowed Margaret to collect a $700 wager–a large sum more than equal to her household expenditures for an entire year.[24]

Mrs. Preston's independence also showed in her conscious efforts to impress upon all that she remained a Wickliffe and thus enjoyed status and wealth in her own right. She customarily signed her name as "Margaret Wickliffe Preston" or "M. W. Preston," not only in her public correspondence, but also in letters to her children. Her many–and often extended–stays at her father's home also reminded contemporaries that she was a member of the Wickliffe clan. "I think she still regards Lexington as her own home," her husband informed the Old Duke early in their marriage, and this identification never changed. Robert Wickliffe's many gifts of land, money, and slaves to his married daughter demonstrated that she was a woman whose means did not depend on her husband's. Margaret's independence as a spouse would allow her on numerous occasions to assert her wishes when she disagreed with him.[25]

Throughout his married years in Louisville, William continued to practice law. Given his strong sense of family, much of his time was taken up with caring for his relatives' interests. Recording deeds and drawing up and enforcing leases occupied his time. Disputes regarding Susan Preston Christy's properties in St. Louis often took her brother there to intercede at court on her behalf, and he also handled cases for his wife's family. With Ben Hardin, his Bardstown friend, Preston defended a Wickliffe relative in 1850 accused of shooting a man. "After a week[']s trial, under most exciting circumstances," a relieved Preston reported, "the jury returned a verdict of 'not guilty.'" Four years later he prepared a brief for his father-in-law's appearance before the Supreme Court and was delighted when the Old Duke won the case. For the remainder of his life Preston would continue to look after legal affairs for his sisters and his in-laws.[26]

While taking care of family litigation, Preston also handled legal matters for other clients. One of his celebrated cases was the divorce of Sally Ward, the daughter of a prominent Kentucky family who had married T. Bigelow Lawrence, a wealthy Bostonian and son of the American ambassador to England. Sally left her husband in 1850 and returned to Louisville, whereupon Lawrence placed an advertisement in the *Louisville Daily Courier* claiming she had deserted him "without just cause." Sally's father then sought a divorce for her in the federal district court in Louisville, and Lawrence contested this request. Preston and James Guthrie successfully defended Sally's petition before the jury, arguing that she had been harshly treated by her husband, who moreover had slandered her in public. Later the divorcée would become a leading Louisville socialite.[27]

In addition to his legal concerns, Preston spent many hours handling business matters. He kept in close contact with the overseer of his farm on the Kentucky River near Carrollton, making personnel decisions, giving advice on agricultural matters, and caring for his finances. Looking after the collection of rents and buying and selling property were other matters that regularly occupied his time, as did the purchase and sale of stocks and bank notes.[28]

But all this took a secondary place in his life, for he soon had an opportunity to serve his country as a soldier in the Mexican War. The conflict that broke out in 1846 between the United States and its southern neighbor–ostensibly over border claims along the Texas frontier–only culminated a decade of increasing antagonism. North American settlers in the Mexican state of Texas had declared independence in March 1836. Their defeat of a Mexican army at the Battle of San Jacinto forced Mexico to recognize the new nation, but that had not ended the dispute.

Texas sought admission to the United States in May 1836. Since slavery was firmly established there, opinion divided on this–supporters of slavery favored annexation, while their adversaries opposed it. Others feared that incorporating Texas would bring war with Mexico. William's cousin, Senator William C. Preston of South Carolina, introduced a resolution in the Senate in January 1838 calling for the admission of Texas, but it was defeated.

William Preston was interested in Texas for several reasons. His brother-in-law was a military officer and secretary of war for Texas, and his Louisville uncle, George Hancock, was a major land speculator there. Interest in Texas lands reached a fever pitch in Kentucky in 1841 when a group of Louisvillians, headed by William P. Peters, received a grant of 8,000 square miles of land in north-central Texas from the Lone Star republic.[29] With Albert Sidney Johnston's help, Preston also invested in Texas real estate that year. As a slaveholder and a person with Texas connections, William's views were "warmly and firmly fixed in favour of annexation." In an 1844 letter to Johnston, he lamented "the narrow limits of our present political parties" and "the fanaticism of Northern abolition" that were delaying the logical and beneficial incorporation of Texas into the Union. That year Texas statehood became an issue in the presidential contest between the Whig candidate, Henry Clay, and his Democratic rival, James K. Polk. Originally opposed to Texas annexation, Clay realized the appeal that this had for many voters and amended his opposition, stating that he supported the acquisition of Texas under certain conditions. Polk harbored no such qualifications: he advocated annexation. Following Polk's election, but before he took office, Congress passed a joint resolution for annexation, and Texas became a state in December 1845.[30]

Texas's admission led to war with Mexico the following year and subsequently the acquisition of half of the territories of the Spanish-American republic. Texas claimed its border was at the Rio Grande, while Mexico argued that its territory stretched northward to the Nueces, a river that flows into the Gulf of Mexico more than one hundred miles to the east of the Rio Grande. Polk's belligerent move in early1846 to send troops under General Zachary Taylor to defend the land between the two rivers resulted in an armed clash with Mexican forces. Congress in May voted to recognize a state of war, 40-2.[31]

Abolitionists opposed the war, viewing the border dispute and the ensuing conflict only as pretexts to expand slavery to newly conquered territories. Most slaveholders favored the war, believing that expansion of the Union was vital. Certainly President Polk viewed the acquisition of territory with favor. Even today, the war's complex origins remain controversial. However, for Mexicans the cause was simple and is expressed in the name they gave the conflict: "The War of North American Intervention." William Preston's correspondence shows that he favored annexing all of Mexico to the United States and considered ownership of the northern Mexican territories from Texas to California necessary for the construction of railroads linking Kentucky and Tennessee to the Pacific.[32]

The Mexican War met mostly with enthusiastic support in Kentucky. Even the emancipationist Cassius M. Clay, who had opposed going to war, joined the army when war was declared. "It appeared that every Kentucky male wished to take up arms," one scholar has noted. More than 10,000 volunteers tried to fill the 2,500 places in three regiments that President Polk asked Governor William Owsley to raise. Seventy-seven of the commonwealth's ninety-nine counties raised volunteer units, and in Louisville war interest was so high that factories closed temporarily because of a shortage of workers. Patriotic feeling and a respect for martial values among the general public abetted the war fervor, but slaveholders were outspoken in their support, hoping that annexation of new territory would lead to the expansion of slavery.[33]

Other more personal motives contributed to the war fervor displayed by so many young men from the commonwealth's leading families. Like William Preston, many of the officers in the Mexican War were sons of Indian fighters and heroes of the Revolution and the War of 1812, and they were eager to display the same valor and patriotism that their fathers had shown. The Mexican War gave them a golden opportunity to emulate the deeds of their forebears. Preston, cousin John C. Breckinridge and brother-in-law Robert Wickliffe Jr., Henry Clay Jr., and numerous other members of the state's elite families went off to war. For them and many others, the honor they sought in the Mexican War was a means of self-identification, and their army experience abroad became a rite of passage for their generation. While many like Preston reached Mexico after the fighting was over, the rigors of military privations and the unhealthy Mexican climate–which managed to kill more invaders than did the Mexican army–proved sufficient to earn them the respect of their peers.[34]

The returning volunteers would provide the commonwealth with a generation of political leaders, and the conflict served as a training ground for the state's officers in the Civil War. These veterans in no small measure owed their electoral and military success to the public's admiration for their service in Mexico. Most notable among these, former Louisvillian Zachary Taylor, descendant of a Virginia Revolutionary War officer, became a national hero due to his victories in northern Mexico, and this led ultimately to his election as president of the United States.

Despite the popularity of the war in Kentucky, a few men–such as Henry Clay–and many women were less enthusiastic. Preston's wife originally believed that the risk of disease in Mexico was a more important consideration than the prospect of military distinction, and Caroline Hancock Preston did not want him to go off to war because William was her only son and important in supporting his family. Robert Wickliffe Jr.'s wife also urged him not to enlist, and John Breckinridge's spouse begged her husband to return home, citing the danger of yellow fever.[35] All of them disregarded the counsel of their families.

While Preston was abroad, his mother died. In her will she divided all of her property equally among her children, except her house and a lot that had been given her by Susan Preston Christy. In the Preston Enlargement, William inherited the land that today is bounded by East Broadway, Barret Avenue, and St. Anthony Place, while his sisters received portions of the subdivision to the south. When settled, this area would be known as the Highlands.[36]

Although William Preston's war record did not include combat, his service permitted him to display his talents as a competent organizer and an effective leader. He had been made captain of the Washington Blues in 1843 and placed in charge of this group of volunteers, a company in the Louisville Legion commanded by his brother-in-law, Jason Rogers. In May 1846 Preston headed a successful effort to raise $50,000 through a public subscription to help transport Kentucky troops to Mexico, and in April of the next year he donated $500 to a fund to repatriate the bodies of soldiers killed at the Battle of Buena Vista, where North American troops under General Taylor defeated the Mexicans. In April 1847 officers of several military groups, including the Washington Blues, met at the courthouse. At this reunion Preston was elected a lieutenant colonel, and Governor Owsley commissioned him to this rank in May. Three months later the army requested two additional regiments from Kentucky, and Preston was mustered into service on 4 October when the Louisville

Chapter III: Husband and Soldier

Legion was incorporated into the Fourth Regiment of Kentucky Volunteers. These infantry troops trained for several weeks seven miles downriver from Louisville.[37]

Following a parade through the city on 1 November, the new officer and his soldiers departed on the *General Taylor* for New Orleans. Placed under the command of General William Butler, the Kentuckians went by ship to Veracruz, arriving eighteen days later. Their first five days aboard *The Pioneer* were pleasant, and Preston exclaimed that "nothing can exceed in beauty the blue waters of the Gulf of Mexico when they are at rest." Just when the soldiers sighted the Mexican coast came "a violent norther" that drove the vessel for five days to the Yucatan peninsula. When the Kentuckians finally landed at Veracruz on 19 November, the fighting already had ended with General Winfield Scott's capture of Mexico City. The coastal fortress of San Juan de Ulloa with its "walls of enormous strength . . . completely commands" the harbor at Veracruz, Preston noted. While encamped for a week along the coast, he studied the site to understand "the masterly manner" in which Scott successfully had laid siege in March 1847 to "one of the strongest and most magnificent fortifications in the world."[38]

During Preston's four-week trip to the Aztec capital, he oversaw the slow progress of his company and the Mexican *arrieros* who were driving some two thousand mules from the yellow-fever-infested tropical lowlands over the Sierra Madre range. Their route took them to the colonial cities of Jalapa and Puebla, where they stopped in each for two days. As for thousands of other North American invaders, the 250-mile journey to Mexico City was a voyage of discovery for the lieutenant colonel. Mexico supplied antiquity, tropical beauty, and grandeur for a romantic generation, and–as a modern scholar has noted–"tales of Mexican adventure . . . poured from the pens of the soldiers." At his wife's urging, Preston kept a dairy of his experiences and impressions on his first trip abroad titled "Journal in Mexico"; later, copies of his journal were made for friends. Immediately he was enthralled by the glories of nature he beheld. "The rich tropical vegetation, the palm trees, . . . great flights of parrots, . . . myriads of flowering shrubs," he observed while climbing westward into the foothills, "presented to the eye of one from the temperate zone a landscape as novel as it was beautiful." With his slave Sam Giles, Preston shot "some singular birds whose name I did not know."

57

Three days later he observed with awe the "snow-crowned and stately crest" of Mount Orizaba.[39]

En route Preston was impressed by many sights. He noted the grandeur of the mountain pass at Cerro Gordo with its "perfectly precipitous cliffs." There General Scott had routed the well-entrenched but poorly provisioned forces under the command of General Antonio López de Santa Anna, who immodestly considered himself the "Napoleon of the West." On leaving the battle site, Preston described the morning as "beautiful beyond description." Below he watched as "the regiments with their trains of white-topped wagons wound slowly on like some vast serpent amid the defiles of the mountains." The troops next encamped several miles beyond Cerro Gordo at El Encero, Santa Anna's massive estate that "is in fact a fortress." The lieutenant colonel admired the house with its "great courts, stables for cattle," and chapel that "give a picturesque air to the building."[40]

On entering Jalapa, Preston noted the "great orange groves bending under the overweight of their golden fruit." In this "Paradise of Mexico," some four thousand feet above the coastal plain, he saw in the market "every product of the torrid and temperate zones–the pineapple, the lemon, the lime, the watermelon, the muskmelon, the peach, the apricot, the apple." After spending four days there, he exclaimed, "Beautiful Jalapa! The remembrance of that unequaled landscape will, for many a year, dwell upon my memory." After marching through arid plains and fertile valleys for days, the troops reached Puebla, "a fine city, built in the Spanish style, with regular streets." Preston was struck by the Alameda, "a beautiful drive, ornamented with statues and fountains," and considered the cathedral "a magnificent structure," with its "gracefully proportioned" twin towers. However, he found its interior "richly decorated with the gorgeous, but barbaric taste manifested in the ecclesiastical edifices throughout Mexico."[41]

Outside of Puebla at Cholula, the Louisvillian climbed the world's largest pyramid. From its summit he beheld "one of the most magnificent views it has ever been my good fortune to behold," "the great volcanoes Iztaccihuatl and Popocatepetl, their snowy crest glistening in the morning sun." While climbing to the top he picked up "numbers of horrible-looking little clay images . . . scattered over the face of the Pyramid"–for him pre-Hispanic art was as distasteful as the baroque religious architecture that the Spanish conquistador had imposed on the indigenous culture. Four days later, after marching through "the unrivaled valley of Mexico," the troops espied "the white towers of the cathedral and the numberless domes and spires" of Mexico City.[42]

In the Aztec capital Preston's regiment was placed under the immediate command of General Scott, a friend of his father-in-law, the Old Duke, and of William's cousin, Senator Preston of South Carolina. William became an admirer of the commander and a friend. The Louisvillian reported that Scott "has been markedly courteous and kind to me while here, extending to me a hospitality and confidence which was as unexpected as it was gratifying." Preston concluded that "Scott's mind is of a rare order" and considered him "a pure, great accomplished and fearless character." "Accomplished as a soldier in the science of war beyond any contemporary," the general, according to the lieutenant colonel, was "carefully read in the elementary principles of law with the most varied historical and belle-lettres acquirements" and possessed "a memory of iron that retains even the most trivial facts."[43] Later Scott would be a house guest of the Prestons in Louisville and Washington.

General Scott's ego and inclination to express controversial views embroiled him in disputes, which in turn detracted from his deeds as perhaps "the ablest American commander between the Revolution and the Civil War." In late 1847 he became involved in a bitter feud with General Gideon Pillow and claimed that Pillow's battle reports had downplayed Scott's role in conquering Mexico City. When President Polk heard of the dispute, he blamed it on "the vanity and tyranny of General Scott" and removed him from command.[44] This antagonized many army officers. The ousted general was quick to defend his actions and showed Preston a "stinging" letter he was sending to the secretary of war. When the pettiness of the charges against Scott became apparent and Congress voted a gold medal for "Old Fuss and Feathers," the general became a national hero. Before leaving Mexico in the spring of 1848, Scott invited his young friend Preston to dine with him, perhaps partaking of the general's favorite menu of cold fowl, port, and champagne.[45]

The Louisville lieutenant colonel's five months in the capital were "occupied by my different duties." One task was looking after his men, who were lodged in the convent of Our Most Holy Mother of

Mercy in the southeastern quarter of the city. The North American troops considered the Mexicans inferior and were enraged when snipers occasionally killed one of their number. Consequently, the victors often showed little respect for the conquered or their property. Clerics complained to Preston that his men were stealing paintings from the cloister and "destroying the fabric of the convent, tearing off and burning the doors, windows and ceiling beams." A representative of the order beseeched Preston to stop "these most dire provocations," and he did so. As a token of thanks, Preston was given an oil painting of the Madonna from the convent.[46]

The Kentuckian's most important assignment was commanding a mule train in April 1848 to and from Veracruz. Eight days after leaving the capital, his 275 wagons carrying 600 sick soldiers reached Jalapa, a resting place for troops before descending to the Gulf coast with its yellow-fever epidemics and malaria. Again Preston was impressed by Jalapa. "The town is about as large as Lexington," he wrote his father-in-law, but the surrounding mountains "are clothed in eternal verdure." From Jalapa the train continued to the coast, accompanied by 50 dragoons, 150 infantry, and 300 teamsters. Preston returned to Mexico City with the mule wagons, this time escorted by 400 cavalry and infantry.[47]

Aware of the success of the Spanish guerrillas against Napoleon in the Peninsular War, Santa Anna hoped that Mexican irregulars would attack Scott's long supply line to the coast, forcing him to abandon the capital. While this proved illusory, Mexican patriots did harass the mule trains. Preston's expedition encountered no guerrillas, but a stagecoach traversing a pass his troops had gone through ninety minutes earlier was attacked, and the driver and a soldier were killed.[48]

The life of an officer in Mexico City was not one of hardship. Preston and two colleagues lived in a mansion belonging to the collector of the customs and a favorite of Santa Anna. "Better than my own at home" was the Louisvillian's verdict on this "beautifully furnished" residence, with its mahogany tables, china, and enormous rooms. Preston also had the services of two slaves, Sam Giles and Bob, a cook who proved a good student of Spanish. The lieutenant colonel brought two horses with him and claimed they were "the most beautiful in Mexico." Several months before leaving Mexico, he gained the services of a local boy named José María, after con-

Depiction of General Winfield Scott's triumphant entry into Mexico City. The Metropolitan Cathedral is in the background and the Government Palace is to the right. Published in John Frost, Pictorial History of Mexico and the Mexican War *(Philadelphia, 1849).*

tracting with his mother to employ him for five years. Disease and ill health were by far the greatest dangers that the soldiers encountered in Mexico, especially yellow fever, cholera, dysentery, and most commonly diarrhea. However, except for a few days of illness early in his stay, Preston was able to report on leaving Mexico that "myself and the servants are uninterruptedly well."[49]

Nor were officers deprived of an active social life. Christmas Day brought them together for "plenty of egg and toddy" furnished by their commander, and that night at his house Preston gave a dinner for friends in his regiment. He reported to Margaret that Bob prepared a meal that "did honor to your training." On another occasion General Scott was Preston's guest. "An excellent corps de ballet," Italian opera, and orchestra performances at the Teatro Nacional, "one of the largest in America," as well as bullfights, equestrian shows, theater offered by a Spanish troupe, and military concerts that always featured "Yankee Doodle" and "Hail Columbia" provided amusement. Two English-language newspapers kept soldiers informed of local events and published news from home.[50]

Though founded in October 1847 by army officers for the "mutual and social benefit of all," the Aztec Club became "an exclusive club." Among 160 officers elected to membership were many who would distinguish themselves as generals in the Civil War: Robert E. Lee, Ulysses S. Grant, Joseph E. Johnston, Joseph Hooker, John B. Magruder, and George B. McClellan. It met in the house of Señor José María Bocanegra, Mexico's former minister to the United States. This club was the center of Preston's social life. There he passed many evenings with old acquaintances from Kentucky and college days in the east.[51] Often he was in the company of his cousin, John C. Breckinridge, who was a major in Kentucky's Third Regiment. He also made new friends through the club, such as Theodore O'Hara, a poet and later an officer with him in the Civil War. As one of five members of the club's finance committee, the lieutenant colonel in May 1848 helped arrange a banquet for 150 to celebrate the overthrow of King Louis Philippe three months earlier and the establishment of the Second French Republic. On the eve of their departure from Mexico, the members of the Aztec Club founded an organization to continue their association. The group held annual meetings for several decades following the war, with Preston an active member.[52]

During much of their stay, the troops in Mexico City were "entirely inactive," Preston reported, while waiting for the prolonged peace negotiations to put an end to their occupation. This allowed the Louisvillian time to observe life in the capital and visit its environs. His impressions and descriptions of Mexico were panegyrical. Soon after his arrival, he asserted, "Mexico [City] is without doubt the most remarkable city of the New World." For Preston the capital's "stately churches, its aqueducts, its palaces, its antiquities, its former and present religion, its mixed and picturesque population combine to render it an object of more interest to the traveler than any other place upon the American continent." The size of the Zócolo or main plaza impressed him, as did the cathedral, "one of the handsomest in the world." "The façade is exceedingly handsome and elaborately ornamented," he opined, and its interior "is gorgeous beyond description"–"the roofs groined and gilded with massive church ornaments" and "the great altar one blaze of gold and silver." Nevertheless, the cathedral's ornamentation "presents a melange of barbaric splendor," he concluded, and "fills the beholder with curiosity and astonishment."[53]

Preston's views of Mexicans were not as positive as his impressions of the architecture of the capital and the countryside. Here his scorn for his host country matched that of his fellow soldiers, who considered Mexicans inferior.[54] "The only thing the Mexican patriot fights for is plunder," he concluded. Following his months in Mexico, Preston was convinced the Spanish had made a mistake in permitting intermarriage. Because "the barriers which separated the races were cast down, the Catilian [*sic*] blood no longer ran pure and unpolluted in the veins of the people," he argued, and this brought "the horrid results of a debased, amalgamated race."[55]

Likewise, Preston looked upon Mexican life with disdain. Some of his opinions displayed his astonishment as a North American at very foreign customs. Observing "crowds of lepers in gaudy and ragged serapes," "wretches in the foulest rags, mendicants, and humble, half naked Indians" crawling on their knees up the baroque nave of the cathedral, the Kentuckian concluded that ecclesiastical charity is "reserved for the priest and is not to be bestowed on suffering humanity. It is for the ornament of the temple and is not to relieve the miseries of a brother. Look at this building, you think of Heaven. Look at the inmates, you think of Hell." Preston considered a bullfight "splendid," but he abhorred the processions and church presentations during Holy Week. "It is impossible for a mind cultivated by the truer teachings of Protestant Christianity to look upon them as aught but mummeries and profanations."[56]

While William was in Mexico, Margaret wrote him many letters on a variety of topics. One subject she emphasized was her ambition for her husband. "Since the year 1753, your Paternal name has taken part, or borne a commission in every war the country has been engaged in," she reminded him. In January 1848 Margaret urged him to earn "the reputation of an able and efficient officer, and perhaps with some military glory to bequeath to your children." A month later, she stressed the role of honor and warned him not to return "Disgraced and Degraded–Great God–Death, anything, but that."[57]

Another recurring theme Mag emphasized was that marriage, in the language of the Episcopal *Book of Common Prayer*, was a "holy estate." Although there was no hint that William ever had been less than chaste, she was intent on warning him against the "profligacy and dissoluteness" that typified army life. He must keep his "honor inviolate" and leave Mexico "with a pure conscience," allowing the couple to "again be happy." Otherwise, "Go to the farthest extremity of the Globe," she warned him, "if your constancy has not been equal to mine."[58]

Despite her insecurity and threats, Margaret assured William that "my love is deep and devoted." Although repentant, she admitted that she had sought "to make you feel that I did not care for you, and I have always endeavored to <u>wound</u>, rather than flatter your vanity." But she confessed, "My first and only wish has been, and is still, to be, the all absorbing feeling of your nature, as you have been of mine." "All the happiness I have enjoyed I have derived from you," she assured him, "and the world is dark without you." The concerned spouse readily admitted her anxiety concerning his health and safety and reminded him in sentimental Victorian terms that "my heart yearns to see you."[59]

Margaret remembered her father's advice concerning marriage—even if she on occasion was unable to follow it–that she must "always strive to make your husband's home and your society agreeable to him if you expect him to prefer home to any other place." In her letters she reminded William of the joys of hearth and family. Margaret wrote of their happiness "when I used to welcome you home" and included many touching details about their children. When Carrie told her mother that she wanted her father to return, Margaret explained that he was away in Mexico so that people would think more of her for being a soldier's daughter. Carrie's reply was, "I don't want Pa shot at, to make people think much of me." Mary was conjugating French verbs and cried when his name was mentioned; Carrie "is growing more handsome every day"; and Poogie "is full of life and mischief"—these were but some of the many vignettes the lieutenant colonel received from the home front.[60]

In his letters William related more than his experiences. He also inquired about his family, vowed to fulfill his responsibilities, and expressed his love to Margaret. "The determination to discharge the duty and pursue the course which I have laid down for the future supports me," he wrote on reaching Mexico. He assured his wife that "my life shall be consecrated to your happiness." Because of their separation, "in this far land my heart sometimes sinks" was a sentiment he often repeated. "What heartfelt pleasure it gives me to hear from home," was another frequent refrain. William was careful to allay Mag's anxiety over his health. Near the end of his Mexican stay, he reported that although he had lost ten pounds, he was much stronger than when he had left Louisville.[61]

While William was away, Margaret Preston took advantage of his absence to try to put the family's finances in order and thereby display her managerial talents. Her father considered her "a great financier" and wrote to his son-in-law that Mag promises "by adding [to] your rents etc [to] have you out of debt before you return." By repaying their debts, Mag told her husband that she would be eliminating "that curse which had darkened some of the happiest moments of our married life." One way she made money was to hire out slaves, a common practice. Margaret found that one servant was "sufficient to wait upon me and mind all the children," so she tried to receive cash for the labors of the other slaves. She asked her father to send some young childless female slaves to Louisville, and he responded, though that did separate them from the rest of their families.[62] Margaret trained them as seamstresses and then sent them to work for others. She already had hired out three male slaves, one of whom worked as a cook at the Galt House and the other two on steamboats. Soon two of her father's slaves became pregnant, and as Wickliffe property these children would have a marketable value. Nephew William Preston Johnston wrote to his namesake in Mexico that Aunt Margaret had "hired out her servants admirably" and was "fully justified in her claim to the title, of a good business manager." The Old Duke assured his son-in-law that the income "from Negroes here alone will be full $2,000."[63]

Mrs. Preston also sold property for her husband while he was in Mexico. In July 1848 an immigrant from Rotterdam and a "Dutchman"– probably a German–bought lots from her. "Our prospects are brighter daily and I believe we will be rich in spite of our extravagance," she optimistically exclaimed. "God help the Dutch for it." Additionally, she noted that the Roman Catholic Church had bought a lot from William's sister, Susan Christy, to build a church. Adjoining this property, Preston owned "a great deal of land . . . which will be enhanced in value by it." Certainly her successes satisfied Margaret. "I know you will acknowledge when you return," she bragged to her husband, "that the part of your business that I have managed entirely myself could not have been better arranged or more to your interest."[64]

When the Treaty of Guadalupe Hidalgo ended the war in February 1848, the United States paid Mexico fifteen million dollars, and the conquered nation granted half of its territory to the victor–all or parts of the future states of New Mexico, Arizona, Colorado, Nevada, Utah, Wyoming, and California. Preston had been part of a war that saw the first real flexing of America's military muscle, but the disputes that surrounded the conflict–slavery and territorial expansion–would continue to increase tensions within the Union.[65]

Preston was disappointed with the treaty, for he believed all of Mexico should have been added to the Union. "The Peace, botched up as it was to secure a feeble administration, against a fancied danger and unpatriotic opposition," he argued, "gave the coup de grace to all our hopes." Nevertheless, he predicted that the future would bring additional conquests: "Let us then forget the present blunder, and look forward to the time when the Flag shall continue its march toward Panama." The peace ended the occupation of Mexico. In June Preston's regiment left Veracruz, and on 18 July thousands turned out in Louisville to welcome them home. Preston returned with his two slaves, the Mexican boy, his horses, a poodle dog, the painting of the Madonna, a Mexican serape, and a pearl necklace for his wife–as well as "a great moustache" that disappeared the next day. He was mustered out of the service on 25 July 1848.[66]

Despite Mag's expressions of love in her letters to William during the Mexican War, she considered her marriage far from blissful. The major problem was William's debts. In correspondence to her father, she often complained of her husband's inability to live within his means. Taxes, payments for street construction and other property developments, his continued gambling, and repayment of loans taken out to cover a variety of expenses–including the purchase of their house–were some of the demands he made against the family's funds. In 1845 William lamented that he owed five thousand dollars to creditors payable that year. The Old Duke opined that the couple was "too hospitable" and considered their entertainment expenses excessive, but he blamed his son-in-law's difficulties on "his family connections," citing "the indebtedness of his brothers in law and sisters." William certainly took seriously his status as the only son in a fatherless family and always tried to help his sisters. This meant on occasion financial assistance, as well as helping with real estate matters. He also devoted a great deal of time as a lawyer to their problems.[67]

Margaret's optimistic predictions that Preston would be out of debt when he returned from Mexico proved far from the truth. In his first month back in Louisville, he calculated that he was $18,000 in debt. William considered selling their house in 1850 to his sister Susan to raise cash, but Margaret opposed this and gained the Old

Duke's support. She claimed her husband was spending too much time and money looking after the affairs of his Preston relatives. Her father concurred, warning her that William's "fortune is too small for his habits of expenditure, with practice he will secure his habit and his health and independence."[68]

On his return to Louisville, Preston decided to embark on a new career. He was frustrated with law as a profession, fearing his life would be spent writing wills and arguing cases before local magistrates, and his partner William Graves had died. The lieutenant colonel's experience in Mexico also contributed to this decision, for there he realized that "I liked campaigning to work." He considered trying to become a colonel, raise a regiment, and stay in the army, but he never pursued this idea.[69] Instead, he turned to public service.

Chapter IV: Legislator

◇

In the years following the war, William Preston became a legislator in Frankfort and Washington. His unhappiness with law as a profession and his determination to attain a position of prominence and power, coupled with his wife's oft-stated ambitions, caused him to seek a government post. While he was in Mexico, Margaret had admonished him, "If you distinguish yourself, the future seems all too bright–If the reverse, I have nothing to hope for in life."[1]

Preston's earlier leadership roles in a host of local groups, his previous party activism as a Whig, and his military service proved invaluable stepping-stones to a succession of electoral positions. First came his selection as a delegate to Kentucky's third constitutional convention in 1849, where he played an important part in shaping the commonwealth's proslavery Constitution of 1850. During the next two years, Preston served in both houses of the state legislature, making valuable contributions to several committees. Then he spent three years in Washington as a Whig congressman and helped advance the legislative agenda of the slaveholding South. After the demise of the Whig party, he became a spokesman for the national Democratic party.

Following the Mexican War, Preston returned to the rapidly changing metropolis of Louisville. In the 1850s its rail lines went southward, and by 1860 trains connected the city with Nashville, Memphis, St. Louis, New Orleans, Cincinnati, and Pittsburgh. Manufacturing became increasingly important to the city's prosperity. An estimated four million dollars had been invested in manufacturing by the mid-1850s, a five-fold increase in fifteen years. Agricultural products, timber, and livestock from the surrounding countryside remained strong contributors to the city's prosperity. William's nephew William Preston Johnston claimed in 1854 that Louisville's slaughterhouses made it the "porkopolis" of the world.[2] On the eve of the Civil War, Louisville counted almost seventy thousand inhabitants. Roughly one-third of these residents were immigrants, particularly Germans and Irish who had entered the United States through New Orleans and East Coast ports.

Nor was cultural life forgotten in this decade of growth. The city's wealthy citizens took the lead in supporting concerts and the theater. Some of the world's most famous musicians performed at Louisville's Mozart Hall at Fourth and Jefferson Streets. In April 1851 the renowned "Swedish Nightingale," Jenny Lind, sang nine songs there in a concert arranged by the impresario P. T. Barnum.[3] Two years later the country's greatest pianist, Louis Moreau Gottschalk, played to a packed house. Ralph Waldo Emerson and Herman Melville were among the American authors who appeared in the city in the decade before the Civil War. Theater performances were offered in German as well as in English, and Italian opera also was heard in the 1850s.[4]

While the Louisvillians' pride in their city may have been excessive, foreign visitors generally were impressed with what they observed. A German was surprised in 1851 by the city's "rapid growth" and noted that its factories were "second only to those of Cincinnati, Pittsburgh, and Saint Louis in importance for the West." When the Hungarian hero Louis Kossuth visited Louisville in 1852, he attended "a creditable concert at Mozart's Hall."[5]

Together with Louisville's growth and development came new social problems. During the interwar years thousands of Germans and Irish settled in cities along the Ohio and the upper Mississippi Rivers, as well as in New Orleans. Overall the South welcomed few immigrants in the decades before the Civil War. Foreigners feared the competition of slave labor there, and the general lack of manufacturing in the largely rural region curtailed job opportunities. By 1860 only ninety-three of the approximately one thousand counties in the South counted more than ten percent of their population as foreign-born. Louisville and Baltimore were among the few southern cities with a large industrial base, and with New Orleans were the only cities with a large percentage of immigrants.[6]

By 1855, only 31,400 of Kentucky's 760,000 inhabitants had been born abroad, but a majority of these new residents had settled in Louisville. Contemporaries estimated that foreigners made up about 30 percent of the city's population in 1852. By 1860, the 13,374 Germans residing in Louisville and the 6,653 Irish made up 34 percent of the city's total.[7]

With the rapid growth of Louisville's foreign population came a fear of immigration. Many native-born complained that aliens were "stealing" their jobs, causing some to speak of a "foreign threat."

Others were suspicious of the immigrants' strange habits–such as beer drinking on Sunday–that clashed with established local mores. More upsetting to conservative Louisvillians were the shocking political ideas of some liberal and even radical German Americans. Many German liberals, known as the Forty-Eighters, fled to the United States following the failure of the 1848 revolutions in their homeland, and some settled in Louisville. In 1854 the Bund Freier Männer, or League of Free Men, a national organization that included liberals, socialists, and atheists, established its headquarters in Louisville. Meeting at Apollo Hall that year, members of the Bund from several cities adopted the Louisville Platform, a manifesto that opposed slavery and the death penalty and favored woman suffrage, the direct election of all office-holders, and a minimum wage.[8] Twenty-seven newspapers throughout the nation eventually adopted this reform program. But more typical of the interests of the city's German Americans were the organizations founded in the 1840s: the Liederkranz or singing association, the Turnverein, a gymnastic society, and the *Louisville Volksbühne* and the *Anzeiger*, both newspapers.[9]

The growth of the Roman Catholic Church in the city was another cause of alarm for many. By the 1850s Catholics had built a cathedral and several churches, and religious orders were active. The Jesuits arrived in 1848 to teach at a school in Louisville, and the Xaverian Brothers established their first American community there six years later. The number of Roman Catholics in Louisville contrasted with the religious convictions of the vast majority of Kentuckians, causing many throughout the commonwealth to view the metropolis with suspicion. Although the state's Catholic population numbered only 24,210 in 1852, a large number of them were among the foreign-born who lived in Louisville. While many of the city's Germans were Protestants, most were Roman Catholics, as were almost all of the Irish. In 1839 St. Boniface Church was established for the city's German-speaking Catholics, and by the 1850s there were three German-speaking congregations. The first Roman Catholic church for Irish Americans was built in 1843.[10]

The city's rapid growth and large ethnic population played an important role in Preston's political career and continued to increase the value of his real estate holdings. A partisan Whig since the1830s, Preston was considered as a candidate for the legislature in 1844, leading him to conclude that if he remained a Whig "I might easily advance." Following the Mexican War he resumed his party activism and in 1849 attended the Whig National Convention in Washington. His Virginia cousin, William Preston, was secretary of the navy in the cabinet of the newly elected President Zachary Taylor, and in January1849 the Kentucky Whig sought to use his family connections and political loyalty to advantage by asking the president-elect for appointment to a foreign post "as a personal favour." Influential friends also wrote to Taylor on his behalf, but to no avail.[11] After this request was denied, Preston entered electoral politics later that year, presenting himself as a candidate to become one of Louisville's three delegates to the state constitutional convention.

In Kentucky advocates of emancipation remained opposed to the state's 1799 charter sanctioning slavery, and they were successful in calling a constitutional convention to prepare a new one in 1849. Throughout the 1840s the opponents of slavery actively had sought to disseminate their beliefs and win converts. Cassius M. Clay launched the *True American* in 1843, Kentucky's famous antislavery paper, and they prepared for the coming campaign for delegates to the constitutional convention. Clay organized a meeting of friends of gradual emancipation in Richmond in early April 1849, and the Rev. Robert J. Breckinridge presided over a meeting in Lexington. At Frankfort in late April, the Friends of Emancipation convened fifty representatives from throughout the state, many of them Whigs and slaveholders.

Slavery was the major issue to be decided at the constitutional convention, and the proslavery forces were determined to impose their will. The issue proved so divisive that it split both the Whig and Democrat parties into proslavery and antislavery factions. However, the proponents of slavery controlled most of the machinery of both parties and selected moderate candidates who had popular appeal. Preston and James Guthrie, a former Democratic legislator, were among the five nominees of the proslavery forces in Jefferson County. William's Lexington cousin, John C. Breckinridge, and Guthrie were among the leaders of the proslavery candidates.

The campaign was a heated one, and debates attracted large and attentive crowds throughout the summer. Partisans on each side condemned the other as "pirates, fanatics, murderers, oligarchs, rapists, bandits, thieves." On one occasion, violence rather than argument prevailed. While speaking at a Madison County engagement, the passionate Cassius Clay was challenged by the son of a proslavery candidate. The meeting turned into a free-for-all. Clay was stabbed and shot at, but his assailant had his intestines cut out when he lunged at the speaker, a massive man adept at fighting and renowned for his skill with the Bowie knife.[12]

The efforts of the emancipationists proved in vain. As elsewhere in the upper South, Kentucky's antislavery advocates failed to attract wide support. Clay's *True American* had 2,700 subscribers outside of the commonwealth, but only 700 in Kentucky.[13] After three days of balloting in August, the proslavery ticket convincingly defeated its opponents throughout the state. The emancipation party did not elect a single delegate to the convention. Despite Clay's oratorical and martial efforts, in Madison County the antislavery candidate polled only 688 of the 3,700 votes cast, while losing to the father of Clay's assailant. In Louisville Preston polled the highest vote, outdistancing the leading emancipationist and a fellow Whig, James Speed, 2,085 to 1,754.[14] Guthrie also was elected and became president of the convention.

The constitutional assembly met regularly in Frankfort during the last three months of 1849 and offered Preston a forum to demonstrate his talents as a political orator and leader. He spoke seventy times before the delegates, making him one of the body's most active members. Slavery was the most important issue of the convention. Since the overwhelming majority favored the institution, the delegates focused on how to safeguard it. In concert with the sentiment of the convention, Preston backed the article on bondage which declared, "The right of the owner of a slave to such slave ... is ... as inviolable as the right of the owner of any property whatsoever." Therefore, "the General Assembly shall have no power to pass laws for the emancipation of slaves without consent of their owners, previous to such emancipation." The new charter also made it a felony for free blacks or mulattos to enter Kentucky.[15]

As a proponent of states' rights, Preston argued that the new charter should define a voter as a "qualified elector of this Commonwealth" rather than as a "citizen of the United States." This the new constitution did. As a staunch defender of individual rights, he opposed outlawing dueling, arguing that duels were needed to defend personal reputations and to prevent assassinations. However, the new charter outlawed dueling, forcing the governor-elect to swear that he had not fought a duel with a deadly weapon.[16]

Preston also proved an ally of Louisville's interests that were being challenged by many rural and small-town delegates. When several members–led by Garrett Davis of Bourbon County, later a United States senator–questioned the patriotism of Kentucky's Roman Catholics and warned of papal plots to subvert democracy, Preston was the first to offer a retort. Since only six of the hundred delegates were Catholics, possibly they had arranged for him, a Protestant, to make this speech. The enemies of Catholics also loathed foreigners of all creeds and questioned their loyalty. To detractors who claimed that Louisville's aliens were not equal in patriotism to other Kentuckians, Preston lauded their services in the recent Mexican War. He also noted that European immigration had "brought to us knowledge of new arts, new modes of agriculture and is developing new means of developing our natural resources."[17] "Grape culture, hitherto unknown," he noted, "had been introduced and was now a thriving industry." As Preston told the delegates, the fear of immigration "exists only in the imagination, and these apprehensions are mere phantoms of the brain."[18]

His defense of immigrants was condemned by nativist spokesmen in Louisville "as pandering to foreigners," and the *Louisville Courier* claimed that in so doing "he will find in the end he will lose more than he can win." Preston, too, feared this. After listening to the harangues of those seeking to limit suffrage, he lamented that "the applause from the galleries at the utterance of sentiments so pernicious, when eloquently urged, makes me tremble for the fate of my country."[19]

Those opposed to foreigners proposed that naturalized citizens must reside for twenty-one years in America before being eligible to vote. This attempt was condemned by the urban delegates. "As Kentucky was the first state . . . that extended the privilege of universal suffrage to every freeman upon her soil," Preston correctly told the convention, "I trust God she will be the last to commence the process of curtailing that right." At a later session, he again challenged the convention, demanding, "Shall we then in Kentucky, be the first to manifest a timidity so unnecessary as the subject of the foreign vote?" He added that such an action might result in violent protests in Kentucky's cities. Other Louisville delegates also weighed in against the proposal, as did Charles Wickliffe, a former governor and Margaret Preston's uncle. After days of debate the measure was decisively defeated, 6-69.[20]

In May 1850, the voters in the commonwealth approved the new, staunchly proslavery charter, 51,351 to 20,302. For Preston, the convention brought a statewide reputation. Even the *Louisville Morning Courier*, an antislavery paper that had opposed Preston's election, was impressed by his performance in Frankfort and predicted he was destined to have a distinguished career in politics. Modern scholars also agree that Preston's role at the convention numbered him among "the most valuable members of the body."[21]

Kentucky's advocates of emancipation never recovered from the overwhelming defeat they suffered in their campaign for delegates to the 1849 convention. Some moderate Whigs who had backed the antislavery slate abandoned the cause, believing that servitude would remain unchallenged in Kentucky. During the 1850s the increasing militancy of abolitionists in the North only hardened the resolve of defenders of slavery, and the publication in 1852 of Harriet Beecher Stowe's popular novel, *Uncle Tom's Cabin*–depicting fugitive slaves fleeing their Kentucky master–provoked indignation. Cassius Clay proved popular in the North throughout the decade, but at home he was reviled by the proslavery majority. After a vigorous campaign for governor in 1851, Clay received 3,600 votes out of 100,000 cast. The following year only 266 Kentuckians voted for the presidential nominee on the abolitionist Free Soil ticket.[22]

By the end of the decade, proslavery sentiment ran so high that the rights of emancipationists were threatened in Kentucky. As elsewhere in the South, mob violence on occasion overrode the rights of the minority. Invited to settle in Madison County and given a tract of land in what became Berea by Cassius Clay, the Reverend John G. Fee, a Bracken County native, opposed slavery on religious grounds. He began establishing antislavery congregations in 1853 and later a school at Berea.[23] In 1857 and 1858 Fee was attacked by mobs for his harangues against slavery, but for him the worst was still to come. When John Brown led a raid at Harpers Ferry, Virginia, in October 1859, attempting to begin a slave revolt, southern whites reacted with anger and fear. Fee's defense of Brown brought immediate demands for him to leave the state. An armed mob descended on his house in December, and he was forced to flee with his family to Cincinnati.[24]

Despite his strong defense of slavery at the constitutional convention, Preston realized that many bondsmen abhorred their condition. The lure of freedom across the Ohio River exerted a strong attraction for Kentucky's enslaved people. "The Negroes are swimming off by the wholesale to Canada," Margaret Preston had written to her father in 1844. That year a house slave had disappeared with $1,100. In 1850 William owned fourteen bondsmen, but one had fled to Pittsburgh. Charles Haws lived there in hiding with his wife Margaret, who wrote to Preston in 1850 asking him "to give Charles his free papers." Based apparently on Preston's agreement to do so, Charles's mother came to Louisville in April 1851 with another letter from his wife imploring Preston to "give liberty to the captive exemplifying the blessed principles of the 'Golden rule.'"[25] Apparently Charles did receive his freedom.

Such experiences did not convince Preston that slavery was an evil. Like most masters, he believed that bondsmen did not run away of their own volition and blamed their escape on the misguided advice or propaganda of others. Margaret Haws's confession that in Pennsylvania the couple was "lubbering under A grate menny disadvantage" perhaps served to confirm Preston's belief that slaves needed to remain in bondage. Nor was his experience with Charles Haws exceptional. Escaped slaves posed a problem for many slaveholders, despite statistics that seemingly demonstrate otherwise. According to the 1850 census, there were only ninety-six fugitives among the commonwealth's 210,981 slaves. However, modern scholars argue that the concern for runaway slaves expressed in the diaries and correspondence of so many owners indicate that such statistics are misleading. "The great majority of slaveholders in the South," one concludes, "were forced at one time or another to deal with runaways."[26]

Following the constitutional convention, Preston was determined to follow the political path. He was so intent on electoral success that he earlier had compromised his word. To be a member of the state constitutional convention in 1849, he had to swear that he had never taken part in a duel. He chose to forget his earlier role in two duels, took the oath, and served as a delegate. Likewise, to become a member of the legislature in 1851 Preston would affirm on his honor that he had not participated in a duel. However, just two years earlier, he was involved in a duel where Captain Henry C. Pope, the cousin of his brother-in-law John Pope, was killed by Preston's friend John T. Gray.[27]

As he had done at the constitutional convention, Preston defended the rights of Kentucky's foreign-born in his campaigns for electoral office. His tolerant attitudes toward immigrants, many of whom were Roman Catholics, can be traced to his schooling at St. Joseph's College in Bardstown, but his defense of aliens also was shaped by economic self-interest. Like many well-to-do slave-owning gentry, William Preston throughout his adult years would be land rich and cash poor. In 1854 he sold property he owned in town on Walnut Street to Louisville's Roman Catholic bishop for $4,500. Preston was particularly aware of the importance of immigrants to the economic progress of the city and profited from their good fortune. The enterprising German and Irish Americans in Louisville were successful in commerce, the trades, and middle-class professions and used much of their wealth to buy property. Fortunately for the Preston family, the original land grant from Governor Thomas Jefferson was adjacent to the growing city of Louisville, so the value of their holdings increased. Although portions of the Preston Plantation east of town—called the Preston Enlargement—had been sold for lots since the 1820s, in the 1850s much of the remaining land was developed with new streets and subdivided into housing sites. The wealth of Louisville's successful immigrants allowed so many of them to purchase these lots that advertisements were printed in both English and German. Contemporaries jokingly called this development "New Hamburg." Today, in the section of the Highlands developed by the Prestons, several streets still reflect their family origins: Christy and Rogers Avenues bear the married names of William's sisters Susan and Josephine. As a large landowner and aristocrat, Preston had little personal contact with the growing urban middle classes—composed of both foreigners and native stock—but his economic fortunes were linked to them.

In the 1850s William Preston entered the electoral arena five times and won on four occasions. He was selected in July 1850 as one of three Whig candidates for Louisville's three seats in the lower house of the general assembly in Frankfort. Preston proved an active campaigner and an effective orator. He gave four speeches in Louisville during the last three days of the campaign, and the Whig press hailed him for the "thrilling appeal" he made on the eve of the polling. On 6 August, all three Louisville Whigs won election. Preston's 1,961 votes put him at the head of the ticket and gave him a three-hun-

THIRD (PERMANENT) STATE HOUSE, FRANKFORT, KY.—Built, 1827-29.

Today known as the Old State Capitol, Kentucky's third capitol building was designed by Gideon Shyrock. Published in Richard Collins, Historical Sketches of Kentucky *(Covington, 1874), 2: 297.*

dred-vote margin over the leading Democratic candidate.[28]

In Frankfort Preston labored in the statehouse designed by Gideon Shryock and constructed in the late 1820s. This Greek Revival structure of Kentucky marble provided an elegant home for the legislature. The portico with its six Ionic columns, the raised dome atop a lantern drum, and the interior with its classical rotunda made this one of the most noble edifices in the state.

Though only a freshman legislator, Preston entered the lower house as a respected member. His role at the constitutional convention and his effectiveness as a campaign orator made him a party leader. When the representatives elected a speaker in November 1850, several voted for Preston before he withdrew. He served on the committees on federal relations and claims and on a committee that considered relocating the state capital. Preston championed legislation of interest to Louisville—such as the establishment of a planetarium there—and on many occasions stated his opinions on pending legislation. Listening to his speeches, Whig observers were struck by "his particularly chaste style and graceful delivery, in which qualities of an orator, he has no superior in either house."[29]

In July 1851 the Whigs nominated Preston for the state senate for the first six Louisville wards. He had no opponent and on 7 August received 1,483 votes in his election to the upper house. During his two years in the senate, Preston was a member of the committees on education and federal relations, serving as chairman of the latter in 1851 and 1852. A defender of public education, the Louisvillian supported the right of the city's school board to increase the education tax and warned against legislative proposals to submit tax measures to the electorate. "The principle of throwing everything before the great mass of the people," he argued, has led to "the downfall of every republic." He also introduced legislation important to Louisville, such as regulating the city's constables, and advocated support of the city's institutions, including the School for the Blind. Preston also promoted railroad interests. He backed the incorporation of the Lousiville and Nashville Railroad Company and brought a bill to punish anyone "for placing obstructions on railroads, so as to endanger life."[30]

But Preston's chief contribution came as chairman of the Committee on Code of Practice, considered "a responsible and honorable position." The Constitution of 1850 called for the legislature to draw up new statutes on civil and penal practice to simplify many legal procedures, and Preston's committee helped do this. The new code proposed a thorough revision of civil law, placing "all members of the profession on a footing of equality." This measure became law during this session, despite the determined opposition of many members of the bar.[31]

A controversial issue faced the general assembly in 1851, the selection of a United States senator. Since the Whigs controlled both houses, the question was who from their party would go to Washington. When the Whigs caucused, they were unable to unite behind a candidate, and a "very unpleasant state of affairs" resulted. In the senate Preston made "an able and powerful address" in mid-November urging party unity, and his "bland and conciliatory course" won him "the confidence and respect of the Senate," a Whig newspaper reported. When his party selected its Senate nominee, Preston "bordered within a hair's breath of winning the stake."[32]

In addition to legislative matters, Preston found time to participate in many Louisville organizations. He gave talks to groups such as the Conversation Club in 1841, and in 1851 he served on the first Board of Trustees for the Louisville Public Schools. Preston became a member of the Abraham Masonic Lodge No. 8 in 1841, and in January 1854 when nine Masons decided to establish a lodge in north-east Louisville, they named it in his honor. Seven months later, at the official organization of Preston Lodge No. 281, he delivered "a very eloquent and appropriate address on the beauties of Masonry," contributed fifty dollars to the organization's orphans and widows fund, and presented a Bible to the new group. Preston Lodge continues today. William remained an active Mason throughout his life, and this membership served him well. His father-in-law was a Mason, as were many Whig leaders and officers in the Mexican War, and during the Civil War several of his Kentucky friends in the Confederacy–Generals John Breckinridge, John Hunt Morgan, and Roger W. Hanson–were Masons.[33]

In 1852 Preston helped organize and spoke at a public reception for Louis Kossuth, the Hungarian republican leader who in 1848-49 had led the briefly successful revolution of the Magyar people against their Austrian overlords. Dominated by a staunch nativist faction opposed to foreigners, the city administration had refused to extend an official invitation to Kossuth during his triumphal tour of the United States. When he arrived in Louisville Kossuth was pleased that "the militia turned out, cannons were fired, and firemen's bells pealed." His speech, delivered in a tobacco warehouse, was "an impromptu affair," and opponents of his visit claimed that a few in the audience "shouted down some of his proposals." The Prestons took him on a ride through town, and he was feted at a multicourse banquet at the Galt House. Later Kossuth remembered that the Prestons "were hospitably kind to me." William also was among the earliest benefactors of St. Boniface Church, the first parish established for German-speaking Roman Catholics. [34]

His growing political prominence, Whig activism, and civic involvement made Preston a natural leader of his party in Louisville. In addition to the high profile he enjoyed in both the state constitutional convention and the state legislature, Preston was an organizer of the Whig state convention in February 1852 and a presidential elector for his friend and his party's unsuccessful candidate later that year, General Winfield Scott. The Kentuckian spoke at the Whig ratification meeting held in late June in Brooklyn, New York, and in July and August he stumped his home state for Scott. In Shelbyville and Bardstown Preston extolled the virtues of the Whig candidate, and party members considered his speech to the Scott Club in Louisville "unusually interesting and eloquent." As contemporary political audiences expected, his partisan monologues always lasted at least an hour and a half, and his popularity as a Whig orator attested to his effectiveness. The *Carrollton (Ky.) Mirror* had nothing but praise for Preston's address there in August 1852: "To say that he made a happy effort is not enough. It was the finest oratory we have listened to for years. . . . His entire speech was replete with eloquence, wit and repartee."[35]

To celebrate the anniversary of General Scott's capture of Mexico City, the Whigs held a barbecue at the Jefferson County Courthouse on 15 September. There a crowd estimated at thirty thousand heard Preston yet again laud the Whig nominee. When Scott visited Louisville in October, he was greeted by Mayor James Speed, a Whig, and was the guest of the Prestons. The general then took his campaign to Indiana. William Preston accompanied him from Jeffersonville to Madison, giving short speeches. Scott carried Kentucky and three other states in the presidential vote, losing to the Democrat Franklin Pierce. Scott, called a "clumsy politician," whose "long-winded, bombastic speeches" failed to appeal, experienced defeat due in part to sectional divisions that split the Whig party into southern and northern wings.[36]

In August 1852, Humphrey Marshall, the Whig congressman from Louisville, resigned to become United States commissioner to China. A special election was called for late November to fill this vacancy, and the district's Whigs by a large majority nominated William Preston as their standard-bearer on the first ballot at their September convention. The Democrat candidate, Calvin Sanders, was not as well known as Preston, but both canvassed vigorously for votes throughout the six-county district. In mid-October the Whig nominee managed to give nine lengthy speeches in as many towns located in three counties. One issue that attracted attention was Sanders's espousal of temperance while campaigning outside of Jefferson County. The *Louisville Daily Courier* reported that the *Louisville Anzeiger* had demanded that Sanders clarify his views on temperance for its German-American readership, and the Democrat assured the newspaper that he would not favor the imposition of prohibition through legislation.

On 20 November, as expected, Preston was elected to Congress, defeating his Democrat opponent by a vote of 6,560 to 4,841. That evening Whig revelers accompanied by several bands converged on the Prestons' Walnut Street residence. There he issued the customary call for unity between the victors and the vanquished and then invited the assemblage into his home for refreshments. Preston's election was in large part a personal triumph. In the presidential canvass held eighteen days earlier, the successful Democratic nominee Franklin Pierce defeated Scott by seventy-two votes in Louisville, but Preston carried each of the city's eight wards, building up a majority there of 1,370 in the congressional balloting.[37]

In July 1853 the Whigs of the Seventh Congressional District nominated Preston for reelection, this time to a full term. The Democratic candidate, Colonel S. S. English of Oldham County, failed to receive the active support of his party and proved a "merely nominal" opponent. Nevertheless, the Whig nominee was "busy as a bee" in his quest for votes. He spoke in late July at the market house and the courthouse in Louisville, drawing large crowds. Predictably, the Whig press lauded his "comprehensive and statesman-like view of things" and praised the "eloquence, power, and impressive beauty of his oratory," which was "frequently interrupted by loud applause." Only a few issues surfaced in the campaign. When Preston urged government support for a railway to the Pacific, the Democrats claimed that this was unconstitutional. English tried to appeal to German and Irish American voters by noting that many Whig leaders were hostile to foreigners, but Preston's record made him immune. On 2 August the incumbent won reelection–by a margin of more than two to one.[38]

Preston spent three years in the House of Representatives. His maiden speech on the House floor was an address in honor of the legislative giant Daniel Webster who had recently died. His fellow Kentucky Whigs selected him to deliver this. "No man has earned a greater reputation in forensic endeavor than Mr. Webster," he declared, adding that "the only statesman whose reputation could challenge comparison" was Henry Clay. In working for the Compromise of 1850, both legislators had "averted the perils that menaced their common country," he argued, thereby drawing "closer the bonds of Union between the North and South." In his speech Preston called upon his classical erudition, including lines in Latin from Cicero and citations from other ancients. Quoting Virgil, he claimed that during the crisis of 1850 Webster had opposed the partisans of discord and "'disdains their empty clamor, and unmoved remains.'" Unlike the other orators that day, the Kentuckian spoke without notes and proudly observed, "It was flatteringly received by the House and the Press seems to have a better opinion of it than its author has." With oratorical skill a highly prized political talent in the years before the Civil War, the newspapers in Louisville were quick to emulate the dailies in the capital and congratulate Preston on the success of his first address.[39]

The Louisville Whig was an outspoken defender of slavery during his years in Congress. When Gerritt Smith of New York spoke on the House floor in December 1853 in favor of abolition and condemned slave owners, the Kentuckian declared himself "unwilling that the remarks which he has uttered should pass without some reply." "I trust to the power of truth to show that the men of the South are not the representatives of a people enduring the odious tyranny that the gentleman asserts," Preston answered. Instead, he argued that southerners were "entertaining far wiser and more practical views than those misguided enthusiasts who would shake to its center a Government planned by patriots and statesmen, and cemented by the public prosperity." God made the European race superior to the African, and "the wisdom of man cannot foresee or penetrate the means by which the civilization of nations is directed by Him," Preston insisted. "Slavery seems to be the price that ignorance pays to intelligence for its tuition in the arts of civilization." Moreover, the "Constitution, solemnly ratified, guarantees to the slaveholding States the protection of their property, and the extradition of fugitive slaves." This institution was a part of the normal hierarchy of humanity, wherein some were naturally subordinate to others. "The abolition of African slavery, and its agitation," he added, "are fraught only with the pernicious consequences to our common country." This address proved so popular that it was reprinted in pamphlet form. Although he would oppose Preston's reelection to Congress in 1855, the editor of the *Louisville Daily Journal*, George D. Prentice, called this defense of slavery "the best speech on the subject that I have ever seen."[40]

The major piece of legislation considered in 1854 was the Kansas-Nebraska bill, which divided much of the nation into hostile pro- and anti-slavery camps. Northern opponents of slavery were determined to outlaw the institution in Kansas and Nebraska, while most southerners vigorously supported the expansion of slavery there. President Franklin Pierce proved too indecisive and unpopular to provide the leadership that might have lessened North-South tension over organizing these territories, and both the Whigs and the Democrats divided along sectional lines, unable to unite their members in the pursuit of common national goals.

In an effort to break the congressional deadlock, Stephen A. Douglas, the politically ambitious Democratic senator from Illinois, decided in January 1854 to offer a compromise to gain southern support. He headed the Committee on Territories and proposed the division of Nebraska into two territories, Kansas and Nebraska, permitting the settlers in each to decide the fate of slavery at a future date. This legislation, Preston argued in a speech before the House, promised "equal rights to the people of the slaveholding, and equal rights to the non-slaveholding States to settle Nebraska and Kansas," so he advocated the measure. He believed the bill would become law, but "the struggle will be close and bitter." He correctly predicted that the divided Whig party "will be annihilated upon it." The Kansas-Nebraska Act proved popular in Kentucky, and Preston received many requests for copies of his speeches favoring the measure.[41] Abolitionists viewed the bill as a southern conspiracy to extend slavery.

Preston had been deeply involved in the bill's passage, first leading a successful parliamentary maneuver in early May to keep the House in session in order to consider the measure and later joining the majority in speaking against an amendment proposed by an Ohio Republican to outlaw slavery in all United States territories. Preston complained that lobbying for the act "kept me up without interruption two days and one night." With backing from President Pierce, most Democrats, and many southern Whigs, the bill passed Congress after more than three months of acrimonious debate.[42] As abolitionists had predicted, this law turned Kansas into an open battleground for five years over the issue of slavery, further inflaming passions in both the North and South.

Another issue that split both parties along sectional lines was the Gadsden Treaty. According to this agreement with Mexico, the United States would purchase approximately thirty thousand square miles of territory to facilitate railroad construction in what would become southern Arizona and New Mexico. But northern legislators tried to defeat the treaty. Preston believed this acquisition would permit "a route for the South to the Pacific," and he "energetically" joined other southern congressmen in the summer of 1854 in arguing for the treaty. "The Gadsden Treaty was passed but with the opposition of the Northern Whigs en masse against it," Preston noted in July. "I found myself again compelled to bid my dearly beloved brethren good bye and go for the bill."[43]

Preston was involved in other legislative duties. His service on the Foreign Relations Committee introduced him to international affairs and provided him with a useful background for his future service as a diplomat. But matters of interest to his constituents and to friends took up much of his time. The Kentuckian successfully offered a resolution to the House "to provide for the issue of new warrants when the warrants have been wrongfully issued." When he argued for this measure before his colleagues, he brandished a fistful of falsified grants and claimed that persons who had "forged land warrants have escaped punishment." When Congress in 1854 was considering a joint resolution offering Winfield Scott a promotion and back pay for his military services, Preston labored on his friend's behalf, for which he received the general's thanks.[44]

Like all congressmen, Preston fought for special projects intended to help his own district. He became particularly involved in a controversy over funds for the customs house in Louisville. Arguing that it would be "a costly economy to construct cheap or inconvenient public buildings," Preston in February 1853 offered an amendment to a treasury bill, adding $162,000 for construction of an adequate customs house in Louisville. This turned into a debate between the eastern and western states, for representatives from the Atlantic seaboard opposed funds to develop inland ports of entry. A Georgia representative attacked this amendment and denied the importance of foreign trade in the West. Preston countered that Louisville's foreign imports had risen to three hundred thousand dollars a year and were growing. However, realizing that his proposal would fail, Preston withdrew it. In February 1854, he introduced an amendment to include an appropriation of $40,000 to complete the existing customs building in Louisville. When his amendment failed, he proposed the same measure the following month, but this time he added appropriations for customs houses in Mobile, Cincinnati, and Wilmington to his motion. The entire monies requested for customs houses in Louisville, Mobile, Cincinnati, St. Louis, and Wilmington, he lectured to the House, "would not be sufficient to build one good frigate." Preston also reminded the representatives that the Democratic secretary of the treasury–his Louisville friend James Guthrie–supported the requested appropriations. The House on 16 March voted 75-64 to include Preston's amendment in the public lands bill. But the following day he won a larger victory when the representatives approved another Preston motion to grant $162,742 to complete and enlarge the Louisville customs house.[45]

Preston was popular with his fellow lawmakers. The Whigs respected his oratorical skills and recognized his talents in marshaling support for legislation. Following his reelection in 1853, he received three votes to become Speaker of the House. But he also was liked by non-Whigs. In part, Preston's sense of humor softened his partisan reputation. When a Whig accused the Democrats of "picayunian" spirit toward appropriations for inland customs houses, the Kentuckian came to his opponents' defense. "I did not know there was any such adjective in the language as 'picayunism,'" he jokingly remarked, to the laughter of the members present.[46]

Despite his outspoken defense of slavery, Preston enjoyed the respect of several important abolitionists. New York's Senator William H. Seward was an antislavery leader and a friend of William II. Channing of Massachusetts, a Unitarian cleric and fellow abolitionist. Channing told the New Yorker that he wished to consider slavery as "a subject of calm and kind conversation between statesmen and Christians, North and South, from whom he can learn and to whom he can comment what he thinks." On hearing this, Seward wrote Preston, "I have presumed so far as to indicate you to him as the character for whom he is seeking."[47]

As might be expected of a partisan Whig, Preston held the Democratic president, Franklin Pierce, in low esteem and complained of his inability to provide leadership. "The President and the administration have no power," Democratic Senator Douglas lamented to Preston in June 1854. Six months later the Louisville Whig wrote his sister, "The administration is at the nadir of powerlessness and with scarcely an apologist left." However, he was impressed with the Democrats' secretary of war, Jefferson Davis. Both William and his wife–using her influence as a member of a prominent Democratic family–lobbied Davis to offer brother-in-law Albert Sidney Johnston a colonelcy. After achieving this goal, Preston remarked of Davis, "Though I am opposed to him politically, he is a man of the highest grade, a true friend and high minded gentleman."[48]

While the Democratic administration might be weak, Preston and other southern Whigs realized in 1854 that their party was no longer a political force. A year earlier he still had held out hope that although his party had been "overwhelmed with disaster, I am one of those who do not believe it is annihilated or dead." But the division of the Whigs over the Kansas-Nebraska bill and the Gadsden Treaty convinced him that this faith was misplaced. "I think it very improbable that there can be any reunion or new coalition between the Southern Whigs and those of the North," he concluded in June 1854. "A schism has long existed in reality–it will hereafter be avowed publicly." However, he still urged "Southern States['] Right Whigs" to "keep their temper for a while, and wait for events . . . instead of joining either the Know Nothings or the Democrats."[49] But many former Whigs were doing just that by 1855.

In his third race for Congress, Preston fell victim in 1855 to the growing fear of foreign immigration expressed by many native-born voters. The American or Know-Nothing party led the protest against the increasing number and influence of foreigners in the United States. Since many of these immigrants were Roman Catholics, the nativists and some Protestant leaders attacked Catholics, charging them with conspiring to overthrow American democracy. In 1854 Know-Nothing candidates lost elections in New York state by a small margin and managed to win campaigns in Massachusetts and Delaware. The following year southern nativists persuaded the American party to endorse slavery.[50]

The rapid growth of Know-Nothing support in both the North and the South came at the same time that the Whig party was being torn apart over the issue of slavery. In Kentucky, as throughout the nation, a majority of the Whigs joined the new party. While many backed the American party's nativist platform, other factors helped to account for Know-Nothing support. Fear of the growing sectional strife led some southern Whigs into the American party, which they viewed as a force able to unite North and South. Other Whigs sided with the new party, in part out of reluctance to join their old adversaries, the Democrats. But not all Whigs flocked to the American party. In Kentucky and elsewhere in the South, many prominent

Whigs became Democrats, viewing the party as a conservative national force that would guarantee their interests.[51]

In 1855 former Whig congressman Humphrey Marshall accepted the nomination of the American party and opposed Preston's re-election bid. A champion of the rights of foreign-born Kentuckians, Preston received their support in his congressional campaigns. He refused to alter his views and join many of his fellow Whigs in their flight to the American party. Preston ran as an independent in 1855 and received the endorsement of the Democrats, who presented no candidate. Their newspaper, the *Louisville Democrat*, became one of his most important advocates. Marshall won the backing of many former Whigs, including the dean of Louisville's journalists, George D. Prentice, who wrote editorials in the *Louisville Daily Journal* in favor of the Know-Nothing nominee. But not all Whigs backed Marshall. In the *Louisville Daily Courier*, former Whig Walter N. Haldeman was outspoken in his support of Preston.

The Know-Nothing and Democratic candidates seeking to become city councilmen and county magistrates also were engaged in heated campaigns in 1855. Intimidation of voters and violence marred the nativists' victories for most of these positions in separate elections held in April and May, and the Know-Nothing candidate, John Barbee, was elected mayor. The new majority on the city council immediately began to carry out its anti-foreign agenda. A German American, Conrad Schröder, was dismissed as a city court interpreter. In July the councilmen refused to issue licenses to several German taverns and declared that no Catholic or foreign-born person could be employed as a schoolteacher. The Preston-Marshall contest continued the emotional encounter between the Know-Nothings and their enemies throughout the summer.

Both congressional candidates actively canvassed their district, attending rallies and speaking before courthouse crowds and at barbecues. Although known, in Preston's words, for his "great corporal ponderosity," Marshall campaigned actively. In Middletown outside of Louisville, several hundred voters enjoyed music, dance, and "good eating" at a July meeting where both candidates gave long speeches. There, as throughout the campaign, Preston stressed his record in the House, particularly his support of the Kansas-Nebraska Act. Marshall, as usual, attacked his opponent for supporting a clause in that legislation permitting foreigners in those territories to vote if they declared their intention to become United States citizens. The American party candidate claimed that he would rather have his right arm severed from his body than to vote for such a provision. In reply, Preston read from the *Congressional Globe* an amendment Marshall had offered while in Congress introducing exactly such a clause into the bill organizing the Oregon Territory. Preston backers gleefully reported that "shouts of derision rose from the audience." Preston's remarks defending his record in Congress before "a very large and enthusiastic multitude" at the Jefferson County courthouse on 1 August were met with "frequent and loud applause," the partisan *Louisville Daily Courier* reported.[52]

The Preston-Marshall campaign was one of the most emotional in the commonwealth's celebrated political history. The major issue of the election "is between Americanism and foreignism," George Prentice's *Daily Journal* informed its readers in July. Although the editor decried the use of "physical force" by members of the American party against their opponents, his paper increased tensions among the electorate. In August the editor warned of the danger of "the importation of foreign paupers" and noted that Preston favored the immigration of "foreign hordes" and was "disposed to go further in the way of securing political privilege to foreigners than almost any other respectable gentleman in our city or district." "Our population are being corrupted and our institutions endangered by an excess of the foreign element," Prentice claimed on 3 August. The next day he wrote, "Notwithstanding our great respect and esteem for Col. Preston, we are compelled to say that we consider his defeat by an overwhelming majority of vital importance." On election eve the Know-Nothing spokesman reminded his readers of the dangers of "Popery," whose "iron heel treads out the life of religious liberty" and would "sap the foundations of all our political edifices."[53]

Preston in turn defended religious freedom and noted the immigrants' essential contributions to the economic and social development of the state. Haldeman in the *Daily Courier* praised Preston for his campaign against bigotry and assailed Marshall for preaching "on all occasions and everywhere, undying and eternal and everlasting and exterminating hostility to the Pope of Rome and his followers." Lamenting that "the anti-Catholic issue is the great one in the contest," the *Democrat* reminded its readers that "on the naturalization laws, religious liberty, and the slavery question, Col. Preston is right."[54]

Marshall defeated Preston on 6 August 1855, an election day so characterized by violence that it is known in the annals of Louisville history as "Bloody Monday." The Know-Nothing-dominated city council refused to authorize enough polling stations or police protection to expedite voting and assure order. Before the precincts opened at six o'clock that morning, so-called "executive committees" of the American party took control of many voting stations in the predominantly German American first and second wards and the Irish American seventh and eighth wards. They admitted only voters displaying a yellow ticket, the sign of Know-Nothing approval. Long lines of immigrants, many with their naturalization papers in hand, were turned away from the polls or chased away as in the case of those waiting in the courthouse yard.[55]

Election day was filled with tension and activity for Preston. A group of Know-Nothing supporters gathered in front of his house on Walnut Street, forcing him to pass through the crowd, while giving a "speech of angry denunciation." He spent the day going from poll to poll encouraging the foreign-born to vote. At one voting station—at an engine house on Main Street—a man threatened Preston with a gun. According to his friend Basil Duke, the congressman "recklessly" moved toward his assailant and kicked his arm, knocking his pistol away.[56]

In some city wards only ten percent of the electorate managed to cast ballots, and few of Jefferson County's three thousand naturalized citizens were able to exercise their franchise. In contrast to his previous electoral successes in Louisville, Preston received only 1,344 of the 4,358 votes cast there instead of the 3,500 his supporters had expected. He lost the district by a margin of 2,000. "Scoundrelism is triumphant," the *Democrat* declared the next day, a partisan verdict that was not an overstatement. Kentuckians also chose the American party candidate for governor, former Whig Charles Slaughter Morehead, sent a majority of legislators from his party to the general assembly, and elected six of the state's ten congressmen.[57]

On this tension-filled day, riots first broke out in the East End of the city. Know-Nothing mobs assailed German Americans, set some of their houses ablaze on Shelby Street, burned down the Ambruster Brewery that afternoon, killing ten German Americans trapped inside, and sacked the German- and Irish-owned taverns and establishments in the Butchertown area. One unit of the state militia, claiming to be acting in defense of public order, joined the mob in the East End. The nativists also set fire to a row of frame houses in a heavily Irish district in the West End–on the north side of Main Street, between Tenth and Eleventh–killed the owner of these tenements, Francis Quinn, and then threw his body into the flames. Preston witnessed this atrocity and began to speak up, until a friend begged him not to involve himself and others "in a fight with a mob, which we were then powerless to quell." To safeguard the Cathedral of the Assumption, Roman Catholic Bishop Martin J. Spalding entrusted the keys to the building to Mayor John Barbee. Only after a search by the mayor found no gunpowder stored in the basement of St. Martin's Church did the mobs threatening to destroy it disperse. After the polls closed at seven o'clock on the hot August evening, a crowd fatally wounded a Catholic priest en route to visit a dying parishioner.[58]

The next day the *Louisville Anzeiger*'s headline read: "20 Men Killed!"–and two out of three killed were foreign-born. "The entire city was under siege through a formally organized armed mob," the German-language daily asserted. While Know-Nothing supporters insisted the riots were caused by "armed foreigners," historians have concluded otherwise. The *Daily Courier* correctly called Bloody Monday "a damnable outrage," while the *Democrat*'s headline, "Louisville Disgraced," did not exaggerate one of the greatest tragedies in the city's history. While similar anti-foreign riots had broken out in St. Louis in 1852 and in the spring of 1855 in Chicago and Cincinnati, Louisville's Bloody Monday proved "the most deadly of the lot," according to one scholar.[59]

Records reveal only a few cases in which damages were ever paid for the violence committed on Bloody Monday. A memorial signed on 6 August by one hundred Louisvillians, including William Preston and James Speed, urged the city to compensate citizens for their losses. But both the Known-Nothing-dominated Board of Aldermen and the state legislature refused to make amends. Of four successful suits pursued by the litigants, the only one that involved a substantial sum was that of the widow of William Ambruster. Attorney Reuben T. Durrett in March 1870 won an award of twenty thousand dollars that the city paid her for the destruction of the Ambruster Brewery and the family's house. Only five persons were indicted following Bloody Monday–two foreigners and three natives–but there were no convictions.[60]

Chapter IV: Legislator

Until his defeat for reelection in 1855, Preston and his family lived in Washington during his three years in the House of Representatives. The couple had enjoyed a lifestyle commensurate with their social rank and William's political ambitions. They purchased a "commodious" residence, allowing them to receive "a crush of company," for entertaining was a necessary complement to political advancement. But buying this house pushed the Prestons further into debt. William took special pride in his wife's good taste in clothes, claiming she "is quite du ton and outdresses everybody." He purchased "a very handsome open calash at New York" for Margaret and reported, "It makes a light and elegant turnout with which she is greatly pleased."[61]

Likewise, William was pleased with Margaret's success as a hostess. Her exploits were designed not only to bring her distinction, but to help his advancement. The Prestons invited society and political figures, as well as members of the diplomatic corps, to receptions, teas, and dinners at their home. William's Lexington cousin, John C. Breckinridge, was a Democratic congressman and often dined with the couple. Visiting Kentuckians, including Mag's uncle, former governor Charles A. Wickliffe, also were their guests. While the menus served are unknown, they no doubt included the many courses of filling foods—fish, beef, and fowl—that diners were accustomed to, from soup to after-dinner liqueurs in copious quantities. "Lucretius [would have been] happy at her feasts," one socialite remarked, "gratified alike by the task possessed and the taste enjoyed"—adding that Mrs. Preston's "eloquent repasts make those of the chief magistrates appear meagre."[62]

William's correspondence in 1854 was filled with comments on yet another "astonishing dinner" produced by Mag, and the next year he wrote that she was preparing "to give a splendid dinner to the judges of the Supreme Court" that promised to be "the greatest triumph of her culinary ambition." Long interested in a foreign post, the Kentucky congressman was careful to invite diplomats to his home, and in 1854 he was "happy in having astonished the foreign ministers" with a memorable soirée. But the heavy entertainment schedule proved wearing. Noting that Lent was strictly observed in Washington, William praised this break in the "gayety for which I am heartily thankful to the parsons." A year later he again was complaining, "We have had a crush of company all winter and I am terribly tired."[63]

But William was not too tired to find time to game. As was often his fate since his student days, "My bad luck continues," he reported in 1854. Once again he found himself "out of cash" and had to have his friend William W. Corcoran, the Washington socialite and philanthropist, "lend me enough money for my present necessities." Six months earlier, Preston had agreed with two others to a card game which would not end "until one or the other lost $5,000." However, despite his wishes, his fellow players insisted that the session stop when William had lost $900.[64]

In addition to recreational pursuits, Preston also found time to participate in a number of civic activities. He was made a member of the Ciceronian Literary Society at Washington's Georgetown College in 1853 and later that year gave a well-received speech at the annual dinner of the Maryland Historical Society.[65] He also contributed to several charities in the capital.

Mrs. Preston's efforts to impress Washington society met with success. The Mount Vernon Ladies Association of the Union, a group of prominent women in the capital, invited her into their ranks. A kinsman, Francis Preston Blair Sr., was an organizer of the Republican party and famous in his own right as a host at his Maryland plantation Silver Spring; he informed Margaret that she was "the very leader of polished life in the capital of the Republic." Her triumphs also made news in Louisville, where gossip had it that she was "decidedly the most admired woman in Washington." William's sister Susan reported that Zachary Taylor's mother had informed her that Mrs. Preston "is my pattern woman." When passing in front of the White House in a carriage in 1853, Kentucky's Senator Joseph Rogers Underwood mentioned to Margaret that one day she might occupy the residence, "if she and her husband did not commit a blunder." Such a suggestion must have reinforced the high hopes that both Prestons harbored and made her hard work as a Washington hostess appear worth the effort. Certainly Margaret continued to dream that her husband one day might occupy the White House. Six years later, when Preston was minister to Madrid, the Spanish envoy in Washington reported that Preston was reputed to have "vague presidential aspirations that originated with his wife."[66]

The couple was happy to have General Scott as a houseguest for seven weeks in early 1855. Congress then was considering a bill to grant Scott the rank of lieutenant general, retroactive to 1847, and allowing him the additional pay due at this rank for the past eight years. The general's "dignity and fine manners," epicurean love of food, and elegance as a conversationalist made him a favorite of the Prestons. His hostess made every effort to indulge the expansive general's voracious appetite. Following his visit, Scott wrote that his stay "will ever be looked back to with delight."[67]

The Louisville congressman and his lady were invited to innumerable social functions. In 1854 President Pierce twice had the couple to the White House for dinner, and Secretary of the Treasury James Guthrie also was their Washington host on many occasions. Francis Preston Blair invited the Prestons to his home. Former Missouri senator and then congressman Thomas Hart Benton and his wife, one of William's cousins, had the couple to dinner several times. Soirées, teas, and dances given by legislators, capital socialites, and foreign ministers also filled their calendar.

The Washington years were good ones for the Preston children. In letter after letter to Kentucky, both parents announced that "the children are all well." "Sunnie is wonderfully stout," and Wick "is as hearty and stout as a butcher's boy," William noted. Margaret reported that all were "fattening on grapes and peaches." She continued teaching them at home, and a white servant was hired to care for the younger children. The parents were pleased that the daughters were making friends and taking advantage of the opportunities offered in the capital. William found the Washington summers "intolerable," so they escaped to Louisville. On trips back and forth to Kentucky, the family found time for vacationing in the healthful mountainous surroundings of White Sulphur Springs in western Virginia, a favorite summer destination for wealthy southerners and politicians.[68]

While the Louisville congressman enjoyed many of his experiences in Washington, he appeared to be less enthusiastic with life there than his wife. In letters to his sister Susan, he vacillated in his opinion of the capital. William often described the city as "dull," the summers there "insufferably hot," and on several occasions declared, "I am growing weary of staying here." Yet at other times he confessed, "I begin to feel as much at home here as in Louisville."[69]

The family's elegant lifestyle in Washington came at a cost. Preston had his sister, Mrs. Susan Christy, look after his Louisville real estate with the help of his banker and financial manager, Frederick Wedekemper. Relatives took an interest in the Prestons' agricultural lands and slaves, more often than not reporting that "your Negroes were well and the farm greatly improved." Just as his wife complained about his costly expenditures, William found her expensive tastes excessive. Once he exclaimed to his sister, "God help Wedekemper and your unfortunate brother." Often Preston lamented, "I need money fearfully," and instructed Susan to consult with Wedekemper and authorize him "to sell for me any and all property he can at such prices as you and he agree." Preston had ample assets to take care of his financial problems–in 1856 the tax rolls credited him with $142,829 in possessions, counting thirty-three tracts of land, eighteen slaves, horses, carriages, and personal effects. Nevertheless, he continued to complain that he was "strongly pressed for money."[70] Although he had tremendous assets, he was intent on holding onto them for his family's later use and for his children's inheritance.

Beside financial difficulties, the Prestons had trouble with one of their slaves, Jane Giles. She was taken to Washington as a nurse for Wick in 1853, but her husband Tom remained in Louisville, where Margaret had hired him out as a cook at the Galt House. In November 1853 Jane escaped while she was accompanying the family on a visit to New York City. Initially, her mistress was distressed "by poor Jane's condition," alone in New York, and General Scott offered to send his orderly to find her if her whereabouts could be determined. "I sopose you wonder why that I left you," Jane wrote to Mrs. Preston in a frank letter on 8 February 1854. "Well I will tell you. Reason one Reason was because you Parted me and my housband as tho we had no feeling." The former slave ended her correspondence asserting, "Mr. Preston he treated me well he would not have sent my husband away had it not been for you." Margaret was appalled by this letter and accepted the belief that a free black probably composed it. William's sister Susan wrote Margaret that she had discovered that Jane had complained of her problems to a New York waiter, and he had encouraged her to flee.[71] Because William Preston was a leading proponent of slavery in Congress, abolitionists were probably happy to offer Jane assistance after her escape.

Following his defeat in 1855 and the demise of the Whig party, Preston became a Democrat. The family returned to Louisville, and in June 1856 he was an at-large delegate to the Democratic National Convention in Cincinnati. Like most southerners, Preston backed

Stephen A. Douglas through the sixteenth ballot, when the "Little Giant" received all twelve of Kentucky's votes. In Washington Preston had been a friend of the Illinois senator, whom he considered "the true friend of honor with the South and able champion of the Kansas Act." While the Pennsylvania politician and diplomat James Buchanan continued to lead Douglas 168-122 on the sixteenth ballot, neither was able to win the two-thirds majority needed for the presidential nomination. According to Preston the Douglas delegates by then were "demoralized by fear," and the Kentuckian believed Douglas's hope for the nomination was doomed. [72]

At that juncture the senator's floor manager, William A. Richardson, approached Preston and showed him a letter from Douglas stating that he would prefer to remove his name should his candidacy endanger the party's prospects for victory. Believing that "further personal adherence to your interests would have been fruitless, and not only detrimental to you but treasonous to the Democratic party and the country," Preston later explained to Douglas, the Kentuckian addressed the convention. After stressing his devotion to Douglas, Preston said that Buchanan was clearly the Democrats' choice and called on supporters of the Illinois senator to put "an end to the useless contest." With the delegates in an uproar, defiant backers of the "Little Giant" shouted, "No!" Then Richardson read the senator's letter to the convention. On the next ballot the Democrats unanimously nominated Buchanan. To mollify the disappointed southerners—and perhaps as Preston and Richardson had discussed—Richardson urged the nomination of John C. Breckinridge for the vice presidency. Preston then presented the name of his Kentucky cousin to the delegates, who nominated Breckinridge to run with Buchanan. [73]

Preston deemed Buchanan's election essential to preservation of the Union. The Kentuckian discounted the chances of the Know-Nothing candidate, Millard Fillmore, and feared that the election of Republican nominee John C. Frémont "will, per se, amount to disunion." "The South has no true friend in the North, but the Democracy," Preston assured Buchanan on the eve of the canvass. Afraid that northerners regarded "the possibility of disunion as a southern gasconade" and the South's defense of slavery as only "electioneering" cant, Preston feared that "nothing short of battle and civil bloodshed will convince the North that the South is in earnest." Should the "Black Republicans" win, he warned that the South must sound an alarm bell "that should make the abolitionist shudder."[74]

Given his belief in the election's importance, Preston worked actively for "Buck and Breck." The Democrats were happy to highlight Preston's support, for the party needed to attract former Whigs to their standard. In September the Louisvillian met with Buchanan and agreed to address rallies at Erie, Belmont, and elsewhere in the Keystone State. In so doing, the Kentuckian noted, "I exerted my voice so much that I am hoarse." He also addressed meetings for the Democratic nominee in Poughkeepsie, New York, Chicago, and his home state. At Tippecanoe battlefield near Lafayette, Indiana, Senator Douglas campaigned for the Pennsylvanian before a crowd of perhaps fifty thousand, considered by Democratic backers "the largest political assemblage ever convened in the West." Among the luminaries who also spoke were Breckinridge, Michigan senator Lewis Cass, and William Preston. Although Cass asked Preston in late October to campaign for the ticket in Michigan, his schedule did not permit this.[75]

In addition to speech making, Preston was occupied with party organization and strategy. In New York he conferred with Governor Horatio Seymour on how to unite the state's badly divided Democrats. While Seymour's "noble ideals" and efforts to promote party harmony impressed Preston, he counseled Buchanan to warn his New York backers that "while the schism continued no cabinet appointment, or first class mission would be conferred upon the State." Fillmore was Buchanan's only serious rival in Kentucky, and there Preston promised the Pennsylvanian to "do all that lies in my power" to convince his Whig friends "to go for the Democracy." In late October he reported to Breckinridge that he had organized two meetings "of our most prominent men" in Louisville and "used every argument with our friends to inflame and stimulate them to action." Remembering how the Know-Nothings had taken control of the balloting on Bloody Monday a year earlier, Preston called together leading Democrats who formed a committee with several American party chieftains to ask the mayor "to press the adoption of such measures as will secure peace and order."[76]

"The election of yesterday has given a new guarantee of the impregnable strength of the Democracy and a new hope for the stability of the Republic and the concord of the States," Preston wrote Buchanan on hearing of his victory in Pennsylvania.[77] Breckinridge became the youngest vice president in the republic's history, and the Democrats carried Kentucky for the first time since 1828. Even in defeat the new Republican party won eleven of the sixteen northern states. Unfortunately, Preston's prediction that "Buck and Breck" would be able to bridge the North-South breach proved too optimistic.

Preston remained involved in local as well as national politics. He supported his good friend Joshua F. Bullitt for appellate judge of Jefferson County in 1857. Bullitt campaigned as a Democrat-backed independent against a Know-Nothing challenger. Both sides expected a closely contested race and prepared to guarantee their supporters' access to the polls on 15 June. On election day Preston and Bullitt went to a polling station in the heavily German first ward to observe the voting. Preston and an American party adversary became involved in a shoving match, and soon both sides were hurling insults and pointing handguns at each other. The nativists pressed charges against Preston for carrying a concealed weapon and drawing his pistol inside the polls. He was tried in Police Court before a twelve-man jury in July. Preston and his defendants claimed that he had been attacked first and argued he had a right to carry a gun, for he correctly surmised that he might be assaulted. Regardless of the details of this incident, Preston displayed personal courage in trying to defend the right of franchise. Following a daylong debate, the jury failed to reach a verdict, and the police judge dismissed the case.[78]

By the late 1850s William Preston enjoyed a national reputation. His political service in Congress, his family's social prominence in the capital, and his campaigning in several states for Buchanan in 1856 brought the Louisvillian wide recognition outside Kentucky. Additionally, the value of his family contacts increased when cousin John C. Breckinridge became vice president. In 1858 these political and personal factors were instrumental in President Buchanan's decision to make Preston his minister to the Court of Spain.

Chapter V: At the Court of Spain

~

From 1858 until 1861 William Preston added an international dimension to his record of public service as United States Envoy Extraordinary and Minister Plenipotentiary to the Spanish Court in Madrid. The growing sectional strife at home would make impossible the purchase of Cuba from Spain, his principal goal, as well as ratification of the treaty he negotiated to settle the long-outstanding difficulties between Washington and Madrid. However, Preston's appeal to the Monroe Doctrine, when protesting Spain's occupation of the Dominican Republic in 1861, marked one of the first times that the United States would invoke this doctrine abroad to assert its foreign policy.

When Augustus Caesar Dodge resigned as minister to Spain in 1858, President James Buchanan considered four candidates for the post. He finally decided on the Louisvillian only after rejecting one aspirant and after the other two had turned down the assignment. The president approached Stephen R. Mallory of Florida, but he decided to remain in the Senate. August Belmont, a prominent New York Democrat and financier, was the candidate of his uncle, Senator John Slidell of Lousiana. But Buchanan wanted Slidell to serve as minister to Paris and feared charges of favoritism if he also appointed Belmont, so the New Yorker was not offered the Spanish assignment. The president asked Slidell's second choice, Senator Judah P. Benjamin of New Orleans, to represent the United States in Madrid, but he preferred to remain a solon. Finally, William Preston was offered this post in September 1858, and he accepted.[1] The Senate unanimously approved his appointment without submitting his nomination for committee consideration as was customary.

From President Buchanan's viewpoint, the Louisvillian was a good man for the Madrid post. The cousin of Vice President John C. Breckinridge had played a role in Buchanan's nomination at the Democrats' 1856 convention in Cincinnati and during the campaign had given speeches for him in New York, Pennsylvania, Illinois, Indiana, and Kentucky. Despite their political association, Preston and Buchanan had never enjoyed a close friendship. Nevertheless, the

Kentuckian's outspoken defense of southern interests, including advocacy of Cuban annexation, made him a logical person to carry forward the president's diplomatic offensive. Not just coincidentally, the appointment allowed Buchanan another opportunity to repay the proslavery Democrats for their support.[2]

In the autumn of 1858 Preston viewed the Madrid offer as a promising step to future advancement. Although his brother-in-law Albert Sidney Johnston urged him to decline the appointment and wait for a more important position, several factors encouraged Preston's acceptance of the Spanish mission. He was actively seeking an appointment in the Buchanan administration, and he did not want to run again for Congress. Preston likewise had decided not to try for the Democratic nomination for governor, although he believed–and probably correctly so–that he would have been able to win the party's endorsement and the election. However, Breckinridge had promised his support to Beriah Magoffin for governor, so the vice president was happy to see Preston accept the Madrid ministry. Another factor influencing his acceptance of the diplomatic post was his wife's desire to live in Europe.[3]

Preston's decision to go to Madrid met with the enthusiastic approval of his family and friends, who believed the post would advance his political ambitions. President Buchanan asserted that the American minister who negotiated the purchase of Cuba would find his name identified "with one of the greatest Events in our history." Preston's father-in-law Robert Wickliffe counseled him not to enter the contest for governor but accept the Spanish post. General Winfield Scott was sorry that Preston was not appointed minister to London or Paris, but maintained that if he should acquire Cuba, "that will more than make up the difference." If Cuba became a United States colony, Scott foresaw Preston as "governor-general of the island, or Secretary of State." Mrs. Preston was encouraged by the general's prediction that in acquiring Cuba her husband would find himself "above all our diplomats save the signers of the Louisiana treaty." Cheered on by such hopes, Preston's wife, nephew William Preston Johnston, and some influential southern Democrats believed the Madrid ministry would help Preston reach the White House, a goal they earlier had urged on him.[4]

Although now remembered for its domestic problems and failures, the Buchanan administration pursued a vigorous foreign policy.

The president sought to overcome growing sectional differences over internal issues such as slavery by building public support for his expansionist goals. As a member of both houses of Congress from Pennsylvania, secretary of state under President James K. Polk, and minister to London, Buchanan had been an outspoken advocate of an American empire, favoring expansion for ideological and nationalist reasons. His belief in Anglo-Saxon superiority convinced him that the migration of white Americans would bring the blessings of democracy and economic prosperity to the inferior peoples of Mexico, Central America, and Cuba. Thus Buchanan believed that the United States was destined to control these lands. As president he continued to emphasize foreign expansion, but found his efforts frequently frustrated. Congress refused to grant his requests to use military force to protect transit routes across Nicaragua, Panama, and the isthmus of Tehuantepec in Mexico or approve his design to make the northern Mexican states of Chihuahua and Coahuila United States protectorates with military bases there. Likewise, his attempt to purchase Baja California and Sonora came to naught.[5]

The key to Buchanan's diplomatic offensive was his attempt to acquire Cuba, the most precious colony in Spain's remaining empire. Strong trade ties between northern ports and Havana and the South's search for additional slave territory had made annexation of the Caribbean isle a popular subject in both the North and South for decades. Thomas Jefferson, John Quincy Adams, James Monroe, John C. Calhoun, and Henry Clay were among the statesmen who believed Cuba should become a part of the American Union. As secretary of state under Polk in 1848, Buchanan had offered Spain one hundred million dollars to purchase the island, but Madrid refused to sell its prized possession.[6]

By the 1850s the issue of Cuba, like so many others, had been turned into a subject of regional controversy. Abolitionists charged that southerners were interested only in gaining the island to guarantee the political power of the slave states, and these northerners created a block adamantly opposed to Cuban annexation. Earlier, in the late 1840s, some slaveholders had contacted those Cubans determined to expel the Spanish. Afraid that the establishment of a republic might mean the end of slavery, some Creoles believed United States annexation would safeguard their interests. These Cubans founded the Club de la Havana in 1848 and collaborated with southern slave owners. Preston corresponded in 1849 with Cristóbal Madan, a Havana conspirator seeking United States assistance against Spain. In 1850-51 hundreds of southerners served with Narciso López, a Venezuelan native who lived in the United States and became a filibuster. He twice invaded Cuba, trying to wrest it from Spanish control.[7]

Mississippi's governor John A. Quitman was among the most outspoken supporters of López, but the cause also proved popular in Kentucky. Two veterans of the Mexican War from the commonwealth, Theodore O'Hara and Thomas Hawkins, and a West Point graduate from the state and former consul in the West Indies, John T. Pickett, visited the filibuster in Washington and urged him to seek recruits in Kentucky. In February 1850 López visited Louisville where he found many supporters. One hundred fifty men from the state volunteered for López's expedition to Cuba in August 1851. They served in a regiment under Colonel William L. Crittenden, a West Point graduate and the nephew of a Kentucky governor. Preston supported their efforts and believed their goal was the "liberation of Cuba." The Spaniards quickly captured the invaders and executed Crittenden and fifty-one of his men on 16 August. López was garroted on 1 September, but 135 of his soldiers were imprisoned and later ransomed. The filibusters' execution was greeted with protest meetings throughout the United States, including one in Louisville.[8]

Many northerners also were attracted to the idea of Cuba under United States control. August Belmont, the New York agent of the Rothschilds, believed the island should be purchased, and in December 1852 he sought to enlist the banking houses in a grandiose scheme. These financial institutions were to warn Madrid that foreign holders of Spanish bonds were frightened by the nation's instability and considering unloading their securities. Faced with a credit crisis, Belmont reasoned, Spain would be forced to sell Cuba to avoid economic and political chaos. Senator Slidell had urged Buchanan in 1854 to consult Belmont about his plan.[9] Such proposals encouraged the belief that Madrid would cede the island.

President Franklin Pierce was willing to offer one hundred and thirty million dollars for Cuba, and he asked Congress in August 1854 to appropriate funds to purchase this "Pearl of the Antilles." But the members decided to postpone action on this controversial request. Disturbed by this delay, the United States ministers in London, Paris, and Madrid–James Buchanan, John Mason, and Pierre Soulé–met in Belgium and issued a declaration in October. In this Ostend Manifesto the three Democrats stated that Cuba "is as necessary to the North American republic as any of its present members." They urged the United States to make an "immediate and earnest effort" to purchase the island, but should Spain not agree to this, the American Union, "by every law, human and Divine, . . . shall be justified in wresting it from Spain." When the three ministers' recommendation was published in the United States, a storm of opposition arose. In the eyes of many, the manifesto linked territorial expansion with naked aggression, instead of associating it with the spread of republican institutions. In addition to hostility at home, the British government criticized the manifesto. The Pierce administration quickly repudiated the ministers' action, but the document furnished yet another point for debate between North and South, as antislavery northerners seized on the incident as evidence of a ruthless slavocracy.[10]

President Buchanan confidently expected his administration would be successful in purchasing Cuba. In his second annual address on 6 December 1858, he expressed this belief and argued that the colony could and should be acquired by "honorable negotiations."[11] He asked Congress for an appropriation to be used as a down payment should Madrid agree to sell the island. Several signs seemed to indicate that Spain at long last might be willing to cede her most important possession. One of the president's early actions had been to meet secretly in 1857 with Christopher Fallón. Born in Spain of Irish parents, Fallón lived in Philadelphia and had business connections with both the European financial community and the Spanish royal family. He was closely associated with the Rothschild banking interests through Belmont, involved in Spanish railroad bonds through his ties with Baring Brothers in England, and represented Léon Lillo et Compagnie of Paris. As the United States agent of the French company, Fallón had invested monies of the Spanish queen mother, María Cristina, in Pennsylvania land purchases.[12]

The Spanish American financier managed to convince an optimistic Buchanan that business pressures could succeed where diplomacy had failed in regard to Cuba. The Madrid government owed more than five hundred million dollars to the Rothschild, Baring, and Lillo banking houses. Fallón and financiers like August Belmont believed that the major parties in Spain "reluctantly" might agree to sell Cuba to pay off this debt. A generous share of the purchase price of Cuba, it was assumed, would find its way into the pockets of the politicians. Corruption was not uncommon among Spanish officials in the mid-nineteenth century, making this proposal seem realistic. Furthermore, the queen mother had earned a reputation in Spain for receiving money in exchange for political favors and was thought to be sympathetic to selling the island. Some believed that she might support a United States scheme to buy the colony in exchange for a monetary gift. María Cristina also had extensive holdings in Cuba, and their value likely would rise if the island came under American control.[13]

With a letter from Buchanan in hand authorizing him "to ascertain whether Spain is willing to sell," Fallón sailed for Europe in December 1857. There he sought to convince European investors and Spanish leaders of the financial advantages that would accrue from America's purchase of the Caribbean isle. In the Old World he met with the impecunious queen mother, worried Spanish bond-holders, and various politicos. From Madrid Fallón wrote Buchanan, "The hostility in Spain to the question of sale of Cuba has greatly increased since 1848," and he noted that the outspoken hostility of many in Congress to acquiring the island was encouraging Spaniards opposed to its cession. Nevertheless, the Spanish American reported, "I feel now convinced that with judicious management the purchase can be made on fair terms, honorable and beneficial to both countries." He therefore urged Buchanan to appoint a new envoy to Madrid and give him carte blanche to negotiate Cuba's purchase at the appropriate time. However, he urged the president to include "no reference to this subject specifically" in the instructions to his new minister to Madrid. "I place great reliance on your ability and sound judgment," Buchanan wrote Fallón in April, after receiving his correspondence from Europe. By then the president was convinced that the right appointee and a large enough supply of money would enable the United States to bring the legendarily corrupt politicians in Madrid to barter away their Caribbean prize.[14]

Before departing for Madrid, Preston visited Washington in December to discuss his assignment. Buchanan's secretary of state, Lewis Cass, told the new minister that the purchase of Cuba was an obvious goal and that he should seek specific instructions concerning this from the president. The secretary believed the new envoy should enjoy full powers to negotiate such a deal. Of his White House meeting the Kentucky diplomat optimistically reported, "The President is polite and lets me have everything my own way. After a long and full interview, he acceded fully to my views."[15] Although Preston's interview with Buchanan focused on Cuba, the envoy's official instructions contained no mention of the island, as Fallón had suggested.

Preston also visited the Spanish minister to Washington, Gabriel García y Tassara, trying to assure him that the United States would not go to war over the Caribbean colony. The Iberian was impressed by Preston as a warm individual. But García y Tassara warned the foreign office in Madrid that the new minister had sympathized with the filibusters' attempts to invade Cuba and was an outspoken proponent of Cuban annexation.

The Spanish public was aware that Buchanan and Preston were intent on acquiring Cuba. Newspapers in Madrid, such as *La América* in November 1858, asserted that the new minister would look for a pretext to start a war between the two nations. The following month the deputies in the Cortes, Spain's parliament, went on record as opposing any discussion of ceding their nation's most prized colonial possession.[16]

On the eve of his departure, the envoy also received advice from Fallón. Buchanan had asked the Spanish American to meet with Preston when he and his family were in Philadelphia, but the two were unable to get together. Instead, Fallón addressed a long letter to the Kentucky minister on 6 January 1859. "You will no doubt find on going to Spain," Fallón wrote, "that every one you meet with . . . will at once repel the idea of a sale of Cuba, and yet this must not be taken as a true indication of the real feeling or sentiments of all." While admitting that he did not know whom Preston should approach, the Philadelphian urged him to try to gain the support of José de Salamanca, a "silent partner in the banking house of Señor Lillo and Cie. of Paris" and the wealthiest industrialist in Spain. Because of the count's influence with the royal family, Spanish politicos, and European financiers, Fallón assured Preston that "if you can enlist his aid you may be perfectly assured of success."[17]

The Prestons' trip to Madrid was a long one. After Washington, they went to Philadelphia, where Margaret had attended school, and there she visited a "milliness" for proper attire. They sailed from New York on 9 January 1859. By then Preston was confident of success in acquiring Cuba. He sincerely believed that "a big pile of <u>cash</u> (not <u>credit</u>) at Madrid" would permit him to "seize any golden opportunity that Fortune might cast upon the current, [so that] I might make a stroke that would not alone signalize me, but benefit my country." Preston thought that twenty million or even ten million dollars would be enough to purchase the island. Here the Kentuckian was repeating the opinion of Fallón, who believed that Cuba was the United States's for the taking, if only the Madrid officials could be given "assurances of success and confidence that the terms of contract if any will be fulfilled."[18]

The day following Preston's departure for Europe, Senator Slidell of Louisiana introduced a resolution requesting an appropriation of thirty million dollars "to facilitate the acquisition of the island of Cuba." The Senate Foreign Relations Committee recommended passage of Slidell's bill and argued that the "acquisition of Cuba may be considered a fixed purpose of the United States." The majority of committee members believed that the Cuban people were "ardently desirous of annexation," and they insisted that United States ownership of the island was important both to national security and to commercial expansion. Representative Lawrence Branch of North Carolina introduced a similar measure in the House that also won committee approval.[19]

In the Senate William H. Seward led the opposition to purchasing Cuba. In his minority report for the Foreign Relations Committee the New Yorker asked, "What is to be the status of the slave population" in Cuba under North American ownership? He considered the cost of purchasing the island prohibitive and warned against the acquisition of "a population different entirely from the citizens of the United States." Seward concluded that Slidell's bill was simply a "great Presidential demonstration, made, I think, to retrieve the sinking and wasting fortunes of an Administration that has championed its own immoderate desires more than the less sanguine expectations of the American people." For Republicans like Seward, Buchanan's Cuban policy proved that proslavery Democrats manipulated the president.[20]

The purchase of Cuba turned immediately into a sectional issue, with most southerners urging passage of Slidell's bill and Republicans denouncing it as a proslavery plot. The *Louisville Daily Courier,* the *Washington Union,* and the *Constitution* in the capital favored the bill. For these newspapers, the annexation of Cuba was "a matter of vital importance to the security of the entire Union in a military point of view, and of incalculable value to all our industrial, agricultural, shipping, manufacturing and commercial interests." Additionally, United States ownership would "release nearly the whole population of Cuba from the chains which bind them to the Spanish throne," for Spain's only "object is to make money out of the people of Cuba." According to the Democrats, opposition to acquiring Cuba was "dictated by a spirit of partisan hostility and jealousy."[21] The *New York Times*, a leading opponent of purchasing Cuba, noted the importance that slavery played in the southerners' proposal. For the *Times* Slidell's bill was a "Thirty Million Scheme," a "dark plot," for "tormenting Spain into parting with what we cannot just at present afford to purchase and can never profitably take by force." According to their opponents, the Democrats were attempting to make a "financial conquest" of the island, but the money they sought "is wanted for purposes of bribery–that if voted it will be spent in purchasing support for the Cuban scheme in the Spanish Court." Preston ignored such negative sentiments and actively campaigned for Buchanan's Caribbean initiative. In December he wrote his friends "to press home upon the country the necessity of consolidated public opinion and full endorsement of the Cuba policy."[22]

Before Preston reached Madrid, the project to purchase Cuba had been defeated by domestic political animosities. Congressional debate on Slidell's proposal divided the pro- and anti-slavery forces. The Louisiana senator stressed that Cuba's sugar plantations and commerce would provide opportunities for investors, and he noted that United States ownership of the island would halt the African slave trade there. Northern Democrats Stephen A. Douglas of Illinois and George E. Pugh of Ohio led Senate backers of the bill, as did Benjamin of Louisiana. Pugh claimed the people of Cuba sought annexation and argued that the United States must exert its right to control the continent. But Republican senators demanded to know why an appropriation was sought before it was known if the Spanish were willing. Those who could answer this question did not dare. Slidell's motion to end discussion of the bill and bring it to a vote failed by a margin of 28 to17 on 9 February, convincing him his measure would not pass. He withdrew it on 26 February, promising to reintroduce another proposal in the next session. Republicans in the

House also opposed United States acquisition of Cuba and managed to prevent a vote on Branch's bill.[23]

Congressional elections in October and November cost the Democrats their majority in the lower house and doomed passage of Slidell's proposal. The president and the Louisianian refused to give up, but their efforts were to no avail. Again in his December 1859 annual message–as in his address a year earlier–Buchanan urged "the acquisition of Cuba by fair purchase," noting that unless Congress concurred, "it will be almost impossible to institute negotiations without any reasonable prospect of success." Slidell reintroduced his measure in 1860, but the Foreign Relations Committee never returned it to the floor. The president again advocated the purchase of Cuba in his December 1860 message, demonstrating his inability to understand the angry sentiments that would burst into war a few months hence.[24]

Buchanan's attempt to use Cuba to unify his party and bring the North and the South together in a territorial enterprise had failed. The problem of slavery proved stronger than the desire for territorial expansion on the eve of the Civil War. The failure to purchase Cuba augured the importance that slavery would assume as an issue in Abraham Lincoln's successful campaign the following year.

After "a rough but not stormy passage" to England, William Preston and his family spent a week in London. They proceeded to Paris, where he was presented to Napoleon III at the Tuileries, a Renaissance palace constructed three hundred years earlier by Catherine de Médici. Like so many others, the Kentuckian was impressed by the charm of the emperor of the French. In Paris the Prestons placed their three older daughters in the convent-school of the Sacré Coeur. Despite the institution's waiver of its rule not to accept Protestants, the parents six months later removed their children to avoid "the bigotry the order evinced." The three children were transferred to a Protestant school, but Carrie did not like it. Next the older girls were sent to the Convent of the Assumption in the suburb of Auteuil.[25]

In Paris Margaret pursued private French lessons to improve her command of the language, and William complained that he was "heartily tired" of too many formal dinners and balls. The couple also found time to purchase and send five shipments of furniture, several carriages, six boxes of carpets, iron skillets, teapots, linens, four containers of porcelain, and two boxes of silver plate to see them through their Spanish stay. Leaving the three older daughters at Autueil, the rest of the family left the French capital by train for Marseilles, where they boarded a ship for Alicante on the Spanish Mediterranean.[26] From there they went by train up to the Castilian plateau, finally reaching Madrid on 4 March.

Unfortunately for Preston, his hope of taking advantage of the divisions among Spain's politicians proved impossible. In the late 1850s the nation was governed by an effective coalition, headed by General Leopoldo O'Donnell, who previously had served in Havana as captain-general, the chief political official on the island. A talented politician, O'Donnell enjoyed the support of the queen and brought together a coalition known as the Liberal Union. Instead of encountering the ministerial instability that characterized nineteenth-century Spain, the American envoy confronted a government and citizenry united in their determination to retain their colonial empire. O'Donnell adroitly used the threat of United States acquisition of Cuba to strengthen his administration. Two months before Preston reached Madrid, the minister of foreign relations, Saturino Calderón Collantes, declared in the Cortes that retention of Cuba was a matter of national "'dignity and honor.'" In January 1859 legislators voted unanimously never to cede the island.[27]

Preston's optimism over the possible cession of Cuba quickly proved to be at variance with what he observed in Spain. Even before he received the news of the failure of Slidell's resolution, the Kentucky envoy realized that no government of any political persuasion would remain in power if it agreed to sell the nation's colonial prize. Spanish public opinion adamantly opposed Buchanan's December 1858 proposal to purchase Cuba. Preston's predecessor in Madrid, Augustus Dodge, reported that the president's speech had created "a good deal of excitement here." This proved an understatement. The press excoriated Buchanan for imagining that Spain would forsake its honor by selling Cuba.[28]

The new minister was concerned about his reception by the government, but was assured he would be well received. When Preston had his first interview on 9 March with Foreign Minister Calderón, the Spaniard warned the American envoy that "any proposition to purchase Cuba would result in the immediate cessation of all intercourse between the two nations." Preston then asked if not men-

Courtesy Special Collections, University of Kentucky
*Isabella II of Spain reigned from 1833
to 1868; from William Preston's album.*

tioning this matter was a condition for seeing the queen, adding that he would not consent to having "any conditions or limitations imposed upon me." Calderón said no, but added that the topic would be poorly received.[29]

In an impressive ceremony at the Royal Palace, the Kentuckian presented his credentials to Queen Isabel II on 13 March. Preston alighted from his coach in the plaza in front of the enormous stone residence, whose interior was a monument of Rococo splendor. Tapestries after cartoons by Raphael covered the walls, large portraits of Spanish monarchs by Goya complemented the many mirrors in the public rooms, and grandiose Baccarat chandeliers gave light. The Louisvillian ascended the marble stairway, where guardsmen in resplendent uniform watched him pass en route to the Throne Room. There, under a ceiling mural depicting Columbus's discovery of the New World–painted by Tiepolo–Preston was introduced to Her Catholic Majesty. Diplomatically choosing to overlook the problems between the two nations, his remarks were "short and bland." He promised "to promote the amicable relations which happily now exist" and carefully refrained from mentioning Cuba during the audience.[30]

Political opposition at home to acquiring Cuba depressed the new envoy. After only one month in Madrid, Preston lamented, "The unpatriotic debates in Congress amused them [the Spaniards] greatly and filled the officials here with joy." Two weeks later he was informing Washington, "It is very bitter to think how party opposition has left the Administration without means, and myself powerless to seize any golden opportunity that fortune may throw in our way." "All attempts to buy without ready money would be idle," he concluded, "and as Congress has not thought fit to grant that, any attempt to negotiate would be useless." Preston wrote Secretary of State Cass in late April, "I have no longer a desire to remain at this Court." The defeat of Slidell's bill, the Louisvillian concluded, proved that "the President is dead politically, and the Republicans sure of triumph." Even worse, it has "checked America in her advancement to Empire" and "withheld the extension of her free institutions in the New World." In May 1859 he informed Buchanan that his mission was "useless."[31]

Against all logic, however, Preston continued to speculate that events might permit the acquisition of Cuba. He thought that perhaps France's aid to the Italian nationalists opposed to Austrian-ruled lands on the peninsula might make the British fear the Mediterranean balance of power was being upset. Should this bring war between France and Britain, Spain might back France. Then, Preston believed, Cuba should be "boldly seized" by the United States. Or perhaps the O'Donnell government would fall, and a new ministry cede the island. But such hopes came to naught.[32]

Unable to advance the grand plan for Cuba, Preston turned his attention to another cause: solving the outstanding controversy between the two nations over the *Amistad* claims. This complex affair had plagued Spanish-American relations since 1839. In April that year a Portuguese slave ship acquired a cargo of blacks in Sierra Leone and sailed to Havana where in June they were sold into slavery. Although this violated an 1817 Anglo-Spanish treaty outlawing the slave trade with Africa, the captain-general issued passports for the fifty-three Africans and they were given Spanish names. The two Spaniards who had bought them placed them aboard the Spanish schooner *Amistad* for the two-day trip to Puerto Principe on Cuba's northwest coast. En route the captives mutinied, killed the captain and the cook, and tried to force their purchasers to sail them back to Sierra Leone. Instead, the white pilots deceived them, and the vessel reached Long Island Sound in August 1839.[33] There an

American brig took the Africans to New London, Connecticut, where they were charged with murdering the ship's crewmen. Under the treaty of 1795 between the United States and Spain, both nations were committed to care for and return to the owner the vessel and merchandise of any kind rescued from pirates and brought into a port of the other country, "as soon as due and sufficient proof shall be made concerning the property."[34]

The two Spaniards claimed they were the owners of the *Amistad's* goods and human cargo and filed suit for restoration of their property. But a group of prominent abolitionists organized a legal offensive to win freedom for the Africans. They argued that the blacks had been enslaved illegally. However, President Martin Van Buren and Attorney General Henry D. Gilpin favored the return of the ship and its cargo as called for by the 1795 treaty, so the abolitionists carried their case to the courts. Southern slave owners backed the president and contended that the Africans' Spanish passports demonstrated they belonged to their purchasers. In January 1840 a federal district tribunal agreed with the Africans' defenders and decided that the blacks were not the property of their supposed owners. On appeal the circuit court upheld this decision. The *Amistad* and its merchandise were sold in October 1840 to repay the claims of the vessel's salvors, an act that enraged the Spanish claimants and their government.

Afraid of angering southern voters in an election year by freeing the mutineers, President Van Buren took the case to the Supreme Court. There, former President John Quincy Adams passionately defended the freedom of the Africans in two speeches, each lasting almost four hours. On 9 March 1841, the high court upheld the lower courts' decisions and declared the blacks free, but the Spanish government refused to accept this disposition of the affair, again demanding indemnification. The thirty-four *Amistad* survivors were returned to West Africa in November 1841.[35]

Following Van Buren, Presidents John Tyler, James Polk, Millard Fillmore, Franklin Pierce, and James Buchanan each recognized the legitimacy of Spanish claims in the *Amistad* affair. With the support of the executive branch, bills were introduced into Congress in 1844, 1847, 1848, 1851, 1852, 1858, and 1859 to appropriate either fifty or seventy thousand dollars to satisfy the *Amistad* claims. Opponents successfully blocked passage of these resolutions, arguing either that the United States should never reimburse illegal slave owners or that the decision of the courts should not be violated.

A second Spanish-North American dispute exacerbated the difficulties between the two nations over the *Amistad* claims. In 1844, following a devastating hurricane, Spanish authorities in Havana issued a decree permitting the importation of certain foodstuffs and building materials into the island duty free for six months. The government in Madrid countermanded the decision of its colonial officials after shipments of goods had left the United States for Cuba. One hundred American exporters were forced to pay $128,635.54 to the customshouse in Havana, thereby trimming profit margins and causing some unanticipated losses. In 1854 Spanish and United States representatives reached an understanding that American claimants would receive full indemnity. But the Madrid government refused to approve the accord until Washington agreed to settle the *Amistad* case.[36]

The outstanding claims of United States citizens led to calls for military intervention. Mississippi's Senator Jefferson Davis in December 1858 urged the seizure of Cuba if Spain did not pay, and the following month Congressmen Thomas L. Anderson of Missouri and Reuben Davis of Mississippi urged war with Spain "to obtain for our people justice of injuries done to them and their property," a course of action endorsed by several important newspapers. When Preston in October 1859 pressed Calderón to agree to full payment of the Havana claims, the Spaniard told him that public pressure would not permit Madrid to do this until Washington agreed to satisfy the *Amistad* claims.[37] Although the Kentuckian protested, it was obvious that the two countries would have to resolve both disputes simultaneously.

In November 1859 Preston and Calderón reached a tentative accord to resolve the *Amistad* and Cuban claims. The Madrid government would agree to pay the Havana claims in full, but without interest, a proposal Secretary Cass supported. Preston and Calderón decided that a convention should be concluded creating a commission to arbitrate all outstanding differences between their governments. In December 1859, President Buchanan recognized the justice of Spain's *Amistad* demands, and the Spanish minister in Washington reported, "The arrangement of the claims appears to be proceeding satisfactorily."[38]

Preston and Calderón signed a "Convention for the Settlement of Claims between the United States of America and Her Catholic Majesty" on 5 March 1860. This document stated that Spain would accept responsibility for paying $128,635.54 to settle the Cuban dispute and immediately turn over $100,000 of this sum to Washington. A three-man board of commissioners was to be created; each government would appoint one member and the third would be chosen by these two arbitrators. They would hear the *Amistad* case and all other claims, determining the amounts due each litigant by a vote of at least two to one. In a complex clause, the agreement stated that eventually the remaining $28,635.54 due the United States for the Cuban claims would be paid if Washington would reimburse the Spanish claimants in the amount agreed upon by the commissioners. If the United States did not do so, the Madrid government would pay the Spanish litigants their determined awards and not surrender this remainder to Washington.[39]

President Buchanan was pleased that this convention promised to end two decades of diplomatic discord between the two countries. He submitted the treaty on 3 May to the Senate, where a two-thirds majority was required for its passage. The Republican solons led the attack on this agreement. They argued the United States could not morally pledge itself to reimburse illegal slave owners in the *Amistad* case in defiance of the previous decisions of the judiciary. On 27 June, by a vote of twenty-six yeas and seventeen nays, an antislavery faction of twelve Republicans and five allies was responsible for the rejection of this attempt to resolve all outstanding Spanish-American disputes. Following his presidency, Buchanan defended the proposed treaty as satisfactory "to all claimants, but unfortunately not to the Senate of the United States," blaming its failure on "the extreme views of the Senate against slavery." The victory of the North in the Civil War–not diplomacy–ended the *Amistad* affair, for after 1865 the United States would not consider offering compensation for the freed Africans.[40]

Preston's other diplomatic duties in Madrid were of an unexciting and often routine nature. Attending state functions; overseeing the actions of United States consuls in such cities as Barcelona, Cadiz, Valencia, Tenerife, Manila, San Juan, and Havana; informing Washington of Madrid's ratification of international accords; and notifying the respective United States agencies of changes in Spanish tariff laws and navigational regulations proved to be time-consuming tasks. Looking after the rather minor problems of American citizens trading with or traveling in Spain, Cuba, Puerto Rico, or the Philippines were other duties that required a great deal of patience and effort. Arrested United States sailors and tourists, complaints from irate Spanish merchants over legal difficulties, and arrangement for the burial of American citizens in the Church of England cemetery in Madrid were but a few of the myriad difficulties the Kentuckian dealt with.[41]

In carrying out his duties, Preston chose his nephew, Robert Wickliffe Woolley, as secretary of the legation. Horatio I. Perry, who was married to a Spaniard and had been at the legation since 1849, continued as chargé d'affaires, and John De Havilland served as translator. While United States heads of mission came and went in the nineteenth century, officials like Perry proved "indispensable," for they gave continuity to the diplomatic service abroad.[42]

Lincoln's inauguration in March 1861 signaled the end of Preston's ministry to Spain, but he continued at his post until 25 May. Aware of his prosouthern politics, the new Republican secretary of state, William H. Seward, pointedly wrote the envoy that the president expected him to report promptly any information about Confederate efforts to gain Spanish support. The Kentuckian informed Seward that no southern agents had come to Madrid and added his belief that Spain's attitude toward the American conflict would depend on the policy of Napoleon III in France. Preston also presented the court with a copy of Lincoln's inaugural address and followed instructions to notify the Spanish government that the United States was closing rebellious southern ports to commerce.[43]

Following Lincoln's election, the dissolution of the Union allowed a confident Spain to expand its Caribbean empire. Preston reported that Spaniards greeted the Republican victory with elation, believing it closed the door on American designs on Cuba. In Washington, García y Tassara realized that the sectional crisis in the United States meant that Washington would be unable to carry out any military action in the Caribbean, and he informed Madrid of this.[44]

In 1858 the provisional president of Santo Domingo, Pedro Santana, had asked Spain to protect his country against threats from Haiti, its western neighbor. O'Donnell's government had given clandestine arms and money to Spanish supporters, and he considered the annexation of Santo Domingo "a noble enterprise." When Santana in March 1861 asked Spain to make his country a protectorate, Madrid was ready to do so. Francisco Serrano, the captain-general in Cuba and a friend of the prime minister, also favored Spanish recolonization and sent troops from Havana to the island. O'Donnell admitted in April to the British chargé in Madrid that the breakup of the Union had encouraged Spain's action. Queen Isabella annexed Santo Domingo in May 1861.[45]

Preston made his greatest contribution to United States diplomacy when he expressed opposition to Spanish intervention in Santo Domingo and concern over rumors that Madrid might send troops to Mexico. In December 1860 he reported to Secretary of State Cass that he had "used a strong tone as to the determination of the United States to permit no occupation of territory, and indeed brought it to the point, that Spain might endure the perils of War and the cost of hostilities in the New World." Made aware by the European press of Spain's invasion of Santo Domingo, Preston energetically protested to the foreign office without waiting for instructions from Washington. In a note of 12 April 1861, he reminded Señor Calderón that the independence of the American republics had been recognized by Spain and that "there is no doctrine in which my government is more fixed than in its determination to resist any attempt of an European power to interfere for the purpose of controlling the destiny of the American republics or reestablishing over them monarchical power." The Kentuckian then sent a full report on 14 April of this recolonization attempt to the Republican administration in Washington, assuring Secretary of State Seward that Spain would remain in Santo Domingo if the United States did not take a firm stand.[46]

Considering the Spanish minister's reply unsatisfactory, Preston again went on the offensive. In his note of 23 April, the Kentucky envoy emphasized the "general policy of the United States . . . first announced in 1823" by President James Monroe and warned Calderón that "Your Excellency can well appreciate the conflict which the annexation of Santo Domingo and the destruction of that policy will inevitably produce between our governments." Preston also was aware of rumors that Spain was considering an invasion of Mexico, so he went on to warn the foreign minister that his government "may well pause before it ventures upon the perilous experiment." When a Madrid newspaper erroneously reported on 27 April that Secretary Seward had assured the Spanish minister in Washington that the Lincoln administration would not protest the Spanish occupation of Santo Domingo, a disappointed Preston wrote in the margin

115

by this article, "This is the last disgrace." In May, four days before leaving Madrid, the Louisvillian fired off yet another warning to Calderón: "For forty years the Government of the United States has avowed its determination to resist any attempt to reestablish monarchical power over the republics of the New World, believing it essential to their independence and prosperity as well as to the interests and just rights of the United States to leave them free from all such intervention." Spanish historians have concluded that Preston's notes to the foreign office offered not only "a sharp protest," but "involved a true threat" to Spain's annexation of Santo Domingo.[47]

The leading historian of the Monroe Doctrine, Dexter Perkins, has asserted that Preston's 23 April defense of United States policy was a "remarkable state paper [that] should hold an important place in the evolution of the Monroe Doctrine." Although constantly invoked at home and deeply rooted in the popular mind, Monroe's 1823 statement of principles was not utilized by American diplomats until decades later. Britain's growing involvement in the Mosquito coast along the Caribbean shores of Nicaragua and northern Honduras in the late 1840s and 1850s brought the first assertion of the Monroe Doctrine as a tool of foreign policy. As minister to London, James Buchanan on 6 January 1854 cited the doctrine in a memorandum to the British foreign secretary, Lord Clarendon, to help justify United States opposition to British dominion there. However, throughout his months-long debate with the foreign office, Buchanan made the Clayton-Bulwer Treaty his principal argument in opposing British intervention in the Mosquito coast. In this accord signed four years earlier, both nations agreed to share control of any future canal through Central America and pledged not to construct fortifications there.[48]

Unlike Buchanan's protests in London, Preston's aggressive remonstrances to the Spanish foreign office from December 1860 through May 1861 rested squarely on the Monroe Doctrine. In addition to Dexter Perkins, other historians have asserted that Preston's sole emphasis on this doctrine to justify American policy made his note of 23 April a "milestone" in United States diplomatic history—and helped make it thereafter a touchstone of foreign relations.[49]

The Republican administration in Washington expressed appreciation for Preston's efforts. Seward agreed with the Louisvillian's protests against Spanish intervention in Santo Domingo. The secretary of state sent a sharply worded note to García y Tassara and instructed Preston's successor in Madrid to remonstrate against Spain's annexation of Santo Domingo. Seward assured Preston in May 1861 that "it gives me great pleasure to add that your official conduct during your residence in Madrid has been entirely acceptable to the President." Lincoln lauded his fellow Kentuckian's "loyal and effective conduct" and complimented "the real zeal with which he has fulfilled his former instructions."[50]

Not all northern partisans concurred. Preston's successor in Madrid was Carl Schurz, a German immigrant prominent as a journalist and an opponent of slavery. As a Republican political leader he had supported Lincoln's nomination in 1860. Schurz claimed that Preston had "most zealously served the interests of the rebellion before openly joining it." Preston's proslavery advocacy also rankled Horatio Perry, a New Hampshire native and Harvard graduate whom Seward had promoted to secretary of the Madrid legation, replacing Robert Woolley. Schurz considered Perry a "sincere and zealous patriot." Perry denounced Preston to Washington for using his official position, money, and time to spread propaganda hostile to the United States. However, neither Schurz nor Perry ever mentioned a single act by Preston to support their assertions. Given the sectional hatred that pervaded public opinion at the outbreak of the Civil War, their accusations concerning the Kentucky envoy's conduct perhaps stemmed more from contempt for his southern allegiance than from his actions. One historian of Spanish-American relations considers Perry's letters to the State Department "self-serving" and concludes that "perhaps Perry and Schurz were too harsh" in their criticism of Preston.[51]

Preston's record of diplomatic disappointments in Madrid obviously can be credited to the growing sectional strife in the United States that doomed to failure attempts to purchase Cuba and to settle the *Amistad* claims. The envoy's advocacy of these causes was consistent with his prosouthern stance. Unfortunately for him, the growing strength of the Republican party in the 1850s was depriving southerners of their northern allies and frustrating their political goals. Preston commented bitterly on the deleterious effect of this North-South animosity on United States foreign policy. "I am crippled by Congress," he wrote to the president in May 1859, "and can only stand as a sentry to watch the enemy but without means to win any victory fortune may offer." Dejected over the Senate's refusal to approve Slidell's resolution and the treaty with Spain, the Kentuckian attacked "the interminable vaporing of Congress" and observed, "I firmly believe that I could do things deemed impossibilities, but for the unhappy party dissension at home, the rancor of the Republicans and the combination of perfidious Democrats against the President." Preston concluded that Buchanan was unequal to the challenges facing him and remarked, "As to old Buck, I have surrendered all hope, long since, that he could help us–I pity him."[52]

The Kentuckian's disappointment with Congress and the president blinded him to other reasons that also made his goal unattainable. He continued to believe that only a lack of sufficient funds was frustrating the acquisition of Cuba. Long after the rejection of Slidell's resolution, Preston assured Washington in October 1859 that the Spanish-Moroccan war that had just begun would have permitted him to acquire the Caribbean colony if only he had thirty million dollars available for the purchase. Obviously the novice diplomat was mistaken. Any acquaintance with Spanish politics of this period demonstrates that Cuba could be wrested from the mother country "only at the price of war."[53]

Preston's preparation and abilities as a diplomat equaled those of most American representatives abroad before the Civil War. In the 1850s high government positions were determined by political factors and customarily awarded to males of social standing. Preferment in the foreign service required neither diplomatic training nor specialization. The Kentuckian's knowledge of the Spanish language and customs was, of course, inferior to that of Washington Irving, who had lived in Spain and written several volumes on Iberian history before serving as United States minister to Madrid in the 1840s. Nevertheless, few envoys were as well prepared as Irving, and Preston in the 1840s as a young adult had mentioned in his speeches and writings the lives of such noteworthy Spaniards as Hernán Cortés, the conquistador of Mexico, and Father Bartolomé de las Casas, the Renaissance humanist who defended the Indians in the sixteenth century.

The Louisville envoy acquired only a rudimentary knowledge of Spanish, but few American emissaries before the Civil War spoke the language of the country to which they were accredited. Preston read French and was able to speak it, with some difficulty, at social functions. Since French was the second language of educated Spaniards and the lingua franca of international relations in the nineteenth century, he could communicate with Spanish officials and members of the diplomatic corps not conversant in English. When negotiating with Spanish counterparts, the envoy did not trust his command of French and requested an interpreter to avoid misunderstandings. Margaret was most straightforward about her husband's language difficulties when she remarked, "Just imagine that he is obliged to say all he has to say in Spanish and French. I die with laughter to see what an exertion it costs him."[54]

The diplomat's impressions of Spain were similar to those of other American contemporaries confronted with the foreign and medieval version of Roman Catholic culture that still dominated the Iberian peninsula. The pre-Lenten carnival days in Madrid appeared to Preston "a scene which seems to delight the people very much but is to me a melancholy sort of foolery." Even less did the Louisvillian appreciate the rigors of Holy Week that often forced members of the upper class and the diplomatic corps to go on foot to their destinations, rather than ride in their carriages. Although not a member of any church, he was a believer and considered himself a Protestant. With his family he attended the only non-Catholic worship services allowed in the capital, held in the home of a British diplomat. Preston often described Spain as "priest ridden," and he reported to Washington with disbelief that the Protestant meetings were attacked by a Madrileño newspaper as gatherings of heretics. For Preston, this proved "to show how far Spain is behind the rest of Europe in religious liberty."[55]

Despite their problems with Spanish customs, the minister and his wife were impressed with Madrid. Shortly after their arrival Preston informed his sister Susan that "Madrid is old fashioned, proud and more expensive than Paris or New York," and he spoke eloquently of the capital's many fountains and "miles of carriages on the Prado," the city's main boulevard. "The Court is brilliant and ceremonious," he reported with pleasure to President Buchanan.[56]

William and Margaret Preston were determined to establish themselves as social leaders in Castile. Asserting that there were no houses for rent suitable for their diplomatic obligations and family needs, Preston decided to lease a large, unfurnished dwelling and "spend at least $10,000 to arrange it." He was satisfied with the results of this decision. In 1861 he bragged that his "house is now very handsome and by far the most comfortable in Madrid." Certainly its imported French furnishings were the envy of less fortunate colleagues. The minister took advantage of his diplomatic immunity from customs duties. In Madrid he ordered wines, liquors, beer, tea, and truffles from France, as well as thousands of cigars and cigarettes from Cuba, to regale his guests.[57]

As ususal, the Prestons employed a large staff, and as in Kentucky they had a problem with one of their slaves. In addition to Spanish maids, Margaret hired a French chef to cater to the gourmet appetites of their guests and sent her black housekeeper, Fanny Green, to cooking school in Paris. William Thompson, a slave who served as a butler in Europe, was accused by Mrs. Preston of overspending and suspected of befriending their French cook. She considered the Frenchman "the greatest villain" and believed he was stealing from her. Thompson ran away and explained why in a letter to William Preston: "I know Mrs always dislike me . . . [and] has no confidence in me witch I feel very much." Nevertheless, the butler assured his former master that "I would go with you sir to the end of the world and would niver git tiard of sirving you."[58]

Lavish entertaining won Preston many friends in the diplomatic circle and among the Spanish aristocrats. In January 1861 guests at a dinner offered by the American minister included the Duke of Tetuán, officials from the foreign office, the British envoy, and heads of mission from other delegations. As the legation's abolitionist chargé d'affaires Horatio Perry observed, Preston "spends his money freely and flatters certain classes here," particularly the aristocratic courtiers and military officers. In addition to hosting elaborate affairs, the Prestons also attended receptions offered by others. Isabel II gave receptions for the diplomatic corps at the Royal Palace. There in the Hall of Columns, under a ceiling mural by Corrado Giaquinto celebrating the "Triumph of Bacchus," the couple socialized with other diplomats, ministers, the royal family, and Spanish grandees. The Kentuckian proudly reported in 1861 that "the Queen thanked me on behalf of the society here for the addition we had made to the social engagements of her capital" and assured him of "'the universal esteem that you have acquired and the special regard that my Husband and I always shall have for you.'"[59]

Preston's cordial relations with the Madrileños, as one historian has noted, allowed him to "feel comfortable in Spanish society," in marked contrast to the difficult associations his predecessors Pierre Soulé and Augustus Caesar Dodge had had with their counterparts. The flamboyant and volatile Soulé became involved in bitter altercations during his ministry, and Dodge never developed friendly associations with Spanish officials. Likewise, Preston's successor Schurz would encounter personality problems in dealing with Spain's diplomats and would leave his post after only six months.[60]

The Prestons' Madrid hospitality was reciprocated. The Louisvillian found the queen "kind and civil to him," and on occasion he was invited to dine with her. The Kentucky couple enjoyed concerts and balls at the Royal Palace given by the queen, as well as a host of dances and dinners offered by the diplomatic corps. A sumptuous affair at the Russian minister's home particularly impressed Margaret soon after her arrival in the spring of 1859. Picnics, teas, and rides in the country with friends were other diversions of the Prestons and fellow members of the diplomatic set.

Unfortunately, both William and Margaret disliked life in Madrid almost from the moment of their arrival. Their correspondence is filled with hopes that soon they might return home. After only one month at his post, Preston wrote his sister Susan, "I wish sometimes that I was back in Kentucky," and two months later his predecessor, Augustus Dodge, reported that "neither he nor his wife are happy in Madrid." When it soon became apparent that Preston had little chance of achieving his goal of purchasing Cuba, he possessed little interest in remaining in Spain. "My sufferings this winter have been beyond your conception," he wrote his sister Susan in early 1860. "My even having come to Europe will be the continuing regret of my days." Only his honor and the embarrassment of returning early from his assignment, Preston claimed, kept him at his post.[61]

The weather and housing problems also contributed to the couple's difficulties. For Preston Spain had become "this land of discomforts." The summer heat in Madrid and the trouble and expense of moving temporarily to a rented house outside of the capital at Aranjuez where the court spent the summers made life disagreeable for the family. On several occasions the Prestons complimented themselves on sending their daughters to school in Paris rather than keeping them in Madrid.[62]

Mrs. Preston's dislike for living in Spain surpassed her husband's.

On arriving in Madrid, she seemed to enjoy the social whirl, but soon she detested the capital. After only four months there, the Lexington spouse declared, "We all suffer dreadfully with homesickness. William often declares that he will stand it no longer, the life here is infernal. . . . I always encourage him in his discontent, and tell him that the children are ready and more than willing and that I am more anxious than they are." Her husband usually respected Mrs. Preston's opinions, and her distaste for Spain certainly colored his impression of life there. The queen's minister to Washington, García y Tassara, realized after meeting the Prestons on several social occasions that Mrs. Preston "appears to play a large role in affairs," and "without entering into either political or diplomatic questions, has a great influence on her husband." She had gained a deserved reputation for forthright speech among friends. In February 1859, after listening with her husband to the queen's address on the opening of the Cortes, the Kentucky lady opined to an American observer, "'It wasn't eloquent!'" Following the death of her father in September 1859, Margaret concluded, "I should return home," asserting that this would be in the best interests of the children.[63]

The Prestons were both happy and distressed with their children's experiences in Europe. Polly, Carrie, and Poogie improved their French in Paris–each wrote letters in French to their father–and the three younger children profited from studying with their mother and several tutors in Madrid. Margaret was proud of young Jessie's talents in reciting her lessons, and Wick learned to speak Spanish "passably." The delighted father reported that during their Christmas visit to Madrid in 1860 the three oldest daughters "have been the belles of the season." Mrs. Preston noted with equal pride that during their visits to Madrid Polly was courted by the son of the British consul and Carrie received the attention of the French minister's son.[64]

Despite the pleasures the parents derived from some of their children's experiences, they were disappointed with many aspects of their development. Both considered the education of the three older daughters in Paris convent schools deficient in arithmetic and deplored their instruction as based on memory. But even worse, the couple lamented the religious instruction the children received at the convent. "I scarcely know them as the straightforward guileless children that left us 14 months since," Margaret complained in 1860, blaming their new conduct on "those Jesuits." She was distressed when, on her return to Madrid, Poogie did not want to go to Protestant services, and once her mother observed her "counting her beads instead of listening to the sermon." "This estrangement of my children from my faith and influence," Mrs. Preston remarked, "causes me great unhappiness." The Old Duke had warned his daughter to keep the children under "the guardianship of the mother and the protection of the father," rather than sending them to convent schools. Remembering this, a contrite Margaret confessed to her husband in 1860, "Oh that the wise admonitions had been heeded, which are now lost to me forever." Like their parents, most of the children enjoyed good health in Europe. However, Sunie suffered from smallpox in Madrid, and Carrie broke her hip in Paris–a misfortune her mother blamed on the "unwholesome food" at the convent.[65]

During the Prestons' years in Madrid, two relatives and a new family friend lived in their home. Nephew Robert Woolley, secretary of the legation, stayed with them, as did another relative, Sidney Christy. He came to Madrid in 1860. Also that year Thomas Wentworth Sydney Beauclerk, a thirteen-year-old English lad, joined the family circle. The son of Lord Charles, the Duke of Saint Alban, and Lady Laura, Sydney had been sent on his mother's death to live with his grandparents in Madrid. His grandfather was the British minister there. Sydney became a fast friend of Wick Preston and a favorite of his sisters. When his grandmother died, he moved in with the Prestons.

Buchanan's minister found Spain expensive. Their Madrid residence, the summer house in Aranjuez, the children's education, and the family's ostentatious lifestyle cost far more than Preston's twelve-thousand-dollar salary. After one month in Madrid, the envoy wrote his sister Susan Christy, "I am greatly pressed here for money to make a creditable appearance, and if the question is between my patrimony and a decent show for the country the acres must go." Counting on the growing wealth of the German immigrants to purchase lots from him, Preston told his sister, "I trust that the Dutch will come in thick." In Louisville his nephew William Preston Johnston helped Christy and Frederick Wedekemper, his financial agent, oversee Preston's assets, selling properties as directed and renting the houses the family owned in Louisville and St. Louis.[66]

William and Margaret spent much of their time in Paris. In the fall of 1859 both were there visiting the three older daughters, while nephew Robert Woolley looked after the three younger Prestons in Madrid. In March 1860, William traveled to the United States, where he remained for half a year, looking after the estate of Robert Wickliffe Sr., who had died in Lexington the previous year. Margaret stayed in Paris with the five daughters and son, and after William's return she again spent several months in the French capital in 1861. Mother and children lived in "very handsome apartments" on the Champs Elysées. This broad avenue ran from the Tuileries Palace and gardens up to the Arc de Triomphe and was lined with imposing three- and four-story stone residences that had become fashionable quarters for the elite during Napoleon III's Second Empire. In Paris Margaret oversaw the children's education and gave Wick his English lessons. Following her husband's instructions, two French women were hired to give daily lessons in French literature and grammar, history, and geography, while other teachers came to give music and dancing classes several times a week. The three older girls had five hours of class a day and sometimes spent five hours on their homework. Polly, the oldest daughter, read Voltaire, Wick repeated verses from La Fontaine, and all of the children took parts in acting out a comédie.[67]

But Paris life consisted of more than lessons for the Preston children. From their apartment windows four stories above the Champs Elysées, they enjoyed watching the emperor pass by in parades celebrating the visits of royalty such as Russia's Grand Duke Nicholas. The girls attended concerts, observed "all the new fashions," and went to parties. Son Wick reported proudly to his father that "Peggy is quite the belle," and Polly, the oldest child, bragged that she had gained access to the palace at Fontainebleau by informing the guard that she was "the daughter of a diplomat."[68]

In Paris, as in Louisville, Washington, and Madrid, Mrs. Preston found time for more than overseeing her children's education and social life. Although she professed to avoid social engagements following her father's death, Margaret attended a series of dinners in 1860 during William's trip to the United States. The following year she also hosted a series of teas and soirées and invited a circle of socially prominent Americans to her Paris drawing room. She designed her entertainments to impress, and this she accomplished. "Ma has been quite a belle last Sunday," Poogie reported in June 1861 to her father in Madrid, "quite a number of visitors called." But not all fell under her spell. One of Margaret's guests became a sharp critic. Mrs. Lizinka C. Brown, the Tennessee widow of a Preston relative, considered her hostess "truely clanish [sic]" and claimed that she "measures people by the length of their purse." She found Mrs. Preston "obsessively kind" and was annoyed at her condescending manner.[69]

By the time the Prestons arrived in Europe, Margaret had changed in appearance and in her attitude toward her husband. She had gained weight, becoming "immensely large"–in the words of an unsympathetic acquaintance–a condition that would contribute to her later physical disabilities and poor health. Margaret also became increasingly critical of William. During the Mexican War she had chided him for being a poor correspondent and warned him of the consequences of infidelity, but during their European years she turned to shrill attacks on what she considered his selfish behavior. While he was in the United States, Margaret "in despair" wrote to her spouse, accusing him of "enjoying yourself too much to write me a long letter" and chastised him for not taking "the trouble to inform me of the important fact of when you will return." In addition, the nagging wife complained constantly of the trials she suffered in Paris. "I will be reduced to starvation if I do not get a remittance," she once informed William, noting that "I have reduced the establishment to two servants." In the same letter Margaret reminded him that she would be "humiliated" if he did not send money for a gold table service.[70]

Guilt was another weapon Margaret employed. Attempting to convince William to shorten his visit to the United States in 1860, she reported that "Wick speaks of you with moist eyes and quivering lips." In Europe Margaret's feelings toward her husband presaged her later, even more hostile behavior. William overlooked his wife's provocative accusations and dutifully responded as she desired. In solicitous letters, he hoped that the "remittances reached you in time to prevent embarrassments" and assured her that "my happiness will be complete when with the blessing of God we are reunited."[71]

While tending to the estate of Robert Wickliffe Sr., Preston spent the spring and summer of 1860 in the United States. He also brought the proposed arbitration treaty to Washington and met with the president. Diplomatic disappointments and personal circumstances had convinced Preston that he should resign his post. "Because the convention with Spain was rejected," he asked Buchanan to accept his resignation. But the Pennsylvanian convinced the Kentuckian that this would "embarrass" his administration and persuaded him to serve in Madrid for the rest of his administration.[72]

Preston attended the Democratic convention that spring in Charleston, South Carolina. Kentucky's Democrats earlier had chosen delegates who backed James Guthrie for the presidency. Vice President Breckinridge said he was not interested in the nomination, but he asked his friend James B. Clay and Preston to look after his interests and his honor at Charleston. The party rejected a southern proposal that the platform include a plank requiring the federal government to protect the rights of persons and property in its territories. This caused most delegates from the lower South to leave the convention. After many ballots, the leading candidate, Stephen Douglas, was unable to garner the two-thirds majority required for nomination. The delegates voted on 3 May to recess the meeting and reconvene on 18 June in Baltimore.

Following the Charleston convention, Breckinridge considered becoming a candidate. He believed that if he were the nominee he would be able to unite the southern and northern branches of the party. Preston also attended the Baltimore convention. There the Douglas backers successfully voted to seat delegations loyal to the Illinois senator to replace the Democrats from Alabama and Louisiana who had left the party. This caused a second secession of delegates, including ten of Kentucky's twenty-four representatives. Those who had walked out of the convention at Charleston and Baltimore met with other dissident Democrats from the Pacific coast and the east, and on June 23 they settled on Breckinridge as their nominee. Senator Stephen A. Douglas of Illinois became the standard-bearer of the regular Democrats. Joining Douglas and Breckinridge as candidates for the White House were Abraham Lincoln of the Republican party and Tennessean John Bell of the Constitutional Union party, who attempted to form a North-South coalition to preserve the Union. Before leaving New York to return to Europe, Preston reflected on the presidential contest: "The case is simple—shall Lincoln and ruin, or the South and the Union triumph?"[73]

Accompanied by Sidney Christy, the Kentucky diplomat left the United States in August and reached Paris in September. There he spent several weeks with his family. With Sidney, the Prestons continued to Spain, boarding a steamship in Marseilles on 2 October bound for Barcelona where the queen and her court were. Just out of the harbor the vessel was blown toward shore by a heavy mistral and was in danger of being wrecked. A Brazilian corvette, *Isabella II*, answered the distress call and took all the passengers aboard. But this ship was pushed against the rocks by the heavy surf. A successful rescue operation was mounted from the shore, and William joined the crew in helping save several passengers. "I was thrown with great forces against the rocks, in attempting to land my children," he reported, "but being a very strong swimmer, succeeded in reaching a landing amid the breakers, though half lifeless." This near-disaster, one historian remarked, seemed "somehow symbolic of the futility of the whole mission." Six days later his tedious journey ended in Barcelona. By 23 October he and his family were back in Madrid.[74] He would remain in the Spanish capital for another seven months.

Following Lincoln's election, Preston in January 1861 penned his letter of resignation, dating it 5 March, the day after the president's inauguration. The minister sent it to his cousin, Vice President John C. Breckinridge, asking him to submit it to the State Department. The Union had been "murdered . . . by the organized Abolitionists of the North," Preston concluded by January. Yet he did not give up hope of preserving the Republic. "Blow to the devil the thought of Southern congresses, rampant harangues and disunion nonsense," he warned his nephew, Robert Woolley. "Sober, serious-minded conversation" still might "get things in order, upset the Republicans, and regain power honestly and nobly."[75]

Preston had his final audience with the queen at her palace in Aranjuez on 24 May 1861. Despite his disappointments, his words to Isabella II were diplomatic and in the expected ornate style: "The remembrance of the distinguished kindnesses of Your majesty and of His Majesty the King will accompany me across the Atlantic; and engraved indelibly in my memory, it always will be nurtured by me with effusiveness and affection." The day following Preston's meeting with the queen, he and his family departed Madrid. Joining them was Wick's English friend, Sydney Beauclerk, whose father agreed to his son's plea to live with them in Kentucky.[76]

Despite Preston's frustrations, the failure to purchase Cuba, and the rejection of the treaty of arbitration, his diplomatic efforts have won respect. In summarizing his contributions, one authority concludes, "His position proved critical and indeed his influence was measurable." Preston's appeal to President Monroe's policy of 1823 to protest Spain's occupation of Santo Domingo marked an important moment in the evolution of the Monroe Doctrine. The envoy's diplomatic skills also have attracted attention. Although a southerner, the Kentuckian's notes to the foreign ministry–in the words of one scholar–"clearly attempted to represent Washington in Madrid," not only during the Buchanan presidency, but during the early months of the Lincoln administration. Likewise, Preston's "cordial relations" with Spanish officials–despite their aversion to his goal of purchasing Cuba–stand out, particularly when contrasted with the problems his immediate predecessors and his successor encountered.[77]

William Preston returned to a very different homeland in 1861. Abraham Lincoln was president and the southern states had seceded from the Union. Back in Kentucky, the Louisvillian cast his lot with the South. As a military commander and a diplomat, Preston would serve the Confederacy in its war for independence.

Chapter VI: Fighting for Southern Independence

⁓

The breakup of the Union following Lincoln's election forced a reluctant William Preston to choose sides. He joined the Confederate army in October 1861 and served as a colonel and brigadier general until January 1864. The Kentuckian fought in the major engagements in the western theater, assisting the commanding general at Shiloh and leading men to battle at Stones River and Chickamauga. His bravery and leadership at the latter affair won him renown throughout the South and abroad. During most of 1863 Preston was in charge of troops guarding valuable saltworks in southwestern Virginia. By 1864 he had served the Confederacy in Kentucky, Tennessee, Mississippi, Virginia, and Georgia.

Despite his southern loyalty and animosity for Republicans, the Louisville aristocrat was not immediately prepared to advocate secession. On hearing in Madrid of Lincoln's election, Preston did not believe that abandoning the Union was the answer. Although he insisted that "no people have ever endured a more deliberate injustice than the South have suffered from the North in the recent election," he still hoped that "Mr. Lincoln's Administration may receive the support of the Democratic party in every measure calculated to restore kind feelings and patriotic forebearance [sic] in the country." Despite the "very gloomy" news from home, the Kentuckian wrote in November 1860, "the South mustn't be too hot, and cut away the Republican bridges." The following month he optimistically predicted, "I somehow think that common sense and courage will soon come to the rescue, and that things will be soon better."[1]

Preston argued that southern legislators could use their powers of budgetary control to force the Republicans to compromise on abolition. "Prudence may yet save the Union," he predicted in January 1861. "We have other remedies than Disunion," he insisted, noting that "the Senate can paralyze the Executive by refusing to ratify his appointment of violent and truculent leaders like [Charles] Sumner and Seward. . . . Again, we might refuse to vote supplies." If Kentucky and the other Border States joined in such opposition, "the cavaliers will get a final settlement," he reasoned, for "there is in the North strength enough to secure a fair adjustment."[2]

Events in the spring of 1861, however, led Preston to espouse southern independence, and by the time he left Spain he had decided to back the Confederacy. On hearing of South Carolina's movement toward secession, the diplomat in January 1861 labeled it a "wild and immeasurable" remedy, admitting, "I may be accused of timidity, and I confess I am timid in joining measures which are to end in the destruction of my country." In February he still pledged, "I will give my best blood and all I have to preserve the Union on just and equal terms," but he also added, "if we are to be menaced or coerced by Northern Fanaticism, I shall try by every means in my power to resist, and on bended knees I wish to implore Kentucky to line our woods with riflemen and let the wave burst over our breasts, before it reaches our Southern brethren." Although he feared that "the sense of shame will drive the South into some rash act . . . in attempting to regain . . . self respect," the capture of Fort Sumter in April convinced Preston that the separation of the North and the South was inevitable. "A great struggle is on us," he predicted in May on leaving Madrid. For the former diplomat, Republican intransigence had forced the South into such a humiliating position that the dreaded act of secession remained the only remedy.[3]

Once the war began, Preston recognized that slavery "doubtless . . . is the most prominent cause, and great heat and passion has [sic] been engendered among my country men by it," but he insisted, "It is not to perpetuate slavery that I have taken sides with the South." "Born in the South, with my friends and kindred there," the Louisville native took up arms for the Confederacy "because I love my country." "I thought it better to remain with two republics, than one tyranny and to let the Southern States depart in peace, instead of pursuing them with fire and sword, and lose the liberties of all." Concerning his northern foes, he claimed, "I do not hate them," and he recognized that "the people on both sides are honest in their rage." But he attacked "the zeal or bigotry of the abolitionists" and blamed the "demagogues and unchristian clergymen, the salaried panderers to popular passions," for forcing the North into "the wicked and foolish endeaver [sic] to reconquer an unhappy alliance."[4] His appeals to ideology and patriotism were common among soldiers and officers on both sides of the Civil War.

On their return from Madrid, the Prestons stopped in both London and Washington. In the British capital he met in June with Confederate agents Edward Anderson and Cabel Huse and informed them that Spain was both unwilling and unable to provide weapons or other assistance for their cause. In Washington he saw William H. Seward to offer a final report on the Madrid mission. Sectional tensions were so high that Lincoln's secretary of state was criticized for listening to such a prosouthern envoy rather than detaining him as a traitor.[5]

The Prestons returned in September not to Louisville but to Lexington, where they resided in Margaret's family home, Wickliffe Place. Like the ex-envoy, most Kentuckians had hoped to avoid a choice between North and South, but the state's strategic location and its importance as a transportation link made this a quixotic wish. As early as April 1861, five companies of volunteers had left Louisville to join the Confederate army, and Union recruiting offices were established.[6] The prosouthern Kentuckians made their way to Camp Boone, just across the Tennessee border from State Line (Guthrie), Kentucky. There, General Simon Bolivar Buckner, the former inspector general of the State Guard, was organizing units from the commonwealth. The month the Prestons returned, southern troops occupied Hickman and Columbus, Kentucky, on the Mississippi River and, in response, Federal forces moved into Paducah. The pro-Confederate governor, Beriah Magoffin, continued to believe the state should remain neutral and demanded that both armies leave the commonwealth. Unionists in control of the general assembly ordered the Confederates out, and when they remained, the government in Frankfort declared its allegiance to the North.

Across Kentucky, slaveholders divided in their support, since the Lincoln administration had not made abolition of slavery a war aim. Many wanted both union and slavery. Still, in Lexington many prominent slave owners favored the Confederate cause, and some stealthily left the city in September to fight for the South.[7] John Hunt Morgan, the head of the Lexington Rifles, had his men remove guns and ammunition from the armory at the fairgrounds on the night of 20 September as they marched off to Bowling Green. There the State Guard with its commander General Simon Bolivar Buckner was controlling the western portion of the commonwealth for the Confederacy.[8]

Afraid that they were subject to arrest for their prosouthern views, William Preston and Roger W. Hanson, a veteran of the Mexican War and state legislator, departed Lexington and rode eastward to Prestonsburg in Floyd County. When Preston realized he would be free to return home, he considered doing so, but at the "urgent request of Breckingridge" he decided to meet his cousin in Virginia "to consult with him as to our course." After talking with Breckinridge, Preston decided to enter the Confederate army. Together with several others, the two cousins traveled by rail from Abingdon, Virginia, to Bowling Green to join General Buckner. In mid-October Preston and Breckinridge went to Richmond, Virginia, to apply for military commissions. A lieutenant colonel in the Mexican War, the former minister was made a colonel on 3 November, instead of brigadier general as he had expected.[9]

The next week Preston addressed the First Regiment of Kentucky Volunteers at Centerville, Virginia. The new colonel's remarks were received with enthusiasm, and the troops "afterwards [made] a very fine vocal serenade for him." He stayed with his nephew, William Preston Johnston, then a lieutenant colonel in the Bluegrass unit, who found his uncle "looking very well, but is gloomy about Kentucky." Brother-in-law Albert Sidney Johnston, the southern commander in the Western Department, made Preston his "volunteer aide-de-camp to the General commanding." In answer to his nephew's offer to try to gain a generalship for him, Preston claimed that he preferred his position under Johnston because of "its independence to administrative favors."[10]

One hundred sixteen representatives from sixty-five Kentucky counties convened the Confederate Sovereignty Convention on 18 November in Russellville. Meeting in the Clark House, a large brick residence, they passed an Act of Secession and organized a provisional government. They appointed Preston as one of three commissioners to go to Richmond to apply for the commonwealth's admission into the Confederate States of America. The southern Congress on 10 December admitted Kentucky to the Confederacy. A "golden opportunity exists," an optimistic Preston assured Jefferson Davis, to take advantage of the "great discontents [that] have been manifested among the Union men in Kentucky." To that end, he urged the president to issue a proclamation guaranteeing that any northern officers who abandoned their positions "would be assured the same rank, pay and command" in the southern army. However, Confederate forces soon were withdrawn from the state, preventing Rebel sympathizers from forming a de facto government—and this of course discouraged volunteers to their cause.[11]

Although not a professional soldier, William Preston would prove to be an effective military officer for the Confederacy. From November 1861 until January 1864, the Louisvillian commanded combat troops in five states. His promotion to brigadier general in the spring of 1862 and his appointment to successively more important commands attested to official recognition of Preston's accomplishments.

The new Confederate colonel did not fully look the part of a military officer. Certainly, he was imposing in appearance, with his sharp features and handsome countenance. His six-foot stature and erect carriage projected a vigorous and commanding air. But the rest of his visage seemed to betray his nonmilitary background. By 1861 Preston carefully parted his hair to obscure—unsuccessfully—his increasingly bald pate. His meticulously trimmed mustache and high forehead, marred by deep furrows while he read, imparted the impression of a dignified intellectual rather than a decisive man of action.

As aide-de-camp to General Johnston, Colonel Preston was kept busy communicating orders from his brother-in-law to subordinates between November and April, 1861-62. During these months the southern forces retreated from Bowling Green through Nashville and central Tennessee to the town of Corinth in Mississippi. Preston also was responsible for providing nonmilitary supplies for Johnston and his staff, a task that included the purchase of goods as varied as books, tablecloths, horses, and lace for uniforms.[12]

The sanguinary Battle of Shiloh marked the climactic moment of Preston's service as a colonel and aide-de-camp.[13] The fall of Fort Henry on the Tennessee River and of Fort Donelson on the Cumberland River to Union forces and the Rebel retreat from Bowling Green and Nashville opened General Johnston to considerable criticism. The commander had been a friend of Jefferson Davis since their days at Transylvania University in Lexington and at West Point, and his son William Preston Johnston was serving as a special aide to the Confederate president. The young Johnston resided in the Davises' Richmond White House, becoming a confidant and friend to both the president and his wife Varina.[14] General Johnston retained the administration's backing, but his lack of military success

Courtesy National Park Service

Published in Albert Dillahunty, Shiloh National
Military Park, Tennessee *(Washington, D.C.,*
1961).

and charges of favoritism made him determined to vindicate his reputation and win a decisive victory.

In late March 1862, Confederate forces from Louisiana under General Daniel Ruggles and from the Gulf Coast under General Braxton
Bragg joined Johnston's troops at Corinth, a railway junction in north-
east Mississippi. The gray army of forty thousand mostly uniniti-
ated warriors was located twenty-three miles south of Brigadier
General Ulysses S. Grant's force of about the same size. The Federals
were encamped around Pittsburg Landing on the Tennessee River
just north of the Mississippi-Tennessee line.

Aware that another Union army of some thirty thousand was
marching from Nashville under General Don Carlos Buell to join
Grant, Johnston decided to attack Pittsburg Landing on 3 April. But

Kentucky Historical Society Special Collections
Episcopal Bishop and Major General Leonidas Polk.

rain, confused orders, and logistical problems delayed the Confederates' march northward. On 5 April Johnston's second-in-command, Louisiana General Pierre Gustave Toutant Beauregard, and General Bragg argued that the postponement of their offensive had allowed the Union army to expect an attack and proposed that the southern troops avoid an engagement. Colonel Preston responded "promptly and warmly" opposing any delay, arguing it would "dishearten the men." Breckinridge and Episcopal bishop and Major General Leonidas Polk concurred, and the commander decided to go ahead with the battle plan. According to Preston, his brother-in-law was determined to make battle and swore to him, "I would fight them if they were a million."[15]

The "sharp volleys of musketry" that Preston noted at 5:30 on the morning of the 6th signaled the start of one of the hardest-fought engagements in American military annals: a Union patrol had come upon a Rebel infantry battalion and the battle was on. It certainly was one of the most successful surprise attacks carried out during the war. Even after the contest was in progress, Grant refused to believe that a Confederate offensive was underway.[16]

The fighting took place on the bluff above Pittsburg Landing near the small log building that was Shiloh Church. More than eighty thousand soldiers remained oblivious to the certain charms of springtime in western Tennessee on a day Colonel Preston described as "remarkably bright and beautiful." Stands of oaks, hickories, and cedars surrounded the "small fields interspersed . . . with bold undulations from the hills bounding the river" that the Kentucky aide-de-camp observed that morning. There, young men–without any previous experience in a major engagement–began in earnest the goal of battle: killing and conquering the enemy.[17]

The southern forces advanced with difficulty along a three-mile front throughout the morning. Preston's observations of the fighting before noon were replete with optimistic comments: "sharp skirmishing," "loud cheers and handsome advance of our troops," "camp carried and firing stopping." But the Rebels encountered particularly stubborn fire along a wooded wagon trail on the Confederates' right flank. This bastion of resistance, dubbed the Hornets' Nest, continued in the early afternoon to block the gray troops from sweeping around the enemy's line of defense toward Pittsburg Landing. Seeing this, the confident Confederate commander encouraged his men sometime after two o'clock to move forward with bayonets and dislodge the blue troops. This they did and Johnston rode to the rear, the sole of one boot ripped by a musket ball and his horse wounded in two places. Three hours later, General Benjamin M. Prentiss was forced to surrender the Hornets' Nest after a fierce Rebel artillery barrage from sixty-two cannons had broken the Union lines.

Just as he was convinced that his men had carried the day, Johnston sent Governor Isham Harris of Tennessee to order a brigade to change position, and on the governor's return to the crest of the small ridge he saw the commander lurch in his saddle. Harris took hold of Johnston, who admitted to being seriously wounded. The governor guided the commander's horse to a protected ravine and placed the general on the ground. William Preston and other members of the general's staff were called to the spot, but his physician, Dr. D. W. Yandell, was attending the wounded elsewhere. Kneeling down, the brother-in-law supported in his arms the head of the fallen leader and "cried passionately, 'Johnston, do you know me?'" The general "smiled faintly, but gave no other sign of recognition." Panicked by the bleeding from his right leg, those present did not think to apply a tourniquet. Preston called for whiskey, and Captain Dudley M. Haydon sought to pour some bourbon down the general's throat. He was unable to swallow it. He had died from a loss of blood from a minié ball that had pierced an artery below his right knee. The general's son later wrote that his father's wound was "not necessarily fatal" and maintained that a tourniquet or the presence of Dr. Yandell probably would have saved his life.[18]

Never in American history had such a high-ranking officer been killed at the head of his troops. "At the moment of victory, after routing the enemy at every point," Preston notified Beauregard that he was now in command and informed him that "the completion of the victory would devolve on him." In Richmond President Davis sent to the Confederate Congress a message on the death of his "long and close" friend that included the "simply narrated" dispatch sent him by Johnston's brother-in-law. Preston and Theodore O'Hara, his friend since the Mexican War, together with five other members of the general's staff, accompanied the body to New Orleans for interment in St. Louis Cemetery.[19]

General Beauregard decided not to continue a sustained attack in the late afternoon on 6 April, believing that his hard-pressed men were exhausted. But by early evening, Grant had amassed an impressive array of fifty-three cannons above Pittsburg Landing to protect his battered army. The following day, reinforced by the overnight arrival of seventeen thousand fresh troops from Buell's army, Union soldiers retook their lost ground and forced the outmanned Confederates to withdraw to Corinth.

Because the South's initial success at Shiloh on 6 April was turned into a Pyrrhic victory the next day, a bitter debate ensued concerning Beauregard's leadership after he assumed Johnston's mantle. Preston, Polk, and other defenders of the slain commander claimed that by not pursuing the fight the Louisianian had forfeited the South's best chance of complete victory. In writing to General Johnston's son, Uncle William emphasized this point, confirming his nephew's belief that "when Beauregard missed the opportunity . . . to attack, all was lost." But the Creole leader and his apologists argued that their exhausted forces were unable to sustain yet another offensive at the end of the day. Regardless of debates over "if history," at Shiloh the South lost the most crucial contest of the war for control of western Tennessee and the lower Mississippi valley.[20]

For his loyal service to Johnston, William Preston was nominated by General Beauregard and President Davis for the rank of brigadier general, a promotion approved by the Senate on 18 April. On his return from New Orleans, Preston reported to the Louisiana commander and was assigned to General Breckinridge, who was reorganizing the First Kentucky Brigade, later affectionately known as the "Orphan Brigade" to its men who fought far from their Bluegrass homes. Breckinridge placed Preston in charge of a new brigade, comprised of three regiments of the Kentucky "Orphans" and an Alabama battery. The brigadier found his new unit lacking in discipline, but soon he reported, "I have . . . got to be popular among the men and getting them entirely under my control and in better organization."[21]

In late May Union pressure forced the Confederates to retreat from Corinth, and Preston's men served as the rear guard. During Breckinridge's leave in Louisiana, the new brigadier was placed in temporary command of the reserve corps. His ten thousand soldiers, three thousand animals, and 250 wagons oversaw the removal of all government supplies from Oxford and Grenada, Mississippi, as they moved southward. He and his men also went to Abbeville where they guarded a nearby railroad bridge over the small Tallahatchie River.[22]

The withdrawal from Corinth found Preston both in bad health and angry over the army's leadership. "On duty every day . . . since Bowling Green," the new brigadier was confined to his quarters "for nine days at a time" because of liver and digestive problems. But his major complaint centered on General Braxton Bragg's execution of the retreat. Six weeks of indecision and delay, in addition to sending "the provision wagons . . . thirty miles in advance" of the troops, brought hunger and a loss of morale. "We lost a fifth of the army," he estimated, "by sickness, straggling and desertion. We cannot show more than 40,000 to 45,000 effectives here now as against 50,000 to 55,000 effectives at Corinth." Preston criticized Beauregard's leadership but particularly blamed Bragg for the army's difficulties, noting that the abrasive general "is a stern and imperious soldier and is endeavoring by excessive severity to establish discipline, but the men are indignant, and I fear trouble. I wish to God the President were here," Preston wrote to his nephew in Richmond. The brigadier's complaints about Bragg only would increase as the war progressed.[23]

On 23 June Preston was instructed to bring his corps by train to Vicksburg to help Major General Earl Van Dorn confront a fleet of enemy gunboats sent there from Memphis and New Orleans, both cities now occupied by Union forces. The brigadier's wagon train went across country gathering up supplies for the beleaguered "Bluff City" on the Mississippi. Returning from Louisiana, Breckinridge resumed command of his troops camped along the river. Hot weather, foul drinking water, mosquitoes, malaria, and dysentery took their toll of the Kentuckians bivouacked near Vicksburg. Preston fell ill with fever and was unable to lead his men as they followed General Breckinridge still further south in his unsuccessful campaign against the bluecoats in control of Baton Rouge. Preston's slave Samuel Giles again served his master in this war as he had in Mexico and helped nurse him back to health. Once recovered, the brigadier assisted Breckinridge in reorganizing the division on its return to Mississippi.[24]

General Braxton Bragg in June 1862 replaced Beauregard as commander of the Army of Tennessee. Major General Edmund Kirby Smith, head of the Army of East Tennessee, favored a Confederate invasion of Kentucky and persuaded Bragg to support an autumn campaign to secure the commonwealth for the South.[25] General Preston advocated this course and, through his nephew William Preston Johnston, urged President Davis both to support this plan and to encourage Bragg to consult with him and other Kentuckians familiar with the "moral and political influence that may be brought to bear" in their native state. "It would . . . please me to see General Preston along," Bragg wrote Breckinridge while planning the Kentucky invasion. When Breckinridge's troops were sent to retake Corinth, Preston and his staff were relieved of their duties at their request to participate in the coming Kentucky campaign. In September, the brigadier optimistically wrote, "I wish to help secure Kentucky forever for the South. The hope makes me well and excites my every energy. I wish on returning to get the men of influence to espouse our cause and enlist their children in our own ranks."[26]

September 1862 marked the apex of Confederate success in Kentucky. Bragg's forces marched into the state through Tompkinsville to the east of Bowling Green, while General Kirby Smith invaded the commonwealth from the southeast. On 2 September eleven thousand Confederates under Kirby Smith marched into Lexington with bands

Kentucky Historical Society Special Collections
William Preston.

playing and colors flying. Loud applause, waving handkerchiefs, and ladies tossing flowers welcomed the conquerors. Two days later, Colonel John Hunt Morgan and his nine hundred men were greeted with "the wildest outburst of enthusiasm" as they paraded in columns of four down Limestone Street to Main and then to the courthouse. For five weeks the strains of "Dixie" and the "Bonnie Blue Flag" replaced those of "John Brown's Body." By late in the month, the line of Confederate control ran from Bardstown in the west to Frankfort, Lexington, and Mount Sterling in the east. Traveling from Mississippi through Chattanooga and Knoxville, Preston and a few cavalrymen in late September joined Kirby Smith's command. General Bragg welcomed Preston's presence, noting that the Kentuckian "has great influence here and will forward our recruiting."[27]

Taking advantage of Confederate control of Lexington, Preston spent five days at Wickliffe Place. He found "the family well," but his wife was "dreadfully lamed" from a broken ankle, making him fear she would have to use crutches the rest of her life. The brigadier remarked with a smile that during his visit he had managed to convince his twelve-year-old son Wick not to accompany him back to the army, since "I showed him his duty was with his mother." In addition to tending to family pleasures, William and Margaret made Wickliffe the scene of "brilliant festivities" for Generals Bragg and Kirby Smith during their brief conquest of the Bluegrass.[28]

Outside of Perryville, near Danville, Confederate and Union forces met on the afternoon of 8 October to determine control of Kentucky. A portion of Bragg's forces, some fifteen thousand men, engaged the bulk of Major General Don Carlos Buell's army of about thirty thousand Federals. To the west of Bragg's army, the Union forces had been advancing from Tennessee into the state, but each side had avoided a major battle. Perryville amounted to an inconclusive afternoon of slaughter. By sunset the two contestants had suffered more than 7,600 casualties in the rolling farmlands edged with maple, oak, and sumac trees displaying their autumn colors. During the next few days the out-manned Rebels were forced to begin a retreat back to Tennessee. Preston missed the decisive battle, for he was with Kirby Smith's army intent on blocking Yankee troops purported to be crossing the Kentucky River at Frankfort. The dashed hopes of the Confederates increased the distrust of southern officers—including Preston and Kirby Smith—for Braxton Bragg. The commander, in turn, became skeptical of the advice of the Kentucky generals, for they had predicted that thousands of volunteers would join their cause during the invasion of the commonwealth. Instead, only several hundred did so.[29]

After the Kentucky campaign, Preston took charge of an Alabama brigade until its wounded leader, General Sterling A. M. Wood, was able to resume his command in late November. The defeated southern forces regrouped around Murfreesboro in middle Tennessee. On 12 December President Davis ordered the formation of a new division of four brigades under Breckinridge's command and placed Preston in charge of one of these units composed of five regiments of soldiers from Tennessee, North Carolina, and Florida. Nine days later an Alabama contingent joined his troops. In late November, General Bragg told his officers to prepare the Army of Tennessee for a "bataille rangée" or well-ordered engagement between the two forces for supremacy in middle Tennessee. By the summer of 1862 desertions had become a problem for the army, and the day after Christmas four men from Preston's unit were shot for taking flight.[30]

Courtesy Oxford University Press

From Battle Cry of Freedom: The Era of the Civil War by James M. McPherson, copyright – 1988 by Oxford University Press, Inc. Used by permission of Oxford University Press, Inc.

Chapter VI: Fighting for Southern Independence

From 31 December through 2 January 1862-63, thirty-five thousand Confederates led by General Bragg attempted to stop forty-two thousand Union troops marching south from Nashville under Major General William S. Rosecrans. The two armies met at Stones River just outside of Murfreesboro.[31] The rugged terrain on either side of the small river was marked by limestone outcrops and hills along its shores, hickory and cedar thickets growing above the dense cover of honeysuckle and catbrier vines, and gently sloping corn and cotton fields. On the evening of 30 December, every soldier knew that battle was imminent. Despite a cold, pelting rain, each side tried to encourage its troops. "Hail Columbia" was heard in the Yankee camp to the north and west of the winding river, while the southerners played "Bonnie Blue Flag" on the opposite bank.

In the foggy half-light of early morning on New Year's Eve, General Bragg's forces struck first, surprising some bluecoats at breakfast. Yelling Confederates on their left flank swarmed into the right side of the Union line and forced the Yankees to give ground in a fighting retreat. In late morning Bragg issued a series of confusing orders to Breckinridge on the extreme right, who sent his brigades forward to attack. But Rosecrans had established a strong artillery position on a cedar-covered rise, Round Forest. Breckinridge's four brigades threw themselves against their opponents with courage and abandon, but they encountered withering fire from the guns atop the hill. They were hurled back after suffering heavy losses.[32]

Although the enemy's advantageous position prevented Breckinridge's troops from capturing the Union battery, Preston's brigade–supported by four artillery pieces–fought valiantly and in a concerted assault took a northern position. The Kentuckian had deployed one of his units far to the right of his main forces, making the Federals aim their fire both to their left and straight ahead. This permitted Preston's troops to charge across an open field and flush Yankee infantrymen from their stronghold, a grove of cedars on the west bank of the river. When the brigade "fell into confusion under a crushing fire," the commander "seized the colors and rode before the line toward the enemy." This encouraged his soldiers, who then "dashed forward over the plain and into the wood." One of Preston's officers, Major John T. Lesley, noted with amazement that following the general's heroic act, "with a joyous shout[,] our boys sprang forward, and were soon in possession of the wood that had lately covered the enemy." On 31 December, one member of the brigadier's staff was killed at his side, another–astride General Albert Sidney Johnston's horse Nelson–fell severely wounded across Preston's mount and covered him with blood, and the visor of the Kentuckian's new cap was struck by the fragment of a shell. That morning his brigade had numbered 1,951 men; by nightfall 54 had died and 384 were wounded.[33]

Believing that Rosecrans would retreat on New Year's Day because of heavy losses, an overoptimistic Bragg telegraphed President Davis that the Army of Tennessee had won a great victory. But the northern forces did not leave the field. Throughout the daylight hours, the exhausted troops on both sides abandoned killing to bury dead comrades, tend to wounds, and prepare for the next round of warfare. This time, no stirring music was heard.

On 2 January the Confederate commander ordered Breckinridge's corps to take a ridge occupied by a Federal division on the east bank and defended by fifty-seven pieces of artillery on high ground across the river. When Breckinridge protested that such an attack could only end in defeat and a senseless loss of lives, Bragg remained firm. On delivering this order to Preston, Breckinridge pointedly told him that the unwise plan was Bragg's responsibility.

Preston's regiments gave up "the bloody cedars" they had taken two days earlier and crossed the river to join Breckinridge as ordered. The troops advanced across an open field in a close-ordered, successive-lines formation, with Preston's men making up the second row of soldiers, about two hundred yards behind the first. These Rebels enjoyed an initial success, capturing the ridge on the east side of the stream. Preston's brigade took "some 200 prisoners." The southern troops then pursued their foes down toward the river. At that moment, the Kentucky brigadier later lamented, Rosecrans moved up fresh batteries on the opposite bank, and "they poured a withering and continual fire on our men on the hill-side, converting the momentary victory into bloody defeat." The heavy enemy fire wreaked havoc among the gray-clad soldiers. Seeing this, Preston grabbed the first flag he saw and "beat all fugitive men and officers over the head with my sabre till I got a handful of men around me." Then rallying them with "a touch of stump speech address," he regrouped them in a ravine and established a new line of defense. The assault failed, but it left another 41 men dead and 245 wounded from Preston's brigade.[34]

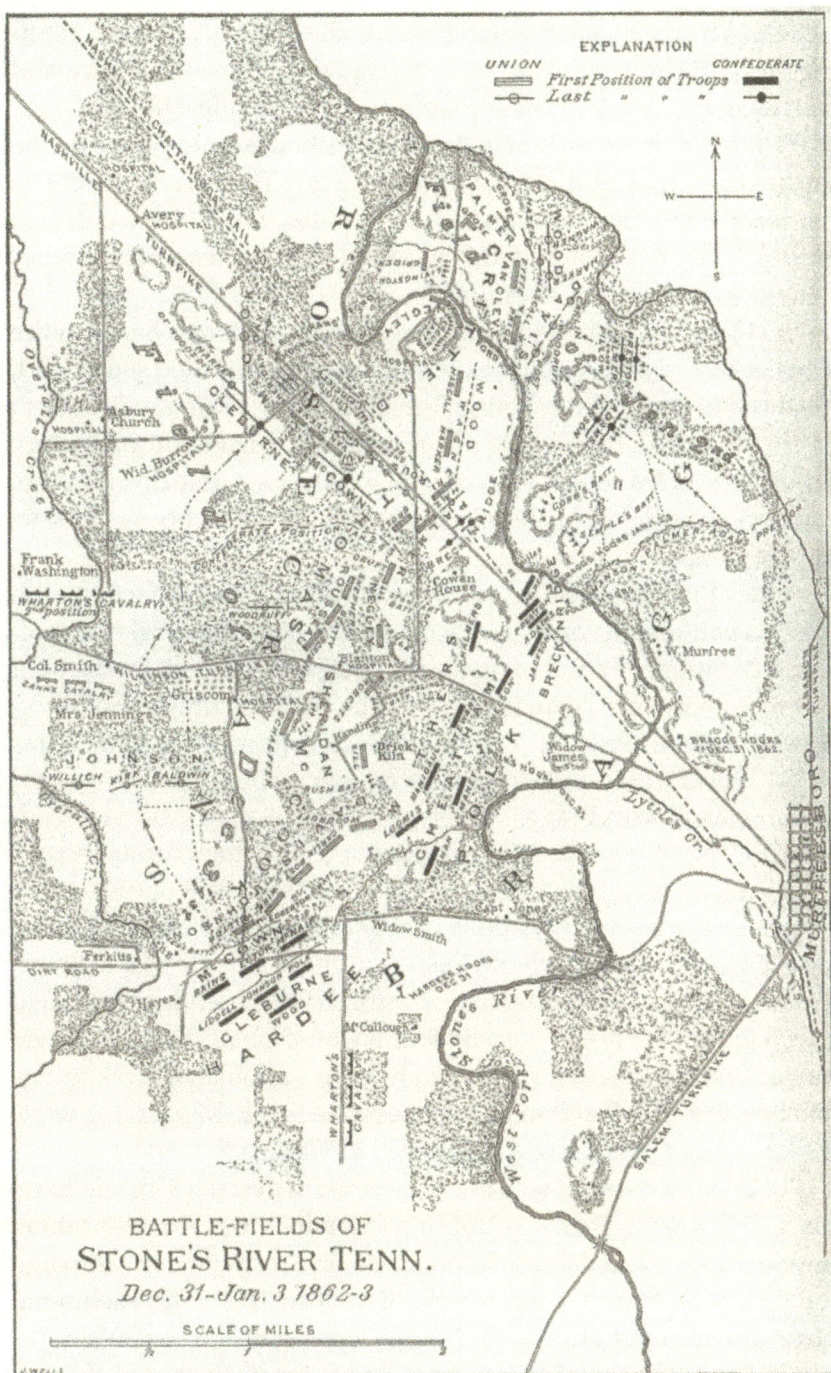

EXPLANATION

UNION — First Position of Troops — CONFEDERATE
— Last " " "

BATTLE-FIELDS OF
STONE'S RIVER TENN.
Dec. 31–Jan. 3 1862-3

SCALE OF MILES

Published in Battles and Leaders of the Civil War, *vol. 3 (New York, 1884).*

Of this tragic engagement the Kentuckian angrily reported, "During the battle both men and officers displayed great intrepidity, and I attribute the repulse Friday 2 January to the manifest hopelessness of the attempt to hurl a single division, without support, against the cardinal position of the whole hostile army. This was apparent to the least intelligent soldier." Murfreesboro was a "concentrated Shiloh," Preston concluded, "with shorter rushes and bloodier struggles, and the same results."[35]

On 3 January, General Bragg decided that his forces had to retire from Murfreesboro. Again the Confederate forces headed southward, this time to congregate around Tullahoma some thirty miles north of the Alabama line. During this retreat, the brigadier took temporary charge of his cousin's division of 5,500 men, while Breckinridge enjoyed a brief leave of absence to be with his wife who was following the troops.

Stones River marked yet another defeat, and dissatisfaction with Bragg's battle plans only increased the disdain of several of the officers–including Kentucky generals Breckinridge and Preston–for their commander. "There is an imbroglio between Bragg and his officers," William Preston Johnston reported from Richmond to his wife, "Breckinridge and Uncle Wm. are said to be the principles [sic] in the quarrel with Bragg." The two cousins were considered leaders of the "Kentucky block" of officers opposed to their commander.[36]

Jefferson Davis sent William Preston Johnston to Tennessee to investigate the accusations made against Bragg, but the president decided to keep him in charge. Nevertheless, according to a biographer of Bragg, the mistakes made at Stones River destroyed his "usefulness as a field commander." In order to stop dissension among his officers, Davis removed Breckinridge and Preston from Bragg's command. Breckinridge and his division full of Bragg's enemies were sent to Mississippi, while the Kentucky brigadier was dispatched to Virginia.[37]

On 28 April Preston was ordered to southwestern Virginia to replace Brigadier General Humphrey Marshall, the Know-Nothing opponent who had defeated Congressman Preston in his campaign for reelection from the Louisville district in 1855. The Richmond government sought to put the best face possible on Preston's transfer; William Preston Johnston explained to his uncle that he was being sent to his new assignment because the president wanted "a man of real ability" there. Certainly Davis was concerned about the army's evident weakness in the Virginia mountains. Ignorant even of the number of men in this military district, he had sent an inspector in May to ascertain the preparedness of the troops there. As feared, the president's agent reported, "Things are in a terrible condition."[38]

Exhausted and ill with fever in April, the Louisville native spent a week in Columbia, South Carolina, with his cousin, General John S. Preston, who found him "in very feeble health" and in need of a "long rest and ease." Nevertheless, his host noted that "his spirits are buoyant as usual–but at times he appears languid." The Kentuckian next went to Richmond for three days and enjoyed visiting William Preston Johnston and conversing with President and Mrs. Davis. "The few days at Richmond have set me up for a year," the thankful uncle reported to his nephew. Later Preston would return to the Confederate capital for several days of relaxation and enjoy playing chess with his nephew–just as the two had done in Louisville decades earlier. The brigadier also traveled to Knoxville to consult with General Buckner before arriving at his new post on 14 May.[39]

Preston's district was important because it included the saltworks that furnished this essential substance for most of the Confederacy east of the Mississippi. William's uncle, General Francis Preston, had established his home in Abingdon, Virginia, and begun the manufacturing of salt in nearby Saltville in the 1790s. The vital Virginia and Tennessee Railroad transported the product and by 1863 became a goal of Union raiders. Although Federal forces attacked Wytheville, Virginia, in July of that year, they were repulsed before they could destroy the rail line. Not until May 1864 did northern troops close the railroad.

The general established his headquarters in Abingdon, just north of Bristol, Tennessee, and quickly concluded that "the command is . . . a mere wild brigade." He relocated the positions of many of the dispersed forces throughout his six-county district along the rail line, so that they could be assembled quickly when needed. In reorganizing his troops, Preston relied on his aides, Captains Joe Blackburn and Harris Johnston, and on George B. Hodge, a dedicated cavalry officer who carefully carried out the general's orders. After "having collected and scraped together all I could find," the Kentucky brigadier counted 2,416 men in his new command. Preston's troops guarded saltworks that produced ten thousand bushels daily and defended an ill-defined two hundred miles of mountainous frontier between Union and Confederate forces in Kentucky, Tennessee, and Virginia. Although Preston was under General Buckner's Department of East Tennessee, the commander granted the Louisvillian full authority in his distant district.[40]

The brigadier spent a good deal of time enforcing discipline among his men, successfully keeping his soldiers and officers in camp at night, and clearing the streets of Abingdon of stragglers. Preston believed in observing a strict military hierarchy. In Virginia he upheld this principle, reporting that he even instructed his officers not "to come to see me except on business with written orders." Two months after the Kentucky brigadier took command, his superior, Major General Buckner, "expressed great gratification at the promptitude of troops and conditions of things" in the southwestern Virginia district. Impressed by Brigadier General John Hunt Morgan's dashing raids against the startled enemy, Preston organized similar sorties from his Virginia base. In July he ordered a small group to sweep into Kentucky, raiding Mt. Sterling and penetrating to Maysville on the Ohio River. His men reported fighting the enemy four times on their "very exciting and somewhat hazardous trip." Such offensive expeditions were designed to force the enemy to maintain a defensive stance.[41]

Once in southwestern Virginia, Preston made excellent use of his good connections to obtain needed supplies for his command. In Tennessee he had discovered the importance of well-placed friends in assisting his unit. At the urging of Mrs. Jefferson Davis, the government in Richmond had sent two thousand pounds of cured pork and "15 or 20 old hams" to Preston's unit the week after the Battle of Stones River. When he found his Abingdon district short of armament, the general immediately asked William Preston Johnston in Richmond to intercede with Colonel Josiah Gorgas, the efficient head of ordnance, to send five hundred rifles. Of course, asking for favors also entailed obligations. "At Mrs. Davis' request," Preston added a major to his Abingdon division in August, for which he received the thanks of the president's wife. Later, as a Confederate diplomat, the Kentucky general sent Mrs. Davis two boxes from the West Indies that included such luxuries as Java coffee, guava jelly, pasta, olives, and English cheese.[42]

In the late summer of 1863, the Confederates decided to undertake a major offensive to check General Rosecrans's advance toward Chattanooga, a vital rail center. This effort led to the Battle of Chickamauga in September. Preston was ordered in August to bring most of his troops south by train from Virginia through eastern Tennessee to form one of the two divisions of General Buckner's corps. The Louisville native's forces numbered four thousand men in three brigades, one artillery battalion, and one group of reserves. From General Robert E. Lee's army in Virginia twelve thousand men under Lieutenant General James Longstreet were detailed to reinforce the western Confederates. The Union capture of Knoxville on 6 September forced these Virginians to travel via Charlotte, Wilmington, and Atlanta to join the Army of Tennessee, still commanded by General Bragg.[43]

After Rosecrans's troops crossed the Tennessee River below Chattanooga, Bragg evacuated the city on 8 September and directed his army into north Georgia. The newly assembled Confederate forces first encountered Rosecrans's men ten days later along Chickamauga Creek a dozen miles south of Chattanooga across the state line. Thick virgin stands of pine, oak, hickory, and maple trees on the mountainsides, interspersed with fields in the lowlands full of cornstalks and pumpkins, offered both sides protection along the six-mile front. Some sixty-six thousand Confederates faced westward, while several hundred yards ahead awaited more than fifty-eight thousand soldiers in the parallel Union lines. Behind the Yankee troops were several spurs of Missionary Ridge where the reddish tinge of the dogwoods, the scarlet of the sumacs, and intimations of color from the massed hardwoods signaled the start of autumn.[44]

On 18 September, the eve of battle, the first cold snap of the season brought scattered frost by daybreak. Although fog clung to the lowlands in the early morning, the sunshine of a dry and dusty Indian summer warmed the afternoon. But the 125,000 warriors on both sides had no chance to heed the change of seasons. Their thoughts were focused on the coming test of arms. The next two days would witness the bloodiest battle of the war in the west.

Throughout the daylight hours on 19 September, Bragg ordered massive assaults against Rosecrans's forces in an attempt to outflank them and cut them off from Chattanooga. But Union troops put up a stout defense, holding the Rebels to small gains. Preston's division took its orders on the first day from General Buckner whose corps made up the left wing of Bragg's army. Only one of Preston's three brigades was sent into action that day–in support of another unit in the late afternoon. By dusk, about 150 of his men had been killed or wounded. During the night, against a backdrop of picket firing and the cries of the wounded, Preston's division was "vigorously engaged in constructing defenses" to strengthen the Rebels' left line. That evening many of Longstreet's troops reached the battlefield, and the general was given command of the Confederates' left flank. Lee's lieutenant exuded confidence, encouraging Bragg's troops who were accustomed to defeats and withdrawals.[45]

After more stubborn fighting the following morning, Longstreet's men charged through a gap in the Union lines, sending Rosecrans and much of his army fleeing toward Chattanooga. Union Major General George Thomas, later known as the "Rock of Chickamauga," organized the remaining troops to prevent a rout. He formed a new line atop Snodgrass Hill, a two-hundred-foot-high ridge that proved all but impregnable, and managed to protect the Federal retreat northward through McFarland's Gap en route to Chattanooga. Determined to take this stronghold, Longstreet launched twenty-five separate assaults against Thomas's right on the south bank of the Union citadel. Simultaneously, General Polk's men were assailing Thomas's left flank on the north slope of the ridge. "In its general aspects the battle of Snodgrass Hill," according to one historian of the encounter, was "the most determined and sanguinary fight of all this grisly meeting of the two armies along the Chickamauga, and comparable in its fury to Gettysburg."[46]

But successive waves of Rebels were repulsed in their efforts to storm this bastion. Three divisions had failed to gain the hill by the middle of the afternoon, when Longstreet ordered Preston's brigades to make an all-out effort to dislodge the Federals protected by artillery and defenses of rocks and logs. Brigadier General Archibald Gracie's and Colonel John H. Kelly's brigades moved up the cleared southern slope of Snodgrass Hill in two lines until only forty paces from the crest. There they stood in the open and traded volleys with the entrenched enemy. The bravery of these troops under fire has won encomia from both contemporaries and later military historians: "Nothing in this battle, marked with gallantry so frequent that it became commonplace, surpassed the courage of these two brigades as they watched their ranks thin minute by minute and still doggedly refused to yield an inch of ground." But glory that day had its price. Gracie's unit suffered the worst losses–698 men killed

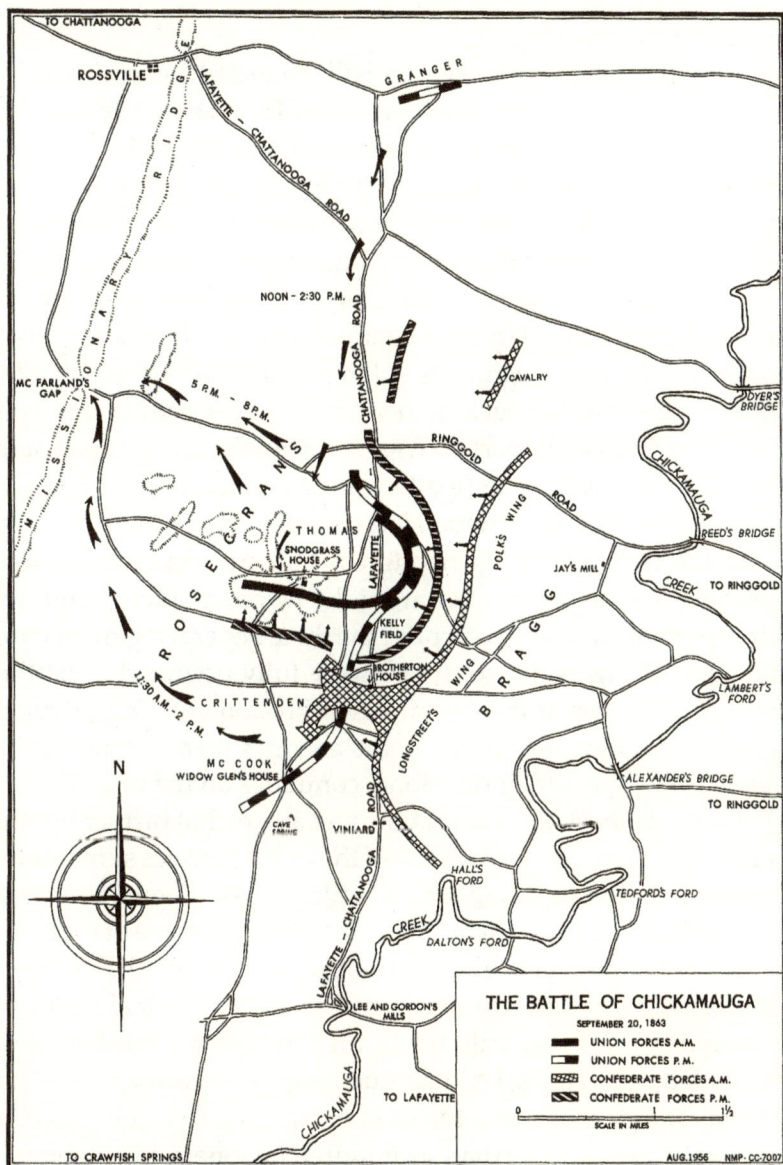

Published in James R. Sullivan, Chickamauga and Chattanooga Battlefield *(Washington, D.C., 1956).*

or wounded out of 2,003. When General Preston presented President Davis with the flag of the brigade's Second Alabama Battalion, this standard had been pierced in eighty-three places by enemy balls. After more than an hour of combat, the remaining exhausted troops retreated down the slope.[47]

During the attack on Snodgrass Hill, blue-clad General James A. Garfield–later President Garfield–reached Thomas shortly after four o'clock with orders from Rosecrans directing the Union forces to withdraw "immediately." But the battle commander refused, arguing that "'it would ruin the army to withdraw it now.'"[48] At sunset the heroic Union general began his organized retreat.

At the end of the day, Preston gained his greatest military success. Although two Union brigades already had abandoned Snodgrass Hill, three regiments still remained entrenched atop this bloody citadel. The Kentucky general took his reserve brigade, commanded by Colonel Robert C. Trigg, and led the charge against the remaining bluecoats, who finally waved a white flag. In planning the attack, the brigadier depended on John Dyer, his courier who owned the farm bordering Snodgrass Hill. He directed Preston's forces in a flanking maneuver around a wooded outcrop and up a ravine, permitting them to surprise the three Federal regiments from Ohio and Michigan. These troops were fully occupied in battling other Confederates at their front when Preston and Trigg directed their men in a bayonet charge to the enemy's rear. Colonel Kelly's brigade soon joined their divisional comrades on the hill.

Exhausted, short on ammunition, and aware that further fighting would mean extermination, many of the brave Yankees surrendered, while others were captured after a futile defense. A retreating Indiana unit fired on the two Rebel brigades, allowing some of the northern prisoners to escape–although most were recaptured. In replying to the Hoosiers' attack, Preston's men let loose the final volleys of the long battle. By nightfall, the Confederates were masters of the field, with the remaining Federals hurrying up the road toward Chattanooga. The Kentuckian's forces had captured two colonels commanding brigades, more than six hundred prisoners, five standards, one piece of artillery, and some two thousand arms. When night fell, the Army of Tennessee had won its "first grand victory," General Longstreet observed. The retreating Federals had left behind some eight thousand men who fell captive and fifteen thousand small arms. But like most victories, this one came at great cost. Of the 4,078 men in Preston's division, 1,014 were wounded and 202 were killed at Chickamauga. Overall, the battle left a third of Bragg's men, some twenty thousand, dead or wounded, while more than sixteen thousand of Rosecrans's forces suffered the same fate.[49]

Chickamauga marked the high point in General Preston's military career. "The gallant manner in which he conducted his division to the assault," General Buckner emphasized, "contributed in a manner second to none to the winning of the key point of the field and thus deciding the fate of the day." But Buckner also looked beyond the Louisvillian's heroism and commended his preparation and leadership of his men: "Upon Brigadier General Preston, and his brigade commanders, . . . I cannot bestow higher praise than to say, that their conduct and example were such as to convert a body of troops, but few of whom had before been under fire, into a division of veterans in their first battle." "Preston dashed gallantly at the hills," General Longstreet observed, adding that the Kentuckian's attack "crippled the enemy so badly that his ranks were badly broken, and by a flank movement and another advance the heights were gained."[50]

A correspondent for the *London Times* present at the battle claimed that Preston's "bearing on the slope of Missionary Ridge, under the setting sun of the 20th September, will . . . rank . . . with any other famous deeds of arms ever witnessed on the earth." The Englishman went on to compare the brigadier's success to that of General Louis C. A. Desaix, whose opportune arrival with fresh troops at the Battle of Marengo was credited with saving Napoleon's forces from certain defeat during his Italian campaign of 1800.[51]

Students of Chickamauga have not been unanimous in praising General Longstreet's determined assault on Snodgrass Hill throughout the afternoon of 20 September. Some have argued that the Virginian should have deployed his troops to outflank the Union bastion and try to cut off the Federals' escape route. But others have excused his actions, maintaining that the commander was unaware of how strongly entrenched the enemy was in the heavily wooded positions around the ridge. As the officer in charge of carrying out Longstreet's plans that afternoon, Preston also received criticism from some quarters. General Gracie's son later insisted that "the delay occasioned in capturing these Federal regiments on Snodgrass Ridge was a mistake; that if Preston's Division had made a pursuit of the enemy, instead of capturing these regiments, greater results would have been obtained." Others faulted the Kentucky brigadier for not pursuing the enemy more quickly once his forces controlled the top of the hill.[52]

Although many glorified General Preston's actions at Chickamauga, he looked back on the struggle with mixed emotions. For him the two-day engagement was a "terrible battle." Certainly he was proud that "my division was engaged in the fiercest combat on the field" and had "stormed the strongest part of the opposite line." But he remained quite aware that the "splendid distinction" of his men came only through their "suffering" and lamented the deaths of so many. Of course, Preston's emotions matched those of many other officers. His cousin, General Breckinridge, on several occasions was seen with tears in his eyes while regarding the faces of the dead killed in battle.[53]

Chickamauga was Preston's last battle. For two years he had fought in engagement after engagement. Like so many other combatants on both sides, he often had been aware of the danger of death. Before Shiloh, his first armed clash, he thought of the possibility of dying on the battlefield and composed "a few lines" to his family "in the hope that they may be delivered to you in case of my death." Following this battle, he wrote his wife, "God knows, shall we ever meet again?" Throughout the remainder of his days as a soldier, his correspondence showed that he was becoming increasingly aware of his own mortality. The hole shot in his cap at Murfreesboro was literally a "close call," and "the winter scene, the frost, the dead and dying" that Preston observed on the banks of Stones River was a stark *memento mori*, "wild enough for a Banquet of Ghouls." Following the carnage at Chickamauga, he reflected on his spiritual life. To his wife he expressed his regret at not being a member of the Episcopal Church, since "my own convictions are with its noble and enlightened doctrines," and he urged her to have "our dear children christened in the Episcopalian Church."[54]

After Chickamauga, Generals Buckner and Longstreet nominated Preston for promotion. "It is a simple act of justice to recommend his appointment as Major General to command the division now under his command," Buckner wrote of his fellow Kentuckian. But Jefferson Davis never agreed to this request, despite the praise showered on the brigadier for his heroism. A major reason for the president's reluctance was the growing animosity of Preston and several other officers toward their commander, Braxton Bragg, whose unfortunate military decisions and contentious personality led to celebrated conflicts with many officers, including Generals Breckinridge, Buckner, Longstreet, Polk, and William J. Hardee. This bitter dispute, of course, weakened the Army of Tennessee's efforts to confront its foes. The so-called political officers–including Preston and cousin John Breckinridge–believed their West Point leader had contempt for their military abilities. Both Bluegrass generals had held Bragg in very low esteem since the failed invasion of Kentucky and since he had ordered their troops at Stones River to charge impregnable positions.[55]

The Louisville brigadier considered Bragg "tyrannical . . . impetuous . . . and narrow minded," "unfit for command." "<u>Bragg is too weak to fight</u>," Preston concluded after Murfreesboro, "<u>and too unpopular to run</u>." The Kentuckian also made his opposition to "Boomerang Bragg" known to his fellow generals, as well as to his nephew William Preston Johnston in Richmond. After Chickamauga, the disgusted Kentuckian concluded that Bragg "has a heart of ice and head of wood." Throughout his service in Tennessee and at Chickamauga Preston carefully showed respect toward his commander, but the brigadier also remained "perfectly willing to give him my opinion that we had no confidence in him."[56]

When Bragg did not pursue the Chickamauga success with a rapid attack on Chattanooga, Preston and several other officers signed a petition addressing their complaints to President Davis in early October. They noted that "it is now certain that the fruits of victory of the Chickamauga have now escaped our grasp" and urged the president to remove Bragg from command of the Army of Tennessee, the Confederacy's second-most important force. Modern historians are all but unanimous in their negative verdicts concerning Bragg's military leadership. "Bragg had little talent for field command," maintained a biographer, who concluded that "he made a major contribution to Confederate defeat." After a visit to Bragg's headquarters and a display of indecision, the southern president left the commander in charge and approved the transfer of several hostile officers to other postings. Because of his support for Bragg, Davis increasingly considered opposition to the military chieftain tantamount to criticism of his leadership.[57]

Preston remained a brigadier in the Army of Tennessee, but he was removed from command of his division. "I have a dull future before me with Bragg," Preston wrote in early October to his nephew in Richmond. The discontented Kentuckian expressed a desire to return to southwestern Virginia and asked, "Is it possible?" General Buckner on 18 October reassigned Preston to his former military district in southwestern Virginia. But Bragg and Buckner were involved in a dispute concerning the latter's East Tennessee command, and Bragg denied that Buckner had the authority to offer an appointment to Preston. Jefferson Davis agreed that Buckner lacked this authority, but the president notified the contentious commander of the Army of Tennessee that Preston would retain his Virginia post, because "it is for the best."[58]

This time Preston held his post in southwestern Virginia for less than three months. In mid-November he returned to Abingdon to take command of 4,208 men. The general was particularly impressed by one of his soldiers, Captain Robert T. Ford, a Louisvillian and a cousin of William Preston Johnston's wife Rosa. At Ford's request, the captain became his commander's aide in late November and proved to be a faithful assistant.[59]

Preston was very depressed after Chickamauga. "I have been so deep in the blues lately," he lamented once back in Virginia. In part this was brought on by his disappointment in his military fortunes– failure to win a promotion and a better command. Because of leaving Bragg's army, "I fear . . . you lost your chance, which was good, for a Div[isio]n.," his nephew William Preston Johnston wrote him in November 1863. The disorder he found in Abingdon on his return also upset him and contributed to his war-weariness. In addition to homesickness, the general's low spirits also were brought on by the fatigue that followed his arduous three-month service with Bragg's forces in Tennessee and Georgia. Aware of his uncle's low morale, William Preston Johnston tried to encourage him with a report that some Kentuckians were backing Preston for the Confederate Senate. Will urged him to consider this, for "if [a] senator you are independent and powerful." But this did not come to pass. On 7 January 1864, Preston was relieved of duty in Virginia and ordered to proceed to Shreveport, Louisiana, to serve General Kirby Smith in the Trans-Mississippi Department. But the same day the Richmond government countermanded these military instructions, offering him a diplomatic post instead.[60]

During his twenty-seven months in the Confederate army, 1861-64, William Preston traveled thousands of miles through Kentucky,

Tennessee, Mississippi, Alabama, Georgia, the Carolinas, and Virginia on horseback and by rail. As an officer, his living conditions were vastly superior to that of the enlisted men, but even commanders encountered diseases, exhaustion, and many discomforts. His slave Samuel Giles performed errands, nursed him, purchased food and supplies, prepared meals, and did laundry. In addition, his master reported, Samuel "has been very good to me in my loneliness." Given army funds in 1863 for a personal servant, the general purchased a slave called "Boy Peter" for this position and a second black named Howard. The master found them loyal servants and became fond of both. When Preston left Virginia in August 1863 to join Bragg's forces, Giles accompanied him, but Peter and Howard were entrusted to a captain in Abingdon. After Chickamauga, Preston sent the two slaves to Richmond to assist nephew William, and enjoined him to "treat Howard and Peter as your own."[61]

The Kentuckian often enjoyed such daily amenities as tablecloths at dinner, and he usually was accompanied by trunks carrying his personal possessions and a box of books. Although visitors from Virginia complained that the food available in the western camps was inferior to what they enjoyed in the Old Dominion, the officers still managed to dine on beef (though often described as "tough"), bacon ("indifferent" in the opinion of some), chicken and eggs (considered "delicacies"), and–rarely–mutton.[62] For entertainment, Preston continued to read classical works in Greek and Latin, played chess, and attended theatrical and musical presentations offered by the soldiers.

As an officer, Preston often boarded with a local family when the army remained in place for several days. After Stones River he resided in a private home in Tullahoma for ten weeks. But while on the march, even his elaborate tented shelters left much to be desired, causing him to complain particularly of "icy rains and wintry bivouacs." At his command in Abingdon he took a house for his headquarters and enjoyed the sedentary existence.[63]

Despite amenities afforded an officer, Preston's life proved difficult. His schedule and the pressures of command brought him almost constant fatigue. In his mid-to-late-forties during the war, he was afflicted by poor health on several occasions, making it difficult for him to carry out his duties. Liver and digestive problems confined him to quarters for nine days in June 1862, and later that month he fell ill with fever at Vicksburg. Before assuming command in southwestern Virginia in April 1863, the brigadier needed to rest from exhaustion. Although his more stationary life in Abingdon allowed him to regain his strength, the general again confessed to feeling "bad" in June 1863 and admitted to losing "thirty five or thirty seven pounds." He also complained of an "acute pain" in his left eye that the doctor diagnosed as "iritis." This condition would continue to afflict him and finally result in blindness in this eye.[64]

In addition to his daily concerns as an officer at war, Preston's greatest worry throughout the conflict was the well-being of his family in Lexington. Before leaving home in September 1861, Preston instructed his wife to remain at Wickliffe Place and to obey United States authorities as long as they provided protection for her and the children. A year later he again insisted that it was "your duty to abstain from any act that could harm you." Should conditions become "so intolerable, so that you cannot stay, seek shelter in Canada, you cannot cross the lines! Do not even think of it." Margaret scrupulously followed this advice.[65]

Throughout the war years, Preston's wife and children in Kentucky encountered hostility from both northern partisans and the Federal government. Margaret attended the Second Presbyterian Church, the church of her mother and stepmother. But the pro-Unionist sentiment of the congregation discouraged her participation and probably caused her to join the Episcopal Church of her father following the war. By early 1862 she complained that "the life we are leading is too gloomy," and she noted that the girls "never go out, even to church." Uncertainty about Preston's safety led to a state of "agonizing suspense" for the whole family. But as Margaret wrote her sister-in-law Susan Christy Hepburn, other southern sympathizers in Lexington suffered more than she. In February 1863 a friend told her a "heartrending" story of Federal soldiers demanding payment of "five hundred dollars or her life."[66]

Despite difficulties, Margaret was able to shelter her children. She helped the younger ones with their lessons and listened as the older daughters recited aloud from French books. Carrie wrote her father that her older sister read "nearly all the time [but] I am sorry that novels predominate." Margaret also tried to bolster the family's spirits. She brought William's library from Louisville to Lexington and ordered new clothing for herself and the children. For her forty-fifth birthday in 1864, Margaret hired a band to dance with friends and family. The children complained of isolation, but they tried to avoid problems. The daughters "were never presented to any officer," but when they encountered Union soldiers, they "always treated them civilly–Hating them most cordially," Polly wrote her father. Only one public display of hostility by a family member was recorded during the war years. When General Kirby Smith's troops entered Lexington in September 1862, daughter Carrie "amused herself by tearing up and trampling on a union flag" that had been removed from a building on Main Street.[67]

Mrs. Preston went out of her way to carry on as if life were normal, and this helped her project an air of confidence that was not lost on Federal authorities. Like other Civil War women without husbands by their sides, she gained even greater autonomy in handling economic affairs. The feminine head of household oversaw improvements at Wickliffe Place. A marble mantle was installed, new curtains and chandeliers were purchased, extensive plumbing repairs were made, and the residence was painted. She advertised for tenants for Ellerslie Farm, watched over the management of Piedmont Farm in Bath County, and rented a stall at the Upper Market House where produce was sold. Margaret continued to hire out her slaves, some of whom worked for the army at Camp Nelson. When a slave ran away in 1862, Union forces apprehended him.

Kentucky's vulnerability to Confederate incursions and growing animosity in the second year of war caused northern officials to react with increasing harshness toward southern sympathizers. Following General Kirby Smith's occupation of Lexington in September 1862, William Preston Johnston reported that Federal army officers had been "very rude and threatening" to General Preston's wife, telling her that they "would make her and her children crawl on their knees . . . and beg for bread" unless they pledged allegiance to the United States.[68] In May 1863 the Lexington Office of the Post Commandant informed Mrs. Preston that "in accordance with 'General Orders No. 66 of the Department of Ohio' yourself and your family will prepare to remove beyond and South of our lines by the 1st day of June next." However, if she felt "disposed to take the oath of allegiance, you will make the same known at this office." Mrs. Preston and her two eldest daughters, Mary Owen and Caroline Hancock, swore an oath not to give "aid, assistance or information" to the enemy.[69]

In an attempt to guarantee their continued residence in Lexington, Margaret Preston mobilized influential friends. In May 1863 her physician, Dr. Dudley Bush, certified that her ankle, badly broken the previous year, still was not completely healed. Although Mrs. Preston no longer needed crutches, she still was lame and would only be able to travel with difficulty, if at all. Joshua F. Speed, a Louisville friend and an advisor of Abraham Lincoln, wrote to the president to assure him of Mrs. Preston's correct conduct. The Louisville Unionist urged him to show "such mitigation of the orders as your good feelings and the facts in the case will warrant, believing as I do that the interests of our cause will not suffer by acts of clemency to meritorious people." Such intervention allowed her and the children to remain in Kentucky, but their situation remained difficult. Fortunately, the children remained in good health–although the father heard that his son had almost lost an eye "in a duel with walnuts."[70]

By the summer of 1863 increasing animosity marked the relationship of Federal forces with prosouthern Kentuckians, as well as with many of their pro-Union neighbors. Two years of war had hardened attitudes on both sides. Troops under General Preston's command in Virginia made raids into Kentucky at Mt. Sterling and Maysville in July 1863. One of his men wrote, "We never for one moment thought of taking a [Kentucky Unionist] Home Guard prisoner, looking upon them simply as an organized hoard [sic] of 'Bush Whackers,' all that were captured were killed. They expected nothing else and asked not for their lives, so they treat our men when taken by them." When Preston heard that General Ambrose E. Burnside, commander of the District of Ohio, was executing southern recruiters in Kentucky, he urged the Confederacy to do the same to Union agents in east Tennessee. "The exact rule of retaliatory justice" should apply, he insisted.[71]

Ironically, one of the most frightening experiences the Prestons had came at the hands of southern soldiers. The three oldest daughters were between Louisville and Lexington on a train attacked by Confederate cavalrymen in July 1863. As related in the diary of a Unionist Lexington teenager, the southern soldiers "destroyed the Misses Prestons' baggage," despite protests that they were daughters of General Preston. Such acts brought daughter Mary to criticize southern raiders in Kentucky for not always acting as Confederate men "'usually do.'"[72]

Margaret Preston and her family were subjected to increased

Union pressure as the war dragged on. Part of the family's property in Lexington was taken for use as a military hospital in late 1863. When reports circulated that Wickliffe Place would be taken over for medical purposes, Union Colonel John Mason Brown, a friend of the family and future husband of Mary Owen, the oldest Preston daughter, interceded with Federal authorities and was able to prevent this. He assured Mrs. Preston that she and her children could continue to reside in their home.[73]

Physical separation and the dangers of war proved difficult burdens for all members of the family. Frequent, though irregular, correspondence united William and his loved ones. His letters to the children were replete with counsel that they "love, obey and comfort your Mother," while assuring them, "You are not far away from my heart." He consoled his wife that "there is a sort of happiness in misfortune if nobly sustained" and reminded her "to let no maternal tenderness prevent" her from seeing that Wick was "thoroughly" educated. His daughters informed him of their activities and their love. After Jessie wrote that he was the pride of the family, Margaret–as she had done while he was in Mexico–begged that "God grant that you may always act as to make us proud of you."[74]

Despite correspondence, the Lexington Prestons–like all those who have seen men go off to war—could never be certain of William's well-being. Fearing possible death, he wrote a letter before the Battle of Shiloh to "My dear son and daughters" in the event "I may not see you again," and the lonesome husband often complained that his estrangement from wife and children "is worse than death." After Shiloh he left "special deposits of money and papers" with William Preston Johnston to be delivered to his family in the event of his demise. On hearing that his hat was pierced by gunfire at the Battle of Stones River, Margaret reported that "Poogie wrote to her father that Mary, Carrie and herself were contending, who should own that cap, but she knew he would award it to the most studious, and she was determined to win the prize." When leaving Virginia in August 1863 to join Bragg's forces, Preston instructed his nephew to take charge of his belongings in Abingdon for delivery to his family in case of an "accident."[75]

Once, in August 1862, Mrs. Preston considered crossing through the military lines to visit her husband who was ill at Vicksburg. She telegraphed her friend Mary Todd Lincoln to intercede for her and arrange for a pass. The next day the president's wife asked Kentucky's military commander, General Jeremiah T. Boyle, to grant this request, and Abraham Lincoln told Mrs. Preston that because of his wife's "early and strong friendship for you, I would gladly oblige you, but I cannot absolutely do it." However, if Boyle or James Guthrie, a Unionist and longtime friend of the Preston and Wickliffe families, would agree to her request, the president promised that permission would be granted.[76] Although she probably would have been able to acquire a pass, Margaret decided not to pursue the matter.

Besides his anxiety over his family's safety, General Preston was concerned about safeguarding his financial interests. In 1861 he valued his fifty-four properties in Louisville at $263,970 and his St. Louis real estate at $100,000. His twenty-seven slaves and personal property increased his assets by $34,500. Not included in these totals were his bonds, stocks, and smaller properties in Kentucky, Indiana, Illinois, and Texas. In addition, his wife's fifty-one slaves, Wickliffe Place, and two farms in Fayette and Bath Counties were worth $238,000.[77]

Despite his Confederate service, Preston managed to protect most of his real-estate holdings, personal property, bonds, and stocks from creditors and confiscation. In a complex legal instrument dated 26 December 1861, the trained lawyer conveyed all his "real and personal property" to two Louisville trustees, his uncle George Hancock and Frederick Wedekemper, who had handled Preston's financial matters since his years in Congress. Later, John Preston, a relative, replaced Wedekemper. The Confederate authorized his trustees "to sell and convey said property for the purpose of maintaining and supporting properly Margaret W. Preston . . . and her children." Hancock and John Preston were enjoined to take no actions without his wife being "a party to it." Through this legal maneuver Preston sought to circumvent legislation forcing rebellious United States citizens to forfeit their wealth because of treason. On 7 July 1862 Preston was indicted for treason by the Fayette County Circuit Court.[78]

William's sister Susan handled her brother's monetary matters during the war. She corresponded with him about his financial affairs and gave instructions to the Louisville trustees. Wealthy in her own right, Susan had experience in managing substantial funds. A successful lawsuit in 1858 had granted her valuable St. Louis properties from the estate of her first husband, Howard Christy. William had traded several Louisville lots in 1860 for some of Susan's Missouri real estate. In addition to his sister, William also instructed his wife to help manage his affairs.[79]

During the war many claims were made against Preston's assets. The trustees collected "large sums of money due William Preston," using the proceeds to make payments to his wife and his creditors. The Kentucky aristocrat in 1861 had many debts resulting from numerous financial transactions and the loans still unpaid from his father-in-law's estate. His sister oversaw the trustees' payments of interest due on her brother's outstanding obligations–particularly notes from the Bank of Kentucky–thereby avoiding foreclosure. Because of the "disturbed conditions," the value of many of Preston's properties in Kentucky fell during the first two years of the war, so he advised his trustees "to keep cool and not sacrifice my property." In February 1863 he predicted that "the Yankee currency in a year will not be worth forty cents on the dollar, and a little property will pay off all my debts." Nevertheless, Susan Hepburn and the trustees decided to sell the Preston house on Walnut Street in Louisville, for they feared that it might be confiscated.[80]

Attempts to postpone or renegotiate Preston's obligations led to a series of legal cases. Nine disgruntled creditors brought suit in early 1862 seeking the repayment of more than $64,000. Other court actions were taken against Preston in Kentucky throughout the war, demanding immediate debt payments. In several cases the trustees were forced by court order to sell his property to satisfy creditors. Preston was worried in January 1863 that "the estates of the family are being swept away." In September of that year the Fayette Circuit Court ordered a public auction of Preston's personal belongings to cover a bank note. More than one thousand dollars were paid for articles belonging to him, such as linens, silver, furniture, horses, cattle, and farming implements. However, relatives and friends repurchased these items from the successful bidders and returned them to the family. Twenty acres of land on Newburg Road southeast of Louisville were auctioned in December 1863 at a marshal's sale to settle a court decision. Not without reason Preston feared in May 1864 that his property "in Kentucky is knocked about fearfully," reporting that $50,000 of his holdings had been sold. And in Indiana some railroad stocks and a large tract of his land near Clarksville, Indiana, were confiscated in April 1863 because of treason and sold at auction for account of the United States. Despite such losses,

Preston remained very wealthy. "I yet have $50,000 to pay friends and $30,000 for myself," he noted in May 1864. Satisfied with the vast amount of real estate he still owned in Kentucky, Missouri, Illinois, and Texas and the value of his remaining bonds and stocks following the war, Preston credited his good fortune to "a deed of trust I drew that baffled the thieves," but he lamented that "they worried, badgered and bedeviled my trustees and family sorely."[81]

The conflict brought one substantial change in the Prestons' antebellum assets. Although Lincoln did not free the slaves in Kentucky during the Civil War, as early as 1862 Preston reported that on his Fayette County lands "Federal troops have run off some of my negroes." Some of the slaves became Union soldiers, thus gaining their freedom. In 1865 he and Margaret lost all their human property under the Thirteenth Amendment.[82]

While Preston was largely successful in safeguarding his property during the war, his financial arrangements led to conflicts with his wife. When Margaret finally saw William's account books, she discovered cash payments to his sister, Susan Hepburn, and real estate dealings between them. Margaret became more upset when she found that her husband had asked her Bath County agent to sell her Piedmont Farm in order to raise cash. The irate wife then asked Susan to reconvey some Louisville property to her that William had left in his sister's trust. When Susan answered that she was uncertain if the property belonged to her, Margaret accused her sister-in-law of stalling and confronted her husband. He had to admit that he had sought to sell Piedmont without consulting her, but concerning the Louisville property, he answered, "It is entirely in her management and I wish it to remain entirely subject to my sister's control." Trying to console his wife, William pleaded with her to trust "my sister's justice and equity" and assured her that their disagreement over finances had wounded him "to the core of my heart." Margaret yielded to her husband's wishes, leaving Susan in control of the Louisville property. William continued to confide in his sister on real estate matters, reminding her that he wanted "this to be in profound confidence between us." The distrust that husband and wife displayed over the control of their property during the war proved a harbinger of the conflicts the two would have over the same subject after 1865.[83]

Despite worrying over the fate of his family and his financial difficulties in Kentucky, William Preston's performance as a Confederate officer was impressive. Yet his success owed no debt to formal training for war. Of the 425 southern generals, Preston was one of 226 who lacked military schooling. A Harvard law graduate and not a West Pointer, his soldiering prior to the Civil War had been limited to captaining a volunteer unit of the Louisville Legion and spending sixteen months as a junior officer in a noncombatant position in the Mexican War. But an avid reader, he had familiarized himself with the contributions of leading military architects–such as the seventeenth-century designer of French fortifications, the Marquis de Vauban–and of the battle tactics of such victors as Napoleon and Admiral Horatio Nelson. The Kentucky "political general" also was familiar with the military theories of Antoine Henri Jomini, a Swiss Napoleonic general whose 1836 *Summary of the Art of War* was considered one of the best works on military strategy by mid-century.

Following the war, the Louisville Confederate argued with the benefit of hindsight that southern forces should have relied on an offensive military strategy to inflict losses on their much more numerous northern enemies. In 1877, Preston summarized his views: "I only feel, as I felt at the time, that not the fort but the field, not serried columns, but loose lines of skirmishes, confusing unsuspected masses of men suddenly concentrated, not the tactics that are the best on the plains of Lorraine or Belgium, but with long marches, sudden assaults, quick retreats and light field works, away from rivers, was the way to fight the Federals."[84]

Failure to follow such a strategy, Preston believed, brought disaster for the South. The humiliating Confederate defeat at Fort Donelson on the Cumberland River he blamed on a mistaken defense of "the foolish mud holes which the West Pointers built for us, after the ideas of Engineers from Vauban to Beauregard." Likewise, concentrations of limited southern military resources at Island No. 10 on the Mississippi and at Vicksburg were for Preston an "error in a military point of view, of attempting such defenses of fixed points by armies of greatly inferior force in cooped up fortifications instead of by light movable columns on open territories." At Shiloh, the Kentuckian argued, "A bold night attack on C. F. Smith's regiment with one skillful and hardy officer . . . and a thundering cannonade" would have captured a whole command–including 3,500 Union soldiers–and given the Confederates a resounding victory.[85]

All wars engender debates about military strategy, and the Civil War was no exception. Particularly because the South lost the conflict, the Confederacy's conduct of the struggle has engaged successive generations of students.[86] Like Preston, many historians have maintained that a bolder military strategy of swift attacks by highly mobile troops should have been the conscious aim of the Rebel forces. Still others have argued that the tactics of the southern generals–such as Robert E. Lee–were in fact too daring and not defensive enough–an opinion at odds with Preston's.[87] The debate between proponents of offensive and defensive military strategies is as old as war itself.[88] Like all such "what-if" theories, the discussion of the Confederacy's proper military policy promises to remain a subject for future generations.

Certainly Preston sought to carry out his theories on the field of battle. The success of his unit at Chickamauga was based on the daring, unsuspected assault he advocated: outflanking the enemy and surprising them with a lightning charge. While leading troops in southwestern Virginia, he organized surprise raids into Kentucky, one penetrating as far as the Ohio River. But Preston did not command an army or draw up battle plans. His responsibility was to implement them. Often this called for the use of common sense, not elaborate military theories. At Stones River Preston's logical decision to disperse his troops, forcing the Federals to fire both to their left and straight ahead, allowed his men to cross an open field and rout the defenders.

Preston's experiences as a civilian permitted him to make contributions to the Confederate army. A well-organized lawyer and a slave owner concerned with discipline, he proved a capable military administrator and organizer. As aide-de-camp for General Johnston, Preston efficiently helped oversee the myriad details involved in running an army–the supplying of provisions, resolving unexpected difficulties, carrying messages, and being aware of the concerns of unit leaders. In southwestern Virginia he reorganized his command and instilled a sense of discipline previously lacking among his 2,400 troops. And with his three brigade commanders, he managed to prepare a largely untested division to face the reality of enemy fire at Chickamauga. As in civilian life, his caring personality, sense of humor, and ability to command the respect of others made him popular among his men–a fact that in large measure contributed to his success at the head of his forces at Stones River and Chickamauga and in southwestern Virginia.

Despite his record of accomplishment in the army as an administrator, organizer, and thoughtful officer, Preston was best remembered by contemporaries for his inspiring–even daring–feats of valor under fire. Like hosts of leaders on both sides, the Kentucky general employed exhibitions of courage to reassure and animate his troops. A friend, General Basil Duke, considered him "one of the boldest men in the army" and faulted him for "being almost reckless in exposing himself to danger." Such conduct by officers was "unquestionably a powerful factor in motivating men to follow them." In the words of one Civil War historian, such acts served as a "direct transfusion of courage from a commander to his men." At Stones River Preston's seizing the regimental flag and urging his wavering forces forward brought both success to his troops and acclaim from officers and enlisted men. His gallantry at Chickamauga's Snodgrass Hill helped lead his troops to victory and won praise not only from the military, but in the press in the South and abroad. The element of luck helped Preston survive such risky–and viewed with hindsight, perhaps rash–feats. Such acts brought the Louisville Confederate renown as a general, as in the case of innumerable war heroes since time immemorial.[89]

Three months after Chickamauga, in January 1864, President Davis named Preston minister to Mexico. This assignment took the Kentucky brigadier to Bermuda, Havana, Halifax, London, and Paris, venues that offered startling contrasts with his life as an officer at war.

Chapter VII: Minister to Mexico

❧

Preston left the battlefield in 1864 to accept one of the most perplexing diplomatic assignments ever undertaken by an American. On 7 January President Jefferson Davis named him envoy extraordinary and minister plenipotentiary to the court of Emperor Maximilian in Mexico. As in Preston's earlier ministry to Spain, circumstances beyond his control doomed this mission to failure.

By the third year of the war the Confederacy had been unsuccessful in attaining its most cherished diplomatic goal: foreign recognition of southern independence. The prosouthern views of French Emperor Napoleon III were known, and his minister in Washington, the Count Edouard Henri Mercier, urged him in March 1862 to establish relations with the Confederacy.[1] President Jefferson Davis's cabinet was particularly disappointed when the governments of Queen Victoria and Napoleon III acquiesced to the Union blockade of their ports. The Confederacy's envoy to Paris, John Slidell, and other southern representatives who spoke with the emperor continued in 1863 to send reports on France's forthcoming recognition. The French minister in Washington reported in 1864 that Lincoln's government was "constantly and very seriously worried about recognition of the South by the Emperor." In London Lord Palmerston, the prime minister, asserted that a northern victory was "improbable," and he also allowed Confederate representatives to believe that British support might be imminent.[2]

The South was confident that the textile industries in Britain and France would require these cotton-hungry powers to accept the Richmond regime. But the Confederacy's international position was not as strong as the government had assumed, and "King Cotton diplomacy" would prove an illusion. Several other factors were important to the two European allies. From the United States Britain purchased large quantities of grain, a necessity that rivaled cotton in the government's calculations.[3] Slavery also "crippled Confederate diplomacy from the start," one historian has observed, but the Richmond cabinet was not willing to recognize this. In Britain and France antislavery societies espoused the northern cause and greeted Lincoln's Emancipation Proclamation with enthusiasm.[4] In France republican enemies of the Second Empire equated a Union victory with the triumph of liberalism, and in Britain, even though many businessmen and aristocrats favored the South, popular suffrage gave pro-Union laborers a voice in determining foreign policy.[5] This was a fact that President Davis and his advisors did not apparently consider. Another factor was a pragmatic one. Neither power wanted to ally with a loser, so both London and Paris followed the battlefield results. Union victories at Gettysburg and Vicksburg in July 1863 discouraged each nation from exchanging diplomats.[6] Despite southern wishes, neither European power in the final analysis would choose to challenge the North until the South's independence seemed probable, by which time international recognition would be relatively unimportant to the Confederacy.

At the outbreak of the war southern agents in Mexico encountered a liberal government sympathetic to the North. President Benito Juárez, an outspoken republican and opponent of slavery, had just won in 1860 a three-year civil war against conservative forces. Despite the obvious antisouthern prejudices of Mexican politicians, Colonel John T. Pickett, a former United States consul in Veracruz and a Confederate Kentuckian, wrote his friend John Forsyth, another southern partisan and a former minister to Mexico, urging the Richmond government to send a secret representative to Mexico City. Forsyth in turn convinced President Jefferson Davis to name Pickett for this assignment.[7]

The Confederacy believed Mexico would realize commercial advantages from a prosouthern or at least a truly neutral foreign policy. For these reasons, many in the North concluded that Juárez's government would establish relations with Richmond, and some northern newspapers in 1861 spoke of "the probable recognition of the Southern Confederacy by the government of Mexico." Consistent with Richmond's illusory belief that nations owed recognition to the South, Pickett's diplomatic instructions reminded him that "it is not the wish of this Government to ask for formal recognition," but should Mexico request it, the Kentuckian should comply.[8]

Pickett proved a poor choice to overcome Mexican hostility toward the South. His racist views of Latins as inferior and "not overscrupulous" were reflected in the haughty attitude he displayed in the Aztec capital. The Lincoln government took advantage of the Mexicans' animosity toward the slaveholders for favoring Texas independence and the Mexican War by appointing Thomas Corwin as minister to the Spanish-American republic. A Kentucky native who had served as governor of Ohio as well as a congressman and senator from that state, Corwin opposed the United States invasion of its southern neighbor in 1846 and had developed a close relationship with Juárez. The Union envoy believed his mission was "to prevent the Southern Confederacy from obtaining any recognition," and promised Juárez's hard-pressed administration an American loan of eleven million dollars.[9] Although these funds were never appropriated in Washington, the Mexican regime granted United States troops in California permission to travel through the northwestern states of the country en route to Arizona. Juárez's friendship with the North convinced Pickett that southern troops should invade northern Mexico and occupy Monterrey, and he wrote Richmond urging the undertaking.[10] Unfortunately for the Confederate Kentuckian, his correspondence was sent through the Mexican mail, and under Juárez's orders his letters were detained at the border. Copies were returned to Mexico City.

After only four months in the capital, Pickett decided in October that Mexico had cast its lot with the North, and he made plans to leave the country. The tall, athletic Kentuckian was a man of "ardent nature." Before returning to Richmond, he purposely provoked a fight with John A. Bennett, an outspoken northern sympathizer. Pickett was placed under arrest. He unsuccessfully demanded a presidential pardon from Juárez–an act that would have recognized his official status and thereby the Confederate government as well. In vain Pickett also sought asylum in the French and Prussian legations. On 15 December, the Mexican administration finally allowed the contentious Kentuckian to depart for Richmond.[11] President Davis, angry at Pickett's undiplomatic conduct, rejected his requests for an interview.

In northeastern Mexico the Confederacy was well represented by José A. Quintero, a Cuban who had settled in Texas. The Richmond government made him its "confidential agent" in Monterrey, where Governor Santiago Vidaurri ruled the states of Nuevo Leon and Coahuila and exercised effective control over the neighboring coastal state of Tamaulipas. A political rival of Juárez, the governor jealously guarded his independence from Mexico City and was known as the "Lord of the North." Vidaurri earlier had contemplated the creation of an independent Republic of Sierra Madre in northern Mexico with himself as president. In 1859 while an exile in Austin, Texas, the Mexican politico became a friend of Quintero. Soon after the Confederate agent arrived in Monterrey, Vidaurri asked the South to annex his state. Realizing that this would involve his nation in a war with Mexico, President Davis declared that such a union "would be imprudent and impolitic in the interests of both parties." Nevertheless, Quintero and Vidaurri reached agreements allowing southern cotton and tobacco to enter Tamaulipas en route to Europe, providing the governor with customs revenues. This Mexican ally also sold the Confederacy blankets, small arms, gunpowder, lead, copper, sugar, and flour.[12]

Discouraged by its lack of success in international affairs, the Confederate state department in late 1863 seized on unexpected events in Mexico that it hoped would bring foreign recognition–and perhaps even entice the French to support the South. In 1861 President Juárez had suspended interest payments on foreign debts.[13] The British, French, and Spanish governments reciprocated by sending a joint expeditionary force to Veracruz in a vain attempt to extract reparations. Early in 1862 French troops, without the support of their European allies, marched toward Mexico City. Despite fierce opposition and even the defeat of the Gallic hosts at Puebla on 5 May, the Juaristas abandoned their capital to Napoleon III's army of thirty thousand and carried on a guerrilla struggle instead.

The French emperor underestimated Mexican opposition to European intervention and stubbornly pursued plans that led to more involvement. This would increase his opposition at home and five years later end in a fiasco abroad. The defeat of France's Mexican adventure was the first major reversal Napoleon III experienced, and the *affaire* is considered by some historians as "the worst decision of his career."[14] But conservative Mexicans in 1862 welcomed European intervention and established a regency headed by General Juan Nepomuk Almonte under the French aegis.

Napoleon III realized that the American Civil War offered him an opportunity to implant a monarchy in Mexico without threat of effective United States opposition. This so-called "Grande Pensée de l'Empereur" was more than an attempt at national aggrandizement by the nephew of Napoleon I. Hopes of economic gain also motivated French investors with substantial claims against Mexico. The Parisian banking house of Jean-Baptiste Jecker had invested fifteen million dollars in Mexican bonds, and Napoleon's half-brother, the Duke of Morny, was a partner in the firm.[15]

In addition to nationalism and profit, a cultural imperative encouraged Paris's New World adventure. The ruler of the Tuileries, under the influence of his Spanish wife Eugénie, believed that the French people had a mission to come to the rescue of their fellow Latins in Mexico. Otherwise, Napoleon surmised, the Spanish-American nation inevitably would be conquered by its much stronger Anglo-Saxon neighbor and lose its Latin culture and Roman Catholic faith.[16]

To help insure Austrian friendship, Napoleon III in 1863 proposed the Hapsburg Archduke Ferdinand Maximilian as emperor of Mexico and promised to support his regime with French troops. The Mexican regency in July 1863 brought together an "Assembly of Notables" that offered the crown to the Austrian prince. Maximilian's wife Charlotte, the daughter of King Leopold I of Belgium, believed her husband was unable to display his true leadership talents in Trieste as governor-general of Lombardo-Venetia.[17] She urged him to accept the imperial throne, and Maximilian agreed.

From Mexico and Europe reports reached Richmond that Maximilian wished to recognize the Confederacy and wanted an official southern agent sent to Mexico City. On 2 November 1863, A. Vigenau, General Almonte's emissary, arrived in Monterrey to seek Governor Vidaurri's support for the new monarchy. Vigenau saw Quintero who reported that "General Almonte had suggested to Emperor Napoleon the propriety of recognizing our independence. Mexico will do so immediately upon the arrival of Emperor Maximilian. . . . General Almonte has been anxiously awaiting for the Government of the Confederate States to send a commissioner to Mexico." Two days later Quintero wrote Almonte, "The hope is fondly cherished by our people that before long a treaty of alliance and perpetual amity containing reciprocal advantages will be made between the subjects of the two nations." The regent replied that he would like the Confederate agent to keep in close touch with him.[18]

From Europe the Confederacy received word that the archduke

Courtesy Special Collections, University of Kentucky

Maxmilian I, Emperor of Mexico, from Wiliam Preston's album.

favored the Confederacy and hoped for a Union defeat. The Austrian prince's father-in-law, King Leopold of Belgium, in 1862 had reminded Napoleon III "how important the recognition of the South" would be for a Mexican empire. "The most serious difficulty" to his regime, Maximilian wrote Napoleon III in the summer of 1863, would be the United States, "an implacable enemy," hostile to monarchy, and a threat to Mexico's borders. Confirming these views, Lincoln's consul in Trieste, Richard Hildreth, informed the archduke in September that he was invited to become emperor not "by the Mexican people, but in fact by the French invaders." "The United States will never tolerate for a day a monarchical government, or any government supported by any European power in Mexico," Hildreth warned, ominously predicting that "whoever aspires to the throne of Mexico will, should he go hither, be exceedingly lucky to escape with his life."[19]

The archduke wanted the South to believe he would establish relations. Captain Matthew F. Maury, a Rebel naval agent in London, wrote Maximilian that Richmond supported his empire. In October 1863 the Austrian replied in English that the Confederacy was "a country which so many ties of conformity of pursuit and interest will unite to Mexico." Mr. John De Havilland, a friend of Jefferson Davis and former resident of Washington, had an interview with Maximilian in November at his Miramar Palace in Trieste. The archduke told him that his government intended to recognize the Confederacy when he reached Mexico City. Another southerner and a former United States minister to Turkey, General James Williams, corresponded with the Hapsburg prince. His advisor, the Baron de Pont, wrote to Williams in December that the Mexican empire was "a natural friend of your country" and, concerning Maximilian, told him "not to fail to acquaint President Davis confidentially of his support towards the South." At Trieste Williams met with the Austrian who told him of his determination to recognize southern independence.[20]

Despite such assurances, the nascent empire had no intention in 1863 of establishing relations with the South. When rumors in September had it that Mexico and the Confederacy were about to sign an alliance, Maximilian's agent in Paris, F. de Arrangoiz, sent the Paris government a letter written in code that this was unfounded, and he remarked that such a step would be contrary to Napoleon's wishes.[21]

Reacting to optimistic reports from Mexico and Europe, the Confederacy on 5 January decided to send a minister to Maximilian's court. President Davis placed William Preston's nomination as envoy extraordinary and minister plenipotentiary to Mexico before the Senate meeting in executive session on 6 January 1864. The chamber approved his appointment, and on the following day Secretary of State Judah P. Benjamin sent Preston his official instructions.[22] The Kentucky brigadier was a logical choice for this mission. In addition to his diplomatic experience in Spain under President Buchanan, Preston knew General Almonte, Mexico's envoy to the Spanish court, who in 1864 was Maximilian's chief advisor.[23] The Kentuckian also had been presented to Napoleon III at the Tuileries in 1859 en route to Spain, and the support of the emperor of the French was crucial to Mexican recognition. The Richmond government named Captain Walker Fearn of Alabama secretary of the new legation and appointed Captain Robert T. Ford, Preston's aide at Abingdon, to the mission, along with Major Charles J. Helm and an army private.

Preston's unexpected appointment forced the general to put several personal matters in order. William Preston Johnston was entrusted with arranging and storing his uncle's papers and was instructed "to keep my things for me or give any thing you choose to my servants, etc." Sam Giles did not accompany his master abroad and was given "a right to have his own time til I return and . . . to return to Kentucky if he prefers it." Giles was afraid to cross the battle lines, so he remained with Preston's nephew in Richmond. Another slave, Watson, was to stay in Virginia. He was promised freedom in the event of Preston's death and given "a paper to that effect." Johnston received $650 for their care. The diplomat-general also gave away his three horses: a sorrel named Shiloh, the bay Chickamauga, and a gray steed, Nelson–General Albert Sidney Johnston's mount–went to Johnston's son.[24]

The Kentuckian was to travel to Mexico, see General Almonte to arrange an official reception by the emperor, and then await Maximilian's arrival. Secretary of State Benjamin stated that "there seems . . . no good reason to apprehend any hesitation on the part of the Emperor in receiving you as the accredited Minister of the Confederacy," and he observed, "Recognition is implied by the public reception of Diplomatic Envoys." In the unlikely event that Washington would acquiesce to Mexican recognition of the South, Preston was to propose the establishment of free trade with Mexico, with each granting the other most-favored-nation status. This would give the Confederacy open access to Mexican gulf and Pacific ports. In the more probable case that the United States would oppose Maximilian's recognition of the South, the Kentuckian was to offer Mexico a ten-year treaty of alliance and win the right of passage for Confederate commerce to the Pacific via the northern states of Sonora and Chihuahua. Preston also was instructed to impress on the French minister in Mexico, the Marquis de Montholon, the benefits his nation would enjoy by signing an alliance with the South.[25]

Benjamin was familiar with politics and economics in both Mexico and France. While a senator from Louisiana in the 1850s, he successfully convinced politicians influential in Napoleon III's government to invest funds in the Louisiana-Tehuantepec Company to build a railroad across the Mexican isthmus. Despite a concession from the Juárez administration to construct this line, the firm by 1860 found itself bankrupt.[26] Given the disappointments he already had suffered in Franco-Mexican affairs, the secretary instructed Preston on how to act if Maximilian denied recognition to the Confederacy. "If any unnecessary delay is made or any doubt or difficulty imposed," Benjamin warned the Kentuckian, "you will return to the Confederacy and cause it to be understood that any future overtures . . . must proceed from Mexico." In January 1864, John Pickett also sought to advise Preston about Mexican matters, but the new envoy disapproved of Pickett's earlier conduct and avoided him.[27]

Napoleon III was aware of the South's expressions of friendship. In January 1863 the French agent in Richmond informed the minister of foreign affairs in Paris, Edouard Drouyn de Lhuys, that President Davis had praised the emperor for recognizing the "sufferings of our heroic people." In August the French diplomat reported that "the successes of our armies in Mexico are very well regarded in Richmond and in all of the South."[28]

Predictably, Washington opposed a foreign emperor in Mexico. Maximilian's regime guaranteed difficult relations between the United States and the governments in both Mexico City and Paris. A delighted South argued that "the future of the Mexican Empire is inextricably bound up with the safety and independence of the Confederacy." Certainly Napoleon III was aware of American hostility. The House of Representatives passed a unanimous resolution against recognizing Maximilian, and the northern press was outspoken in declaring the Mexican empire an affront to the Monroe Doctrine. The Lincoln administration informed the French envoy in Washington that no representative of Maximilian would be received. Paris also learned that "the hardly reassuring noises about the nature of relations between France and the United States" had even upset the New York stock market.[29] Throughout Maximilian's four years in Mexico, the emperor never gained complete control of the nation, and Washington continued to recognize Juárez's opposition government.

To avoid problems with France and Mexico while the United States was at war, Secretary of State William H. Seward adroitly allayed French fears that the Lincoln administration would react militarily against Maximilian's regime or would sever diplomatic relations with Paris. The American secretary assured French agents in Washington that the United States was particularly "proud" of maintaining good relations with Europe, especially with Napoleon III, and that every effort would be made to continue this happy condition. Seward made no formal protest to the emperor about the French invasion, but he warned Paris that the American public opposed their intervention. At the same time the secretary assured Juárez's minister in Washington, Matías Romero, that United States policy was dictated by "its major interests and that recognition of Maximilian was diametrically opposed to them."[30] Seward's success in placating France and his efforts to keep Napoleon III and Maximilian from exchanging diplomats with the Confederacy, while continuing to recognize Juárez's Mexican regime, have won praise from generations of historians in the United States and abroad.[31] Northern diplomats in Paris and Mexico City also went out of their way to assure Drouyn de Lhuys and Maximilian's secretary of state, Fernando Ramírez, that Seward would not permit hostile public opinion to alter the United States' correct relations with their governments.[32] This cautious northern policy kept Mexico and France from moving toward the Confederacy, while carefully denying recognition to Maximilian.

In February 1864 Preston's appointment appeared in the press, and Seward referred to his mission as a "new intrigue" by the South. The secretary of state told Matías Romero that the Confederacy's belief in recognition by the new emperor "probably had been suggested by the French Government." However, Seward maintained that Maximilian would not receive Preston. Unconvinced, Romero feared that such "an alliance is rather probable between the traitors [Maximilian's government] and the Confederates."[33]

The Mexican envoy carried on a successful campaign against Maximilian, lobbying congressmen and gaining public support. In March 1864 a "Great Banquet" was given in honor of Romero at Delmonico's Restaurant in New York. Poet William Cullen Bryant, former governor and senator Hamilton Fish, and historian George Bancroft were among the diners who enjoyed the ten-course feast. That autumn the Mexican diplomat visited General Ulysses S. Grant at his headquarters, and the commander assured him that he would be happy to serve Juárez's government "in the glorious enterprise of defending Mexican independence."[34]

The French minister in Washington led Napoleon to believe that the United States would alter its opposition toward Maximilian's government. While Seward had not recognized the Austrian prince as the ruler of Mexico, the secretary of state pointedly reminded the French envoy that neither had the United States officially protested the archduke's acceptance of the throne. The Gallic diplomat believed that much of Washington's hostility toward Maximilian was a transitory matter of electoral politics. Referring to the Monroe Doctrine, the Frenchman reported to Paris in January 1864 that "it would be very dangerous for a presidential candidate to repudiate it too openly." Encouraged by his envoy in Washington, Napoleon III in 1864 hoped that United States recognition of the Maximilian regime would be forthcoming after the autumn presidential election, reinforcing the emperor's determination not to make any overtures toward the South. For Napoleon Washington's acceptance of Maximilian would be of greater value to both emperors than any treaty with the Confederacy.[35]

Another reason for France's reluctance to recognize the South was British opposition. The French emperor tried to convince Rebel agents that his sympathies rested with their cause, but he argued that his nation could only act toward the American war in concert with the British.[36] "France will not move in the American question," a Confederate agent in Europe assured Benjamin in 1862, "unless England leads the way." John Slidell soon realized that "Napoleon's friendly advances were always forestalled of fruition by British reluctance to cooperate." Despite the influence of British businessmen and politicians who favored southern recognition, the cabinet opposed this.[37] Nevertheless, southern sympathizers in Britain did their part. In April 1862 two members of Parliament, William S. Lindsay and John A. Roebuck, met twice with Napoleon, who told them that he would follow Britain's lead, and in June they unsuccessfully sponsored a bill to recognize the Confederacy.[38]

Reports that London would exchange diplomats with Richmond continued to circulate in the autumn of 1863. In September Maximilian's agent, Fernando de Arrangoiz, sent a letter in code from London that "the English government seems ready to recognize the Confederate States," and the pleased archduke so informed Napoleon. The Austrian added that southern independence was "a true necessity for the Mexican Empire." "I am very happy about what you said concerning the intentions of the English government concerning the Confederate States," Napoleon replied, but more realistic than the archduke, the emperor of the French added, "I admit that I still doubt their resolution."[39]

By mid-1863 Britain's continuing refusal to exchange ministers enraged Secretary Benjamin, and he decided London would not change its policy. He expelled the British consuls from the South and decided to try to convince France unilaterally to grant recognition. For Benjamin, William Preston's mission was more than an attempt to establish relations with Maximilian. The secretary hoped that a Confederate-Mexican alliance would lead Napoleon to exchange envoys.[40]

The French emperor continued to assure Confederate partisans that he sympathized with their cause, and he expressed his disappointment with Britain's refusal to join him in recognizing the Richmond government. However, a disillusioned Secretary Benjamin concluded on 23 June 1864 that "there has been bad faith and deception in the course pursued by the Emperor." France's reluctance to establish relations with the South would determine Maximilian's refusal to receive a Confederate minister.[41]

Diplomatic responsibilities took Preston to the Bahamas, Cuba, Bermuda, England, France, and Canada in 1864, but not to Mexico. In mid-January the Kentuckian and Captain Fearn, the legation's secretary, left Wilmington, North Carolina, and successfully ran the Union blockade. In Nassau they boarded another vessel bound for Havana, arriving there 7 February. The other three members of the Mexican mission reached Cuba later. When Preston discovered that Maximilian's arrival in Mexico had been postponed until at least April, he decided to remain in Havana until the new emperor reached Mexico City. "I do not think it wise for me as Envoy of the Confederate States to manifest too much solicitude as to recognition to Mexico," the Kentuckian wrote Benjamin in February. "Therefore, it seems to me that it is far better to wait here," a decision that pleased the secretary.[42] Preston's reception by the regent, General Almonte, would not fulfill the Confederacy's goal, recognition of southern independence.

Preston expected to remain only a few weeks in Cuba, but continued delays in the emperor's schedule and diplomatic uncertainties forced the envoy to stay on the island for four months. He lived in a boarding house run by an American woman, Eliza Hammond. Playing chess and reading filled Preston's leisure hours, and on several occasions he visited "La Luisa," the estate of his wealthy planter friend, Adolfo Molinero. Despite such diversions, "waiting the slow events abroad" and "the yellow fever around me" had turned the Kentuckian's Havana stay into a trial.[43]

Before departing for Mexico, Maximilian had made a triumphal progress through Europe. He paid official visits to the queens of Spain and Great Britain. In Paris Maximilian was received by his benefactor with a reception usually reserved for crowned heads. The Mexican flag flew above the Tuileries when Napoleon III descended the staircase of honor to welcome the blond Hapsburg and his enthusiastic wife. At opera and theater performances and at gala dinners, receptions, and balls, the capital's elite and the diplomatic corps turned out. Two foreign agents were conspicuously absent. The American minister, William L. Dayton, following instructions from Washington, declined invitations to greet the Austrian. Nor did the Rebel envoy John Slidell meet the archduke. The southerner's request for an audience was not granted.[44] Slidell reasoned that the Austrian had avoided him in order not to offend the Lincoln administration and claimed that the archduke still wished to recognize the South. Despite Maximilian's refusal to see him, the southern diplomat confidently informed Preston that the new emperor considered French recognition of the Confederacy so important that he made it "almost a condition precedent to his definite acceptance of the throne."[45] Before departing for Veracruz, the Austrian monarch received the blessing of Pope Pius IX at the Vatican.

Preston optimistically concluded in March that Maximilian would receive him "at the earliest moment he can obtain the acquiescence of Louis Napoleon." The Kentuckian promised not to "proceed to Mexico until a favorable moment occurs, or until I am informed that the Emperor will be in a condition to act promptly in regard to the subject of my mission." In his correspondence in April, May, and June with Secretary Benjamin, President Davis, John Slidell in Paris, and the French envoy to Mexico, the Marquis de Montholon, Preston stated that he would not go to the Aztec capital, for Maximilian had not yet expressed an interest in seeing him.[46]

By early June, Preston was wondering if predictions that the emperor would recognize the South were "accurate, or if there were not a misapprehension, as to the inclinations of Maximilian." Nevertheless, the envoy believed that the Austrian would realize that relations with the South were "essential to the safety and stability of Mexico." In mid-June Maximilian made a triumphal entrance into the capital, heralded by church bells, artillery salvos, and shouts of "Viva!" Preston sent Captain Ford to Mexico City to inquire of Montholon and Almonte if the emperor would set a date for an official audience. From Richmond Secretary Benjamin wrote Preston, "We await with lively interest the account of your proceedings."[47]

From Mexico Montholon informed Paris that Preston had contacted the new emperor. The French envoy reported that Maximilian wanted to "observe the strictest neutrality" in the Civil War and "did not think the moment had come to tell Mr. Preston to present himself." Montholon said that he was going to tell the emperor that this was the correct policy. A confidential report from Captain A. M. Toutant Beauregard, a southern agent in Mexico, reached Preston in late June, warning him not to try to see the new emperor at that time.[48]

Unable to carry out his assignment from Havana and finding the Spanish captain-general hostile to his presence, Preston decided in June to sail for Europe to consult with the Confederate agents in London and Paris. "The inference to be drawn from my absence, and the probable indifference of the Confederacy to send a minister to Mexico," he reasoned, "will do no harm." Preston was convinced that United States pressure on the French emperor was keeping Maximilian against his will from granting recognition. The Kentuckian wrote President Davis in late June that General Robert E. Lee's forthcoming victory in Virginia over General Ulysses S. Grant "will decide everything" and bring the victorious South immediate international acceptance. Preston planned to return to Cuba in September, the earliest date he might expect replies from Ford, Montholon, and Almonte. On 29 June the Kentuckian sailed on a British steamer for Southampton, leaving Captain Fearn, Major Helm, and the private attached to the mission in Havana. Subsequent reports from Ford in Mexico City confirmed the envoy's reluctance to approach the emperor.[49]

Preston was in Europe from 22 July to 25 August, visiting London and Paris. James Mason, the Confederate envoy to Britain, and Slidell assured him that Maximilian sincerely sought to recognize the Confederacy. From the British capital Preston wrote Ford in August to make yet another attempt to arrange an official reception and to inform the Mexicans that if Maximilian would not receive him "no further overture will be made by the Government to that of the Emperor and that any future intercourse between the two nations must be inaugurated by a mission from Mexico to the Confederacy." The Kentuckian hoped "to determine definitively" Maximilian's stand.[50]

In Paris the Kentucky diplomat met with José Manuel Hidalgo y Esnaurrizar, Maximilian's minister to France, and in a conversation in French the Mexican assured his guest of his "sympathy for the

Confederacy." However, Hidalgo stated that recognition of the South would be tantamount to war with the United States, an assertion Preston strongly refuted. So frank and argumentative was their interview that the Mexican later told another Confederate agent that he considered their "conversation menacing, though violating no personal courtesy." Certainly Benjamin would have considered Preston's fervid defense of Confederate recognition a violation of his instructions. While in France the Kentuckian also visited his niece Henrietta, William Preston Johnston's sister. A Roman Catholic convert, she was living in a convent in Orleans, although she was not a nun.[51]

After his discussion in Paris with Señor Hidalgo, Preston was more aware than ever that Napoleon III held the key to Mexican recognition of the Confederacy. "The only impediments are at Paris," he wrote Benjamin in August. "Every effort should be directed to remove or obviate these obstacles, instead of essaying it at Mexico where none exist except the inhibition of the Emperor of France."[52]

In England the Kentuckian found time for relaxation while a guest at Shepperton Manor, the Middlesex country home of William Lindsay. This Tory merchant of "great wealth and influence" owned one of the largest shipping concerns in the world. An advocate of free trade, Lindsay was a leader of southern sympathizers in Parliament. The long weekend at Shepperton offered the American the most pleasant days he had enjoyed during four years of war, causing him to remark, "The contrast is great to the wild scenes through which I have been so recently passing."[53] In late August he left Liverpool and sailed for Canada.

Like her husband, Mrs. Preston and her children journeyed abroad in 1864. That year in Lexington the family suffered from the increasingly hostile attitude of Union officials in Kentucky toward southern partisans, as the bitter war entered its fourth year. The Federal commander, General Stephen G. Burbridge, decided in May to crush local opposition. He promised to execute four Confederate prisoners for each Unionist killed by guerrillas and tried to force the wives of southern officers from the state. Other acts had engendered opposition. Lincoln's Emancipation Proclamation in September 1862 did not free the slaves in Kentucky, but many Unionists were slaveholders and opposed the measure. Many more Kentuckians objected to the enlistment of blackss, both freedmen and slaves, in the United States army. This was begun in February 1864, and over twenty thousand Kentucky African Americans were signed up by the end of the war. "You should see the wild confusion, in the domestic arrangements of Lex. caused by the enlisting of negroes," Polly wrote her father. "Mama has lost 7 or 8 and will doubtless lose more."[54]

Morgan's raid on Lexington in June 1864 lasted only a few hours, but it exacerbated tensions between the Union forces and southern sympathizers. "Life is most unpleasant–After John Morgan's raid, searched, insulted, and hated, and I dread things growing much worse instead of better," Margaret lamented to her husband. That summer Lincoln gave military courts jurisdiction over "guerrilla-marauders," and in July martial law was declared in Kentucky. General Burbridge's "General Orders No. 59" declared that any southern sympathizers within five miles of a guerrilla "outrage" would be subject to arrest and banishment.[55]

Forewarned that she would be ordered to leave Kentucky and sent into Confederate territory, Margaret and three children left in early July 1864 for Canada via New York City. Poogie was ill and remained in Lexington with sisters Mary and Caroline who looked after her. Soon these daughters also traveled to Canada. Margaret and four of the girls lived together in Montreal, while Poogie was a boarding student at the Sacré Coeur Convent School in Sault au Recollet near Montreal. Wick attended a school in nearby Lennoxville, but his mother missed her "beautiful boy" and made him often visit the family in Montreal. President Davis's daughter Margaret and son Jefferson Jr. were classmates of the Preston children in Canada.[56]

All seven Prestons adjusted well to life in exile. A family friend reported, "Mag Preston is flourishing at Montreal with Lordlings and generals in her train." Aunt Susan visited them and became "absorbed in the girls." Captain Robert Ford's wife Alice also had fled Kentucky to live in Montreal, and she reported to her cousin Rosa Johnston in Richmond, Virginia, that Wick is "an idol" with his mother, who fortunately "doesn't hesitate to acknowledge it."[57]

When Preston's ship reached Montreal, his wife and children and his sister Susan greeted him on 6 September 1864. He had not seen his family since the autumn of 1862, during the brief Confederate occupation of Lexington. While awaiting news from Mexico City and instructions from Richmond, the general remained in Montreal from September until mid-December. Since this visit "involved no delay prejudicial to the public service," Preston wrote Benjamin, "I trusted it would not be unreasonable if after having been separated from them by three years of constant service, if I should visit them for a few weeks on my return." William also took advantage of his Canadian visit to settle his accounts with his sister Susan for taking care of his interests and gave her the deed to a St. Louis property purchased in 1860. He still remained in her debt for $5,611.[58]

While Preston was in Europe, he was sharply criticized by Secretary of State Benjamin for violating diplomatic instructions. On receiving copies of Preston's letters to Almonte and Montholon, the Richmond diplomatic chief accused the Kentuckian of soliciting recognition from Maximilian. In his letter of 22 July, Benjamin pointedly reminded the envoy that President Davis likewise was disappointed with him. The administration insisted that international acceptance was a self-evident right due the South. Benjamin was particularly upset that Preston in his correspondence with Montholon sought "to lay before the Emperor the evidence of our right to recognition." Likewise, the secretary disapproved of the Kentuckian's efforts to convince Almonte that the Confederacy desires "only to be fairly heard by other nations as to the evidence upon which we rest our claims to independence." However, since "it seems out of our power to modify the situation as created by those letters," Benjamin authorized Preston to wait until September to see if Maximilian would agree to receive him.[59]

Not until Preston arrived in Canada in September did he receive Benjamin's critical letter of 22 July. The envoy then wrote the secretary of state and "regretted" that he had considered his actions a "violation of instructions." The Kentuckian countered that his correspondence with Montholon and Almonte was "private and confidential" and marked as such, rather than official in nature. Although Preston insisted that Benjamin had misconstrued the meaning of the missives, the Kentuckian wrote to Ford the same day that it was indeed "fortunate" that Benjamin's instructions countermanding Preston's letters "did not arrive in time" to stop Ford from attempting once more to arrange an audience with Maximilian.[60]

The Benjamin-Preston dispute highlighted two different points of view on how Confederate diplomacy should be carried out. The cautious approaches of President Davis and his New Orleans secretary came from their fear that the South would only compromise its inherent rights and the dignity of its cause by soliciting recognition abroad. By contrast, Preston believed that no logical opportunity should be discarded to gain Mexican recognition, so he sought to argue the Confederacy's case. The Kentuckian's letter to Montholon in Mexico City did elicit a long and valuable response. The French minister took the envoy's request for an official audience to Maximilian, who explained he had "a great desire" to receive Preston. Nevertheless, the emperor urged the Confederate to postpone his trip to Mexico because he was about to leave the capital on a tour of the restive cities in the north. The envoy informed Benjamin that Maximilian's schedule would force him into "the disagreeable necessity of eluding official intercourse with our government till his own troubles are removed."[61]

Preston was not alone among the Confederate agents abroad who were accused by the Richmond government of exceeding their instructions in their zeal to gain recognition. Two months after faulting the Kentuckian for disobeying his orders, Benjamin chastised his minister in London, James Mason, for proceeding "beyond what the state of the case would warrant" in his interview with the British prime minister. Likewise, Benjamin criticized Slidell for his "painful solicitations" to Napoleon III.[62]

With the advantage of hindsight, Benjamin's cautious diplomacy is easy to criticize. His unawareness of the South's real international position led him to the illusory belief that foreign powers would be forced to recognize the Confederacy, and like President Davis he overestimated the dependence of Britain and France on cotton. As the cautious diplomatic approaches the secretary advocated toward France and Mexico demonstrated, he underestimated the importance of foreign recognition and aid to the survival of the Confederacy.[63] A more audacious, pragmatic policy abroad, such as Preston pursued, might have offered the South a better chance of success in its international affairs.

But such "what-if" theories cannot overlook the difficulties under which southern diplomats labored. They were forced to represent a regime that upheld slavery and whose military suffered more defeats as the war progressed. Despite his defects, Benjamin's international experiences and outlook, as well as his fluency in French and Spanish, had prepared him like few other Confederates to handle foreign affairs. He remains one of the few southern diplomats who have won the praise of many historians.[64]

Although Preston believed Benjamin's criticism was intended to "terminate my mission," the Kentuckian would not admit defeat. On 10 October he wrote Ford in Mexico City, instructing him to make a final attempt, not "officially or semi-officially but only privately," to see if Maximilian would not agree to receive Preston. By early November Preston finally admitted that the "probabilities" were that the emperor would not establish relations.[65]

The envoy extraordinary remained in Canada for three months. Believing that there was little hope of Mexican recognition, Preston was "reluctant to go forward to Mexico or to Havana" until he had an answer from Mexico City concerning an audience with the emperor. In late November the ships in Nova Scotia began "shifting to Bermuda for the winter" before Preston received his reply from Ford. He was to meet the Kentuckian on the British island off North Carolina in the event that the emperor refused to receive him, so the diplomat sailed from Halifax on 13 December for Bermuda.[66]

In Mexico Ford had followed Preston's August instructions to seek an audience with the emperor, but he encountered no success. The Marquis de Montholon in late September promised the Confederate captain that Maximilian would give the South an answer on his return to Mexico City, following his tour of the provinces. The emperor returned to the capital on 29 October, but Ford received no word. The southern agent then informed the foreign ministry that he would leave Mexico on 10 November, unless he heard from Maximilian. Again, silence greeted Ford's efforts, and he departed Mexico City on 5 December for Havana. There the three other members of the legation joined him en route to Bermuda. They reached the British island on 27 December, ten days after the arrival of their chief from Nova Scotia. Their mission was now ended. The emperor had no intention of recognizing the Confederacy in late 1864. From Paris Hidalgo wrote to Maximilian on 30 December that Drouyn de Lhuys, the French foreign minister, had informed him that Mexico must do nothing that would upset the North.[67]

Preston left Canada in December 1864, but his wife and children remained there until the following October. By 1865 Carrie and Jessie were attending a convent school in Montreal, while the other siblings lived with their mother. In January William arranged for Sydney Beauclerk to return to England for his education, a decision Margaret seconded. "It was dreadful having him in the house with my

MRS. SUSAN P. HEPBURN.

Published in W. F. Meffert, History of Preston Lodge No. 281, F. and A. M., Held at Louisville, Kentucky, from January 19, 1854, up to January 19, 1904 *(Louisville, 1903).*

daughters after he grew up," she affirmed. On a visit to Boston in January, mother and son were searched and briefly placed under arrest by zealous officials, but a better fate awaited the daughters on their incursion into the United States. In February they were taken to New York City by Susan Hepburn on a shopping trip, but their mother criticized her sister-in-law for this expensive outing. Margaret complained to Wick, "I wish your Aunt Susan would get another husband and mind her own affairs and let me and mine alone. It is improper her taking my daughters to spend money in New York when I am with so little money that I fear I cannot pay my board." Despite such worries, husband William saw to it that his wife was "able to draw money from her resources in Kentucky to support herself and my family in Canada."[68]

The Confederate envoy was unable to return to Richmond from Bermuda as he had planned. By early 1865 few blockade-runners were able to reach ports in the Carolinas. On the night of 19 January 1865, trying to enter Wilmington, North Carolina, Preston's ship was almost captured by Union gunboats. After another two weeks in Hamilton, Bermuda, the Kentuckian tried unsuccessfully to reach Charleston, South Carolina, but his vessel was unable to pass through the Yankee flotilla and proceeded to Nassau in the Bahamas. In February he sailed to Havana, where he met Camille Armand Jules Marie, Prince Polignac. The romantic Frenchman was returning to France, after commanding a Confederate division in Texas. Louisiana governor Henry Allen was sending him to Paris to lobby for French recognition, and he was received by Napoleon III just before the end of the war. On 1 April the Kentuckian and his secretary, Captain Fearn, sailed from Cuba to Matamoros, Mexico, on the Rio Grande River. On the Texas side were Union troops, so they traveled upriver and then crossed into the Confederacy where they met twenty southern cavalrymen, who toasted their arrival with cheers and a bottle of rum.[69]

In Texas the Kentuckian joined General Kirby Smith's troops defending the Trans-Mississippi Department. After hearing of Lee's surrender to Grant at Appomattox on 9 April, the southwestern Confederates debated what course to follow. En route from the Mexican border to the commander's headquarters in Shreveport, the southern diplomat visited General John B. Magruder in Houston, where the two "talked very freely" and agreed that the isolated Trans-Mississippi forces should continue to fight. Magruder implored the Kentuckian to convey his opinion to Kirby Smith and wrote the commander, "I am happy to have had my own views confirmed by his [Preston's] right and enlightened judgment." On 23 April Kirby Smith announced Lee's surrender and urged his troops to continue their struggle.[70]

General Kirby Smith was happy to add Preston to his army. Both had fought together during the Kentucky and Tennessee campaigns of 1862 and were good friends. Preston again met other trusted Confederates in Texas. General Simon Bolivar Buckner had been transferred to the Trans-Mississippi Department the previous year and was serving as Kirby Smith's chief of staff. The southwestern commander promoted the Kentucky diplomat and brigadier general to major general. But by this date there was no longer a Confederate government in distant Richmond to approve–or disapprove as President Davis had done in October 1863–his promotion to major general.

Preston was placed in charge of the Polignac Division. Prince

Polignac had served the Confederacy as a general until 1865. The little Frenchman was affectionately called "Polecat" by his troops who could not pronounce his name. His bravery against Union gunboats on the Washita River brought him fame, and in April 1864 his forces played a major role in the southern victory at Mansfield, Texas.[71]

When Preston inherited Polignac's Division, the war was almost over. Despite Kirby Smith's decision to continue fighting, his soldiers began to leave their units for their homes in Texas, Louisiana, and Arkansas, and some fled into Mexico. On 8 May news arrived that General Joseph Johnston in North Carolina had taken the last Confederate army in the east out of the war on 26 April. Some of Kirby Smith's officers still opposed surrender, including Preston who did all in his power "to make head for a campaign."[72] But on 14 May four hundred soldiers at the Galveston garrison mutinied. Further resistance was impossible. Accompanied by Generals Sterling Price and Joseph Brent, Buckner met Union General Edward R. S. Canby on 26 May and agreed to surrender terms, subject to Kirby Smith's approval. On 2 June aboard the Federal steamer *Fort Jackson* at Galveston, the gaunt, balding Confederate commander signed the military convention negotiated a week earlier. The last Confederate army had laid down its arms. The Civil War was over. Meanwhile, following Kirby Smith's instructions, Preston had tried to make arrangements with the semiautonomous officials in northern Mexico to permit passage through their territories of what was dubbed "the grand emigration expedition."[73]

Throughout the war, Preston was confident that the Confederacy would emerge from the conflict an independent nation. The Kentuckian was aware in 1862 and 1863 of the Union's advantage in troops and supplies, but he believed that the southern forces in both the west and Virginia would defeat their adversaries. While attempting to carry out his diplomatic mission to Mexico, he remained optimistic and in June 1864 predicted for General Lee "a triumph for our arms so dazzling that all governments and monarchs will throw open their courts for our welcome." That summer the envoy engaged in more wishful thinking when he noted that "the west it is feared will break into revolution–Kentucky and Indiana are mutinous." Later in 1864 when a southern military victory appeared improbable, Preston believed that a stalemate on the battlefield would lead to a popular demand for peace in the North.[74]

Finally, after failing to reenter the Confederacy from Bermuda in early 1865, Preston abandoned hope of a Confederate victory. But he still expected the South to retain its independence. In a letter to his son in February, William stated that he was "very anxious" for peace and hoped for it based on "any terms that I did not consider idle or humiliating." Otherwise, the Kentuckian remarked, he "would prefer fighting on to the slightest dishonor"–clearly believing that the Confederacy would not surrender.[75]

Preston's return from Texas to Kentucky took six months and carried him through Mexico and the Caribbean to England and then to Canada. In the company of five generals and three governors, Preston undertook what he referred to as "our Mexican hegira." Preston left San Antonio, Texas, 17 June, on horseback and traveled with the other Confederates through a dusty landscape dotted with cacti and maguey plants. They reached Monterrey, Mexico, eleven days later. With "an old champagne hamper with wines and liquors and edibles," the group then "progressed in state" to San Luis Potosi, where Rebel agent Quintero served as their host. Next they departed for Mexico City, spending eight pleasant days there in late July.[76] The English minister, a Preston acquaintance from Madrid days, looked after them.

Following their trip from the capital down to the Gulf Coast, Preston and two Confederate officers sailed from Veracruz on 1 August for Havana. The Kentuckian then took passage to St. Thomas. Unable to find a steamer there for Halifax, he left for England. Former Secretary of State Judah P. Benjamin was a fellow passenger on this almost tragic voyage. Fifty miles out of port, the vessel caught fire at night and limped back into St. Thomas with the flames barely under control. On a second ship Preston and Benjamin arrived in Southampton on 1 September. The Kentuckian spent more than three weeks in England, staying first with his parliamentary friend William Lindsay in Middlesex and then visiting Stratford-upon-Avon and other sites in Warwickshire with his cousin, General John S. Preston of South Carolina. The Kentuckian also found time to see other Confederates in England, including Benjamin, who remained abroad until his death in 1884.

After a fortnight at sea, Preston debarked on 11 October at Quebec City where his family welcomed him. The Prestons spent three weeks together in Montreal. When friends wrote that "there was great danger of confiscation of Mrs. Preston's property from her long absence," Margaret and the children returned to Lexington, leaving William in Canada with his nephew William Preston Johnston and cousin John C. Breckinridge. But Preston detested his exile. "I am so unhappy here . . . my life is so intolerable," he complained.[77]

In early December 1865, William wrote his sister Susan that he was so eager to join his family that "there is scarcely any sacrifice, short of the abject surrender of all past feeling that I would not make." Susan resided in Washington in 1865 and was a good friend of Montgomery Blair. He was a distant relative and political protégé of Missouri Senator Thomas Hart Benton, the husband of Preston's cousin, Elizabeth Preston McDowell. Blair became postmaster general under Lincoln and was a strong supporter of President Andrew Johnson. Preston considered the president a good man and praised him for being "a firm opponent of the Know Nothing party even to the peril of his life." Johnson's moderate policies toward the defeated South met with the Kentucky Confederate's approval, while the opposing proposals of the Radical Republicans met with his scorn. "I believe the Radicals will attack the President soon and furiously," he predicted, "and that the South ought to stand by him like one man, irrespective of party." Preston urged Susan to express his "views to Mr. Blair, incidentally but very strongly" and to ask him to help prepare a parole for her brother. Both Susan Hepburn and Montgomery Blair saw James Speed, Preston's friend from Louisville and President Johnson's attorney general, who arranged for the general's return.[78]

By late 1865, Preston was resigned to the consequences of the Union victory. In addition to his support for Johnson's moderate policies toward the South, the Confederate Kentuckian also favored the abolition of slavery, "so as to leave no future and useless seeds of discord." No doubt hostile to Maximilian for not recognizing the Confederacy, Preston in December 1865 reaffirmed his earlier support of the Monroe Doctrine. "I am also strongly opposed to Empire in Mexico, and believe it must fail," he asserted, "even without being pushed over by the United States though I should like to see Maximilian toppled at a proper time, by the United States government."[79]

Preston left Canada on 15 December 1865 and traveled to Washington where James Speed approved his parole. In his first electoral contest, Preston in 1849 had defeated Speed, an antislavery Whig, to become a delegate to rewrite the state's constitution. Not all Unionists favored the general's return, and despite Speed's help the ex-Confederate encountered hostility. Several northern newspapers had labeled Preston a "traitor" who should not be allowed back in Kentucky. When crossing into the United States at St. Albans, Vermont, a customs agent recognized Preston as a Confederate general. He was laden with expensive purchases, and the official assessed a duty on a new wolf-skin traveling coat. Preston protested, demanding that he send notice of this imposed tax to the "Honorable James Speed, Attorney General, Washington City."[80]

The ex-Confederate "reported to Grant, who was very civil, and gave me a safeguard ag[ainst] all his Myrmidons, which was countersigned by Speed and I returned home declining to ask audience or pardon." The attorney general wrote to the district attorney in Louisville, telling him, "Do not have Col. Preston arrested or disturbed." Speed made a point of informing General John M. Palmer of this instruction. Palmer was military commander in Kentucky and an "ardent abolitionist," which made him unpopular throughout the state. Speed also arranged for William Preston Johnston's return to Kentucky that December "without fear of arrest."[81]

In December 1865, four years and three months after leaving Lexington to join the Confederacy, the Civil War finally had ended for William Preston. For the rest of his life Kentucky again would be his home.

Chapter VIII: After the War

❦

Back in Lexington in December 1865, William Preston resided there for the remaining twenty-two years of his life. He devoted his energies to managing Margaret's family home and her land in Fayette County, as well as helping his children and their spouses. After the war his relationship with his wife became strained, but outwardly both projected a harmonious front. The former general also dedicated himself to finances and to handling legal problems related to his real-estate interests. Politics still demanded much of his time. Preston served in the Kentucky legislature and played an active role in the state and national Democratic party. As expected of one enjoying such a prominent social status, he participated in a wide variety of civic activities.

Although Lexington became the family's home, Preston confessed in 1866 that "my inclinations are for Louisville as it is the place of my birth." However, his residence there was sold during the war, and he was financially unable to purchase another. "Fortune may turn her wheel," Preston speculated, "and give me once more a home" in Louisville, but this was not to be.[1]

In Lexington the Prestons lived at Wickliffe Place. This house on the northwest corner of Second and Jefferson Streets was constructed between 1818 and 1825 by Colonel John Todd, the father of Margaret's stepmother, Mary Owen Todd Russell. Originally called Glendower, the mansion was a rambling one-story Federal structure. In 1865 the building was surrounded by twenty-seven acres, bounded by Jefferson, Second, Third, and Georgetown Streets. Its front faced Second Street, and the middle third of the façade was a slightly projecting pavilion with two rectangular windows on each side of a large entrance door, covered by a small portico and approached by wide stone steps. On either side of this pavilion was a recessed, covered veranda that shaded three large windows. Like so many Lexington residences, the brick mansion was painted white. A typical Bluegrass limestone wall separated the front lawn from the street and a semicircular drive brought visitors to the front door. Although several fireplaces heated the large structure, Mrs. Preston often com-

C. Frank Dunn Collection, Kentucky Historical Society Special Collections
"Preston Place," William Preston's home in Lexington.

plained that the mansion was "frightfully cold and uncomfortable" in the winter. In summer two great elms on the front lawn cooled the house.[2]

In addition to Glendower, Colonel Todd owned Ellerslie, a two-story dwelling, surrounded by 1,750 acres, just outside of Lexington on the Richmond Pike. The house was built about 1787 by Levi Todd and was the birthplace of Robert S. Todd, Mary Todd Lincoln's father. Margaret Preston inherited this estate, as well as 3,000 acres around Mt. Sterling, Kentucky, from her father in 1859. In the summer of 1884 the Lexington Water Company acquired several hundred acres at Ellerslie. Today a reservoir and Mentelle Park are located on Colonel Todd's former property.

Colonel Todd gave Glendower to his only daughter, Mary Owen Todd Russell. When she was widowed, the family of her deceased husband contested her right to the mansion and other properties, but the court rejected their claim. Margaret and her siblings moved into Glendower after their father, Robert Wickliffe, wed the heiress, and the residence was renamed Wickliffe Place. Mary Owen Todd Wickliffe willed the Lexington house to Margaret Wickliffe Preston, her favorite stepdaughter.[3]

After returning to Lexington, Preston substantially altered

Wickliffe Place. "The house," he reported to his sister Susan Hepburn, "is comfortable, the outbuildings dilapidated, the grounds unenclosed and neglected." Preston set out to remedy this. In the 1870s he converted the rear of the residence into a conservatory and constructed two wings of two stories behind the building. Where they joined the original dwelling, he added two three-story towers, each with prominent pilasters, corbeled brickwork under the roof and windows, and widely overhanging roofs, supported by brackets and topped with pointed finials. The altered building created three sides of a rectangle, forming a courtyard with a large walnut tree in the middle. The transformations, especially the ornate, neo-Romanesque towers and the courtyard, changed the Federal structure into one resembling an Italian villa, a popular postwar style. Paths behind the house led to a formal garden, stables, a coach house, and a greenhouse. The residence came to be known as Preston Place and remained in the family until 1903. The landmark was razed in 1942.[4]

The interior of Preston Place reflected the ostentatious decor of the Victorian period. In the hall a dark red carpet led from the entryway to the back courtyard. Two sets of double doors on the right of the hallway gave access to parlors, each with black marble mantels and rosewood furniture. Family portraits adorned the walls. One parlor opened into the library. On the left side of the hall was the formal drawing room, with gilded furniture, landscape paintings, and an oil of the Madonna, given to Preston in 1847 for protecting a convent in Mexico City. Behind the drawing room were the formal and family dining rooms. The kitchen had a range that occupied one wall and an enormous brick oven.

Ellerslie also was in need of repair, and Preston began "working away with some prodigal negroes who have left the sty and trying to fix up the shattered place." He hired an overseer for the farm, but personally looked after its restoration and management. The first tasks included building new fencing, constructing barns, and purchasing livestock. Sam Giles, the childhood playmate whom he had manumitted, worked for him at Ellerslie. "Marse" Preston also had the help of another former slave, Charles Robinson, who was a minister. Often in the fields his old owner "swore like a trooper" and "laughed heartily." Once, told that Robinson would be preaching the next day, a contrite Preston joked, "'Well, then, sir, . . . I beg your pardon for swearing in your presence. I should not have done it if I had known.'"[5]

To make the farm profitable, Preston leased the mansion and parcels of land. Several former slaves lived on the property and worked "on the shares," Preston noted in 1869, "giving me one half the crop." By the 1880s six hundred acres were leased to Bernard J. Treacy for his Ashland Park Stock Farm. An artificial ice pond on the tract was used by Timothy Anglin, whose large icehouse sold more than five thousand dollars worth of ice annually. In addition to Ellerslie, Preston oversaw the hiring of managers and leasing lands on other farms the couple owned, not to mention renting and selling his real estate in Louisville and St. Louis. Despite these activities, the former general noted a year after returning to Kentucky, "My life is as tranquil as it was for several years past, eventful and active."[6]

The Prestons continued to borrow large sums of money following the Civil War. The return of the Fayette County properties to good condition involved expenditures, as did the family's ostentatious lifestyle. Preston negotiated loans with local banks. Legal problems, a complement to major real estate interests, also led the couple further into debt. Preston was forced to practice his skills as a lawyer in Lexington, Louisville, and St. Louis to defend his property rights and those of his sister Susan Hepburn. Margaret also was involved in lawsuits concerning her inheritance. One claimant in 1881– twenty-two years after the Old Duke's death–demanded a $250,000 settlement. The following year Margaret lost this case and was forced to borrow $222,000 at 7 percent interest to pay her creditors. Until her death–twelve years after her husband's demise–she continued to be besieged by legal challenges.[7]

Although Preston constantly complained he needed money and spoke of trying "to keep up appearances," the value of the family's holdings in Fayette County alone was estimated for tax purposes in 1869 at $143,450, an enormous fortune. And this sum did not include real-estate investments elsewhere: 479 acres in Bath County, 480 acres near Robinson, Illinois, another 300 acres at Mann's Lick outside of Louisville, claims to 1,376 square miles of land north of Dallas, Texas, and Preston's properties in Louisville and St. Louis. In addition to real estate, he owned $7,500 in Louisville municipal bonds in 1880 and many stocks–particularly railroad equities.[8]

"I have more land than money," Preston wrote nephew William Preston Johnston in 1867, "and am generally hard up for the latter." The years following the war were difficult ones in Kentucky. Land values in Lexington decreased by a quarter between 1862 and 1872.[9] In Louisville Preston observed in 1868 that "rents are falling rapidly" and the prices of town lots remained "dull." However, land sales in Louisville, often to enterprising German immigrants as in earlier years, continued to bring in income for the remainder of his life. Although agricultural prices in Kentucky remained depressed following the Civil War, his efforts to restore Ellerslie farm to profitability proved successful. But as Mrs. Preston stressed to her son in 1873, "The income from Ellerslie will barely enable us to live in a very simple way."[10]

The Lexington mansion was the scene of both family events and social functions. Margaret had given birth to five of the couple's six children there and three of the daughters were married in the drawing room, while receptions following the weddings of the other two daughters at Christ Church were also held in the house. Until marital difficulties led the two to live separate lives in the mid-1870s, the Prestons continued to be known for their lavish entertaining. The rooms on the first floor were arranged so they could be opened into a grand salon for receptions and dances, and the family received visitors in the drawing room. Sunday afternoons were devoted to callers, who were served what Margaret called "son-in-law punch," for she insisted no one was the worse for having imbibed it.[11]

In line with the elaborate tastes and expectations of their guests, the quality, quantity, and preparation of their table was exceptional. The former envoy dispensed large sums on imported wines, and he bragged that he spent more money than any other person in Kentucky purchasing such difficult-to-acquire delicacies as oysters and oranges from the fashionable Galt House Hotel in Louisville. When guests came to dinner, they ate at a long table that sat twenty-four and with the only gold service in Lexington–specially ordered Dresden china purchased when the couple lived in Madrid–and gold-plated tableware. The repasts were elaborate culinary displays. Two soups–a *crème* and a consommé–began the typical feast, followed by fish and meat courses, with a punch offered between them. Next came a salad, then a frozen cream dessert and choice of pastries. Wines and liqueurs accompanied the dishes. The fare at Preston Place became famous in the Bluegrass, and some guests reputedly joked that one could become inebriated and return to sobriety three times in the course of a meal there.[12]

The Prestons employed a number of house servants, and Margaret was proud that foreigners from five nations worked for the family in 1867. A Norwegian served as coachman, his wife toiled in the kitchen, and his son was employed as the drawing-room servant. The gardener was an Englishman whose wife was a cook. Three others came from Germany, Ireland, and Ethiopia. The diverse origins of the kitchen staff caused Mrs. Preston to remark, "They cannot talk to each other and consequently cannot quarrel." Her favorite servant was the former slave and Paris-trained chef Fanny Green, who introduced several French specialties to the Bluegrass. Preston Place guests long remembered such dishes as her *crème de volaille*. Margaret collected recipes for her table and oversaw the preparation and serving of meals.[13]

For William and Margaret Preston family life brought both pleasure and pain. One of the positive developments was the newfound importance of religion in their lives. Nominally Presbyterian, William had been married in Christ Church in Lexington. During the Civil War he urged his wife and children to become Episcopalians. Mrs. Preston had attended the Second Presbyterian Church of her mother and stepmother in Lexington, but its congregation was pro-Union. She became a member of Christ Church where her father had been a vestryman. The parish traced its origins to 1796, and in 1849 the present building, an imposing Gothic Revival brick structure with a square tower dominating its façade, was consecrated at the corner of Market and Church Streets. The rector, the Rev. Jacob Shaw Shipman, had managed to hold the divided congregation together during the war, and although a New Yorker, he was popular with his prosouthern members. In February 1866 Margaret, Wick, and daughter Mary Owen were confirmed at Christ Church by the Rt. Rev. Benjamin B. Smith, the first bishop of Kentucky. This "gave me great satisfaction," the proud paterfamilias reported, "for no one has felt more deeply than myself the vacuum of a life without complete religious faith." Although he was never confirmed, William became a loyal layman and often expressed his thankfulness for God's blessings.[14]

The Prestons were active in the church. William regularly paid fees for the family's pew at the front of the nave, and the Rev. Shipman became a friend of the family. Margaret and her daughters Sunie and Jessie in the late 1860s helped teach three hundred youngsters at the Negro Sunday school sponsored by the parish. Mrs. Preston enjoyed the experience and found "the little darkies brighter and more docile than the white children." Religion was also a part of their home life. "My house is becoming powerfully Episcopalian," William noted in 1868. The family observed the liturgical calendar, causing William to complain that "the season of Lent makes everything very dull," and in theology they favored the Anglo-Catholic beliefs propounded by Edward B. Pusey, a leader of the Oxford Movement in the Church of England.[15]

The five Preston daughters were sources of parental pride. Each young lady had pursued her education in Kentucky and in France, studying the humanities and acquiring the expected social graces. All also enjoyed active social lives, which the senior Prestons oversaw with interest and pleasure. The couple often commented on their girls' beaux, showing satisfaction in the social standing, as well as the personalities, of their suitors.[16]

The daughters married prominent men, thereby fulfilling their parents' expectations. The oldest girl, Mary Owen, took a cousin, John Mason Brown, as her husband in 1869. A graduate of Yale University, he was a northern officer and attorney from one of the state's most illustrious families. During the war he had helped protect his future mother-in-law's property in Lexington. Preston liked Brown, but resented his Union service. However, he confessed to his nephew William Preston Johnston that he hoped the "past will not be bequeathed to the future."[17] In 1873 the couple moved to Louisville. In 1870 Mary Owen's younger sister, Caroline Hancock, married Robert A. Thornton, a Virginia Confederate veteran, who was practicing law in Lexington with General John C. Breckinridge. Eight years later, middle-daughter Margaret wed George M. Davie, a graduate of Princeton and Democratic politician. He was in a Louisville law firm with John Mason Brown. Davie and Brown helped organize the city's celebrated park system and helped to found the Filson Club, a group interested in Kentucky's history.

The two youngest Preston daughters, Susan and Jessie, attended a convent school in New York until 1871, when they returned to live at Preston Place. In the summer they traveled with their mother to the fashionable White Sulphur Springs in West Virginia, a Mecca for former Confederate officers, including General Robert E. Lee, and to the East Coast, where they were introduced to their future spouses.[18] Both sisters were married in Lexington in 1890. Susan wed former Union general William F. Draper of Hopedale, Massachusetts, in May. A successful businessman, he was a co-owner of George Draper and Sons, a company that manufactured cotton machinery, and president of two regional railroads and a director of many enterprises. Draper was active in Massachusetts Republican politics, serving in Congress and as ambassador to Italy. The youngest Preston daughter, Jessie Fremont, in November married Draper's younger brother, George Albert. Like William, George co-owned George Draper and Sons and became active in Republican politics as a member of the party's state committee. Susan had a daughter, while Jessie bore a girl and a boy who lived beyond childhood.

The Prestons' son Robert Wickliffe (Wick) never lived up to his parents' lofty expectations. Born in 1850, the only male heir was subject to such strong parental pressures admonishing him to excel that even the most subservient of sons might have been expected to rebel. Wick proved anything but subservient! His father urged him to remember "the unimpeached honor of generations of gentlemen from whom you are descended," and his mother reminded him that his grandfather Robert Wickliffe "looked to you to sustain his name." But such admonitions made little impression.[19]

Wick's academic performance distressed his parents. His father could not accept the son's less-than-mediocre record; after all, William Preston had been an assiduous student of the classics and believed that an educated male should possess a thorough background in the liberal arts. On his return to Lexington he reread Virgil and Homer in 1866 in order to encourage Wick by his example, but the son showed little interest. The next year he was sent with Sydney Beauclerk, their charge since Madrid days, to the Kentucky Military Institute. When Colonel R. T. P. Allen publicly reprimanded Wick for being late to school, the youth returned home.[20]

His father then sent Wick to Washington College, later Washington and Lee University, in Lexington, Virginia, where William Preston Johnston was professor of history and belles lettres. Preston had advised his nephew on curricular reforms that Johnston introduced at the college and happily sent his son there in December 1867. When Preston heard in March that Wick was studying for his examinations, the father wrote him that this "news was the most agreeable I have had for some time." Letters from his father instructing him to

Courtesy Special Collections, University of Kentucky

William Preston's only son, Robert Wickliffe "Wick" Preston.

"avoid billiards," "<u>read honestly</u> and <u>attend faithfully</u> the lectures," and "devote a half hour each to Greek and Latin daily" did not motivate the youth. Nor did the attention of William Preston Johnston and Robert E. Lee, the college president, have much effect. Wick considered Lee "courteous, and manly looking," but was disappointed to find him "a quiet grisly looking old gentleman." The discouraged elder Preston had to scold his son in 1868 for ranking thirtieth out of as many students at Washington College. "I implore you, therefore, my dear son," wrote his distressed father, "not to let me be mortified by having to withdraw you from college."[21]

Equally distraught at their son's performance, Margaret Preston warned him in 1867, "If you knew how fearful I am of your doing wrong you would do right." After receiving a photograph of Wick with a bottle of whiskey in one hand, his mother denounced this as a "cruel" gesture. When she heard that he was interested in a young woman she disliked, the forthright Mrs. Preston wrote, "You know too well my opinion of her to think that I would ever receive her into

Courtesy Special Collections, University of Kentucky

"Ugly Club of '69 [1869]"; Frank Page, Va., Edmund Berkeley, Va., Wickliffe Preston, Ky., Samuel Ammen, Va., Gabriel Santini, La., Sheppard Clarke, Ala., John Barlow, Ky., and Hill Carter, Va.

my family." On another occasion his mother admonished him, "God grant you wisdom to choose a Christian wife and not a ball room belle." Meanwhile, Sydney Beauclerk was earning an engineering degree at Rensselaer Polytechnic Institute in Troy, New York.[22]

Preston withdrew Wick from Washington College and sent him to the University of Virginia in 1869. His record there was poor. He often wrote his father asking for–and always receiving–more money and requesting permission to drop courses. By January 1871 Preston again implored his son, "I hope you will not mortify me by being dismissed from the university." Aware of the limitations placed on women, his mother admonished Wick: "Your sisters are talented but they are proscribed. They cannot do anything to sustain the family and their hopes naturally center upon you, because a career is opened to you, which is denied to them."[23]

Next the family sent Wick north to school in the summer of 1871. "You have been pronounced insubordinate at two colleges," Mrs.

Preston emphasized, "do maintain a better character in the North than you did in the South." First the twenty-one-year-old went to Exeter Preparatory School in New Hampshire for tutoring and then to Yale University, but his sojourn there proved typically brief. In 1872 he attended law classes at Harvard University, but did not pursue a degree.[24]

Following his academic failures, Wick spent the next decade as a playboy. A handsome man well over six feet tall, the affable Wick had many friends. In 1872, while at White Sulphur Springs, he informed his mother: "I am always pleased to be considered a good dancer, inasmuch as I think cultivated heels are socially of more value than cultivated brains." His many travels gave him ample opportunities to dance. He visited friends for extended stays in London, New York, Boston, Cincinnati, St. Louis, Chicago, New Orleans, and Jacksonville and spent his summers at resorts.[25]

By 1878 Wick was in New York doing legal work for his friend William C. Whitney, who headed the counsel's office for the city. There the Kentuckian proofread documents and researched company records. His father urged him to study while in New York and become a lawyer, and Preston's friend, former governor Samuel J. Tilden, tried to encourage him in this effort. But Wick would have none of this. He informed his father that his colleagues in the legal department were "mere machines" and the "office too chaotic for reading you recommend." Instead, he relished going to the races and dances with Whitney. Dining at Delmonico's Restaurant, rides in Central Park, and parties with scions of the Belmont, Astor, Fish, Morgan, and Whitney clans were activities he enjoyed more. The youth's salary of $1,500 did not begin to support his tastes, so again he sent his father letters with the same refrain: "I need more money." In epistles home in 1875, Wick affirmed that he was "unfit for business" and concluded he "must marry rich, being fit for nothing else."[26]

In 1878 his disappointed father realized that "the social and fashionable attractions of the city" left his son "but little time for reading and work." To Samuel Tilden, Preston lamented, "It seems that taste is not hereditary or at least, I fear it is not." But his mother continued to lecture him, insisting that he owed it to his family to "make yourself a lawyer." By 1881 Preston recognized that his son was "strong and handsome," but considered him "a man without a plan."[27]

Despite his deficiencies, Wick pleased his parents in matrimony.

Courtesy Special Collections, University of Kentucky
Mrs. Robert Wickliffe Preston.

The son surprised them in December 1882 when he announced his engagement to Sarah (Sallie) Brant McDowell of St. Louis, grand-daughter of one of William's cousins, Governor James McDowell of Virginia. The couple had met in Paris in 1860 where Sallie's father was a doctor, and Wick had visited her in St. Louis. She was a talented young woman whose wealth surpassed $400,000; Sallie was enthusiastically accepted into the family. Preston was so happy with her influence on his son that he considered her "the crowning glory of my life."[28]

After living with the McDowells, the newlyweds moved to Lexington in 1883 where they lived at Lakewood, a restored house at Ellerslie. The following year they resided in Washington, D.C., but by 1885 Lexington again became their home. The younger Prestons had three children, but their firstborn died in infancy. The other two, Margaret and William, were named for their Preston grandparents. Wick assisted his father during the latter's last two years of life in running Ellerslie. The two Preston men shared such tasks as ordering cedar posts for fencing, overseeing the tobacco crop and livestock, hiring employees, handling land transfers, and negotiating loans. Wick's special interest was breeding thoroughbred horses.[29]

But marriage did not dissuade Wick from reverting to the frivolous conduct that characterized his youth. In 1885 a friend bet the Kentuckian $300 he could not ride his bad-tempered filly up Franklin Street in front of the Maryland Club in Baltimore. Wick accepted, and in December many spectators watched him try. Surprisingly, the horse refused to move after Wick mounted. He unsuccessfully whispered into her ear and finally resorted to whipping the filly. She made a great jump that failed to dismount her rider, who then "by good management" got her to walk down the street, turn around, and pass the club. The Kentuckian's success was reported in the *National Police Gazette*, together with a cartoon showing the Bluegrass rider whispering to the filly.[30]

Despite concerns about Wick, William and Margaret generally took great pleasure in their family. Caroline Preston and husband Robert Thornton remained in Lexington, and their three babies were indulged with favors by their maternal grandparents. Mary Owen and John Mason Brown had four offspring, and Margaret and George Davie one who survived infancy. Both the Browns and the Davies resided in Louisville, so William and Margaret saw their families often. In December 1872 Preston reported that his first two grandchildren, born in 1871 and 1872, were "rebellious" and "robust." Next March the doting grandfather noted that these "two fine little grandsons" were beginning to talk. "A little granddaughter Margaret Howard Thornton comes to greet us," he reported in 1873, "and make happy our Christmas fireside."[31]

Always generous parents, the Prestons gave their children money until their marriages, property as wedding gifts, and assistance following their vows. Caroline, for example, received a lot in Louisville and land in Texas. When daughter Margaret Davie had health problems and difficulties with her husband, her parents offered support. This middle daughter suffered from an illness she labeled dysentery, but it probably was a form of bulimia. At least once she had to be placed in a sanatorium. To help her, her mother and father went to Louisville to care for her family. When Margaret found herself in debt or wanted expensive clothing, she hesitated to ask her husband for funds and her father sent money instead. Wick also received large doses of financial help after his wedding.[32]

Preston's concern for others extended beyond his family. He retained his benevolent attitude toward the blacks who had labored for him. As several historians have emphasized, violence against African Americans was commonplace in Kentucky in the decades following the war.[33] Lynchings and night murders by gangs killed perhaps 1,400 of the freedmen in the commonwealth by 1885. Preston despised such acts. "Boy Peter" Thompson, a slave who had served the general during the war, lived with his family on rented land at Ellerslie. He was killed in front of his wife and an infant child "by a band of marauders" in January 1871. "The wretched Ku-Klux went to poor Peter's . . . at midnight and murdered him," Preston wrote his son. "I have brought his family to town. . . . The county is degenerating fearfully." The murderers sent Thompson's former master a note informing him they were mad that a black had a house when many poor whites did not. Alone in Lexington when this happened and frightened by this violence, Margaret never slept thereafter without a night watchman.[34]

Samuel Giles, Preston's slave for four decades, rented land at Ellerslie in 1871. Following Thompson's murder, the Prestons ceased leasing property to blacks. Giles and his family were sent to Bath County, where his former master provided him some land and a house. However, the ex-slave lived close to poverty in his last years and was forced in 1885 to ask for a cow to "do some better" for his wife and children. Preston also showed some concern for other former slaves. Until his death the "Dear Old Master" received requests to provide "a good young horse," pay bail to a jailer, and send money from several who had worked for him. Many times Preston sent assistance.[35]

Like her husband, Margaret believed in the racial superiority of whites, but this did not stop her from demonstrating her paternalistic feelings toward African Americans. When Wick left a lecture at Harvard because a black student was present, his mother chastised him:

> How can you with the philanthropic blood of the Howards in your veins object to any of God's creatures getting an education? You do yourself such gross injustice by such conduct for at home you . . . are beloved by all the negroes. . . . You need not make them your equal, any more than I do because I commune with them at God's altar who is no respecter of persons–I hope you will show those Northern people that you have more sympathy for the negro than they have.[36]

Preston did not confine his generosity to family members and former slaves. Following the Civil War, he also gave to ex-Confederates in need. In 1867 Jefferson Davis and his family were living in Lennoxville, Canada, and the Kentucky general joined several others "in a private way to contribute something to relieve his embarrassment." Preston also developed a reputation for his gifts to impecunious Confederate veterans who came to him for assistance.[37]

Despite the pleasure both Prestons took in their family and their interest in others, difficulties arose between William and Margaret that turned their marriage into a contentious relationship–almost ending in divorce. To friends William Preston always claimed that "I have been residing at home happily so far as my private life is concerned," and for public consumption Margaret carefully tried to project the image of a devoted wife. But reality was otherwise. Her hostility toward her husband stemmed from discoveries she made in 1864. During the war she saw his account books and found that he and his sister Susan were involved in real-estate transactions and that he had loaned her money. Then Margaret learned that William had tried to have her Bath County agent sell the Piedmont Farm she had inherited. Ever after, she refused to trust him in financial matters and insisted that her husband keep separate accounts for her Piedmont Farm.[38] Margaret was determined to pass her property on to her children and believed her husband's efforts to raise money through land sales was deleterious to their social status and economic well-being.

Their next marital crisis came in 1868, this time over spousal infidelity. While her husband was in Washington, Margaret opened a letter to him from a "Fannie Caldwell" of South Abington, Massachusetts, who asked for money from her former lover. William claimed never to have heard of his supposed paramour. Suspicious of male conduct, his wife had warned him–apparently without cause–that he must keep his "honor inviolate" while away during the Mexican War. She chose not to believe him concerning Fannie and wrote, "It is unnecessary for you to return to investigate for I do not intend to see you and you cannot force yourself into my presence." "I shudder to think that your blood flows in the veins of my children." Margaret then informed him, "This of course severs our relations as husband and wife."[39]

William answered his wife, asking that the matter "be resolved not in passion, but with decency and deliberation." But he also threatened to file for divorce. Preston went to Boston where he hired a detective who found that Fannie was really William R. Emerson of Baltimore. The constable of Massachusetts confirmed that Emerson was a "scamp and mean impersonator," who was in jail for having "duped" other wealthy husbands. In late May William gave his wife a sworn statement from a Boston justice of the peace stating these facts.[40]

The Prestons' marital discord reached another crescendo in December 1874 when Margaret asked William for a divorce. Following a quarrel over money matters, she left William in Lexington and went to stay with her oldest daughter, Mary Brown, in Louisville. She wrote, "I could not preserve my own self respect if I contemplated for a moment ever returning to your house until money matters which have created so many fearful scenes are so arranged that it can never again cause a disturbance." Margaret claimed, "[I] never again expect to hold with you the relation of a wife." She asked her husband to renounce all rights to her inherited property, promising she would do the same regarding his, and threatened to hire Isaac Caldwell, a Louisville attorney, to represent her in court.[41]

Mary Brown interceded with her father, telling him that his wife would be satisfied if he promised to give her the income from the Ellerslie and Piedmont properties. After visiting his mother, Wick told his father she sought a divorce and demanded the income from her farms.[42] The children opposed their mother's plans, and she dropped the subject.

But relations between the spouses did not improve. Two years later the two were arguing so much over finances that Wick informed his father, "I deem it necessary to stay away." While living with her sister in Trimble County, Margaret in October 1884 asked William to give her a formal agreement separating their properties or she would file for divorce. He answered that no court would grant a divorce, for to obtain this, "abandonment, desertion, adultery or felony on my part, would have to be proven by you." However, he would consent to a division of properties and physical separation, but he called the demand "unjust and cruel." "As to your person you have for many years, at intervals, had most complete liberty," William asserted, "and I as a gentleman have always respected your rights as a lady, and never invaded your wishes." Meanwhile, he informed her that he was "waiting patiently to see what course you would determine to pursue against me, to establish your famed legal rights." Receiving her husband's consent to a voluntary separation, Margaret did not pursue divorce proceedings.[43]

In addition to money and charges of infidelity, other issues engendered disputes between the spouses. Son Wickliffe became a source of conflict. Margaret blamed his difficulties on her husband, for William had insisted that he attend Washington College and the University of Virginia. However, she argued that he should have been sent north where he would have had fewer friends to distract him. She considered her husband "over indulgent" toward their son and complained to Wick that he "never tells me any of his plans in regard to you."[44]

As a consequence of their disputes, the couple was living apart as much as possible by the mid-1870s. Their marriage became one of financial relationships rather than mutual respect and love. When Preston Place was rebuilt in the 1870s, they arranged for separate bedrooms. After the marriage of the two oldest daughters, Margaret spent many winter months in Louisville, either at the Galt House or at their homes. Assisting them and visiting the grandchildren made her absences from Lexington appear maternal in nature and disguised her desire not to be with her husband. Margaret suffered from ill health and lameness–a problem that dated back to her broken ankle during the war, aggravated by being overweight. She spent time convalescing at her daughters' homes in Louisville. This, too, made her separation from her husband appear less obvious. In September 1878 when George Davie formally requested daughter Margaret's hand in marriage, her mother was embarrassed that she did not know her husband's address.

By the 1880s Margaret had surrendered her reputation for being an elaborate hostess and tried to avoid entertaining. She beseeched her husband in 1883 to "spare me what seems almost worse than death, a houseful of people and bills running up at the butchers and the grocers." Following her demand in 1884 for separation or divorce, she lived in Louisville with the Davies until William's death. He spent his last three years at Preston Place alone or in the company of his two youngest, unmarried daughters. In the summer his wife traveled to White Sulphur Springs, Hygeia Springs at Old Point, Virginia, and later Bar Harbor, Maine, in the company of her children. William enjoyed staying at Newport, Rhode Island, and Cape May, New Jersey, fashionable seaside resorts, accompanied by a servant and sometimes his son.[45]

Beside his marital problems, Preston was plagued in his last decades with poor health. The pain he first felt in his left eye in 1863 continued after the war. In early 1878 he suffered "a large hemorrhage into the vitreous" and a "sudden loss of sight" in this eye. Dr. E. Williams, his ophthalmologist in Cincinnati, ordered "total abstinence from reading and writing" and made him wear an eye shade. Rest and an operation brought no cure. By May he had lost vision in his left eye, and "my right eye is well, but not strong." Preston lived the remainder of his life dreading "blindness and an unhappy old age," but he never lost sight in his other eye. A liver ailment, another illness he first experienced during the war, brought intermittent suffering and physicians' prescriptions to follow a "strict diet."[46] Attacks of neuralgia also afflicted him, despite the pills he ingested. By the 1880s Preston was very deaf and investigated hearing aids, but there is no evidence he used any.[47]

No doubt during his fifties and sixties Preston suffered from the aches and pains of advancing years and fear of total blindness, but his pessimism regarding his health was perhaps as much psychological as physical. In August 1878 Preston visited Dr. Samuel D. Gross in Philadelphia. He had been the Prestons' neighbor in the 1840s while head of surgery at the Louisville Medical Institute and later became president of the American Medical Association. Dr. Gross examined his friend and found "no disease about him whatever."[48]

In the 1870s Preston's children reported that their father was "much depressed," "most despondent," and "frequently excited." His wife complained in 1872 that he spent too much time sleeping during the day, and Wick lamented that his father often was "in bed all day," "sulking heavily." For two decades Preston's correspondence demonstrated his sense of depression. In June 1877 he wrote, "I have not been well and all works wrong with me, every way," and seven years later he claimed, "I am not well . . . my case is irremediable." But his most frequent complaint was "I am here all alone."[49]

Preston's pessimism in old age brought with it reflections on faith and intimations of mortality. In 1874 he assured friend Henry Watterson, "I fear God, cher Henri, and I do not fear any other." "Time begins to pull at me," he wrote three years later, "though without bringing me to earth." "I have almost flown my flight, and now flag with weary wings over the abyss," William warned his sister Susan in 1881. "But I was never afraid of Hell, because I believe in the Mercy and Wisdom of God, the Maker of all things." Preston continued to express such thoughts until death. "Seventy years are on me, and the snow flakes angrily against my window panes," he ruminated before Christmas in his last year. "All is ended henceforward for me. My struggle with men is over; my contemplation of God and his mysteries begin in earnest."[50]

Despite infirmities, marital problems, and bouts of depression, William Preston in his last five years actively pursued two time-consuming business affairs. One dealt with a Lexington transaction and coincided with the progress the city was experiencing in the 1880s. Its population grew and new institutions, buildings, and services appeared. The cornerstone for the Kentucky Agricultural and Mechanical College–the predecessor of the University of Kentucky–was laid in 1880, and two years later the first telephone service was inaugurated, some electric lights were erected on Main Street, and mule-drawn streetcars were appearing. A new courthouse was completed in 1884. But nothing better represented the progress of the times than the city's new waterworks. In November 1883, Preston became one of three founders of the Lexington Hydraulic and Manufacturing Company, established under an act of the legislature that permitted Lexington to condemn land at Ellerslie for a reservoir. The corporation contracted with the city to construct and maintain a water system to supply a population of thirty thousand and agreed to a rate schedule. The Prestons sold much of their Ellerslie property to the company. In 1884 a large lake was dug by convict laborers, but their employment was opposed by many denizens, who held a rally to protest their presence.

On 30 January 1885, a large crowd gathered at Main Street and Cheapside to watch as firemen shot a column of water as high as the new courthouse, and then they "swarmed out to the waterworks for the dedication ceremonies." The sale of land and William's interest in the corporation provided cash, but Margaret was intent on also retaining fishing privileges at the reservoir for her family.[51] This was accomplished and the Ellerslie Fishing Club was founded with her husband as its president. The lake, later enlarged, remains today on the south side of Richmond Road near the beltway around the city.

A potentially much more valuable concern engaged Preston's energies in the early1880s: Texas lands. In 1841 the Republic of Texas granted approximately 12,000 square miles of territory in north-central Texas, just north of where Dallas soon would be founded, to a group of Louisvillians, headed by William P. Peters.[52] He and his partners formed the Texas Association to colonize this land. With the help of his brother-in-law, Albert Sidney Johnston, then secretary of state for the republic, Preston also invested in real estate in 1841, but in south Texas. By the 1850s Dallas was developing into an important town, increasing the value of the adjacent Peters Colony.[53] William's Louisville uncle, George Hancock, was a major land speculator, and in 1852 he purchased 46 percent of the association's stock and became its president.

After the Civil War, the Texas legislature, dissatisfied with the slow development of the Peters Colony, tried to rescind its grant. Preston was sent to Texas in 1872 to urge the association's lawyer, A. A. Casseday, to prosecute their rights more vigorously. However, the land dispute continued on without resolution when Hancock died in 1875. Preston then inherited his interests and became the "Chief Agent and Trustee" of the association. He engaged John W. Buchanan of Louisville, who handled his property transactions there, to pursue the corporation's Texas claims.[54]

In 1881 Preston took the offensive in attempting to defend the Texas Association's right to its huge grant. As he prepared to go to Texas to press the group's claim, Preston wrote his sister, "I hope yet to set [*sic*] in sunshine and gold. Monte Carlo dreams." In the suit "William Preston complainant vs. Wm. C. Walsh [Commissioner General of the Texas Land Office] defendant," his Louisville sons-in-law, John Brown and George Davie, argued the case in 1882 before the United States Circuit Court in Austin. They maintained that the association had carried out its responsibility to colonize its lands and therefore was entitled to ownership. The justices concurred, declaring "the complainant's arguments are found to be true and supported by proof." When new shares in the company were issued in 1883, Preston owned 2,068 of these 5,504 equities.[55]

But the Texas gold was not to be. The state took the circuit court's decision to the Supreme Court. With many prominent Kentuckians involved in the claim—many were his relatives and friends like Reuben T. Durrett—Preston asked the Kentucky General Assembly in Frankfort to pass a resolution calling upon the governor and the state's members of Congress to champion their cause. This the legislature did, but to no avail. Claiming that the association had done "almost nothing" to carry out their obligations under the original grant, the justices on the high court overturned the circuit court's decision. Although deprived of the enormous wealth that the Texas lands would have brought him, Preston still owned considerable property in the Lone Star State. Among his important holdings there were 1,344 acres in Cherokee County and another 640 acres in Hale County.[56]

Despite separation from his wife, poor health, and his disappointment over the Texas claim, Preston enjoyed a modicum of personal happiness in his final years. While remaining close to their mother, his daughters also were solicitous of his well-being. Their visits with grandchildren to Preston Place and his stays with them punctuated his days alone with pleasure, as did the return to Lexington of son Wick and Sallie two years before his death. The close relationship between William and his sister Susan remained essential to each and offered great consolation. "We both will never be separated in heart or feeling," he assured Susan in 1881, as "the dawn of a brighter life is at hand for us both." For her he was the "best" brother "I believe a sister was ever blessed with." One surprise that touched Preston came from Sydney Beauclerk, who by the 1880s was an engineer in Irasburg, Vermont. He named his first son Preston after his surrogate father.[57]

Activities Preston had long enjoyed continued to bring satisfac-

213

tion. He played chess with friends and whist with his daughters, listened to Strauss's music at a Lexington soirée, and studied Greek and Latin classics–despite his eye problems. Correspondence allowed him to keep in touch with old friends–even though his handwriting had deteriorated badly. Letters from William Preston Johnston, the first president of Tulane University in New Orleans, enlivened his days. Although Preston's wish "that chance, or good fortune, may enable us to meet again" proved a vain hope, he and Jefferson Davis remained epistolary friends. In 1886 Preston's son-in-law George Davie urged him to read the works of Herbert Spencer, the English social philosopher. "I have not read with sufficient care Mr. Spencer's books," Preston admitted, but "I believe that I will, as a pleasure in my old age, and so as to keep me up to the times, until I retire finally."[58]

Preston's many personal problems did not prevent him from continuing to lead an active public life. Following the Civil War, his interest in politics continued unabated. The Confederate veteran excoriated the Reconstruction policies of the Radical Republicans toward the South, particularly the Freedmen's Bureau with its goal to help former slaves adjust to their new status through education and economic aid. For Preston, the Radicals' control of the national government was a "disgrace" and their actions for "my people and State are quite intolerable." Nevertheless, the partisan Democrat noted with special pleasure, "The sentiment of Kentucky is almost unanimous against the present policy at Washington."[59]

After the Civil War, conservatives in Kentucky cast their lot with the Democratic party in opposing the Radicals in Congress. Many "Unionist Democrats," as well as former Whigs loyal to the Union, resented emancipation and united with the prosouthern Democrats. The majority only reluctantly conceded the abolition of slavery. The state legislature in 1865 refused to ratify the Thirteenth Amendment ending the institution and also rejected the other two civil rights amendments, the Fourteenth and the Fifteenth.[60] The Freedmen's Bureau met with hostility, and in 1871 the Democratic-controlled legislature refused to pass a law against mob violence. The prosouthern leaders came to dominate the party and control the state politically for the remainder of the century, and it became a decided political benefit to have served in the Confederate army.[61]

Preston's comments on the Lexington balloting in January 1866 showed both satisfaction and bitterness over the Democrats' success: "Yesterday the drums and fifes were beaten, the Conservatives having carried the City Election against the Radicals. The drum and fife! They should have been heard in front of our bayonets at Shiloh and Chickamauga." Later that year he reported: "The Democracy won a great victory last summer with Confederates in disguise."[62]

Many Democratic leaders wanted Preston to be their standard-bearer for governor in 1867. Friends and editorials in several newspapers throughout the state implored him to announce. "The Confederates are urging me to run for Governor next year," Preston wrote in December 1866. "Personally I do not wish to enter the lists, but, peradventure, my constitutional liking for rows, broils and all Hibernian pleasures may bring me into the ring." In the end, he chose not to. When the state's Democrats met in Frankfort in February 1867, his name was put forward, but he withdrew his candidacy "before the Convention in graceful speech." The fortunes of the Republican party in Kentucky reached their nadir that year. The Democrats elected John L. Helm governor, and the Republicans lost all nine congressional races and barely made a showing in Louisville.[63]

In 1868 Preston was drawn into an active role in Democratic politics. In March, as a delegate to the state convention, he nominated the meeting's president. Preston was encouraged by the conservatives' control there and reported, "I had things pretty much my own way." Also a delegate in July to the national convention in New York City, he led half of the commonwealth's delegation in support for Union general Winfield Scott Hancock of Pennsylvania for the presidency. When former New York governor Horatio Seymour finally won the nomination after twenty-one ballots, Preston then presented the name of Frank P. Blair Jr. to the convention for vice president, and he was selected. Blair, a Preston kinsman from Maryland, believed in states' rights and white supremacy. At the courthouse in Lexington that summer, Preston addressed a rally for Seymour and the state candidates, and although Republican Ulysses S. Grant won the presidency, in Kentucky the Seymour-Blair ticket defeated Grant by a vote of almost three to one.[64]

Preston received a pardon from the United States government in 1868, granting him full rights as a citizen. After returning to Kentucky he had stated in 1866 that he had "too delicate a stomach to ask for pardon," but two years later Congressman James B. Beck urged him to apply for one. Preston swore an oath of allegiance in

October 1868 and in December signed a printed letter accepting President Johnson's warrant of pardon.[65]

Weeks after receiving his pardon, Preston was elected to the Kentucky General Assembly. Democrat Robert C. Rogers had been chosen by the voters in 1867 to represent Fayette County in the legislature for two years, but he resigned in early December 1868. The county's Democratic committee met 7 December and unanimously nominated Preston as its candidate to fill Rogers's term. In accepting their selection, Preston rationalized that his service in Frankfort would "advance the local interests of the county." Democratic newspapers in Kentucky reported with glee that "the entire Radical press of the country is greatly exercised of the nomination of General Preston for the Legislature." Lexington's *Kentucky Gazette* claimed that the candidacy of a former Confederate general proved that "all our white men stand in equality before the law." Preston had no opposition and was elected on 26 December. He certainly felt at home in Frankfort, for so many southern veterans were legislators that some considered the general assembly "scarcely more than the meeting of a Confederate regiment."[66]

In Frankfort Preston advocated state financial aid to develop the commonwealth's depressed economy. Considering transportation improvements essential to rebuilding Kentucky's prosperity, he introduced a measure that became known as the "ten million dollar bill." This called for issuing state bonds to subsidize railroad construction. But the proposal encountered a storm of opposition from those who claimed that such government aid would "render the credit of the State auxiliary to that of a private individual or a corporation" in violation of the state constitution. Preston countered this argument when he addressed his constituents at the Fayette County Courthouse in early May. Demonstrating his "great familiarity with the statistical reports," he spoke for two hours. The legislator noted that many Kentuckians were driven away by not having the "proper avenues of enterprise open to them" and insisted that state assistance to public improvements was essential. However, it was not those contemptuous of such government aid that defeated the ten-million-dollar bill. Rather, the powerful Louisville and Nashville Railroad lobby killed this proposal. Preston enjoyed being back in politics, but his wife did not. She complained to Wick, "I will be called upon every Saturday night to entertain members of the Legislature that your father may bring home with him." He decided not to be a candidate for reelection in 1869.[67]

In 1876 and 1880 Preston actively supported Democratic presidential candidates. A friend of New York governor Samuel J. Tilden, the party's nominee in 1876, the Kentuckian attended meetings of the Democratic Executive Committee that year and met with Tilden at his New York City home on 24 September to discuss campaign strategy. The Saturday before the election, Preston addressed a rally in Lexington and predicted, "The republicans would bully or cheat the Democracy by counting out as many Southern States as might be necessary to continue their power." In the balloting the Republican candidate, Rutherford B. Hayes of Ohio, lost Kentucky by 62,000 votes and received 264,000 fewer votes nationwide than Tilden.[68] However, contested returns from Florida, Louisiana, and South Carolina and the ineligibility of one elector from Oregon placed twenty electoral votes in doubt. The candidate who won these disputed votes would win the White House.

Southern Democrats were adamant in their determination to gain the presidency for Tilden. Preston's friend Henry Watterson, the renowned editor of the *Louisville Courier-Journal*, had been elected to Congress from Louisville in 1876 and idolized Tilden, considering him "the nearest approach to the ideal statesman I have ever known." The week following the election, Watterson joined J. Stoddard Johnston, Preston's cousin, in urging Tilden to declare his intention to take the oath of office. "There is but one hope," Preston counseled his party in mid-November, "and that is instant and intrepid action."[69]

Tilden made Watterson his spokesman in Congress to deal with the disputed election. The Democratic-controlled House and the Republican majority in the Senate were unable to agree on which candidate was entitled to the contested electoral votes, and a stalemate ensued. In mid-December, Preston, Watterson, and Johnston joined several others at Tilden's home on Grammercy Park, with Preston the most outspoken in urging the New Yorker to take the offensive and claim his victory. On 8 January in a *Courier-Journal* editorial, Watterson asked Kentucky's Democrats to send "at least ten thousand unarmed men" to Washington in February to participate in a "peaceful army of one hundred thousand men" in support of Tilden's inauguration. A week later the Louisville congressman met with Tilden and tried to convince him to endorse such a rally.[70]

On 17 January more than two thousand gathered at the Liederkranz Hall in Louisville to hear Preston, Basil Duke, and Cassius M. Clay–Kentucky's famous spokesman for emancipation who had become a Democrat–give "vehement" addresses demanding Tilden's election. But the New York governor demurred. Watterson attributed Tilden's inaction to his idealism and believed he lost the White House because of this.[71]

The Democratic candidate's refusal to act on this advice disappointed his supporters, Preston included, and led to a negotiated settlement. In late January Congress appointed an electoral commission to determine the legal electors, and its members voted 8-7 along party lines in favor of Hayes. Southerners engaged in a filibuster to prevent his election, but it became obvious that the Democrats could not elect Tilden. This impasse encouraged compromise. Watterson and several southerners met with Hayes supporters on 26 February at the Wormley House, a Washington hotel. At such meetings the two parties carried on negotiations and cobbled together an agreement.[72] Many southern congressmen would vote to accept the presidential electors committed to Hayes and help the Republicans organize the House of Representatives. In exchange the Republican nominee when president would end the last vestiges of Reconstruction by removing Federal troops from the South and appointing southerners to government posts. In addition, Hayes would direct more federal spending to the region and offer government support for a railroad linking Memphis and New Orleans to the Pacific. Some of the elements of the compromise, such as the removal of Federal troops from the South, represented measures that the Republicans already intended to carry out.

The details of the compromise remain a mystery. Although years later Democrats urged Watterson to give "evidence that the presidency was stolen by Hayes," the Louisvillian decided that these "matters should remain a sealed book in my memory."[73] What is known is that the Democrats' filibuster ended, and many southern congressmen joined Watterson in accepting the decision of the electoral commission. Hayes became president on 4 March and Reconstruction ended.

Although Preston considered Tilden's defeat a "humiliation," he concurred with the pragmatic solution reached with the Republicans. Because of the secrecy that surrounded the compromise, Preston's precise role in the affair is uncertain. However, during the election and afterward he and Watterson corresponded often–sometimes in coded verses that remain undecipherable.[74] By late January Tilden's inaction convinced Preston that he would not be elected, and the general probably encouraged Watterson to force the Republicans to grant the South favors before acceding to a Hayes presidency.

Concerning two matters included in the compromise, Preston had strong views that accorded with Watterson's: obtaining a federal subsidy for the Texas and Pacific Railroad and the appointment of southern Democrats to federal positions. Preston likely reinforced his Louisville friend's determination to stress these two items in his dealings with the Republicans. The Texas and Pacific Railroad's plan to link the South with the Pacific was the project of Thomas Scott, the railway czar. Throughout his adult life, Preston had been concerned with railroads. He owned rail stocks and had backed the incorporation of the Louisville and Nashville Railroad in the state legislature in 1851. As an owner of Texas lands, Preston had long championed Scott's rail line. The Kentucky general and the Pennsylvania railwayman had become friends, and Preston served on his Pacific Railroad Committee. In mid-January 1877 Scott wrote him to come to Washington to emphasize "the necessity of every Southern man coming into line so that this great highway may be built."[75]

Preston's other concern, the appointment of southerners to government posts, was one he shared with other ex-Confederates. His nephew, William Preston Johnston, had been in line to become a district attorney general for Kentucky with Tilden's election. Johnston had been in Washington working with Watterson, lobbying Democrats to stand behind their candidate. On discovering in late January that southern congressmen were negotiating with Hayes's representatives, Johnston wrote his uncle and told him, "I consider it of the utmost importance to you to be here as soon as you can. I know this." Preston traveled to the capital in early February, but it is not known with whom he spoke or the subjects of his conversations. By early March he had met with Tilden in New York.[76]

Although agreed to by Republicans, federal subsidies to the Texas and Pacific Railroad were never granted, but President Hayes did appoint many ex-Confederates to government positions, pleasing Watterson and Democratic legislators. In recognition of his support for Watterson and the compromise, Preston exercised influence in nominating Democrats for federal positions. Congressman J. C. S. Blackburn wrote the general in October 1877 to tell him of "the number of appointees taken from Kentucky" and "to assure you that the ability to comply with any request of yours is all that is necessary to ensure its accomplishment." Preston's influence in securing federal appointments became well known, causing many hopeful applicants to ask him to write to President Hayes in support of their qualifications.[77]

In 1880, at the state Democratic meeting in June at the Lexington Opera House, Preston gave a speech in favor of Tilden, as did Cassius Clay, who wrote Tilden that Preston's endorsement was "very able." Preston then served as a delegate to the Democratic national convention, but in 1880 the party chose former Union general Winfield Scott Hancock to run for the presidency. The Kentuckian became so outspoken for the Pennsylvania nominee that Republicans considered Preston one of several advisors who controlled him. In a hostile political cartoon by Thomas Nast, published in *Harper's Weekly*, the Kentucky Confederate was depicted as tweaking the nose of the subdued candidate.[78]

Finally in 1884 the Democrats placed their man in the White House. Grover Cleveland of New York owed his victory to the southern Democrats, and he appointed many to government posts. William Preston wanted to be named minister to Spain again and encouraged his friends to lobby the president. Kentucky's attorney general wrote Cleveland, assuring him that naming Preston "would certainly meet with the most cordial approval of the people of Kentucky," while the chairman of the state's Democratic party informed the president that his appointment would please the "Democracy of Kentucky." Many of Preston's supporters praised him "as an able, accomplished diplomat" and stressed that he would be a good negotiator in talks concerning Cuban tobacco and sugar quotas, matters of importance to the southern states. In mid-March Preston went to Washington and spoke with Cleveland and his secretary of state, Thomas F. Bayard, about the Madrid position.[79] However, the Kentuckian did not become minister to Spain.

In the postwar years Preston's public role was not limited to politics. He participated in many state and national organizations. In 1872 two groups merged to form the Kentucky Agricultural and Mechanical Society and held annual exhibitions in Lexington. Preston became its first president. Two months after the founding of a new incarnation of the Kentucky Historical Society in October 1878, he joined the organization. The Louisville native also belonged to several organizations there. Preston resumed his membership in his Masonic lodge in 1866, taking care to pay the dues he owed for the war years, and in the prestigious Pendennis Club. He was a founding member in 1886 of the city's Harvard Club. The father-in-law of John Brown and George Davie and a longtime friend of Reuben Durrett, all founders of the Filson Club, Preston was unanimously elected to membership on 5 October 1885.[80]

Outside of Kentucky Preston belonged to several organizations. He remained active in the Aztec Club, founded in Mexico City during the Mexican War, and attended several of its reunions in New York City. In 1868 he became a vice president when the Harvard University Law School Association was founded. When in Washington, D.C., he often stayed at the Metropolitan Club, where he was a member. In New York he belonged to the Manhattan Club, founded in 1865 by prominent Democrats such as Samuel Tilden, August Belmont, and John Van Buren, the president's son, and to the socially prominent Knickerbocker Club.[81]

The general was most visible to the public in his role as a popular speaker. In Louisville William Preston joined the governor and several dignitaries in 1871 in giving addresses at the inauguration of the Industrial Exposition Building, a two-story brick structure at the corner of Fourth and Chestnut Streets. The next year Preston was chairman of a banquet and ball offered by the city of Louisville during the visit of His Imperial Highness, the Grand Duke Alexis of Russia. On the duke's arrival in January 1872, a thousand bystanders applauded his progress up Main Street to the new Galt House Hotel. There, Preston, as head of the reception committee, welcomed him and lauded "the unaltered friendship" existing between Russia and the United States. That evening the duke led the Grand Quadrille with a pleased Mrs. Preston.[82]

Many audiences in Lexington asked Preston to deliver talks. In June 1877 he gave the graduation address at the Sayre Female Academy, and on 31 July 1883 Preston greeted President and Mrs. Chester A. Arthur on behalf of the city at the Phoenix Hotel on Main Street. Wickliffe and Sallie Preston rode in the presidential coach that took the Arthurs to lunch at Ashland. Next the guests toured the Ashland Park Stock Farm on the Ellerslie grounds. The next day the president dedicated the Southern Exposition in Louisville. There 1,500

Courtesy Filson Historical Society

William Preston, portrait by Nicola Marchall.

industrial, agricultural, and commercial displays attracted 770,000 visitors during the next hundred days. Mrs. Preston was not in Lexington that July, but at White Sulphur Springs. The presidential couple stopped there on their return to Washington, and she was presented to them.[83]

Several of Preston's addresses were given to groups of Confederate veterans. In September 1874 he delivered an oration in Frankfort at the interment of "Heroes of the Mexican War," praising them for their "manly courage" that "established our power on the Pacific coast." In his presentation, Preston included a eulogy for Trimble County's Theodore O'Hara, the poet-soldier who had fought at Buena Vista, participated in Narciso López's invasion of Cuba, and been a member of General Albert Sidney Johnston's staff. The next year, on 17 June, Preston delivered an oration in memory of General John C. Breckinridge, in the great hall of the Louisville Free Public

Library. After the governor called the meeting to order, Preston defended the Confederate cause for which his cousin fought: "In my belief the ideas of Democratic freedom for which he sacrificed his brilliant position are not dead but will survive. The sacred flame of Liberty is nourished, not extinguished, by the blood of freemen." The *Louisville Courier-Journal's* headline reporting this address read: "The Greatest Living Kentuckian on the Greatest Dead Kentuckian. Magnificent Oration of General William Preston." At a reunion of the veterans of the Orphan Brigade assembled in Glasgow in August 1885, Preston gave a toast and a talk in memory of Shiloh and Albert Sidney Johnston. The next year the general mounted a horse at the Cynthiana train station, rode to the courthouse where members of the Orphan Brigade had gathered for a banquet, and offered an address.[84]

In 1887 Preston's declining health prevented him from giving a presentation at the Filson Club. As a youth William had spoken with several associates of Colonel John Floyd, and at Reuben Durrett's request he agreed to speak on this pioneer surveyor of Kentucky. However, he was unable to prepare this talk.

A month before his seventy-first birthday, William Preston died on 21 September 1887 of "rheumatic gout," perhaps attributable to heart problems and the effects of aging. During the summer he had become ill after supervising repairs to a building at Ellerslie, and his health continued to deteriorate. To recuperate, Preston traveled to White Sulphur Springs with his daughter Margaret and his nephew W. P. Johnston. Although he and his wife had an argument in June over the Ellerslie farm accounts, she came to West Virginia to be with him on discovering his critical condition. While dying at White Sulphur Springs, Preston did receive joyous news. He learned that his family name would continue for another generation, for on 28 August Wick's wife Sallie gave birth to a son, named William Preston for his grandfather. As Preston's condition became worse, Evelina, a cook and former slave, gave him opium and morphine. Preston's obituaries stated that he died at home in Lexington surrounded by his family, but this account might have been related for the benefit of contemporaries who would have expected such an ending. Given his state of health on leaving White Sulphur Springs, he perhaps expired while on board the train returning to his home state.[85]

Preston had written his will in West Virginia on 13 August 1887, and in it he directed that his property in Kentucky, Texas, Missouri, and elsewhere should be used to retire his debts. He gave a monthly payment of $100 for life to "my beloved sister, Susan P. Hepburn," while to "my wife" he bequeathed "all household and kitchen furniture" and other domestic property. The remainder of his estate was to be divided equally among his children.[86]

The general's body lay in the drawing room at Preston Place, where Lexington friends paid their respects, before it was taken to Louisville for burial. Since Christ Church Cathedral was undergoing renovation, services were held at Calvary Episcopal Church on Fourth Street. Basil W. Duke, Henry Watterson, and Simon Bolivar Buckner marched in the funeral cortege with the family and other mourners from the church up Broadway to Cave Hill Cemetery, where Preston was laid to rest on land adjacent to his grandfather's grant from Governor Jefferson.[87]

Until her death in 1898, Margaret Wickliffe Preston resided at Preston Place, where she lived with her son, daughter-in-law, and their two children. Today at Cave Hill Cemetery a twenty-foot obelisk and two Kentucky coffee trees mark the graves of William and Margaret Preston. Nearby are the remains of both Confederate and Union veterans.[88]

In its obituary, the *Louisville Courier-Journal* called William Preston "The Last of the Cavaliers."[89] In many ways that was correct. Scion of a distinguished Virginia family, a man who enjoyed high social station and landed wealth by birth and through marriage, William Preston defended the interests of his class and his region–slavery, territorial expansion, and states' rights–as a legislator, diplomat, and soldier. The defeat of these interests doomed his political, diplomatic, and military efforts. Despite his paternalistic treatment of African Americans, he shared the racial prejudices of most southern whites of his day, convinced that blacks were inferior, and acted accordingly. But the South with its gentry-directed society based on landed wealth found that the postwar United States was directed by a class of urban entrepreneurs whose wealth came from commerce, finance, technology, and industrial expansion. Preston's class no longer ruled.

Although Preston championed the political rights of the foreign-born who were helping transform urban America, he realized he was isolated from such changes in society. But Preston was aware of the nation's altered social and economic fabric. At the time of the

Centennial Exposition in Philadelphia, he extolled the "good me-chanics" and "magnificent" machinery transforming his country. In his last years he confessed that he had "many friends among the rich and exalted in station, and was almost universally liked by the poor and humble, but that he had never succeeded in especially com-mending himself to "the great 'respectable' middle class." As his friend General Basil Duke remarked, the former soldier and diplo-mat was "more a representative of an order that had passed away than of the society which knew him in his later years."[90] In death, William Preston became even more of a heroic figure to a generation of Kentuckians for whom the Old South and the Civil War were becoming more and more the substance of legend.

Abbreviations Used in Notes

ADP   Affaires Diverses Politiques, Archives du Ministère des Affaires Etrangères, Quai d'Orsay, Paris, France

AKM   Archiv Kaiser Maximilian von Mexiko, Haus-, Hof- und Staatsarchiv, Vienna, Austria

BC   Simon Bolivar Buckner Collection, H. E. Huntington Library, San Marino, California

B-E   Brown-Ewell Family Papers, Filson Historical Society, Louisville

BFP   Breckinridge Family Papers

CEU   Correspondencia, Estados Unidos, Archivo del Ministerio de Asumtos Exteriores, Madrid, Spain

CHP   Charles Hay Papers, Special Collections and Archives, Margaret I. King Library, University of Kentucky, Lexington

CPC   Correspondence Politique des Consuls, 1863-64, Archives du Ministère des Affaires Etrangères, Quai d'Orsay, Paris, France

CPEU   Correspondence Politique, Etats Unis, 1864, Archives du Ministère des Affaires Etrangères, Quai d'Orsay, Paris, France

CSA   Records of the Confederate States of America, 1861-1865 (John T. Pickett Papers), Manuscript Division, Library of Congress, Washington, D.C.

CSR   Compiled Service Records of Confederate Generals and Staff Officers and Nonregimental Enlisted Men, Microfilm Publication, microcopy 331, National Archives, Washington, D.C.

DC   Davie Collection, Preston Family Papers, Filson Historical Society, Louisville

DIDS   Diplomatic Instructions of the Department of State, 1801-1906, National Archives, Washington, D.C.

Abbreviations Used in Notes

DPR   Diplomatic Post Records, National Archives, Washington, D.C.

DTB   Dicken-Troutman-Balke Papers, Special Collections and Archives, Margaret I. King Library, University of Kentucky, Lexington

DUSMS   Despatches of U.S. Ministers to Spain, 1792-1906, Microfilm Publication, microcopy 31, National Archives, Washington, D.C.

ERP   Expedientes relativos a Preston, Wm., Archivo del Ministerio de Asuntos Exteriores, Madrid, Spain

FCHQ   *Filson Club History Quarterly*

FHS   Filson Historical Society, Louisville

JBP   James Buchanan Papers, Historical Society of Pennsylvania, Philadelphia

JC   Joyes Collection, Preston Family Papers, Filson Historical Society, Louisville

JDP   Jefferson Davis Papers, Special Collections and Archives, Transylvania University, Lexington

JFP   Johnston Family Papers, Filson Historical Society, Louisville

LC   Library of Congress, Washington, D.C.

LEUM   Legación de los Estados Unidos Mexicanos en Francia, Embajada de México, Mexico City, Archivo Histórico Diplomático Mexicano, Mexico City

LM   Legación de México en los Estados Unidos, Archivo Histórico Diplomático Mexicano, Mexico City

LPP   Lincoln Presidential Papers, Manuscript Division, Library of Congress, Washington, D.C.

M-BC   Mason-Barret Collection, Special Collections, Howard-Tilton Library, Tulane University, New Orleans

Od'O   Quai d'Orsay, Paris, France

Abbreviations Used in Notes

OR   *War of the Rebellion: A Compilation of Official Records of the Union and Confederate Armies*, 129 vols. (Washington, D.C., 1880-1901)

PEU   Política, Estados Unidos, 1856-1860, Archivo del Ministerio de Asuntos Exteriores, Madrid, Spain

PJFP   Preston-Johnston Family Papers, Special Collections and Archives, Margaret I. King Library, University of Kentucky, Lexington

RKHS   *The Register of the Kentucky Historical Society*

RWP   Robert Wickliffe Preston

SHC   Southern Historical Collection, University of North Carolina Library, Chapel Hill

UK   University of Kentucky, Lexington

WLP   William Preston Letters, Special Collections and Archives, Margaret I. King Library, University of Kentucky, Lexington

WP   William Preston

WPA   William Preston, account books, letter-books, letters, etc., Special Collections and Archives, Margaret I. King Library, University of Kentucky, Lexington

W-PFP   Wickliffe-Preston Family Papers, Special Collections and Archives, Margaret I. King Library, University of Kentucky, Lexington

WPJ   William Preston Johnston

WPP   William Preston Papers, Special Collections and Archives, Margaret I. King Library, University of Kentucky, Lexington

Notes

1. Boyhood

1. Reuben T. Durrett, "In Memoriam of William Preston," paper delivered in 1887 at the Filson Club (now the Filson Historical Society), Louisville, Ky. William Preston's gravestone in Cave Hill Cemetery, Louisville, Ky., incorrectly gives his birth date as 15 Oct. 1816, a mistake included in *The Prestons of Smithfield and Greenfield in Virginia* (Louisville, 1982), 241, by genealogist John Frederick Dorman. Preston recognized 16 Oct. as his birthday; see William Preston (hereafter WP) to Margaret Wickliffe Preston, 16 Oct. 1861, box 54, Wickliffe-Preston Family Papers (hereafter W-PFP), Special Collections, Margaret I. King Library, University of Kentucky (hereafter UK).

2. Letitia [Preston] Floyd to Rush Floyd, 22 Feb. 1843, Breckinridge Family Papers (hereafter BFP), UK; Orlando Brown, *Memoranda of the Preston Family* (Frankfort, Ky., 1842), 3-6; Patricia G. Johnson, *William Preston and the Allegheny Patriots* (Pulaski, Va., 1976), 2-3.

3. William Preston Johnston (hereafter WPJ), "My Father's Family," Mason-Barret Collection (hereafter M-BC), Special Collections, Howard-Tilton Library, Tulane University; Dorman, *The Prestons*, 1-4.

4. Johnson, *William Preston*, 7-9, 14, 85-95; Dorman, *The Prestons*, 14-17.

5. Gail S. Terry, "Family Empires: A Frontier Elite in Virginia and Kentucky, 1740-1815" (Ph.D. diss., College of William and Mary, 1992), 4.

6. *Southwest Virginia and the Valley* (Roanoke, Va., 1892), 406; Sarah S. Hughes, *Surveyors and Statesmen: Land Measuring in Colonial Virginia* ([Richmond], 1970), 92, 99, 102-5, 111, 130, 159, 162-63; Johnson, *William Preston*, 75-81; Dorman, *The Prestons*, 14-17.

7. For the traditional account of the discovery of the Ohio River by the French, see Francis Parkman, *The Discovery of the Great West: La Salle* (1869; reprint, New York, 1956), 21-22, and John Finley, *The French in the Heart of America* (New York, 1915), 58; Thomas P. Abernethy, *Three Virginia Frontiers* (Gloucester, Mass., 1962), 62-64.

8. Neal O. Hammon, *Early Kentucky Land Records, 1773-1780* (Louisville, 1992), xiii, 44, 46, 280, 422; idem, "The Fincastle Surveyors at the Falls of the Ohio," *Filson Club History Quarterly* (hereafter FCHQ) 47 (1973): 17-18; Hambleton Tapp, "Colonel John Floyd, Kentucky Pioneer," FCHQ 15 (1941): 3-4; Anna M. Cartlidge, "Colonel John Floyd: Reluctant Adventurer," *Register of the Kentucky Historical Society* (hereafter RKHS) 66 (1968): 325-27; Johnson, *William Preston*, 120, 163; George H. Yater, *Two Hundred Years at the Falls of the Ohio: A History of Louisville and Jefferson County* (Louisville, 1979), 13; Carl E. Kramer, "The Origins of the Subdivision Process in Louisville, 1772-1932," in "An Introduction to the Louisville Region: Se-

lected Essays," ed. Don E. Bierman ([Louisville], 1980, mimeographed), 25, 27.

9. Neal O. Hammon, "The Fincastle Surveyors in the Bluegrass, 1774," *RKHS* 70 (1972): 292; idem, *Early Kentucky*, 44, 46; John Floyd to William Preston, 19 May 1776, in Neal O. Hammon and James R. Harris, eds., "'In a Dangerous Situation': Letters of Col. John Floyd, 1774-1783," *RKHS* 83 (1985): 213.

10. Albert H. Tillson Jr., *Gentry and Common Folk: Political Culture on a Virginia Frontier, 1740-1789* (Lexington, 1991), 80; Hammon, "The Fincastle Surveyors in the Bluegrass," 292; Johnson, *William Preston*, 181, 238, 248, 277-92; Dorman, *The Prestons*, 18-20; John Frederick Dorman, "General William Preston," *FCHQ* 43 (1969): 301.

11. "Dec. 1, 1779. Thomas Jefferson, Gov. of Va.," box 119, W-PFP; M. A. Allgeier, *Highland Neighborhood History* (Louisville, [1979]), 5; Hammon, "Fincastle Surveyors at the Falls of the Ohio," 19.

12. Terry, "Family Empires," 62; Johnson, *William Preston*, 75, 84, 107, 310.

13. Johnson, *William Preston*, 107, 226; Hughes, *Surveyors*, 161; L. Floyd to R. Floyd, 22 Feb. 1843, BFP, UK; Humphrey Marshall, *The History of Kentucky*, 2 vols. (Frankfort, 1824), 1: 38; Tapp, "Colonel John Floyd," 12.

14. Dorman, *The Prestons*, 58-60; "Major William Preston," portrait by Aurelius O. Revenaugh, Filson Historical Society (hereafter FHS), Louisville, Ky.; John M. Brown, *Memoranda of the Preston Family* (Frankfort, 1870), 1- 40.

15. Francis Preston to William Preston, 13 Sept. 1808, Joyes Collection (hereafter JC), Preston Family Papers, FHS; Meriwether Lewis to WP, 25 July 1808, in James R. Bentley, ed., "Two Letters of Meriwether Lewis to Major William Preston," *FCHQ* 44 (1970): 173.

16. Marshall, *History of Kentucky*, 1: 31.

17. Yater, *Two Hundred Years*, 4-37; Ben Casseday, *The History of Louisville from Its Earliest Settlement till the Year 1852* (Louisville, 1852), 247; J. Stoddard Johnston, ed., *Memorial History of Louisville from Its First Settlement to the Year 1896*, 2 vols. (Chicago, 1896), 1: 71-76; Reuben T. Durrett, *The Centenary of Louisville* (Louisville, 1893), 21, 76-77; Richard C. Wade, *The Urban Frontier: The Rise of the Western Cities, 1790-1830* (Cambridge, Mass., 1959), 50–53, 64-65.

18. Durrett, "In Memoriam of William Preston," 6; Allgeier, *Highland Neighborhood*, 23.

19. Yater, *Two Hundred Years*, 15; Clay Lancaster, *Antebellum Architecture of Kentucky* (Lexington, 1991), 72-73; Holman Hamilton, *Zachary Taylor: Soldier of the Republic* (1941; reprint, 1966), 31, 37.

20. Dorman, *The Prestons*, 60; "Preston, William," in Katharine G. Healy, comp., "Calendar of Early Jefferson County, Kentucky, Wills," *FCHQ* 6 (1932): 177; "The W. Preston dower Examd., 30 June 1824," in Ludie J. Kinkead and Katharine G. Healy, eds., "Calendar of Division Book No. 1 Jefferson County Court, 1797-1850," *FCHQ* 8 (1934): 121; Eliza Madison to Caroline Hancock Preston, 12 March 1821; J. Cabell Breckinridge to Caroline Preston, 10 Sept. 1821, JC.

21. Terry, "Family Empires," 251. For the accomplishments and offices of the members of the Preston family, see Dorman, *The Prestons*.

22. Caroline Hancock Preston to Maria Preston Pope, 12 Jan. 1840, JC.

23. *The Louisville Directory for the Year 1836* (Louisville, 1836), 45; *The Louisville Directory for the Year 1841* (Louisville, 1841), 84; *The Louisville Directory for the Years 1843-44* (Louisville, 1843), 121.

24. Bennett H. Young, *History of the Texts of the Three Constitutions of Kentucky* (Louisville, 1890), 59; *Louisville Directory for the Year 1836*, v, vii; Durrett, *Centenary of Louisville*, 98-99; Hamilton, *Taylor: Soldier*, 31-32.

25. Frances Trollope, *Domestic Manners of the Americans* (1839; Barre, Mass., 1969), 28; Margaret H. (Mrs. Basil) Hall, *The Artistic Journey: Being the Outspoken Letters of Mrs. Basil Hall Written during a Fourteen Months' Sojourn in America* (New York, 1931), 266; Karl Anton Postal, quoted in Dorothy C. Rush, "Early Accounts of Travel to the Falls of the Ohio: A Bibliography with Selected Quotations," *FCHQ* 68 (1994): 261.

26. *Louisville Directory for the Year 1832* (Louisville, 1832), 138-39.

27. C. H. Preston to M. P. Pope, n.d., 1829, 12 June 1840, JC; C. H. Preston to WP, 28 April, 21, 22 Sept. 1832, box 43, W-PFP.

28. Wade, *Urban Frontier*, 125; M. P. Pope to WP, 26 Jan. 1835, JC; Susan Preston to WP, 5 July 1832, box 43, W-PFP.

29. WP to Albert Sidney Johnston, 16 Dec. 1839, Papers of Albert Sidney Johnston, M-BC; [M. P. Pope] to WP, 26 Jan. 1835, JC; S. Preston to WP, 8 June 1833; C. H. Preston to WP, 6 Jan., 21 July 1832, box 43, W-PFP.

30. C. H. Preston to WP, 28 Aug. 1832, box 43, W-PFP; WP to George M. Davie, 3 Oct. 1886, Charles Hay Papers (hereafter CHP), UK; C. H. Preston to M. P. Pope, 27 June, 18 Sept. 1828, 28 May 1835, JC; C. H. Preston, "Recipe Book," handwritten, 1827 (catalogued as a separate work and not part of any collection), FHS.

31. S. Preston to WP, 8 June 1833, C. H. Preston to WP, 28 Aug., 12 Oct. 1832, box 43, W-PFP; Eugene F. Genovese, "'Our Family, White and Black': Family and Household in the Southern Slaveholders' World View," in Carol Bleser, ed., *In Joy and in*

Sorrow: Women, Family, and Marriage in the Victorian South (New York, 1991), 69, 87.

32. Joan E. Cashin, *A Family Venture: Men and Women on the Southern Frontier* (New York, 1991), 21; WPJ, *The Johnstons of Salisbury* (New Orleans, 1897), 100; C. H. Preston to WP, 28 Aug. 1832, box 43, W-PFP.

33. Casseday, *History of Louisville*, 165.

34. WP to M. P. Pope, 27 Oct. 1832, JC; WP to S. Preston, 1, 14 May, 1 June 1834, 10 July 1842, Davie Collection (hereafter DC), Preston Family Papers, FHS.

35. J. Winston Coleman, *Historic Kentucky* (Lexington, 1968), 48; Marion B. Lucas, *A History of Blacks in Kentucky*, vol. 1, *From Slavery to Segregation, 1760-1891* (Frankfort, 1992), 33.

36. WPJ, quoted in Dorman, "General Preston," 302; WPJ, *The Johnstons*, 196; C. H. Preston to M. P. Pope, 27 Nov. 1826, JC.

37. Walter H. Rankins, *Historic Augusta and Augusta College* (Augusta, Ky., 1985), 8-12; Lewis Collins, *Historical Sketches of Kentucky* (Cincinnati, 1847), 209, 210; Lancaster, *Antebellum Architecture*, 156; Coleman, *Historic Kentucky*, 75; Walter H. Rankins, *Augusta College, Augusta, Kentucky, First Established Methodist College, 1822-1849* (Frankfort, 1957), 10-12, 24, 33.

38. "'Edgewood,' The Ben Hardin House," pamphlet, CHP; WP quoted in Lucius P. Little, *Ben Hardin: Times and Contemporaries* (Louisville, 1887), 164, 388, 611; WP to S. Preston, [20] June 1834, [9] June 1835, DC.

39. WPJ, quoted in Dorman, "General Preston," 302; WP, "Some Reflections on the Study of Greek Authors," handwritten, 3 Nov. 1876, in the preface of his copy of Johann Scapula, *Lexicon graeco-latinum* (Oxford, England, [1820]), annotated copy in William Preston, account books, letter-books, letters, etc. (hereafter WPA), UK.

40. WP to C. H. Preston, 19 Nov. 1832; WP, list of expenses, n.d. 1832; Henrietta Preston Johnston to WP, 11 Aug. 1832; C. H. Preston to WP, 25 July 1832, S. Preston to WP, 8 June 1833, box 43, W-PFP.

41. Lancaster, *Antebellum Architecture*, 176-78; Martin F. Schmidt, *Kentucky Illustrated: The First Hundred Years* (Lexington, 1992), 121; H. Edward Richardson, *Cassius Marcellus Clay: Firebrand of Freedom* (Lexington, 1976), 10.

42. John B. Boles, *Religion in Antebellum Kentucky* (Lexington, 1976), 52-66; Clyde F. Crews, *An American Holy Land: A History of the Archdiocese of Louisville* (Wilmington, Del., 1987), 95-96.

43. Richardson, *Cassius Marcellus Clay*, 10-11; Roberta Baughman Carlée, *The Last*

Gladiator: Cassius M. Clay (Berea, Ky., 1979), 10.

44. WPJ, *The Life of General Albert Sidney Johnston* (New York, 1879), 23; WPJ, quoted in Edwin Porter Thompson, *History of the Orphan Brigade* (Louisville, 1898), 195-96; H. P. Johnston to WP, 17 Nov. 1832, box 43, W-PFP.

2. Youth

1. WP to S. Preston, 7 Jan. 1836, WP to A. S. Johnston, 3 June 1837, William Preston Papers (hereafter WPP), UK; WP to S. Preston, 1 May 1834, 3 May 1847, DC.

2. George Hancock to WP, 13 Jan. 1834, 19 Aug. 1836, WP to C. H. Preston, 26 July 1835, box 43, W-PFP.

3. WP to C. H. Preston, 24 Sept. 1836, WP to S. Preston, 7 Feb., 19 Aug. 1837, DC; [M. P. Pope] to WP, 26 Jan. 1835, JC; WP to S. Preston, 15 Oct. 1836, WPP.

4. WP to S. Preston, 7 Jan. 1836, WPP; WP to S. Preston, [n.d.] Jan. 1835, DC; C. H. Preston to M. P. Pope, 26 Jan. 1835, JC.

5. Unless otherwise cited, the source for Preston's studies at Yale are his handwritten notes, "Some Reflections on the Study of Greek Authors," appended to a copy of Scapula, *Lexicon graeco-latinum*, found in WPA.

6. WPJ, quoted in Dorman, "General William Preston," 302; Clement Eaton, *The Mind of the Old South* (Baton Rouge, 1967), 293-97.

7. WP to S. Preston, 1 June 1834, 12 April, 3 May 1837, DC.

8. WP to A. S. Johnston, 3 June 1837, WPA; Simon Greenleaf, form letter, 19 Dec. 1837, S. Greenleaf to WP, 20 Nov. 1838, box 43, W-PFP; Harvard University, *Quinquennial Catalogue of the Law School of Harvard University, 1817-1834* (Cambridge, Mass., 1935), 13.

9. B. C. Prestman, notice, 10 March 1837, box 43, W-PFP; Steven M. Stowe, *Intimacy and Power in the Old South: Ritual in the Lives of the Planters* (Baltimore, 1987), 12-13, 30-33.

10. Bertram Wyatt-Brown, *Southern Honor: Ethics and Behavior in the Old South* (Oxford, 1982), 360; Eaton, *Mind of the Old South*, 289; J. Winston Coleman Jr., *Famous Kentucky Duels: The Story of the Code of Honor in the Bluegrass State* (Frankfort, 1953), 69-83; James Speed letters, 1844, box 46, W-PFP.

11. S. Preston to WP, with a note by Margaret Wickliffe to WP, 30 April [1835], box 43, W-PFP; WP to C. H. Preston, 24 Sept., 12 Nov. 1836, DC; WP to S. Preston, 7

Jan. 1836, 2 Feb., 1837, WPP.

12. Allen J. Share, *Cities in the Commonwealth: Two Centuries of Urban Life in Kentucky* (Lexington, 1981), 38; Casseday, *History of Louisville*, 202; *Louisville Directory for the Year 1836*, 68.

13. F. Garvin Davenport, *Ante-Bellum Kentucky: A Social History, 1800-1860* (1943; reprint, Westport, Conn., 1983), 75; Carl E. Kramer, "City with a Vision: Images of Louisville in the 1830s," *FCHQ* 60 (1986): 432-35; Alexis de Tocqueville, *Journey to America*, trans. George Lawrence (Garden City, N.Y., 1971), 92, 284, 362.

14. WP to A. S. Johnston, 22 Feb. 1839, WPJ, "Extracts from My Journal," Sept. 1848, M-BC; R. Wickliffe Sr. to R. Wickliffe Jr., 21 May 1844, Dicken-Troutman-Balke Family Papers (hereafter DTB), UK.

15. H. Levin, ed., *The Lawyers and Lawmakers of Kentucky* (1897; reprint, Easley, S.C., [1982]), 607; WP to A. S. Johnston, 22 Feb. 1839, M-BC.

16. WP to A. S. Johnston, 19 April, 16 Dec. 1839, M-BC; Charles P. Roland, *Albert Sidney Johnston: Soldier of Three Republics* (Austin, Texas, 1964), 83.

17. WP to R. Wickliffe Jr., 25 July 1844, DTB; Arthur C. Cole, *The Whig Party in the South* (1913; reprint, Gloucester, Mass., 1962), vii, 38, 58, 69; Edward Pessen, "Society and Politics in the Jacksonian Era," *RKHS* 81 (1984): 15; idem, *Jacksonian America: Society, Personality, and Politics*, 2d ed. rev. (Homewood, Ill., 1978), 325; Arthur M. Schlesinger Jr., *The Age of Jackson* (New York, 1958), 154.

18. Charles G. Sellers Jr., "Who Were the Southern Whigs?" *American Historical Review* 59 (1954): 346; Maurice G. Baxter, *Henry Clay and the American System* (Lexington, 1995), 110, 122; idem, *One and Inseparable: Daniel Webster and the Union* (Cambridge, Mass., 1984), 504.

19. WP to A. S. Johnston, 16 Dec. 1839, 15 Feb., 28 Aug. 1840, M-BC; Charles St. Harper to WP, 18 Feb. 1839, box 43, W-PFP.

20. William J. Cooper Jr., *The South and the Politics of Slavery, 1828-1856* (Baton Rouge, 1978), 95, 136; WP to M. Wickliffe, n.d. [1840], 26 Oct. 1840, box 44, W-PFP; Richardson, *Cassius Marcellus Clay*, 34.

21. R. Wickliffe Jr. to WP, 13 April, 16 Oct. 1838, box 43, 14 Nov. 1839, box 40, WP to M. Wickliffe, 12 Nov. 1840, box 44, W-PFP.

22. C. H. Preston to M. P. Pope, 12 Jan. 1840, JC; WP to A. S. Johnston, 14 Jan. 1839, M-BC; WP to S. Preston, 28 Dec. 1839, DC.

23. WP to M. Wickliffe, 26 Oct., 4 Nov. 1840, n.d. [1840], box 44, R. Wickliffe Sr. to

WP, copy of deed, 7 May 1857, box 91, W-PFP; WP to A. S. Johnston, 28 Aug. 1840, M-BC.

24. "Mrs. Preston," *Louisville Courier-Journal*, 8 Feb. 1888; 3 Feb. 1859 entry, Benjamin Moran Diary, Manuscript Division, Library of Congress (hereafter LC); WP to R. Wickliffe Jr., 25 July 1844, DTB.

25. M. Wickliffe to Mary O. T. R. Wickliffe, 27 July [1835?], box 39, Mary Todd Lincoln to M. W. Preston, 23 July 1853, box 48, W-PFP; William H. Townsend, *Lincoln and the Bluegrass: Slavery and the Civil War in Kentucky* (Lexington, 1955), 292-93; Randolph Hollingsworth, "She Used Her Power Lightly: A Political History of Margaret Wickliffe Preston of Kentucky" (Ph. D. diss., University of Kentucky, 1999), 42-46. In addition to Hollingsworth's dissertation, for biographical material on Margaret Wickliffe Preston, see Andrea S. Ramage, "Bluegrass Patriarch: Robert Wickliffe and His Family in Antebellum Kentucky" (M.A. thesis, University of Kentucky, 1993); Andrea S. Watkins, "Patriarchical Politics: Robert Wickliffe and His Family in Antebellum Kentucky" (Ph.D. diss., University of Kentucky, 1999).

26. WP to S. Preston, 28 Dec. 1839, DC; "Mrs. Preston," *Louisville Courier-Journal*, 8 Feb. 1888.

27. George Ranck, *History of Lexington, Kentucky: Its Early Annals and Recent Progress* (Cincinnati, 1872), 382; Hollingsworth, "She Used Her Power Lightly," 103; George R. Poage, *Henry Clay and the Whig Party* (1936; reprint, Gloucester, Mass., 1965), 16; Robert V. Remini, *Henry Clay: Statesman for the Union* (New York, 1991), 569, 653, 691.

28. James C. Klotter, *The Breckinridges of Kentucky, 1760-1981* (Lexington, 1986), 306; George G. Shackelford, *George Wythe Randolph and the Confederate Elite* (Athens, Ga., 1988), xi, 1, 166-70; Merrill D. Peterson, *The Great Triumvirate: Webster, Clay, and Calhoun* (New York, 1987), 167.

29. J. Winston Coleman Jr., *Slavery Times in Kentucky* (Chapel Hill, 1940), 21, 32; Andrea S. Ramage, "Love and Honor: The Robert Wickliffe Family of Antebellum Kentucky," *RKHS* 92 (1996): 52, 116.

30. Robert G. H. Kean, *Inside the Confederate Government: The Diary of Robert Gatwick Hill Kean*, ed. Edward Younger (New York, 1957), 131; Zachariah F. Smith, *The History of Kentucky* (Louisville, 1886), 661; 3 Feb. 1859 entry, Benjamin Moran Diary; Belle Brittan, *Belle Brittan on a Tour at Newport, and Here and There* (New York, 1858), 69; "William Preston," portrait by Aurelius O. Revenaugh, depicting Preston ca. 1850, FHS.

31. Duke, *Basil Duke*, 196; "General William Preston," copy print of a carte de visite showing Preston in his Confederate uniform, FHS.

32. WP, *Remarks of Mr. Preston of Kentucky* (Washington, [1853-54]), 3, a reprint of Preston's speech in the House of Representatives, 20 Dec. 1853; WP to "My dear son and daughters," 3 April 1862, Johnston Family Papers (hereafter JFP), FHS.

33. WP to A. S. Johnston, 23 Aug. 1848, M-BC; WP to "My dear son and daughters," 3 April 1862, JFP.

34. WP to Robert Wickliffe Preston (hereafter RWP), 10 Feb. 1865, DC.

35. WP to "My dear son and daughters," 3 April 1862, JFP; Lucas, *History of Blacks in Kentucky*, 43.

36. Lowell H. Harrison and James C. Klotter, *A New History of Kentucky* (Lexington, 1997), 168; Coleman, *Slavery Times*, 32-33, 45; Ramage,"Bluegrass Patriarch," 56; Lucas, *History of Blacks in Kentucky*, 29, 44; R. Wickliffe Sr., *Speech on the Negro Law* (Lexington, 1840); R. Wickliffe Sr. to WP, 29 Dec. 1849, box 46, W-PFP; John B. Boles, *Black Southerners, 1619-1869* (Lexington, 1983), 86; Eugene D. Genovese, *Roll, Jordan, Roll: The World the Slaves Made* (New York, 1972), 32.

37. Asa F. Martin, *The Anti-Slavery Movement in Kentucky Prior to 1850* (1918; reprint, New York, 1970), 13, 31-32, 48-57.

38. Milly C. to M. O. T. R. Wickliffe, 10 March 1833, M.O.T.R. Wickliffe, statement, 9 March 1841, box 39, W-PFP.

39. William L. Miller, *Arguing about Slavery: The Great Battle in the United States Congress* (New York, 1996), 10, 28-30; David B. Cheesebrough, *Clergy Dissent in the Old South, 1830-1865* (Carbondale, Ill., 1996), 43; Lowell H. Harrison, *The Anti-Slavery Movement in Kentucky* (Lexington, 1978), 39-45; Henry H. Simms, *Emotion at High Tide: Abolition as a Controversial Factor* (Richmond, Va., 1960), 18.

40. David L. Smiley, *Lion of Whitehall: The Life of Cassius M. Clay* (Madison, Wisc., 1962), 21; Richardson, *Cassius Marcellus Clay*, 17, 23; Carlée, *Last Gladiator*, 29; Carl N. Degler, *The Other South: Southern Dissidents in the Nineteenth Century* (New York, 1974), 59.

41. William L. Garrison, quoted in Simms, *Emotion at High Tide*, 27; John C. Calhoun quoted in William B. Hesseltine and David L. Smiley, *The South in American History* (Englewood Cliffs, N.J., 1960), 162, 165.

42. Drew Gilpin Faust, ed., *The Ideology of Slavery: Proslavery Thought in the Antebellum South, 1830-1860* (Baton Rouge, 1981), 1-4; John David Smith, "Slavery and Antislavery," in *Our Kentucky: A Study of the Bluegrass State*, ed. James C. Klotter (Lexington, 1992), 121.

43. William J. Cooper Jr., *Liberty and Slavery: Southern Politics to 1860* (New York,

1983), 178-80; Simms, *Emotion at High Tide*, 131.

44. Larry E. Tise, *Proslavery: A History of the Defense of Slavery in America, 1701-1840* (Athens, Ga., 1987), xiv, 8-14, 249; Coleman, *Slavery Times*, 302; Roland, *Johnston*, 107.

45. Stanley Harold, *The Abolitionists and the South, 1831-1861* (Lexington, 1995), 178; Cheesebrough, *Clergy Dissent in the Old South*, 43; Harrison, *Anti-Slavery Movement in Kentucky*, 45-46; Martin, *Anti-Slavery Movement in Kentucky Prior to 1850*, 108; Lucas, *History of Blacks in Kentucky*, xv.

46. Stephen Aron, *How the West Was Lost: The Transformation of Kentucky from Daniel Boone to Henry Clay* (Baltimore, 1996), 144; John H. Franklin, *The Militant South, 1800-1861* (Boston, 1956), 85-86; Peter Kolchin, "In Defense of Servitude: American Proslavery and Russian Proserfdom Arguments, 1760-1860," *American Historical Review* 85 (1980): 815.

47. Clement Eaton, *The Freedom-of-Thought Struggle in the Old South* (New York, 1964), 268-69; James Oakes, *The Ruling Race: A History of American Slaveholders* (New York, 1982), 195.

48. WPJ, "Extracts," Aug. 1848, M-BC; WPJ to Rosa Johnston, 24 July 1862, JFP; WP to Gen. Almonte, 6 June 1864, DC.

49. WP quoted in R. Sutton, ed., *Report of the Debates and Proceedings of the Convention for the Revision of the Constitution of the State of Kentucky* (Frankfort, 1849), 810.

50. Ibid., 810, 879.

3. Husband and Soldier

1. Young, *History and Texts of the Three Constitutions of Kentucky*, 69; Yater, *Two Hundred Years*, 61; Lucy B. Slater, "Kentucky Biographical Notebook: William Burke Belknap, 1811-1889," *FCHQ* 66 (1992): 581-83; *Picture of Louisville: Directory and Business Advertiser for 1844-1845* (Louisville, 1844), 59.

2. Davenport, *Ante-Bellum Kentucky*, 57; Clyde F. Crews, "Roots of a Renaissance: Cultural Visitors in Nineteenth- and Twentieth-Century Louisville," *FCHQ* 69 (1995): 277-88; Rexford Newcomb, *Old Kentucky Architecture: Colonial, Federal, Greek Revival, Gothic, and Other Types Erected Prior to the War Between the States* (New York, 1940), plates 113-14.

3. Johnston, *Memorial History of Louisville*, 2: 83; Davenport, *Ante-Bellum Kentucky*, 21; Charles Dickens, *American Notes* (1842; Greenwich, Conn., 1961), 193-94.

4. M. O. T. R. Wickliffe to M. W. Preston, 27 March 1840, DC; M. W. Preston to

WP, 16 Aug. [1841], box 44, W-PFP.

5. Melville O. Briney, *Fond Recollections: Sketches of Old Louisville* (Louisville, 1955), 9, 10; *Picture of Louisville*, 313; John Louis Dugan, "James Guthrie: His Interests in Internal Improvements in Kentucky from 1820-1869" (M.A. thesis, University of Florida, 1952), 1-2, 17-18, typescript in FHS; Slater, "William Burke Belknap," 582.

6. [WP], "Household Furniture," [1844], M. W. Preston to R. Wickliffe Sr., 19 March [1843], 6 Dec. [1845], R. Wickliffe Sr. to WP, 30 Oct. 1841, box 44, M. W. Preston to R. Wickliffe Sr., 1 Dec. 1845, box 45, W-PFP; WP to Susan Preston Christy, 10 July 1842, DC.

7. Hollingsworth, "She Used Her Power Lightly," 264; Henry Tanner, comp., *The Louisville Directory and Business Advertiser for 1859-60* (Louisville, 1859), 186; M. W. Preston to R. Wickliffe Sr., 19 March [1843], box 44, 1 Dec. 1845, box 45, W-PFP; Ramage, "Bluegrass Patriarch: Robert Wickliffe and His Family," 63.

8. WP to R. Wickliffe Sr., 10 May 1845, box 44, M.W. Preston to WP, 20 Aug. [1848], box 45, W-PFP.

9. Hollingsworth, "She Used Her Power Lightly," 166-68; WP to M. W. Preston, 9 Feb. 1842, WP to R. Wickliffe Sr., 25 Feb. 1844, 10 May 1845, R. Wickliffe Sr. to WP, 3 June 1847, box 44, S. Christy to WP, 26 April 1850, box 74, W-PFP.

10. R. Wickliffe Sr. to WP, 30 Oct. 1841, box 44, R. Wickliffe Sr. to M. W. Preston, 16 Sept. 1846, deed of R. Wickliffe Sr., 12 Oct. 1848, box 45, W-PFP.

11. R. Wickliffe Sr. to WP, 14 Dec. 1850, box 46, Rosa V. Johnson to WP, 10 Jan. 1851, M. W. Preston to WP, 7 Aug. [1852], box 47, W-PFP; WP to S. Christy, 16 Nov, 3 Dec. 1850, DC.

12. WP to S. Christy, 24 Dec. 1854, box 74, R. Wickliffe Sr. to M. W. Preston, 6 Dec. 1855, box 151, W-PFP.

13. R. Wickliffe Sr. to WP, 13 Jan., 10 May 1848, M. W. Preston to R. Wickliffe Sr., 1 Dec. 1845, M. W. Preston to WP, 26 Aug. 1846, box 45, W-PFP.

14. M. W. Preston to R. Wickliffe Sr., 1 Dec. 1845, WP to R. Wickliffe Sr., 2 March 1846, box 45, 20 March 1854, box 50, M. W. Preston to WP, 19 Sept. 1859, box 46, W-PFP.

15. Hollingsworth, "She Used Her Power Lightly," 162; WP to S. Christy, 2 Feb. 1848, 11 Dec. 1850, DC; Sally H. Woolley to WP, 2 Feb. 1844, box 44, R. Wickliffe Sr. to M. W. Preston, 28 Dec. 1849, box 46, 3 Dec. 1854, box 50, W-PFP.

16. Roland, *Albert Sidney Johnston*, 51; WP to A. S. Johnston, 28 Aug. 1840, M-BC; Arthur Shaw, *William Preston Johnston: A Transitional Figure of the Confederacy* (Baton

Rouge, 1943), 1-25.

17. Roland, *Albert Sidney Johnston*, 145; WP to A. S. Johnston, 25 Feb. 1843, 23 Aug. 1848, M-BC.

18. WPJ, "Extracts from My Journal," M-BC; Shaw, *William Preston Johnston*, 17-26, 30, 34.

19. Aron, *How the West Was Lost*, 125-26; E. Turner to WP, 11 Feb. 1846, box 45, M. W. Preston to M. O. T. R. Wickliffe, 17 May 1843, M. W. Preston to R. Wickliffe Sr., 7 Oct. 1844, [28 Jan. 1845], box 44, W-PFP.

20. Samuel D. Gross, *Autobiography of Samuel D. Gross, M.D., with Reminiscences of His Time and Contemporaries*, vol. 2 (Philadelphia, 1887), 16; Reuben T. Durrett, quoted in Mary Florence Taney, *Kentucky Pioneer Women: Columbian Poems and Prose* (Cincinnati, 1893), 96; Durrett, "In Memoriam of William Preston."

21. M. W. Preston to R. Wickliffe Sr., 15 June 1843, 8 Nov. 1845, box 44, W-PFP; Davenport, *Ante-Bellum Kentucky*, 27.

22. John Rowan to WP, 30 May 1842, Mrs. John Rowan to M. W. Preston, 30 May 1842, box 44, Mary H. Wickliffe to S. Christy, n.d. Sept 1848, box 74, W-PFP.

23. M. W. Preston to R. Wickliffe Sr., 19 March [1843], WP to R. Wickliffe Sr., 8 Nov. 1844, box 44, M. W. Preston to WP, 1 July [1846], box 45, 24 April 1849, box 49, W-PFP; WP to S. Christy, 16 Nov. 1850, DC.

24. M. W. Preston to R. Wickliffe Sr., [29] Sept. 1843, 13 Nov. 1844, box 44, W-PFP.

25. Hollingsworth, "She Used Her Power Lightly," 8-9; WP to R. Wickliffe Sr., 24 March 1845, box 45, W-PFP.

26. M. W. Preston to R. Wickliffe Sr., 9 Dec. [1842], box 44, W-PFP; WP to S. Christy, 16 Nov. 1850, 3 Jan., 23 Nov. 1854, DC.

27. *Louisville Daily Courier*, 25 May 1850; Briney, *Fond Recollections*, 15-23.

28. Neville Green to WP, 25 Nov. 1841, box 44, W-PFP.

29. Norman E. Tutorow, *Texas Annexation and the Mexican War: A Political Study of the Old Northwest* (Palo Alto, Calif., 1978), 20-21, 70-73, 114-15; Patricia E. Hill, *Dallas: The Making of a Modern City* (Austin, Tex., 1996), xix; William R. Hogan, *Texas Republic: A Social and Economic History* (Norman, Okla., 1946), 11; Rupert N. Richardson, *Texas: The Lone Star State* (New York, 1943), 191.

30. A. S. Johnston to WP, 27 Nov. 1841, WP to R. Wickliffe Sr., 3 April 1844, box 44, W-PFP; WP to A. S. Johnston, 7 March 1844, M-BC; Poage, *Henry Clay and the Whig Party*, 140.

31. Glenn W. Price, *Origins of the War with Mexico: The Polk-Stockton Intrigue* (Austin, 1967), 152, 165-67; Tutorow, *Texas Annexation*, 123-27.

32. John H. Schroeder, *Mr. Polk's War: American Opposition and Dissent, 1846-1848* (Madison, Wisc., 1973), 162; Price, *Origins of the War with Mexico*, 36-37, 168; Seymour V. Connor and Odie B. Faulk, *North America Divided: The Mexican War, 1846-1848* (New York, 1971), 3; Agustín Yáñez, *Santa Anna: Espectro de una sociedad* (Mexico City, 1985), 161; Edmund P. Gaines to WP, 15 June 1847, JC; WP to A. S. Johnston, 23 Aug. 1848, M-BC.

33. Richardson, *Cassius Marcellus Clay*, 58; Damon R. Eubank, "A Time of Enthusiasm: The Response of Kentucky to the Call for Troops in the Mexican War," *RKHS* 90 (1992): 324, 330, 343; Richard G. Stone Jr., *A Brittle Sword: The Kentucky Militia, 1776-1912* (Lexington, 1977), 57.

34. Damon Eubank, "A Time for Heroes, A Time for Honor: Kentucky Soldiers in the Mexican War," *FCHQ* 72 (1998): 174-75, 181, 184, 190-92.

35. Eubank, "Heroes," 187, 191-92; Hamilton, *Zachary Taylor*, 21-27, 231-42; M. W. Preston to WP, 13 May 1846, box 45, W-PFP; C. H. Preston to William Owsley, 16 Sept. 1847, Military Correspondence, CHP.

36. C. H. Preston, will, 9 April 1842, prepared by the Louisville Abstract and Loan Association, CHP; Allgeier, *Highland Neighborhood History*, 8.

37. Thomas C. Cherry, *Kentucky: The Pioneer State of the West* (New York, 1923), 242; Notice, 30 April 1847, box 45, W-PFP; William Owsley, Commision, 25 May 1847, and "Field and Staff Muster-in Roll," 10 Oct. 1847, CHP; Frank H. Heck, *Proud Kentuckian: John C. Breckinridge, 1821-1875* (Lexington, 1976), 21-22.

38. WP, "Journal in Mexico," 1, 14, 20 Nov. 1847. A handwritten copy of this diary was made by William Preston Johnston in August 1848, M-BC. A typescript of "Journal in Mexico" was made in 1927 by Preston Brown, William Preston's grandson; microfilm, FHS. An edited version of the diary was privately printed by the family as *Journal in Mexico* (n.p., n.d.). All citations from "Journal in Mexico" are from the typescript. WP to M. W. Preston, 24 Nov. 1847, box 45, W-PFP.

39. WP, "Journal," 26, 29 Nov., 6 Dec. 1847; Robert W. Johannsen, *To the Halls of the Montezumas: The Mexican War in the American Imagination* (New York, 1985), 145, 160-62; M. W. Preston to WP, 13 Nov. 1847, box 45, W-PFP.

40. WP, "Journal," 30 Nov. 1847; Wilfrid H. Callcott, *Santa Anna: The Story of the*

Enigma Who Once Was Mexico (Hamden, Conn., 1964), 139; Yáñez, *Santa Anna*, 179.

41. WP, "Journal," 1, 6, 8 Dec. 1847.

42. Ibid., 8, 16, 18 Dec. 1847.

43. Charles W. Elliott, *Winfield Scott: The Soldier and the Man* (New York, 1937), 279; WP to R. Wickliffe Sr., 14 March 1848, box 45, W-PFP.

44. John S. D. Eisenhower, *Agent of Destiny: The Life and Times of General Winfield Scott* (New York, 1997), 325; Johannsen, *To the Halls of the Montezumas*, 118; Otis A. Singletary, *The Mexican War* (Chicago, 1960), 101; Polk quoted in Dean B. Mahin, *Olive Branch and Sword: The United States and Mexico, 1845-1848* (Jefferson, N.C., 1997), 166; Timothy D. Johnson, *Winfield Scott: The Quest for Military Glory* (Lawrence, Kan., 1998), 210-11.

45. John E. Weems, *To Conquer a Peace: The War between the United States and Mexico* (Garden City, N.Y., 1974), 442-43; Mahin, *Olive Branch and Sword*, 188; Connor and Faulk, *North America Divided*, 132; WP to R. Wickliffe Sr., 14 March 1848, WP to M. W. Preston, 25 April 1848, box 45, W-PFP; Alfred H. Bill, *Rehearsal for Conflict: The War with Mexico, 1846-1848* (New York, 1947), 321; Eisenhower, *Agent of Destiny*, 145.

46. WP to M. W. Preston, 24 Nov. 1847, Manuel Escamilla to WP, n.d. [1848], box 45, W-PFP; Elizabeth M. Simpson, *Bluegrass Houses and Their Traditions* (Lexington, 1932), 10.

47. WP to R. Wickliffe Sr., 20 April, 7 May 1848, box 45, W-PFP.

48. WP to R. Wickliffe Sr., 7 May 1848, box 45, W-PFP; John S. D. Eisenhower, *So Far from God: The U.S. War with Mexico, 1846-1848* (New York, 1989), 347-50; James I. Dantic, "The Kentucky Volunteer Foot Soldier in the Mexican War," *RKHS* 95 (1997): 264; Bill, *Rehearsal for Conflict*, 309.

49. [WP] to [M.W. Preston], [1848], 20 March 1848, Mona Guadalupe Corona and WP, Certificate, 26 May 1848, box 45, W-PFP; WP to S. Christy, 16 Jan., 19 May 1848, DC; Dantic, "The Kentucky Volunteer," 266-69; WP to Howard F. Christy, 7 April 1848, DC.

50. Ralph W. Kirkham, *The Mexican War Journal and Letters of Ralph W. Kirkham*, ed. Robert R. Miller (College Station, Tex., 1991), 79, 97; [WP] to [M. W. Preston], [1848], box 45, W-PFP; George Wilkins Kendall, *Dispatches from the Mexican War*, ed. Lawrence D. Cress (Norman, Okla., 1999), 408-9; Richard B. Winders, *Mr. Polk's Army: The American Military Experience and the Mexican War* (College Station, Tex., 1997), 131.

51. Winders, *Mr. Polk's Army*, 135; Eisenhower, *So Far from God*, 347; James B. Fry, printed letter to Aztec Club members, 1 Sept. 1887, box 70, W-PFP; WP to H. F. Christy, 7 April 1848, DC.

52. Heck, *Proud Kentuckian*, 21; Nathaniel C. Hughes Jr. and Thomas C. Ware, *Theodore O'Hara: Poet-Soldier of the Old South* (Knoxville, 1998), 35; D. Scully, notice, 3 May 1848, box 45, W-PFP; Elliott, *Winfield Scott*, 555.

53. WP to R. Wickliffe Sr., 8 April 1848, box 45, W-PFP; WP, "Journal," 19 Dec. 1847.

54. E. Kirby Smith, *To Mexico with Scott: Letters of Captain E. Kirby Smith to His Wife*, ed. Emma Jerome Blackwood (Cambridge, Mass., 1917), 210; James M. McCaffrey, *Army of Manifest Destiny: The American Soldier in the Mexican War, 1846-1848* (New York, 1992), 210.

55. WP to M. W. Preston, 13 March 1848, box 45, W-PFP; *Congressional Globe*, 33rd Cong., 1st sess., 20 Dec. 1853, 73.

56. WP, "Journal," 19 Dec. 1847; WP to R. Wickliffe Sr., 7 May 1848, box 45, W-PFP.

57. M. W. Preston to WP, 16, 21 Jan., 28 Feb. 1848, box 45, W-PFP.

58. From "The Form of Solemnization of Matrimony," *The Book of Common Prayer* (New York, n.d.), 300; M. W. Preston to WP, 11 March, 13 May 1848, box 45, W-PFP.

59. M. W. Preston to WP, 22 Feb., 13 Nov. 1847, 16 Jan., 11, 30 March 1848, box 45, W-PFP.

60. R. Wickliffe Sr. to M. W. Preston, 18 Feb. [1842], box 44, M. W. Preston to WP, 22 Feb., 13 Nov., n.d. Dec. [1847], 16 Jan. 1848, box 45, W-PFP.

61. WP to M. W. Preston, 24 Nov. 1847, 13 March, 30 May, n.d. [May] 1848, box 45, W-PFP.

62. M. W. Preston to WP, n.d. Dec. [1847], R. Wickliffe Sr. to WP, 13 Jan. 1848, box 45, W-PFP; Oakes, *The Ruling Race*, 40; Hollingsworth, "She Used Her Power Lightly," 64-65; Ramage, "Bluegrass Patriarch," 63.

63. R. Wickliffe Sr. to WP, 13 Jan., 17 April 1848, S. Christy to M. W. Preston, 14 May 1848, WPJ to WP, 8 Jan. 1848, box 45, W-PFP.

64. M. W. Preston to R. Wickliffe Sr., 8 July 1848, M. W. Preston to WP, 30 May 1848, box 45, W-PFP.

65. Weems, *To Conquer a Peace*, 455-56.

66. WP to A. S. Johnston, 12 Aug. 1848, M-BC; WPJ, "Extracts," [July 1848]; "Field and Staff Muster-out Roll," 25 July 1848, CHP.

67. WP to A. S. Johnston, 13 May 1845, M-BC; R. Wickliffe Sr. to R. Wickliffe Jr., 21 May 1844, DTB; WP to S. Christy, 22 Sept. 1849, DC.

68. R. Wickliffe Sr. to M. W. Preston, 24 Jan. 1850, box 46, W-PFP; WP to A. S. Johnston, 23 Aug. 1848, M-BC.

69. WP to A. S. Johnston, 23 Aug. 1848, M-BC; WP to R. Wickliffe Sr., 14 March 1848, box 45, W-PFP.

4. Legislator

1. M. W. Preston to WP, 16 Jan. 1848, box 45, W-PFP.

2. Robert E. McDowell, *City of Conflict: Louisville in the Civil War, 1861-1865* (Louisville, 1962), 13; Yater, *Two Hundred Years*, 57; WPJ to WP, 17 Jan. 1854, box 49, W-PFP.

3. William Mallalieu, "The Origins of Louisville Culture," FCHQ 38 (1964): 154; Briney, *Fond Recollections*, 84.

4. Davenport, *Ante-Bellum Kentucky*, 34; Crews, "Roots of a Renaissance," 278.

5. Moritz Busch, *Travels between the Hudson and the Mississippi, 1851-1852*, trans. Norman H. Benzer (Lexington, 1971), 211; Louis Kossuth, quoted in *History of the Ohio Falls Cities and Their Counties*, vol. 1 (Cleveland, 1882), 160.

6. Degler, *The Other South*, 115; Claudia D. Goldin, *Urban Slavery in the American South, 1820-1860* (Chicago, 1976), 13, 16, 52; Cole, *Whig Party in the South*, 308.

7. James P. Sullivan, "Civic and Business Advancements in Louisville's Rioting Decade 1850-1860" (M.A. thesis, University of Louisville, 1958), 60, 65; Casseday, *History of Louisville*, 247.

8. Cole, *Whig Party in the South*, 314; Sister Agnes Geraldine McGann, *Nativism in Kentucky to 1860* (Washington, D.C, 1944), 61-62; Yater, *Two Hundred Years*, 65.

9. William G. O'Toole and Charles E. Aebersold, trans., "Louisville's Bloody Monday Riots from a German Perspective," *FCHQ* 70 (1996): 421 [excerpts from "Die Kulturfortschritte von Louisville, Ky."], in a souvenir edition of the *Louisville Anzeiger*, 21 June 1914; Erna O. Gwinn,"The Liederkranz in Louisville, 1877-1959," *FCHQ* 55 (1981): 40; Tracy McMahan Liebert, "The Germans in Louisville, Ken-

tucky, in the 19ᵗʰ Century" (M.S. thesis, Georgetown University, 1993), 5-6,17, 20.

10. *Louisville Democrat*, 6 July 1855; Sullivan, "Civic and Business Advancement," 60; Clyde F. Crews, *Presence and Possibility: Louisville Catholicism and Its Cathedral* ([Louisville], 1973), 44-46; Yater, *Two Hundred Years*, 65.

11. WP to R. Wickliffe Sr., 29 April 1844, box 44, WP to Zachary Taylor, 24 Jan. 1849, box 46, W-PFP; Garnett Duncan to Taylor, 15 May 1849, CHP.

12. Dugan, "James Guthrie," 17-20; William W. Freehling, *Secessionists at Bay, 1776-1854*, vol. 1 of *The Road to Disunion* (New York, 1990), 469; Smiley, *Lion of Whitehall*, 135-42.

13. Harold, *Abolitionists and the South*, 128; Richardson, *Cassius Marcellus Clay*, 46.

14. Harrison, *Anti-Slavery Movement*, 57-58; Young, *Three Constitutions*, 53; *Louisville Morning Courier*, 9 Aug. 1849; Smiley, *Lion of Whitehall*, 142.

15. Young, *Three Constitutions*, 53, 71; Kentucky Constitution (1850), art. 10, sec. 2; art. 13, sec. 3.

16. Young, *Three Constitutions*, 71; Don C. Seitz, *Famous American Duels* (New York, 1929), 29.

17. McGann, *Nativism in Kentucky*, 34; *Louisville Morning Courier*, 20 Nov. 1849.

18. Preston quoted in Carl R. Fields, "Making Kentucky's Third Constitution, 1830-1850" (Ph.D. diss., University of Kentucky, 1951), 276; *Report of the Debates and Proceedings of the Convention for the Revision of the Constitution of the State of Kentucky, 1849* (Frankfort, 1849), 1021.

19. Quoted in McGann, *Nativism in Kentucky*, 34; Preston, quoted in Frank F. Mathias, "The Turbulent Years of Kentucky Politics, 1820-1850" (Ph.D. diss., University of Kentucky, 1966), 344.

20. Temple Bodley, *History of Kentucky*, 2 vols. (Chicago, 1928), 2: 224, 507, 1021; *Louisville Morning Courier*, 21, 22 Nov. 1849; Charles J. Bussey, "James Guthrie: Kentucky Politician and Entrepreneur," in *Kentucky Profiles: Biographical Essays in Honor of Holman Hamilton*, ed. James C. Klotter and Peter J. Sehlinger (Frankfort, 1982), 60; McGann, *Nativism in Kentucky*, 36, 41; Fields, "Making Kentucky's Third Constitution," 287.

21. Young, *Three Constitutions*, 73; *Louisville Morning Courier*, 20 Oct. 1849; Harrison and Klotter, *A New History of Kentucky*, 117.

22. Smiley, *Lion of Whitehall*, 142; Coleman, *Slavery Times in Kentucky*, 147, 318.

23. Franklin, *Militant South*, 89; Richard D. Sears, *The Day of Small Things: Abolitionism in the Midst of Slavery, Berea, Kentucky, 1854-1864* (New York, 1986), 1.

24. Cheesebrough, *Clergy Dissent*, 44-45; Victor B. Howard, *The Evangelical War against Slavery and Caste: The Life and Times of John G. Fee* (Selinsgrove, Pa., 1996), 117, 126; Sears, *Day of Small Things*, 293.

25. M. W. Preston to R. Wickliffe Sr., 16 Dec. 1844, box 44, Margaret Haws to WP, 21 Oct. 1850, box 46, 7 April 1851, box 47, W-PFP; "Population, 1850, Jefferson County," *Population Schedule of the Seventh Census of the United States, 1850* (Washington, D.C., 1963), microcopy 432, roll 225.

26. John H. Franklin and Loren Schweninger, *Runaway Slaves: Rebels on the Plantation* (New York, 1999), 241, 249-51, 276-77; Haws to WP, 7 April 1851, box 47, W-PFP (the misspellings in this quote are found in the original letter); Lucas, *History of Blacks in Kentucky*, 62.

27. For Preston's involvement in the duel, see his 1849 correspondence with Dudley M. Haydon and John T. Gray, box 46, W-PFP.

28. F. Wedekemper to WP, 11 Feb. 1854, box 48, W-PFP; Advertising leaflets, n.d., M-BC; *Louisville Morning Courier*, 2, 3, 5 Aug. 1850; *Louisville Daily Journal*, 6 Aug. 1850.

29. Newcomb, *Kentucky Architecture*, 7, plates 102-8; *Louisville Morning Courier*, 7 Nov., 5, 14 Dec. 1850; *Journal of the House of Representatives of the Commonwealth of Kentucky*, 1850-51 (Frankfort, 1850), 4, 6-20, 68, 77, 181, 449-55.

30. *Louisville Daily Courier*, 17 July, 19 Nov., 5, 9, 22 Dec. 1851; *Journal of the House of Representatives of the Commonwealth of Kentucky*, 1851-52 (Frankfort, 1851), 1, 21, 47.

31. *Louisville Daily Courier*, 13, 17 Nov. 1851.

32. Ibid., 17, 27 Nov., 15 Dec. 1851.

33. Thomas S. Shove et al. to WP, 29 Sept. 1841, box 44, W-PFP; Reuben T. Durrett, "The Early Bench and Bar of Louisville," in Johnston, *Memorial History of Louisville*, 2: 302; William C. Simpson, interview with Peter J. Sehlinger, 29 May 2001; W. H. Meffert, *History of Preston Lodge No. 281, F. and A.M., Held at Louisville, Kentucky, from January 19, 1854, up to January 19, 1904* (Louisville, 1903), 19, 33, 350; J. Winston Coleman Jr., *Masonry in the Bluegrass* (Lexington, 1933), 122, 142-43, 149.

34. *Louisville Journal*, 13 March 1852; "Louisville from 1850 to 1870," in Johnston, *Memorial History of Louisville*, 1: 98; John H. Komlos, *Kossuth in America, 1851-1852* (Buffalo, N.Y., 1973), 148; Donald S. Spencer, *Louis Kossuth and Young America: A*

Study of Sectionalism and Foreign Policy (Columbus, Mo., 1977), 121; Louis Kossuth, quoted in *History of the Ohio Falls Cities*, 1: 160; McGann, *Nativism in Kentucky*, 54.

35. *Louisville Daily Courier*, 25 Feb., 3 July, 12, 26 Aug. 1852; *Carrollton (Ky.) Mirror*, quoted in *Louisville Daily Courier*, 30 Aug. 1852.

36. *Louisville Daily Courier*, 15 Sept., 2, 6 Oct. 1852; Johnson, *Winfield Scott*, 213.

37. *Louisville Daily Courier*, 20 Sept., 11 Oct., 13 Nov., 8 Dec. 1852.

38. Ibid., 21, 23 July, 30 Nov. 1852, 4 Aug. 1853; *Louisville Daily Democrat*, 26 July 1853.

39. *Congressional Globe*, 32nd Cong., 2nd sess., 15 Dec. 1852, 64; WP to S. Christy, 27 Dec. 1852, DC; *Louisville Daily Courier*, 25 Dec. 1852.

40. *Congressional Globe*, 33rd Cong., 1st sess., 20 Dec. 1853, 72-73; WP, *Remarks of Mr. Preston of Kentucky*; George D. Prentice to WP, 9 Jan. 1854, box 48, W-PFP.

41. *Congressional Globe*, 33rd Cong., 1st sess., 6 April 1854, 860; WP to R. Wickliffe Sr., 26 Jan. 1854, box 49, W-PFP; Christopher M. Paine, "'Kentucky Will Be the Last to Give Up the Union': Kentucky Politics, 1844-1861" (Ph.D. diss., University of Kentucky, 1998), 196.

42. *Congressional Globe*, 33rd Cong., 1st sess., 11, 20 May 1854, 1180, 1240; WP to S. Christy, 14 March 1854, DC; Cooper, *South and the Politics of Slavery*, 352-57; David Donald, *Charles Sumner and the Coming of the Civil War* (New York, 1960), 250-59.

43. WP to R. Wickliffe Sr., 2 July 1854, box 49, W-PFP.

44. Winfield Scott to WP, 9 Feb. 1854, box 48, W-PFP; *Congressional Globe*, 33rd Cong., 1st sess., 13 Feb. 1854, 414.

45. *Congressional Globe*, 33rd Cong., 1st sess., 1 Feb. 1854, 308, 310; 15 March 1854, 635-36; 16 March 1854, 653; 17 March 1854, 663.

46. Ibid., 33rd Cong., 1st sess., 17 March 1854, 663.

47. William H. Seward to WP, 26 Dec. 1853, box 48, W-PFP.

48. WP to R. Wickliffe Sr., 22 June 1854, box 49, W-PFP; WP to S. Christy, 3 Jan. 1855, DC; WP to Eliza Griffin Johnston, 4 March 1855, M-BC; Roland, *Albert Sidney Johnston*, 169.

49. Cooper, *South and the Politics of Slavery*, 360; WP to N. Wolfe, 20 Dec. 1853, box 48, WP to R. Wickliffe Sr., 22 June 1854, box 49, W-PFP.

50. Winthrop S. Hudson, *Religion in America* (New York, 1965), 240; Ira M. Leonard and Robert D. Parmet, *American Nativism, 1830-1860* (New York, 1971), 100.

51. E. Merton Coulter, "The Downfall of the Whig Party in Kentucky," *RKHS* 23 (1925): 167; Degler, *Other South*, 115-16; Robert F. Durden, *The Self-Inflicted Wound: Southern Politics in the Nineteenth Century* (Lexington, 1985), 68; Avery O. Craven, *The Growth of Southern Nationalism, 1849-1861*, vol. 6, *A History of the South*, ed. Wendell H. Stephens and E. Merton Coulter (Baton Rouge, 1953), 238; R. McKinley Ormsby, *A History of the Whig Party, or Some of Its Main Features* (Boston, 1859), 351; Cole, *Whig Party*, 325.

52. Fred J. Hood, comp., *Kentucky, Its History and Heritage* (St. Louis, 1978), 128; O'Toole and Aebersold, "Louisville's Bloody Monday Riots," 421-22; WP, quoted in Little, *Ben Hardin*, 612; *Louisville Democrat*, 20 July 1855; *Louisville Daily Courier*, 2 Aug. 1855.

53. *Louisville Daily Journal*, 9 July, 2, 3, 4, 5, 8 Aug. 1855; Betty Congleton, "George Prentice and his Educational Policy" (Ph.D. diss., University of Kentucky, 1961), 281.

54. *Louisville Daily Courier*, 2, 3 Aug. 1855; *Louisville Democrat*, 7, 16 July 1855.

55. McGann, *Nativism in Kentucky*, 94-101; Wallace S. Hutcheon Jr., "The Louisville Riots of August 1855," in Hood, *Kentucky, Its History and Heritage*, 130-31; Yater, *Two Hundred Years*, 69; *Louisville Anzeiger*, 7 Aug. 1855.

56. Basil Duke, quoted in "The Illustrious Dead," *Louisville Courier-Journal*, 26 Sept. 1887.

57. *Louisville Journal*, 9 April, 7 Aug. 1855; *Louisville Daily Courier*, 7, 8, 9, 10 Aug. 1855; *Louisville Democrat*, 7, 8 Aug. 1855; Emmet V. Mittlebeeler, "The Aftermath of Louisville's Bloody Monday Election Riot of 1855," *FCHQ* 66 (1992): 198; Wallace Turner, "Kentucky in a Decade of Change, 1850-1860" (Ph.D. diss., University of Kentucky, 1954), 44-45.

58. O'Toole and Aebersold, "Louisville's Bloody Monday Riots," 423; Blanton Duneuer to WP, [1876?], box 63, W-PFP; Hutcheon, "Louisville Riots," 131; Crews, *Presence and Possibility*, 44; *Louisville Daily Courier*, 7, 8, 9, 10 Aug. 1855; *Louisville Democrat*, 7, 8 Aug. 1855; Mittlebeeler, "The Aftermath," 198-99.

59. *Louisville Anzeiger*, 7 Aug. 1855; Hutcheon, "Louisville Riots," 132; *Louisville Journal*, 7 Aug. 1855; *Louisville Daily Courier*, 9 Aug. 1855; *Louisville Democrat*, 7 Aug. 1855; David Grimstead, *American Mobbing, 1828-1861: Toward Civil War* (New York, 1998), 232.

60. Mittlebeeler, "The Aftermath," 205-9, 216-19; McGann, *Nativism in Kentucky*, 108-9.

61. WP to S. Christy, 27 Dec. 1852, 8 Feb.1853, 4 Feb., 8 June 1854, 18 Feb. 1855, DC.

62. WP to R. Wickliffe Sr., 12 Dec. 1854, box 49, Francis Preston Blair Sr. to M. W. Preston, 19 Jan. 1855, box 50, W-PFP.

63. WP to R. Wickliffe Sr., 19 Feb., 13 March 1854, box 49, [Feb. 1855], box 50, W-PFP; WP to S. Christy, 31 Jan. 1855, DC.

64. WP to S. Christy, 3 Dec. 1854, DC; [illeg. signature], note, 29 June 1853, box 48, W-PFP.

65. William H. Travers to WP, 26 Dec. 1853, box 48, W-PFP.

66. S. Christy to M. W. Preston, 29 Jan., 6 June 1854, box 74, F. P. Blair Sr. to M. W. Preston, 19 Jan. 1855, box 50, Christie Johnson to WP, 8 Oct. 1858, box 51, W-PFP; Joseph R. Underwood to wife, 27 Feb. 1853, CHP; Gabriel García y Tassara to Primer Ministro de Estado, 27 June 1859, Correspondencia, Estados Unidos, Archivo del Ministerio de Asuntos Exteriores, Madrid (hereafter CEU).

67. WP to S. Christy, 18 Feb. 1855, DC; Johnson, *Winfield Scott*, 218; Elliott, *Winfield Scott*, 631; Eisenhower, *Agent of Destiny*, 145; Scott to WP, 22 Feb. 1855, box 50, W-PFP.

68. M. W. Preston to WP, 19 Sept. 1850, box 46, Mr. and Mrs. [T. H.] Benton to WP, 13 Jan. 1854, box 48, Franklin Pierce to WP, 4 March, 14 Oct. 1854, James Guthrie to WP, 17 March 1854, box 49, WP to S. Christy, 24 Dec. 1854, box 74, W-PFP; WP to S. Christy, 8 Feb. 1853, 5 July 1854, WP to George Hancock, 2 July 1854, DC.

69. WP to S. Christy, 8 Feb., 10 June, 5 July 1854, 3 Jan. 1855, DC.

70. Frederick Wedekemper to WP, 4 March 1854, Charles W. Woolley to WP, 16 July 1854, box 49, W-PFP; WP to S. Christy, 14 March, 8 June 1854, 4 June 1859, DC; "Taxbooks of Kentucky Counties, Jefferson County," 1856, East District, microfilm reel 73-0197, Kentucky Historical Society Library, Frankfort, Ky.

71. Hollingsworth, "She Used Her Power Lightly," 67-68, 122-23; S. Christy to M. W. Preston, 29 Jan. 1854, 15 Jan. 1855, box 74, Jane Giles to M. W. Preston, 8 Feb. 1854, box 49, W-PFP. The misspellings in this quotation are found in the original letter.

72. WP to Stephen A. Douglas, 7 June 1856, Stephen A. Douglas Papers, Special Collections, Regenstein Library, University of Chicago.

73. Robert W. Johannsen, *Stephen A. Douglas* (New York, 1973), 519; William E. Smith, *The Francis Preston Blair Family in Politics*, vol. 1 (New York, 1933), 340; Dorman, "General William Preston," 304; Thompson, *Orphan Brigade*, 366.

74. WP to John C. Breckinridge, 19 Sept. 1856, vol. 187, BFP, LC; WP to James Buchanan, 15 Oct. 1856, James Buchanan Papers (hereafter JBP), Historical Society of Pennsylvania, Philadelphia.

75. WP to J. C. Breckinridge, 19 Sept., 20 Oct. 1856, vol. 187, BFP, LC; Willard Klunder, *William Lewis Cass and the Politics of Moderation* (Kent, Ohio, 1996), 280-81; Johannsen, *Stephen A. Douglas*, 535.

76. WP to J. Buchanan, 27 June 1856, JBP; WP to J. C. Breckinridge, 20 Oct. 1856, vol. 187, BFP, LC.

77. WP to J. Buchanan, 15 Oct. 1856, JBP.

78. *Louisville Democrat*, 17 June 1857; *Louisville Daily Courier*, 10, 11, 13 July 1857; *Louisville Journal*, 10 July 1857.

5. At the Court of Spain

1. James Buchanan to Stephen R. Mallory, 7 July 1858, J. Buchanan to Judah P. Benjamin, 31 Aug. 1858, JBP; WP to Lewis Cass, 6 Oct. 1858, Despatches of U.S. Ministers to Spain, 1792-1906, National Archives, Washington, D.C., Microfilm Publication, microcopy 31 (hereafter DUSMS).

2. Peter J. Sehlinger, "William Preston, Kentucky's Diplomat of Lost Causes," in *Kentucky Profiles*, eds. Klotter and Sehlinger, 79; Gabriel García y Tassara to Saturino Calderón Collantes, 4 Jan. 1859, CEU; Philip G. Auchampaugh, *James Buchanan and his Cabinet on the Eve of Secession* (Lancaster, Pa., 1926), 10.

3. A. S. Johnston to WP, 1 Sept. 1858, JFP; WP to S. Christy, 8 Oct. 1858, DC; Robert E. May, *The Southern Dream of a Caribbean Empire, 1854-1861* (Baton Rouge, 1973), 164-65.

4. J. Buchanan to S. R. Mallory, 7 July 1858, JBP; WP to S. Christy, 8 Oct. 1858, DC; Winfield Scott to M. W. Preston, 6 Oct. 1858, box 51, W-PFP; WPJ to S. Christy, 15 Nov. 1855, 4 Feb. 1856, JC.

5. Frederick M. Binder, *James Buchanan and the American Empire* (Selinsgrove, Pa., 1994), 274-75; Louis M. Sears, *A History of American Foreign Relations*, rev. ed. (New York, 1935), 246-51, 306; Donathon C. Olliff, *Reforma Mexico and the United States: A Search for Alternatives to Annexation, 1854-1861* (Tuscaloosa, 1981), 87, 102-3.

6. Philip S. Klein, *President James Buchanan: A Biography* (University Park, Pa., 1962), 191-92.

7. Josef Opatrny, *U.S. Expansionism and Cuban Annexationism in the 1850s* (Prague, 1990), 167, 252; see WP correspondence with Cristóbal Madan, box 43, W-PFP;

Charles H. Brown, *Agents of Manifest Destiny: The Lives and Times of the Filibusters* (Chapel Hill, 1980), 42-88; May, *Southern Dream*, 25-30; idem, *Manifest Destiny's Underworld: Filibustering in Antebellum America* (Chapel Hill, 2002), 28-32.

8. Robert E. May, *John A. Quitman: Old Southern Crusader* (Baton Rouge, 1985), 240; Anderson C. Quisenberry, *Lopez's Expedition to Cuba, 1850-1851* (Louisville, 1906), 46; Tom Chaffin, *Fatal Glory: Narciso López and the First Clandestine U.S. War against Cuba* (Charlottesville, 1996), xxi-xxii, 78-79, 98, 214-15; *Lexington Gazette*, 23 Sept. 1874; Brown, *Agents of Manifest Destiny*, 42-56, 89.

9. Irving Katz, *August Belmont: A Political Biography* (New York, 1968), 22-25; John Slidell to J. Buchanan, 17 June, 6 Aug. 1854, JBP.

10. Ostend Manifesto quoted in David Potter, *The Impending Crisis, 1848-1861* (New York, 1976), 190-91; Gavin F. Henderson, "Southern Designs on Cuba, 1854-1857, and Some Other European Opinions," *Journal of Southern History* 5 (1939): 375; Klein, *Buchanan*, 234-41; Binder, *Buchanan*, 200-210.

11. Two historians, Allan Nevins, *The Emergence of Lincoln*, vol. 1, *Douglas, Buchanan, and Party Chaos, 1857-1859* (New York, 1950), 446-49, and Paul A. Varg, *United States Foreign Relations, 1820-1860* (East Lansing, 1979), 216-18, argue that Buchanan considered the purchase of Cuba impossible but championed this policy to please slaveholders. However, Buchanan was not subservient to slaveholders' interests. As president he sought to end filibustering. See Robert E. May, "James Buchanan, the Neutrality Laws, and American Invasion of Nicaragua" in *James Buchanan and the Political Crisis of the 1850s*, ed. Michael J. Birkner (Selinsgrove, Pa., 1996), 138.

12. J. Buchanan to Christopher Fallón, 14 Dec. 1857, JBP; Binder, *Buchanan*, 253; Roy F. Nichols, *The Disruption of American Democracy* (New York, 1948), 228; May, *Southern Dream*, 164.

13. Nichols, *Disruption of American Democracy*, 227-29; James W. Cortada, *Spain and the American Civil War: Relations at Mid-Century, 1855-1868, Transactions of the American Philosophical Society*, vol. 70 (Philadelphia, 1980), 24; Amos A. Ettinger, *The Mission to Spain of Pierre Soulé, 1853-1855* (New Haven, 1932), 708; Binder, *Buchanan*, 253-54, 256.

14. J. Buchanan to C. Fallón, 14 Dec. 1857, in James Bassett Moore, ed., *The Works of James Buchanan*, 12 vols. (New York, 1960), 10: 165; J. Buchanan to C. Fallón, 19 April 1859, CHP; C. Fallón to J. Buchanan, 14 Jan., 12, 24 Feb. 1858, JBP; Binder, *Buchanan*, 253-56.

15. L. Cass to WP, 3 Jan. 1859, Diplomatic Instructions of the Department of State, 1801-1906 (hereafter DIDS), National Archives, Washington, D.C.; WP to WPJ, 17 Dec. 1858, M-BC.

16. G. García y Tassara to Primer Secretario de Estado, 27 Dec. 1858, *Política, Estados Unidos, 1856-1860* (hereafter PEU), Archivo del Ministerio de Asuntos Exteriores, Madrid; G. García y Tassara to S. Calderón, 21 Dec. 1858, CEU; *La América* (Madrid), 8 Nov. 1858; *The Times* (London), 27 Dec. 1858.

17. J. Buchanan to C. Fallón, 8 Dec. 1859, C. Fallón to WP, 6 Jan. 1859, JBP; Raymond Carr, *Spain, 1808-1939* (Oxford, Eng., 1966), 281-82.

18. May, *Southern Dream*, 166; WP to WPJ, 17 Dec. 1858, WP to Reuben T. Durrett, 14 Dec. 1858, M-BC; C. Fallón to WP, 6 Jan. 1859, JBP.

19. *Congressional Globe*, 35ᵗʰ Cong., 2ᵈ sess., 9 Feb. 1858, 909; Craig L. Kautz, "Beneficial Politics: John Slidell and the Cuba Bill of 1859," *Louisiana Studies* 3 (1974): 124; *New York Times*, 27 Jan. 1859; May, *Southern Dream*, 169-70.

20. Kautz, "Beneficial Politics," 126; *New York Times*, 27 Jan. 1859; May, *Southern Dream*, 176-77; Elbert B. Smith, *The Presidency of James Buchanan* (Lawrence, Kan., 1975), 77.

21. *Louisville Daily Courier*, 11 Jan., 19 Feb. 1859; *Washington (D.C.) Constitution*, 9, 18 June 1859; *Washington (D.C.) Union*, 30 Dec. 1858.

22. *New York Times*, 21, 25 Jan., 14 Feb., 1 March 1859; WP to R. Durrett, 14 Dec. 1858, M-BC.

23. Binder, *Buchanan*, 256-57; *Congressional Globe*, 35ᵗʰ Cong., 2ᵈ sess., 453, 747, 909; May, *Southern Dream*, 182; Moore, *Works of James Buchanan*, 10: 349; Kautz, "Beneficial Politics," 124-27; French E. Chadwick, *The Relations of the United States and Spain: Diplomacy* (New York, 1909), 271.

24. Moore, *Works of James Buchanan*, 10: 349; *Congressional Globe*, 36ᵗʰ Cong., 1ˢᵗ sess., 3; Kautz, "Beneficial Politics," 128; Chadwick, *Relations of the United States and Spain*, 272.

25. WP to S. Christy, 24 Feb., 27 Sept. 1859, DC; George P. Gooch, *The Second Empire* (London, 1960), 17.

26. WP to S. Christy, 24 Feb. 1859, DC; Expedientes a William Preston, 24 Nov. 1859 through 30 March 1861, legajo 195, no. 10.446, Expedientes relativos a Preston, Wm. (hereafter ERP), Archivo del Ministerio de Asuntos Exteriores, Madrid.

27. Calderón quoted in Cortada, *Spain and the American Civil War*, 26; Carr, *Spain*, 260.

28. Augustus C. Dodge to L. Cass, 2 Jan. 1859, Despatches of U.S. Ministers to Spain, 1792-1906, DUSMS, roll 40; *El Diario* (Madrid), 5 Jan. 1859.

29. Jerónimo Bécker, *Historia de las relaciones exteriores de España durante el siglo XIX*, 3 vols. (Madrid, 1924-26), 2: 389; WP to L. Cass, 9 March 1859, DUSMS, roll 40; WP to S. Christy, 9 April 1859, M-BC.

30. Cortada, *Spain and the American Civil War*, 27; *Gazeta de Madrid*, 13 March 1859.

31. WP to S. Christy, 9 April 1859, M-BC; WP to L. Cass, 25 April 1859, WP to J. Buchanan, 8 May 1859, DUSMS, roll 40.

32. WP to J. Buchanan, 7 May 1859, JBP; WP to L. Cass, 25 April, 23 Oct., 1, 15 Nov. 1859, DUSMS, rolls 40, 41.

33. For details of the *Amistad* affair, see Howard Jones, *Mutiny on the Amistad: The Saga of a Slave Rebellion and its Impact on American Abolition, Law and Diplomacy* (New York, 1987) and R. Earl McClerdon, "The *Amistad* Claims: Inconsistency of Policy," *Political Science Quarterly* 48 (1933): 386-412.

34. Article 9, Treaty of 1795, *Treaties, Conventions, International Acts, Protocols and Agreements between the United States and Other Powers, 1776-1909*, comp. William M. Mallory, 4 vols. (Washington, D.C., 1910), 2: 1644.

35. Paul G. Nagel, *John Quincy Adams: A Public Life, a Private Life* (New York, 1997), 379; Samuel Flagg Bemis, *John Quincy Adams and the Union* (New York, 1956), 384-415; Jones, *Mutiny on the Amistad*, 205; William A. Owens, *A Black Mutiny: The Revolt on the Schooner Amistad* (Baltimore, 1953), 302.

36. Miller, *Arguing about Slavery*, 399-403; McClerdon, "The *Amistad* Claims," 405; A. C. Dodge to Spanish Foreign Office, 7 March 1859, S. Calderón to WP, 26 Oct. 1859, Notes to the Spanish Govt., Diplomatic Post Records (hereafter DPR), National Archives, Washington, D.C.

37. *Congressional Globe*, 35th Cong., 2d sess., 296, 703; *Washington (D.C.) Union*, 24 Dec. 1858; WP to L. Cass, 14 Oct. 1859, DUSMS, roll 41.

38. WP to L. Cass, 27 Nov. 1859, L. Cass to WP, 18 Jan. 1859, DUSMS, roll 41; McClerdon, "The *Amistad* Claims," 407; G. García y Tassara to S. Calderón, 6 Feb. 1860, CEU.

39. "Convention for the Settlement of Claims between the United States of America and Her Catholic Majesty," 5 March 1860, DUSMS, roll 41; WP to L. Cass, 6 March 1860, DUSMS, roll 41; McClerdon, "The *Amistad* Claims," 408.

40. McClerdon, "The *Amistad* Claims," 410; Buchanan quoted in George T. Curtis, *Life of James Buchanan, Fifteenth President of the United States*, 2 vols. (New York,

1883), 2: 223-24; Jones, *Mutiny on the Amistad*, 218.

41. See WP, Despatches, *passim*, 1859-61, DUSMS, rolls 40-41; see U.S. Embassy, Spain, Preston, Wm., Department of State, Record Group 84, National Archives, Washington, D.C.

42. Cortada, *Spain and the American Civil War*, 110; Claude M. Fuess, *Carl Schurz: Reformer, 1829-1906* (New York, 1932), 86.

43. William H. Seward to WP, 9 March 1861, DIDS; WP to Seward, 14, 22 April 1861, DUSMS, roll 41.

44. WP to L. Cass, 3 Dec. 1860, DUSMS, roll 41; Kinley Brauer, "Gabriel García y Tassara and the American Civil War," *Civil War History* 21 (1975): 10.

45. *Gazeta de Madrid*, 20 May 1861; Dexter Perkins, *The Monroe Doctrine, 1826-1867* (Baltimore, 1933), 274-86.

46. WP to L. Cass, 3 Dec. 1860, CHP; WP to S. Calderón, 12 April 1861, Notes to the Spanish Government, DPR; Bécker, *Historia*, 2: 389; WP to W. H. Seward, 14 April 1861, DUSMS, roll 41.

47. WP to S. Calderón, 23 April 1861, Notes to the Spanish Government, DPR; WP, note beside article in *El Público* (Madrid), 27 April 1861, WP to S. Calderón, 21 May 1861, box 54, W-PFP; Bécker, *Historia*, 2: 396.

48. Perkins, *The Monroe Doctrine*, 291; Binder, *Buchanan*, 178-80; Wilbur Devereux Jones, *The American Problem in British Diplomacy, 1841-1861* (Athens, Ga., 1974), 72, 131-32.

49. Cortada, *Spain and the American Civil War*, 34.

50. W. H. Seward to WP, 1 May 1861, Lincoln, quoted in Seward to Horatio I. Perry, 9 May 1861, DIDS; Abraham Lincoln to Queen Isabel II, 25 March 1861, ERP.

51. Carl Schurz to A. Lincoln, 11 Nov. 1861, in Schurz, *Speeches, Correspondence and Political Papers of Carl Schurz*, ed. Frederick Bancroft, vol. 1 (New York, 1913), 193; Carl Schurz, *Reminiscences, 1852-1863*, 2 vols. (New York, 1907), 1: 254-55; H. I. Perry to W. H. Seward, 20 April, 27 May 1861, DUSMS, roll 41; Cortada, *Spain and the American Civil War*, 108, 110.

52. WP to J. Buchanan, 7 May 1859, JBP; WP to WPJ, 16 Feb. 1860, WP to S. Christy, 16 Feb. 1860, M-BC; WP to S. Christy, 20 Jan. 1860, DC.

53. WP to L. Cass, 23 Oct. 1859, DUSMS, roll 41; see the correspondence of G. García y Tassara to S. Calderón, 1858-61, legajo 1469-70, CEU; Sehlinger, "William

Preston, Diplomat," 92-93.

54. WP, "Journal"; WP, *The Slave Question* [pamphlet] (n.p., [1854]), speech in Congress, 20 Dec. 1853; WP to L. Cass, 9 March 1859, DUSMS, roll 40; M. W. Preston to S. Christy, 14 July 1859, DC.

55. WP to S. Christy, 8 March, 9 Nov. 1859, DC; WP to L. Cass, 25 April 1859, DUSMS, roll 40.

56. WP to J. Buchanan, 7 May 1859, JBP.

57. WP to S. Christy, 9 April 1859, 20 Jan. 1861, M-BC; Expediente relativo a Preston, 23 Oct., 24 Nov., 9, 31 Dec. 1859, 7 Nov. 1860, legajo 195, no. 10. 446, ERP.

58. *Louisville Times*, 20 March 1940; William Thompson to WP, 7 June 1860, box 53, M. W. Preston to WP, [June 1860], box 54, W-PFP. The misspellings in the Thompson letter are found in the original.

59. Duke of Tetuán to WP, 16 Jan. 1861, Andrew Buchanan to WP, [Jan. 1861], box 54, W-PFP; H. I. Perry to W. H. Seward, 20 April 1861, DUSMS, roll 42; WP to S. Christy, 17 Feb. 1861, DC.

60. Cortada, *Spain and the American Civil War*, 108.

61. WP to J. Buchanan, 7 May 1859, JBP; Mary Owen Preston to M. W. Preston, 20 March, 24 April 1859, box 52, R. W. Woolley to M. W. Preston, several letters, May-Aug. 1859, box 54, W-PFP; WP to S. Christy, 9 April 1859, M-BC; G. García y Tassara to S. Calderón, 27 June 1859, CEU; WP to S. Christy, [March (?) 1860], DC.

62. WP to S. Christy, 14 July 1859, 20 Jan. 1860, DC; WP to S. Christy, 9 April 1859, M-BC.

63. M. W. Preston to S. Christy, 14 July 1859, DC; M. O. Preston to M. W. Preston, 20 March 1859, box 52, M. W. Preston to WP, [May 1860], box 53, W-PFP; G. García y Tassara to S. Calderón, 27 Dec. 1858, CEU; G. García y Tassara to S. Calderón, 4 Jan. 1859, PEU; 3 Feb. 1859 entry, Benjamin Moran Diary, Manuscript Division, LC.

64. Robert W. Woolley to M. W. Preston, 1 Sept. 1859, box 52, W-PFP; WP to S. Christy, 20 Jan. 1859, 17 Feb. 1861, DC; WPJ to Rosa Johnston, 7 Nov. 1861, JFP; May, *Southern Dream*, 184.

65. Hollingsworth, "She Used Her Power Lightly," 174; M. W. Preston to WP, 25 [May] 1860, Robert Wickliffe Sr. to M. W. Preston, 11 July 1859, box 53, W-PFP.

66. Sydney Beauclerk to Charles Beauclerk, [April 1861], box 54, W-PFP; clipping from unnamed newspaper, 3 Feb. 1938, CHP; L. Cass to WP, 21 Dec. 1858,

DIDS; WP to S. Christy, 9 April 1859, M-BC.

67. R. Woolley to M. W. Preston, 1 Sept. 1859, box 52, M. W. Preston to WP, 25 May 1860, [June 1860], M. O. Preston to WP, 15 May 1860, box 53, W-PFP; Lizinka C. Brown to [Rebecca Hubbard], 23 Aug. 1860, Brown-Ewell Family Papers (hereafter B-E), FHS.

68. M. O. Preston to WP, [June (?)], 15 July 1860, Margaret H. W. Preston to WP, 30 June 1861, RWP to WP, 29 June 1861, box 54, W-PFP.

69. M. W. Preston to WP, 16 July 1860, M. H. W. Preston to WP, 30 June 1861, box 54, W-PFP; L. C. Brown to [name missing], [Jan. 1861], B-E.

70. [L.C. Brown] to [R. Hubbard], 23 Aug. 1860, B-E; M. W. Preston to WP, [June] 1860, box 54, W-PFP.

71. M. W. Preston to WP, 6 July 1860, WP to M. W. Preston, 27 June 1860, box 54, W-PFP.

72. WP to [J. C.] Breckinridge, 8 Jan. 1861, box 54, W-PFP; May, *Southern Dream*, 184-85.

73. Heck, *Proud Kentuckian*, 82-83; WP to S. Christy, 3 May 1860, WP to WPJ, 6 Aug. 1860, DC; Klotter, *Breckinridges of Kentucky*, 114.

74. WP to Susan [Christy] Hepburn, 9 Nov. 1860, DC; May, *Southern Dream*, 185; WP to J. C. Breckinridge, 8 Jan. 1861, box 54, W-PFP; WP to L. Cass, 9, 23 Oct. 1860, DUSMS, roll 41.

75. WP to R. Woolley, 6 Nov. 1860, WP to J. C. Breckinridge, 8 Jan. 1861, WP to the Secretary of State, 5 March 1861, box 54, W-PFP; WP to S. Hepburn, 17 April 1861, DC.

76. *Gazeta de Madrid*, 26 May 1861; S. Beauclerk to C. Beauclerk, [April 1861], C. Beauclerk to WP, 14 April 1861, box 54, W-PFP.

77. Cortada, *Spain and the American Civil War*, 108.

6. Fighting for Southern Independence

1. WP to WPJ, 10 Dec. 1860, 13 Jan. 1861, M-BC; WP to S. Hepburn, 9 Nov. 1860, DC.

2. WP to J. C. Breckinridge, 8 Jan. 1861, box 54, W-PFP; WP to WPJ, 10 Dec. 1860, M-BC; WP to S. Hepburn, 17 Feb. 1861, DC.

3. WP to WPJ, 13 Jan., 4 May 1861, M-BC; WP to S. Hepburn, 17 Feb. 1861, DC.

4. WP to "My dear son and daughters," 3 April 1862, JFP.

5. James M. McPherson, *What They Fought For, 1861-1865* (Baton Rouge, 1994), 16; Stephen E. Ambrose, *Citizen Soldiers: The U.S. Army from the Normandy Beaches to the Bulge to the Surrender of Germany, June 7, 1944-May 7, 1945* (New York, 1997), 14; Edward C. Anderson and Cabel Huse to L. P. Walker, *The War of the Rebellion: A Compilation of the Official Records of the Union and Confederate Armies* (hereafter *OR*), 129 vols. (Washington, D.C., 1880-1901), Series IV, 1: 539.

6. For accounts of Kentucky's role in the Civil War, see J. Stoddard Johnston, *Kentucky*, vol. 9, *Confederate Military History*, ed. Clement A. Evans (1899; reprint Secaucus, N.J., ca. 1970s); Lowell H. Harrison, *The Civil War in Kentucky* (Lexington, 1975); E. Merton Coulter, *The Civil War and Readjustment in Kentucky* (Chapel Hill, 1926); Thompson, *Orphan Brigade*; William C. Davis, *The Orphan Brigade: The Kentucky Confederates Who Couldn't Go Home* (Garden City, N.Y., 1980); Stone, *A Brittle Sword*, 61-78; idem, *Kentucky Fighting Men, 1861-1945* (Lexington, 1982), 1-25; James L. McDonough, *War in Kentucky: From Shiloh to Perryville* (Knoxville, 1994); Kent Masterson Brown, ed., *The Civil War in Kentucky: Battle in the Bluegrass* (Mason City, Iowa, 2001).

7. Stone, *A Brittle Sword*, 62, 66-67. For Lexington during the Civil War, see Ranck, *History of Lexington*; J. Winston Coleman Jr., *Lexington During the Civil War* (Lexington, 1938); William H. Perrin, ed., *History of Fayette County, Kentucky With an Outline Sketch of the Blue Grass Region by Robert Peter* (1882; reprint, Easley, S.C., 1979).

8. For biographies of several Kentucky Confederate generals, see Arndt M. Stickles, *Simon Bolivar Buckner: Borderland Knight* (Chapel Hill, 1940); Johnston, *Life of General Albert Sidney Johnston*; Roland, *Albert Sidney Johnston*; William C. Davis, *Breckinridge: Statesman, Soldier, Symbol* (Baton Rouge, 1974); Lucille Stillwell, *John Cabell Breckinridge* (Caldwell, Idaho, 1936); Heck, *Proud Kentuckian*; Cecil F. Holland, *Morgan and His Raiders* (New York, 1942); Edison H. Thomas, *John Hunt Morgan and his Raiders* (Lexington, 1975); James A. Ramage, *Rebel Raider: The Life of John Hunt Morgan* (Lexington, 1986).

9. WP to M. W. Preston, 16, 25 Sept. 1861, box 54, W-PFP; Stickles, *Buckner*, 92-107; William C. Davis, "John C. Breckinridge," *RKHS* 85 (1987): 206; Judah P. Benjamin to Albert S. Johnston, 3 Nov. 1861, *OR*, Series I, 1: 504.

10. WPJ to Rosa [Johnston], 9 Nov. 1861, WPJ to WP, 19 Feb. 1862, M-BC; Gen. Johnston, Orders, 15 Feb. 1862, Compiled Service Records of Confederate Generals and Staff Officers and Nonregimental Enlisted Men (hereafter CSR), microcopy 331, reel 202, National Archives, Washington, D.C.

11. George W. Johnson to Jefferson Davis, 21 Nov. 1861, *OR*, Series IV, 1: 539; WP

to J. Davis, 28 Dec. 1861, *OR*, Series I, 7: 801.

12. WP, "Memoranda of Albert Sidney Johnston's death; Battle of Shiloh &c," Records of Adjutant General's Office, RG 94, Entry 286, Special File 1790-1946, National Archives, Washington, D.C., published with an introduction by Peter J. Sehlinger, "'At The Moment of Victory . . .' : The Battle of Shiloh and General A. S. Johnston's Death as Recounted in William Preston's Diary," *FCHQ* 61 (1987): 315-45.

13. This battle has engendered a vast literature. The two most complete accounts are Wiley Sword, *Shiloh: Bloody April* (New York, 1974) and James L. McDonough, *Shiloh–in Hell before Night* (Knoxville, 1977). Other oft-cited works are D. W. Reed, *The Battle of Shiloh and the Organizations Engaged* (Washington, D.C., 1913); Otto Eisenschiml, *The Story of Shiloh* (Chicago, 1946); Joseph W. Rich, *The Battle of Shiloh* (Iowa City, 1911); Thomas Worthington, *Shiloh: Or the Tennessee Campaign of 1862* (Washington, D.C., 1872).

14. See Shaw, *William Preston Johnston*; "William Preston Johnston," *Southern Historical Society Papers*, vol. 27 (Richmond, Va., 1899), 294-95; Jacob Cooper, *William Preston Johnston: A Character Sketch* (New Haven, Conn., 1900).

15. For Preston's view of the battle and its preparations, see Sehlinger, "'Moment of Victory,'" 329-35; WP to William Polk, 1 Dec. 1874, CHP; A. S. Johnston quoted in Johnston, *Life of General Albert Sidney Johnston*, 569.

16. Preston quotes on this battle taken from WP, "Memoranda."

17. WP, Report to Thomas Jordan [?], 20 April 1862, *OR*, Series I, 10: 403-5.

18. Johnston, *Life of General Albert Sidney Johnston*, 615; idem, "Albert Sidney Johnston and the Shiloh Campaign," *Century Illustrated Monthly Magazine* 29 (1885): 627. For accounts of Johnston's death, see WP, "Memoranda," and Roland, *Albert Sidney Johnston*, 336-39.

19. Jefferson Davis to Senate and House of Representatives, 8 April 1862, in James D. Richardson, ed., *A Compilation of the Messages and Papers of the Confederacy Including the Diplomatic Correspondence, 1861-1865*, 2 vols. (Nashville, 1902), 1: 209; Hughes and Ware, *Theodore O'Hara*, 116.

20. WPJ to WP, 20 July 1862, M-BC. For this debate, see Johnston, *General Albert Sidney Johnston*, 627-39; Roland, *Albert Sidney Johnston*, 339-42; Larry J. Daniel, *Shiloh: The Battle that Changed the Civil War* (New York, 1997), 305.

21. *Journal of the Congress of the Confederate States*, 7 vols. (Washington, D.C., 1904), 2: 194; WP to WPJ, 30 May 1862, JFP. For the history of this unit, see Davis, *Orphan Brigade*; Thompson, *Orphan Brigade*.

22. See Archer Jones, *Confederate Strategy from Shiloh to Vicksburg* (Baton Rouge, 1961).

23. WP to WPJ, 14 June 1862, M-BC.

24. Thompson, *Orphan Brigade*, 114-15; *Lexington Leader*, 22 Sept. 1887; "General Preston's Will," *Louisville Courier-Journal*, 26 Oct. 1887.

25. See Grady McWhiney, *Braxton Bragg and the Confederate Defeat*, vol. 1, *Field Command* (New York, 1969); Joseph H. Parks, *General Edmund Kirby Smith, CSA* (Baton Rouge, 1954).

26. Braxton Bragg to J. C. Breckinridge, 8 Aug. 1862, *OR*, Series I, Vol. 16, Part 2, 995; WP to WPJ, 19 Sept. 1862, M-BC.

27. McDonough, *War in Kentucky*, 148-49; Thomas, *John Hunt Morgan*, 52; Coleman, *Lexington During the Civil War*, 25; Gary Donaldson, "'Into Africa': Kirby Smith and Braxton Bragg's Invasion of Kentucky," *FCHQ* 61 (1987): 444-65; Perrin, *History of Fayette County*, 72; WP to WPJ, 19 Sept. 1862, M-BC; B. Bragg to Leonidas Polk, 30 Sept. 1862, *OR*, Series I, Vol. 16, Part 2, 892.

28. WP to WPJ, 1, 22 Nov. 1862, M-BC; Glenn Tucker, *Chickamauga: Bloody Battle of the West* (New York, 1961), 354.

29. For the battle of Perryville, see Kenneth W. Noe, *Perryville: This Grand Havoc of Battle* (Lexington, 2001), and Hambleton Tapp, "The Battle of Perryville," *FCHQ* 9 (1935): 158-81; Thomas L. Connelly, *Army of the Heartland: The Army of Tennessee, 1861-1862* (Baton Rouge, 1967), 252-71; Edward A. Pollard, *The Lost Cause: A New Southern History of the War of the Confederates* (New York, 1866), 332; Steven E. Woodworth, *Six Armies in Tennessee: The Chickamauga and Chattanooga Campaigns* (Lincoln, Nebr., 1998), 7; Brown, *Civil War in Kentucky*, 287; William W. Freehling, *The South vs. the South: How Anti-Confederate Southerners Shaped the Course of the Civil War* (New York, 2001), 59-60; Stephen D. Engle, *Don Carlos Buell: Most Promising of All* (Chapel Hill, 1999), 304-12.

30. WP to WPJ, 9 June, 1, 22 Nov. 1862, M-BC; Thompson, *Orphan Brigade*, 151; G. W. Brent, Special Order, No. 22, 12 Dec. 1862, *OR*, Series I, Vol. 20, Part 1, 448; Larry J. Daniel, *Soldiering in the Army of Tennessee: A Portrait of Life in a Confederate Army* (Chapel Hill, 1991), 111.

31. See Thomas L. Connelly, *Autumn of Glory: The Army of Tennessee, 1862-1865* (Baton Rouge, 1971), 44-68; idem, *Civil War Tennessee: Battles and Leaders* (Knoxville, 1979); Thompson, *Orphan Brigade*, 184-99; Johnston, *Kentucky*, 154-66; Duke, *Reminiscences*, 207; Stanley F. Horn, *The Army of Tennessee* (Indianapolis, 1953).

32. Leonard E. Brown, "Fortress Rosecrans: A History, 1865-1900," *Tennessee His-*

torical Quarterly 50 (1991): 135-36; Russell F. Weigley, *A Great Civil War: A Military and Political History, 1861-1865* (Bloomington, Ind., 2000), 196.

33. J. C. Breckinridge to B. Bragg, 12 Jan. 1862, *OR*, Series I, Vol. 20, Part 2, 777; WP to WPJ, 26 Jan. 1863, M-BC; WP, Report, 12 Jan. 1862, *OR*, Series I, Vol. 20, Part 1, 812; Thompson, *Orphan Brigade*, 199; John T. Lesley to R. W. Woolley, 10 Jan. 1863, *OR*, Series I, Vol. 20, Part 1, 818; B. Bragg, Report, 23 (?) Feb. 1863, *OR*, Series I, Vol. 20, Part 1, 674; Smith, *History of Kentucky*, 659.

34. Grady McWhiney and Perry D. Jamieson, *Attack and Die: Civil War Military Tactics and the Southern Heritage* (Tuscaloosa, 1982), 85-86; WP to WPJ, 26 Jan. 1863, M-BC; James L. McDonough, *Stones River: Bloody Winter in Tennessee* (Knoxville, 1980), 177; WP, Report, 12 Jan. 1862, 813; Perrin, *History of Fayette County*, 679-80; B. Bragg, Report, 23 (?) Feb. 1863, 679.

35. Peter Cozzens, *No Better Place to Die: The Battle of Stones River* (Urbana, Ill., 1990), 212; WP to Theodore O'Hara, 12 Jan. 1863, *OR*, Series I, Vol. 20, Part 1, 813; WP to [Thomas] Jordan, 29 March 1863, M-BC.

36. WP to WPJ, 26 Jan. 1863, WPJ to Rosa [Johnston], 28 Jan. 1863, M-BC.

37. Connelly, *Autumn of Glory*, 69-90; Don C. Seitz, *Braxton Bragg: General of the Confederacy* (Columbia, S.C., 1924), 271-302; Klotter, *Breckinridges of Kentucky*, 124; McWhiney, *Braxton Bragg*, 374.

38. WPJ to WP, 21 April 1863, George B. Hodge to WPJ, 27 May 1863, M-BC.

39. John S. Preston to WPJ, [April 1863], WPJ to Rosa [Johnston], 4 May, 30 June 1863, WP to WPJ, 2 June 1863, M-BC.

40. Ella Lonn, *Salt as a Factor in the Confederacy* (New York, 1933), 25-27; Kenneth W. Noe, *Southwest Virginia's Railroad: Modernization and the Sectional Crisis* (Urbana, Ill., 1994), 56-63, 132-33; WP to WPJ, 2 June, 26 July 1863, WPJ to WP, 23 June 1863, M-BC; Perrin, *History of Fayette County*, 680; Stickles, *Simon Bolivar Buckner*, 223.

41. WP to WPJ, 18 June 1863, JFP; WP to WPJ, 26 July 1863, M-BC; WP to John H. Morgan, 5 June 1863, John Hunt Morgan Papers, Southern Historical Collection (hereafter SHC), University of North Carolina, Chapel Hill; Perrin, *History of Fayette County*, 680; Robert J. Breckinridge to [WPJ], 8 July 1863, M-BC.

42. W.A. Bradford to WP, 9 Jan. 1863, WP to WPJ, 2 June 1863, 28 June 1864, WPJ to WP, 23 June, 13 Aug. 1863, M-BC.

43. WP to WPJ, 24 Aug. 1863, M-BC.

44. See Tucker, *Chickamauga*; Peter Cozzens, *This Terrible Sound: The Battle of Chickamauga* (Urbana, Ill., 1992); Connelly, *Autumn of Glory*, 201-34; Duke, *Reminiscences*, 208-12; Robert W. Ikard, "Lieutenant Thomas Reports on Chickamauga: A Comparison of Immediate and Historical Perspectives of the Battle," *Tennessee Historical Quarterly* 44 (1985): 417-38.

45. WP, Report, 31 Oct. 1863, OR, Series 1, Vol. 30, Part 1, 413; Jeffry D. Wert, *General James Longstreet: The Confederacy's Most Controversial Soldier* (New York, 1993), 310.

46. Richard O'Connor, *Thomas: Rock of Chickamauga* (New York, 1948), 38-50; Tucker, *Chickamauga*, 334.

47. WP, Report, 31 Oct. 1863, *OR*, Series I, Vol. 30, Part 1, 413-19; Tucker, *Chickamauga*, 352-57.

48. Thomas, quoted in Tucker, *Chickamauga*, 359.

49. John Bowers, *Chickamauga and Chattanooga: The Battle that Doomed the Confederacy* (New York, 1994), 150; WP, Report, 31 Oct. 1863, 418-19; WP to Simon B. Buckner, 20 Sept. 1863, S. B. Buckner to Gilbert Moxley Sorrel, 11 Nov. 1863, Simon Bolivar Buckner Collection (hereafter BC), H. E. Huntington Library, San Marino, Calif.; Robert C. Trigg, Report, 26 Sept. 1863, *OR*, Series I, Vol. 30, Part 2, 431-32; John H. Kelly, Report, 25 Sept. 1863, *OR*, Series I, Vol. 30, Part 2, 441-42; Tucker, *Chickamauga*, 354-57, 367-69; Connelly, *Autumn of Glory*, 225; Johnston, *Kentucky*, 179-80; Perrin, *History of Fayette County*, 681-82; James Longstreet, *From Manassas to Appomattox: Memoirs of the Civil War in America* (1896; reprint, New York, 1991), 456; Herman Hattaway and Archer Jones, *How the North Won: A Military History of the Civil War* (Urbana, Ill., 1991), 453.

50. S. B. Buckner to William S. Cooper, 1 Oct. 1863, CSR, microcopy 331; S. B. Buckner to G. M. Sorrell, 11 Nov. 1863, BC; James Longstreet to G. W. Brent, n.d. Oct. 1863, *OR*, Series I, Vol. 30, Part 2, 289.

51. *Times* (London), 24 Nov. 1863; *Louisville Courier-Journal*, 22 July 1917. For Desaix's heroic role, see Gunther E. Rothenberg, *The Art of Warfare in the Age of Napoleon* (Bloomington, Ind., 1980), 44-45; Owen Connelly, *Blundering to Glory: Napoleon's Military Campaigns* (Wilmington, Del., 1987), 65-70.

52. Tucker, *Chickamauga*, 352-53; Connelly, *Autumn of Glory*, 224; Archibald Gracie to S. B. Buckner, 8 Oct. 1907, and A. McMahan, "Fourth Discussion," n.d., 2-3, BC.

53. WP to M. W. Preston, 23 Sept. 1863, M-BC; Davis, "Breckinridge," 207. See also Gerald F. Linderman, *Embattled Courage: The Experience of Combat in the American Civil War* (New York, 1987).

54. WP to "My dear son and daughters," 3 April 1862, JFP; WP to M. W. Preston, 19

April 1862, CHP; WP to WPJ, 26 Jan.1863, WP to M. W. Preston, 23 Sept. 1863, M-BC.

55. S. B. Buckner to W. S. Cooper, 1 Oct. 1863, CSR; WP to WPJ, 26 Sept. 1863, M-BC; Connelly, *Autumn of Glory*, 69-92, 235-78; Stickles, *Buckner*, 237-44; Lloyd J. Graybar, "The Buckners of Kentucky," *FCHQ* 58 (1984): 207-8; Thomas L. Connelly and Archer Jones, *The Politics of Command: Factions and Ideas in Confederate Strategy* (Baton Rouge, 1973), 49-70.

56. WP to WPJ, 26 Jan. 1863, M-BC; WP to Dudley M. Haydon, 14 Nov. 1863, Dudley M. Haydon Papers, Houghton Library, Harvard University.

57. W. M. P[olk]. to J. Davis, 4 Oct. 1863, *OR*, Series I, Vol. 30, Part 2, 65-66, copy in BC; McWhiney, *Braxton Bragg*, 389, 392; Bell Irvin Wiley, *Embattled Confederates: An Illustrated History of Southerners at War* (New York, 1964), 53-54; Paddy Griffith, *Battle Tactics of the Civil War* (New Haven, Conn., 1987), 45-46, 122. See Steven E. Woodworth, *Jefferson Davis and His Generals: The Failure of Confederate Command in the West* (Lawrence, Kan., 1990), 238-45; Alf J. Mapp Jr., *Frock Coats and Epaulets: The Men Who Led the Confederacy* (Lanham, Md., 1996), 110.

58. WP to WPJ, 3 Oct. 1863, WPJ to WP, 10 Nov. 1863, M-BC; WP to Robert McKee, 17 Oct. 1863, Robert McKee Papers, Alabama Department of Archives and History, Montgomery; S. B. Buckner to WP, 18 Oct. 1863, CSR; G. W. Brent to S. B. Buckner, 20 Oct. 1863, S. B. Buckner to G. W. Brent, 21 Oct. 1863, BC; Rosa Johnston to WP, 5 Nov. 1863, Tucker Family Papers, SHC.

59. Kinloch Falconer, "Field Return . . . ," *OR*, Series I, Vol. 30, Part 4, 765; WP to WPJ, 23 Nov. 1863, M-BC.

60. WP to WPJ, 17, 24 Nov. 1863, WPJ to WP, 19 Nov. 1863, M-BC; K. Falconer, "Field Return . . . ," *OR*, Series I, Vol. 31, Part 3, 40-41; J. Withers, Special Order No. 5, *OR*, Vol. 34, Part 2, 858; Johnston, *Kentucky*, 254; J. P. Benjamin to WP, 7 Jan. 1864, Records of the Confederate States of America, 1861-1865 (known as the John T. Pickett Papers; hereafter CSA), Manuscript Division, LC.

61. WP to "My dear son and daughters," 3 April 1862, JFP; WP, Vouchers, 31 Jan., 11 April 1863, CSA; WP to WPJ, 24 Aug., 17 Nov. 1863, WPJ to WP, 10 Nov. 1863, M-BC.

62. WP, "Memoranda"; Fitzgerald Ross, *A Visit to the Cities and Camps of the Confederate States* (London, 1865), reprinted in Richard B. Harwell, ed., *The Confederate Reader* (Secaucus, N.J., 1957), 226-27.

63. William C. Davis, *Diary of a Confederate Soldier: John S. Jackman of the Orphan Brigade* (Columbia, S.C., 1990), 3; Larry J. Daniel, *Soldiering in the Army of Tennessee: A Portrait of Life in a Confederate Army* (Chapel Hill, 1991), 92; WP to WPJ, 26 Jan 1863, J.C. Breckinridge to S. Cooper, 31 March 1863, WPJ to WP, 28 May 1863, M-BC.

64. WP to WPJ, 14 June 1862, M-BC; WP to WPJ, 18 June 1863, JFP; Jack D. Welsh, *Medical Histories of Confederate Generals* (Kent, Ohio, 1995), 176.

65. Joshua F. Speed to Abraham Lincoln, 22 May 1863, Lincoln Presidential Papers (hereafter LPP), LC; WP to M. W. Preston, 17 Nov. 1862, CHP.

66. Pew receipts, Second Presbyterian Church, Lexington, Ky., 1862, box 101, W-PFP; C[harlotte] Mentelle, *A Short History of the Late Mrs. Mary O. T. Wickliffe* (Lexington, 1850), 17; M. W. Preston to S. Hepburn, 5 Jan. 1862, 16 Feb. 1863, DC.

67. Caroline H. Preston to WP, 31 Aug. 1863, box 54, books and furniture inventory, 15 March 1862, box 55, receipt from Henry A. Saxton, 17 Feb. 1864, box 102, M. O. Preston to WP, 17 Aug. 1864, box 48, W-PFP; Frances D. Peter, *Window on the War: Frances Dallam Peter's Lexington Civil War Diary*, ed. John David Smith and William Cooper Jr. (Lexington, 1976), 10.

68. Henry Walker, "Power, Sex, and Gender Roles: The Transformation of an Alabama Planter Family during the Civil War," in *Southern Families at War: Loyalty and Conflict in the Civil War South*, ed. Catherine Clinton (New York, 2000), 181-86; see bills and receipts, boxes 101, 102, and M. W. Preston to Mr. Dean, 28 Jan. 1862, W. K. Anderson to Willis True, telegram, 25 Nov. 1862, M. W. Preston to General Fry, 27 Dec. 1863, Piedmont Farm accounts, box 55, rental receipt, box 101, W-PFP; WPJ to Rosa [Johnston], 24 Oct. 1862, M-BC.

69. J. C. Sigfried to M. W. Preston, 19 May 1863, box 55, W-PFP; see Benjamin F. Cooling, *Fort Donelson's Legacy: War and Society in Kentucky and Tennessee, 1862-1863* (Knoxville, 1986), 79; Harrison, *Civil War in Kentucky*, 84-85; Mark Grimsley, *The Hard Hand of War: Union Military Policy Toward Southern Civilians, 1861-1865* (New York, 1995), 3-4; U.S. War Dept. File, no. 206, Dept. O, 1863, CHP.

70. Dudley Bush, 24 May 1863, U.S. War Department File, CHP; D. H. Thompson to [WP], 12 May 1863, WP to WPJ, 17 Nov. 1863, M-BC; J. F. Speed to A. Lincoln, 22 May 1863, LPP.

71. WP to WPJ, 7 June 1863, R. J. Breckinridge to J. Davis, 8 July 1863, M-BC.

72. Peter, *Window on the War*, 33; M. O. Preston to WP, n.d. June 1864, quoted in Scott J. Lucas, "'Indignities, Wrongs, and Outrages': Military and Guerrilla Incursions on Kentucky's Civil War Homefront," *FCHQ* 73 (1999): 361; Hollingsworth, "She Used Her Power Lightly," 246-47.

73. M. W. Preston, Union Provost Marshal File, National Archives, Washington, D.C.; Dorman, "General William Preston," 307-8.

74. WP to RWP, 28 Nov. 1861, box 54, M. W. Preston to WP, 4 March 1865, box 56,

W-PFP; WP to M. W. Preston, 17 Nov. 1862, CHP.

75. WP to "My dear son and daughters," 3 April 1862, WP to WPJ, 30 May 1862, JFP; WP to RWP, 2 Feb. 1863, M. W. Preston to S. Hepburn, 16 Feb. 1863, DC; WP to WPJ, 24 Aug. 1863, M-BC.

76. Mary Todd Lincoln, *Mary Todd Lincoln: Her Life and Letters*, ed. Justin G. Turner and Linda Levitt Turner (New York, 1972), 131; Abraham Lincoln, *Complete Works of Abraham Lincoln*, ed. John Nicolay and John Hay, 12 vols. (New York, 1905), 8: 13; Townsend, *Lincoln and the Bluegrass*, 292-93.

77. [WP], untitled note, [March 1861], box 54, WP, Indenture, 9 Jan. 1866, box 56, W-PFP.

78. WP, Trust, 26 Dec. 1861, quoted in WP, Indenture, 9 Jan. 1866, box 56, bench warrant, Fayette Circuit Court, 7 July 1862, box 55, W-PFP; William H. Townsend, *Lincoln and His Wife's Home Town* (Indianapolis, 1929), 326.

79. WP, Indenture, 13 Feb. 1862, M-BC; Elija Gilpin to Mrs. Albert [S. Johnston], 9 Feb. 1858, JFP; WP to M. W. Preston, 28 Nov. 1861, box 54, W-PFP.

80. WP, Indenture, 9 Jan. 1866, box 56, W-PFP; WP to S. Hepburn, 2 Feb. 1863, M-BC.

81. WP, Indenture, 13 Feb. 1862, Suit, Louisville Chancery Court, 10 June 1864, *Henry Griswold* v. *William Preston Johnston, Rosa Johnston, William Preston, etc.*, 7 Oct. 1864, R. W. Woolley to WPJ, 2 Jan. 1863, Marshal's Sale, 14 Dec. 1863, WP to WPJ, 4 May 1864, WP to WJP, 4 May 1864, M-BC; Hollingsworth, "She Used Her Power Lightly," 248; receipts, box 101, W-PFP; *Lexington Leader*, 22 Sept. 1887; Collins, *Historical Sketches of Kentucky*, 1: 122; WP to I. G. Walker, 2 Dec. 1866, William Preston, Misc. Papers, FHS.

82. WP to WPJ, 22 Nov. 1862, M-BC.

83. Hollingsworth, "She Used Her Power Lightly," 126-27; WP to M. W. Preston, 8 April 1864, box 74, WP to M. W. Preston, 30 May 1864, box 54, M. W. Preston to WP, 26 June 1864, box 48, WP to S. Hepburn, 3 June 1864, box 74, W-PFP.

84. Steven E. Woodworth, *No Band of Brothers: Problems in the Rebel High Command* (Columbia, Mo., 1999), 131; WP to WPJ, 13 Oct. 1877, M-BC.

85. WP to WPJ, 13 Oct. 1877, M-BC.

86. For a review of various evaluations of the South's military strategy, see Archer Jones, "Military Means, Political Ends: Strategy," in Gabor S. Boritt, ed., *Why the Confederacy Lost* (New York, 1992), 43-77. Studies concerned with southern military strategy include McWhiney and Jamieson, *Attack and Die*; Edward Hagerman,

The American Civil War and the Origins of Modern War: Ideas, Organization, and Field Command (Bloomington, Ind., 1988); Archer Jones, *Civil War Command and Strategy* (New York, 1992); Richard M. McMurry, *Two Great Rebel Armies: An Essay in Confederate Military History* (Chapel Hill, 1989).

87. Two military historians who support conflicting views on this point and their arguments are: T. Harry Williams, "The Military Leadership of North and South," in David Donald, ed., *Why the North Won the Civil War* (Baton Rouge, 1960), 33-54, maintains that "concentrated mass offensives," not the Confederacy's "almost wholly defensive" strategy, offered the South the best hope of victory; Alan Nolan, *Lee Considered: General Robert E. Lee and Civil War History* (Chapel Hill, 1991), 69-106, argues that "the only grand strategy that afforded [the South] a chance to win the war" was a defensive one.

88. See Thucydides, *The Peloponnesian War*, in favor of the Athenians' need to wage a defensive war and Donald Kagan, *Fall of the Athenian Empire* (Ithaca, N.Y., 1987), for a review of the debate between defenders and opponents of this strategy from fifth-century B.C. contemporaries of the Peloponnesian War to the present.

89. McWhiney and Jamieson, *Attack and Die*, 14-18; Basil Duke, quoted in *Louisville Courier-Journal*, 26 Sept. 1887; James M. McPherson, *For Cause and Comrades: Why Men Fought and Died* (New York, 1997), 60; Linderman, *Embattled Courage*, 46-47.

7. Minister to Mexico

1. Daniel B. Carroll, "Henri Mercier and the American Civil War," in *Diplomacy in an Age of Nationalism: Essays in Honor of Lynn Marshall Case*, ed. Nancy N. Barker and Marion L. Brown Jr. (The Hague, 1971), 114; Henry Blumenthal, "Confederate Diplomacy: Popular Notions and International Realities," *Journal of Southern History* 32 (1966): 154.

2. Judah P. Benjamin to John Slidell, [17 Aug. 1863], Affaires Diverses Politiques (hereafter ADP), Archives du Ministère des Affaires Etrangères, Quai d'Orsay (hereafter Qd'O), Paris; Louis M. Sears, "A Confederate Diplomat at the Court of Napoleon III," *American Historical Review* 26 (1921): 256, 262; L. de Geofroy to Edouard Drouyn de Lhuys, 4 April 1864, vol. 131, Correspondence Politique, Etats Unis (hereafter CPEU), Qd'O; F. de Arrangoiz to Baron de Pont, 13 Sept. 1863, Archiv Kaiser Maximilian von Mexiko (hereafter AKM), Haus-, Hof- und Staatsarchiv, Vienna; J. Slidell to Napoleon III, [8 June 1863], ADP.

3. Allan Nevins, *War for the Union*, 4 vols. (New York, 1959-71), 1: 97; Owsley, *King Cotton Diplomacy*, xv; Charles M. Hubbard, *The Burden of Confederate Diplomacy* (Knoxville, 1998), 177-78; D. P. Crook, *Diplomacy during the American Civil War* (New York, 1975), 109.

4. Robert E. May, ed., *The Union, the Confederacy, and the Atlantic Rim* (West Lafayette, Ind., 1995), 17; Emory M. Thomas, *The Confederate Nation, 1861-1865* (New

York, 1979), 172; Henry Blumenthal, *France and the United States: Their Diplomatic Relations, 1789-1914* (Chapel Hill, 1970), 76; Howard Jones, "History and Mythology: The Crisis over British Intervention in the Civil War," in May, *The Union, the Confederacy, and the Atlantic Rim*, 51.

5. Serge Gavronsky, *The French Liberal Opposition and the American Civil War* (New York, 1968), 245-47; Lynn M. Case, *French Opinion on the United States and Mexico, 1850-1867: Extracts from the Reports of the Procureurs Généraux* (New York, 1936), passim.

6. Mapp, *Frock Coats and Epaulets*, 355; Hubbard, *The Burden of Confederate Diplomacy*, 177; Thomas, *Confederate Nation*, 176-77.

7. J. Pickett to John Forsyth, 13 March 1861, J. Forsyth to Jefferson Davis, 20 March 1861, CSA.

8. *New York Herald*, 13 March 1861; Robert A. Toombs to J. Pickett, 17 May 1861, CSA.

9. J. Pickett, "Personal Draft of Mission," sent to R. Toombs, 17 May 1861, CSA; Thomas Corwin quoted in Thomas D. Schoonover, *Dollars over Dominion: The Triumph of Liberalism in Mexican-U.S. Relations, 1861-1867* (Baton Rouge, 1978), 14.

10. M. de Azmacama to Juan Antonio de la Fuente, 20 Aug., 16 Oct. 1861, legajo 40, Legación de los Estados Unidos Mexicanos en Francia, Embajada de México, Paris (hereafter LEUM), Archivo Histórico Diplomático Mexicano, Mexico City; J. Pickett to William Browne, 2 Oct. 1861, CSA.

11. Quisenberry, *Lopez's Expedition to Cuba*, 44; J. Pickett to R. Toombs, 29 Nov. 1861, CSA; *Trait d'Union* (Mexico City), 19 Nov. 1861.

12. Ronnie C. Tyler, *Santiago Vidaurri and the Southern Confederacy* ([Austin, Tex.], 1973), 11-15, 54, 98-101; José A. Quintero to R. M. T. Hunter, 17 Aug. 1861, Quintero to J. P. Benjamin, 5 July 1862, CSA; Davis quoted in James M. Callahan, *The Diplomatic History of the Southern Confederacy* (1901; reprint, New York, 1968), 76.

13. M. Turgot to M. Knüsel, 17 Sept. 1861, Consular Correspondence, Mexico, Schweizerisches Bundesarchiv, Bern, Switzerland.

14. G. P. Gooch, *Second Empire*, 25; Brian D. Gooch, *The Reign of Napoleon III* (Chicago, 1969), 51.

15. Nancy N. Barker, *The French Experience in Mexico, 1821-1861: A History of Constant Misunderstanding* (Chapel Hill, 1979), 177, 187; Charles Dupin, "Mémoires du Méxique," AB XIX-171, Dossiers du Méxique, Papiers des Tuileries, Archives Nationales, Paris; Crook, *Diplomacy during the American Civil War*, 201.

16. Nancy N. Barker, *Distaff Diplomacy: The Empress Eugénie and the Foreign Policy of the Second Empire* (Austin, Tex., 1967), 87; Kathryn A. Hanna, "The Roles of the South in French Intervention in Mexico," *Journal of Southern History* 20 (1954): 4.

17. Nancy N. Barker, "France, Austria, and the Mexican Venture," *French Historical Studies* 3 (1963): 245.

18. J. A. Quintero to Juan N. Almonte, 4 Nov. 1863, Almonte to Quintero, 5 Dec. 1863, CSA.

19. Baron de Pont to José Manuel Hidalgo y Esnaurrizar, 12 Sept. 1863, AKM; King Leopold to Maximilian, 27 Oct. 1862, quoted in Egon C. Corti, *Maximilian and Charlotte of Mexico*, trans. Catherine A. Phillips ([Hamden, Conn.],1968), 186; Maximilian to Napoleon III, 10 Aug., 12 Sept. 1863, Richard Hildreth to Maximilian, n.d. Sept. 1863, AKM.

20. Maximilian to Matthew F. Maury, 24 Oct. 1863, Baron de Pont to James Williams, 2, 26 Dec. 1863, AKM; J. P. Benjamin to J. Slidell, 28 Jan., 20 Sept. 1864, CSA. See Owsley, *King Cotton Diplomacy*, 517-21, for a discussion of the first Confederate contacts with Maximilian.

21. F. de Arrangoiz to Baron de Pont, 14 Sept. 1863, AKM.

22. Kean, *Inside the Confederate Government*, 131; *Journal of the Congress of the Confederate States*, 3: 519.

23. WP to J. P. Benjamin, 6 June 1865, "Letter-book of General William Preston, 1864-65," DC.

24. WP to WPJ, 15 Jan. 1864, M-BC.

25. J. P. Benjamin to WP, 7 Jan. 1864, CSA.

26. For a description of this Franco-North American *affaire*, see Barker, *French Experience in Mexico*, 160-72.

27. J. P. Benjamin to WP, 7 Jan. 1864, J. Pickett to Jefferson Davis, 11 Jan. 1864, CSA.

28. Alfred Paul to Drouyn de Lhuys, 13 Jan., 24 Aug. 1863, Correspondence Politique des Consuls, 1863-64, Archives du Ministère des Affaires Etrangères (hereafter CPC), Qd'O.

29. J. P. Benjamin to WP, 7 Jan. 1864, CSA; Gauldrée-Boilleau to Drouyn de Lhuys, 22 Jan., 2 Feb. 1864, Etats Unis, vol. 15, CPC.

30. Jules Treilhard to Drouyn de Lhuys, 9 Feb. 1864, vol. 131, CPEU; James M. Callahan, *American Foreign Policy in Mexican Relations* (New York, 1967), 291, 295; Seward quoted in Ralph Roeder, *Juarez and His Mexico: A Biographical History* (New York, 1947), 596.

31. See Frederic Bancroft, *The Life of William H. Seward*, 2 vols. (New York, 1900), 2: 419, 429-30; James M. Callahan, *Evolution of Seward's Mexican Policy* (Morgantown, W. Va., 1909), 61; Jay Monaghan, *Diplomat in Carpet Slippers: Abraham Lincoln Deals with Foreign Affairs* (Indianapolis, 1945), 368-70; Norman B. Ferris, *Desperate Diplomacy: William H. Seward's Foreign Policy* (Knoxville, 1976), 155-70; Glyndon Van Deusen, *William Henry Seward* (New York, 1967), 368, 372, 487-88; John M. Taylor, *William Henry Seward: Lincoln's Right Hand* (New York, 1991), 303; Manuel Rivera Cambas, *Historia de la intervención europea y norte-americana en México y del Imperio de Maximiliano de Habsburgo*, (Mexico City, 1961), 2B: 556.

32. John Bigelow to Drouyn de Lhuys, 23 Feb. 1865, vol. 25, Mémoires et Documents, Etats Unis, 1848-65, Qd'O; Fernando Ramírez to J. M. Hidalgo, 25 July 1864, legajo 41, LEUM.

33. Seward quoted in Arnold Blumberg, *The Diplomacy of the Mexican Empire, 1863-1867* (Philadelphia, 1971), 17; Matías Romero to Minister of Foreign Relations, 10 March 1864, Legación de México en los Estados Unidos (hereafter LM), Archivo Histórico Diplomático Mexicano, Secretaría de Relaciones Exteriores, Mexico City.

34. M. Romero to Minister of Foreign Relations, 11 Jan. 1864, in Matías Romero, *Correspondencia de la Legación mexicana en Washington durante la intervención extranjera, 1850-1868*, 7 vols. (Mexico City, 1871), 4: 7-8; Walter V. Scholes, *Mexican Politics During the Juárez Regime, 1855-1872* (Columbia, Mo., 1957), 109; Jasper G. Ridley, *Maximilian and Juárez* (New York, 1992), 177; Romero to Minister of Foreign Affairs, 31 July, 28 Oct. 1864, LM.

35. Hanna, "Roles of the South," 14; Gauldrée-Boilleau to Drouyn de Lhuys, 22 Jan. 1864, CPC; Alfred J. and Kathryn A. Hanna, *Napoleon III and Mexico: American Triumph over Monarchy* (Chapel Hill, 1917), 141.

36. Blumenthal, *France and the United States*, 81; Eugene H. Berwanger, *The British Foreign Service and the American Civil War* (Lexington, 1994), 109; Weigley, *A Great Civil War*, 310.

37. Pierre A. Rost to J. P. Benjamin, 13 Sept. 1862, CSA; Louis M. Sears, *John Slidell* (Durham, N.C., 1925), 188; Ephraim D. Adams, *Great Britain and the American Civil War*, 2 vols. (New York, 1925), 1: 294.

38. Henry Blumenthal, *A Reappraisal of Franco-American Relations, 1830-1871* (Chapel Hill, 1959), 150; Charles P. Roland, *An American Iliad: The Story of the Civil War* (Lexington, 1991), 170.

39. F. de Arrangoiz to Baron de Pont, 13 Sept. 1863, Maximilian to Napoleon III, 27 Sept. 1863, Napoleon III to Maximilian, 2 Oct. 1863, AKM.

40. *Richmond (Va.) Sentinel*, 14 Oct. 1863; Berwanger, *British Foreign Service*, 108; Roland, *An American Iliad*, 170; D. P. Crook, *The North, the South, and the Powers, 1861-1865* (New York, 1974), 340; James G. Randall and David Donald, *The Civil War and Reconstruction*, 2d ed. (Lexington, Mass., 1969), 512; Pierce Butler, *Judah P. Benjamin* (Philadelphia, 1906), 354.

41. Henry Hotze to J. P. Benjamin, 11 July 1863, CSA; Adams, *Great Britain*, 295; J. P. Benjamin to J. Slidell, 23 June 1864, CSA; Hanna, "Roles of the South," 13-14.

42. WP to J. P. Benjamin, 13 Feb. 1864, "Letter-book."

43. WP to S. Hepburn, 14 Feb. 1864, 10 March, 1865, DC; WP, "Memoranda Book," box 56, W-PFP; WP to WPJ, 4 May 1864, M-BC.

44. Joan Haslip, *The Crown of Mexico: Maximilian and His Empress Carlota* (New York, 1971), 203-4; J. Slidell to J. P. Benjamin, 16 March 1864, in Richardson, *Compilation of the Messages and Papers of the Confederacy*, 2: 634.

45. James Mason to J. P. Benjamin, 16 March 1864, in Virginia Mason, *The Public Life and Diplomatic Correspondence of James M. Mason with Some Personal History by His Daughter* (Roanoke, Va, 1903), 475; WP to J. P. Benjamin, 28 April 1864, "Letter-book."

46. WP to J. P. Benjamin, 4 March, 9 April, 2 June 1864, WP to J. Davis, 2, 28 June 1864, WP to J. Slidell, 6 May 1864, WP to Marquis de Montholon, 8 June 1864, "Letter-book."

47. WP to J. P. Benjamin, 1, 6 June 1864, "Letter-book"; José Luis Blasio, *Maximiliano íntimo: El Emperador Maximiliano y su corte* (Mexico City, 1905), 1-2.

48. Marquis de Montholon to Drouyn de Lhuys, 28 June 1864, Correspondence Politique, Méxique, Qd'O; WP to J. P. Benjamin, 29 June 1864, "Letter-book."

49. WP to J. P. Benjamin, 24 June 1864, WP to J. Davis, 28 June 1864, "Letter-book"; Robert T. Ford to WP, 18 June 1864, CSA.

50. WP to R. T. Ford, 20 Aug. 1864, "Letter-book."

51. WP to J. P. Benjamin, 18 Aug. 1864, "Letter-book"; WP to WPJ, 19 Aug. 1864, M-BC.

52. WP to J. P. Benjamin, 18 Aug. 1864, "Letter-book."

53. WP to S. Hepburn, 10 Aug. [1864], "Letter-book"; *Dictionary of National Biography* (London, 1921-22), s.v. "Lindsay, William Shaw."

54. Ronald R. Alexander, "Central Kentucky during the Civil War, 1861-1865" (Ph.D. diss., University of Kentucky, 1976), 178, 181; Harrison, *Civil War in Kentucky*, 76-91; M. O. Preston to WP, 5 June 1864, box 48, W-PFP.

55. M. W. Preston to WP, 26 June 1864, box 48, W-PFP; Harrison, *Civil War in Kentucky*, 77.

56. WP to WPJ, 19 Aug. 1864, M-BC; Caroline Preston to WP, [July 1864], box 48, M. W. Preston to WP, [10 April 1865], box 56, W-PFP; Gerry Van der Heuvel, *Crowns of Thorns and Glory: Mary Todd Lincoln and Varina Howell Davis: The Two First Ladies of the Civil War* (New York, 1988), 226, 230.

57. Elizabeth Blair Lee, *Wartime Washington: The Civil War Letters of Elizabeth Blair Lee* (Urbana, Ill., 1991), 485; Alice Ford to Rosa Johnston, 29 Aug. 1864, M-BC.

58. Diary and account book, 8 Oct. 1864, WPA; WP to J. P. Benjamin, 10 Nov. 1864, "Letter-book."

59. J. P. Benjamin to WP, 22 July 1864, in Richardson, *Compilation of the Messages and Papers of the Confederacy*, 2: 663.

60. WP to J. P. Benjamin, 10 Nov. 1864, WP to R. T. Ford, 10 Nov. 1864, "Letter-book."

61. WP to J. P. Benjamin, 10 Nov. 1864, "Letter-book."

62. J. P. Benjamin to J. Mason, 20 Sept. 1864, CSA; J. P. Benjamin to J. Slidell, 8 Jan. 1864, CSA.

63. For criticism of Confederate diplomacy, see Crook, *Diplomacy during the American Civil War*, 14-16; Robert D. Meade, "The Relations between Judah P. Benjamin and Jefferson Davis," *Journal of Southern History* 5 (1939): 473-78; Blumenthal, "Confederate Diplomacy," 151.

64. May, *Union, the Confederacy, and the Atlantic Rim*, 15; Eli N. Evans, *Judah P. Benjamin: The Jewish Confederate* (New York, 1987), 127, 156.

65. WP to R. T. Ford, 1, 10 Oct. 1864, WP to Charles J. Helm, 10 Nov. 1864, "Letter-book."

66. WP to C. J. Helm, 29 Nov. 1864, "Letter-book"; WP to RWP, Dec. 18, 1864, DC.

67. R. T. Ford to WP, 28 Sept. 1864, M-BC; R. T. Ford to Fernando Ramírez, 9 Nov. 1864, R. T. Ford to C. J. Helm, 8 Dec. 1864, CSA; J. Hidalgo to Maximilian, 30 Dec.

1864, AKM.

68. WP to WPJ, 22 Oct. 1865, WP to S. Hepburn, 10 March 1865, M-BC; Margaret H. Preston to WP, 31 Jan. 1865, M. W. Preston to RWP, 19 Feb. 1865, M. W. Preston to WP, 20 March 1865, box 56, W-PFP.

69. Stephen R. Wise, *Lifeline of the Confederacy: Blockade Running during the Civil War* (Columbia, S.C., 1988), 205-11; WP to RWP, 10 Feb. 1865, WP to S. Hepburn, 10 March 1865, DC; Ella Lonn, *Foreigners in the Confederacy* (Gloucester, Mass, 1965), 86-88; WP, "Memoranda Book," box 56, W-PFP.

70. John B. Magruder to E. Kirby Smith, 28 April 1865, *OR*, Series I, Vol. 48, Part 2, 1288-91; Stickles, *Simon Bolivar Buckner*, 265-66.

71. WP to E. Kirby Smith, 18 Dec. 1865, E. Kirby Smith to WP, 18 Dec. 1865, box 56, W-PFP; Linderman, *Embattled Courage*, 45; Robert L. Kerby, *Kirby Smith's Confederacy: The Trans-Mississippi South, 1863-1865* (New York, 1972), 249; Lonn, *Foreigners in the Confederacy*, 448.

72. Brigitte Hamann, ed., *Mit Kaiser Max in Mexiko: Aus dem Tagebuch des Fürsten Carl Khevenhüller, 1864-1867* (Vienna, 1983), 157; WP to Varina Davis, 1 Nov. 1865, Jefferson Davis Papers (hereafter JDP), Special Collections and Archives, Transylvania University Library, Lexington.

73. Kerby, *Kirby Smith's Confederacy*, 420, 424-26; Robert E. Shalhope, *Sterling Price: Portrait of a Southerner* (Columbia, Mo., 1971), 280; Andrew F. Rolle, *The Lost Cause: The Confederate Exodus to Mexico* (Norman, Okla., 1965), 50; Stickles, *Simon Bolivar Buckner*, 270; F. L. Claibourne to H. N. Frisbie, 22 May 1865, *OR*, Series I, Vol. 48, Part 2, 538.

74. WP to J. Davis, 28 June 1864, WP to W. M Gwinn, 28 June 1864, "Letter-book."

75. WP to RWP, 10 Feb. 1865, DC.

76. For details of Preston's trip from Texas to Canada, see WP to A. C. Jones, 16 Nov. 1865, CHP; Carl Rister, "Carlota, A Confederate Colony in Mexico," *Journal of Southern History* 11 (1945): 35; WP, "Memorandum Book," box 56, W-PFP; *Revue de la Quinzaine de l'Estafette* (Mexico City), 29 July 1865.

77. Evans, *Judah P. Benjamin*, 320; Robert E. Meade, *Judah P. Benjamin: Confederate Statesman* (London, 1943), 321; WP to V. Davis, 1 Nov. 1865, JDP; WP to WPJ, 22 Oct. 1865, M-BC; WP to S. Hepburn, 5 Dec. 1863, DC.

78. WP to S. Hepburn, 5 Dec. 1865, DC; Elbert B. Smith, *Francis Preston Blair* (Cambridge, Mass., 1980), 389; S. Hepburn to WPJ, 10 Dec. 1865, M-BC.

79. WP to S. Hepburn, 5 Dec. 1865, DC.

80. *Cincinnati Gazette*, 21 April 1865; WP to Collector of Customs, 16 Dec. 1865, box 56, W-PFP.

81. WP to I. G. Walker, 2 Dec. 1866, DC; James Speed to Joshua Lewis, 22 Dec. 1865, and John M. Palmer, 22 Dec. 1865, box 56, W-PFP; Stuart S. Sprague, "Slaver's Death Knell," *FCHQ* 65 (1991): 458; McDowell, *City of Conflict*, 181; S. Hepburn to WPJ, 10 Dec. 1865, M-BC.

8. After the War

1. WP to E. Kirby Smith, 4 Sept. 1866, DC.

2. Simpson, *Bluegrass Houses*, 2-3, 8-9; M. W. Preston to RWP, 18 Dec. [1868], Preston-Johnston Papers (hereafter PJFP), UK; Coleman, *Historic Kentucky*, 139; *Lexington Leader*, 30 June 1938.

3. Coleman, *Historic Kentucky*, 89; Lancaster, *Antebellum Architecture*, 70-71; Hollingsworth, "She Used Her Power Lightly," 309; Frank Dunn, *Old Houses of Lexington*, 3 vols. (Frankfort, n.d.), 2: 530; Simpson, *Bluegrass Houses*, 5; Robert Wickliffe, *Will of Robert Wickliffe* (n.p., n.d.), UK.

4. WP to S. Hepburn, 7 Jan. 1865 [1866], JC; Lancaster, *Antebellum Architecture*, 66; Hambleton Tapp and James C. Klotter, *Kentucky: Decades of Discord, 1865-1900* (Frankfort, 1977), 283; Simpson, *Bluegrass Houses*, 8; Coleman, *Historic Kentucky*, 139; undated clipping, *Lexington Leader*, CHP.

5. WP to S. Hepburn, 7 Jan. 1865 [1866], JC; *Louisville Courier-Journal*, 26 Sept. 1887. For the interior of Preston Place, see Simpson, *Bluegrass Houses*, 8-13.

6. WP, account book, 14 April 1869, box 86, W-PFP; George W. Ranck, *Guide to Lexington, Kentucky: With Notices Historical and Descriptive of Places and Objects of Interest, and a Summary of the Advantages and Resources of the City and Vicinity* (Lexington, 1883), 76-77; Hollingsworth, "She Used Her Power Lightly," 310-11; WP to WPJ, 21 Oct. 1866, box 13, W-PFP; WP to WPJ, 8 Nov. 1867, M-BC.

7. WP to RWP, 18 Aug. 1868, WPP; WP to RWP, [1873], PJFP; M. W. Preston to William Lindsay, 15 July [1881], 9 Oct. [1882], 7, 19 Oct. [1890s], William Preston Letters (hereafter WLP), UK.

8. WP to RWP, n.d. 1872, WPP; WP to I. G. Walker, 2 Dec. 1866, DC; "Preston, Genl. Wm.," "Taxbook," Fayette County, 1869; WP, "Diary," 8 Oct. 1864, 6 Dec. 1880, 4, 22 Nov. 1883, WPA.

9. WP to WPJ, 8 Nov. 1867, M-BC; Ranck, *History of Lexington, Kentucky*, 383, 404;

Harrison and Klotter, *New History of Kentucky*, 216.

10. WP to WPJ, 26 April 1868, M-BC; James Buchanan to WP, 27 July, 20 Aug. 1886, box 70, W-PFP; M. W. Preston to RWP, 19 Jan. [1873], PJFP.

11. Simpson, *Bluegrass Houses*, 10-12; undated clipping, *Lexington Leader*, CHP.

12. M. W. Preston to RWP, 30 Oct. [1867], WPP; Simpson, *Bluegrass Houses*, 11-12.

13. M. W. Preston to RWP, 30 Oct. [1867], WPP; Benjamin Buckner, quoting his father, Judge Buckner, *Louisville Times*, 20 March 1940; Rosa V. J. Jeffreys to M. W. Preston, n.d., box 80, W-PFP.

14. Clay Lancaster, *Vestiges of the Venerable City: A Chronicle of Lexington, Kentucky* (Lexington, 1978), 85; Frances Keller Swinford and Rebecca Smith Lee, *The Great Elm Tree: Heritage of the Episcopal Diocese of Lexington* (Lexington, 1969), 10, 248, 281; [George Thomas] Chapman Record Book, 4 Feb. 1866, Archives, Christ Church Cathedral, Lexington; WP to WPJ, 6 Feb. 1866, M-BC.

15. WP, "Diary," 23 Nov. 1880, WPP; Margaret Wickliffe Preston Johnston, autobiographical statement, n.d., M. W. Preston to RWP, 19 Jan. [1868], PJFP; WP to WPJ, 26 April 1868, M-BC; WP to RWP, 8 March 1868, WPP; Swinford and Lee, *The Great Elm Tree*, 285.

16. WPJ to Rosa Johnston, 9 Nov. 1861, JFP.

17. For information on the Preston children and their families, see Dorman, *Prestons of Smithfield and Greenfield*; WP to WPJ, 28 Aug. 1869, M-BC.

18. WP to WPJ, 14 July 1871, M-BC; WP, "Diary," [n.d.] Sept. 1879, WPP.

19. WP to RWP, 17 July 1876, PJFP; M. W. Preston to RWP, 19 Feb. 1865, WPP.

20. R. T. P. Allen to WP, [28 Jan. 1867], M. W. Preston to WP, 28 March 1867, box 57, W-PFP; Sydney Beauclerk, obituary, unidentified newspaper clipping, [1938], CHP.

21. WP to WPJ, 18 Sept.1866, 18 March 1867, box 13, RWP to WP, 22 Dec. 1867, box 57, W-PFP; Shaw, *William Preston Johnston*, 101; WP to RWP, 8, 21 March 1868, WPP; WP to RWP, 15 March 1868, 8 March 1870, 1 March 1872, PJFP.

22. M. W. Preston to RWP, 15 Dec. 1867, 18 Aug. [1867], WPP, and 9 March [1869?], 4 Aug. [1869], PJFP; Sydney Beauclerk, obituary.

23. RWP to WP, [1870], M. W. Preston to RWP, 5 Aug. [1870?], PJFP.

24. M. W. Preston to RWP, 5 Aug. [1871], PJFP; Hollingsworth, "She Used Her

Power Lightly," 180.

25. RWP to M. W. Preston, 27 July 1872, box 61, RWP to WP, 31 July 1876, box 63, W-PFP.

26. RWP to WP, 28 April, 29 Sept. 1875, [Jan. 1878], 18 Feb., 27 March, 14 Nov. 1878, box 64, W-PFP.

27. WP to Samuel J. Tilden, 30 March 1878, Samuel J. Tilden Papers, New York Public Library, New York City; M. W. Preston to RWP, 1 Sept. [1878], box 64, W-PFP; WP to S. Hepburn, 23 Dec. 1881, DC.

28. WP to RWP, 4 Dec. 1882, M. W. Preston to RWP, 4 Dec. 1882, PJFP; RWP to WP, 16 June 1882, box 67, W-PFP; M. W. P. Johnston, autobiographical statement.

29. S. F. Frost to RWP, 18 Jan. 1884, PJFP; WP to RWP (numerous letters), 1884-86, PJFP; E. Polk Johnson, *A History of Kentucky and Kentuckians*, 3 vols. (Chicago, 1912), 3: 1492.

30. *National Police Gazette*, 26 Dec. 1885; Simpson, *Bluegrass Houses*, 13-15.

31. WP to S. Hepburn, 11 Sept. 1885, DC; WP to WPJ, 9 Dec. 1872, 24 Dec. 1873, M-BC; WP to Elizabeth Carrington, 27 March 1873, CHP.

32. Margaret Preston Davie to WP, [1884], box 70, 1 Oct. [1884], box 68, [1885], box 69, RWP to WP, I.O.U., 2 April 1885, box 69, WP to Caroline H. Preston, 28 April 1885, box 69, Jessie Preston to WP, 24 July 1887, box 71, W-PFP; Hollingsworth, "She Used Her Power Lightly," 198.

33. See Harrison and Klotter, *New History of Kentucky*, 218; George C. Wright, *Racial Violence in Kentucky, 1865-1940: Lynchings, Mob Rule, and "Legal Lynchings"* (Baton Rouge, 1990), 19-20, 41; Otis A. Singletary, *Negro Militia and Reconstruction* (Austin, Tex., 1957), 26-44; Ross A. Webb, "'The Past is Never Dead; It's Not Even Past': Benjamin P. Rumkle and the Freedmen's Bureau in Kentucky, 1866-1870," *RKHS* 8 (1986): 344-48; Lucas, *History of Blacks in Kentucky*, 187-98; Victor B. Howard, *Black Liberation in Kentucky: Emancipation and Freedom, 1862-1884* (Lexington, 1983), 88-99.

34. Marion B. Lucas, "Kentucky Blacks: The Transition from Slavery to Freedom," *RKHS* 91 (1993): 412; *Lexington Kentucky Gazette*, 11 Jan. 1871; WP to RWP, 22 Jan. 1871, WPP; Note to WP, 23 Jan. 1871, box 60, W-PFP; Hollingsworth, "She Used Her Power Lightly," 187.

35. Robert W. Beasley to WP, 16 March 1868, box 57, Robert Thompson to WP, 30 Aug. 1870, box 60, Joseph Smith to WP, 29 Dec. 1870, box 59, Samuel Giles to WP, 8 June 1885, box 69, W-PFP.

36. M. W. Preston to RWP, [1872], PJFP.

37. Lewis E. [Haine] to WP, 28 Jan. 1867, J. F. Gibson to WP, 11 Nov. 1867, box 57, W-PFP; Duke, *Reminiscences of General Basil Duke*, 215.

38. WP to E. Kirby Smith, 4 Sept. 1866, DC; WP, 30 Jan. 1883, "Inventory of Debts 1883," box 88, W-PFP.

39. M. W. Preston to WP, 13 May 1848, box 45, Fannie Caldwell to WP, 6 May 1868, WP to M. W. Preston, telegram, 13 [May] 1868, M. W. Preston to WP, [May 1868], box 57, W-PFP.

40. WP to M. W. Preston, 16 May 1868, [late May 1868], Edward J. Jones to WP, 27 May 1868, James Leeds to WP, 29 May 1868, box 57, W-PFP; *Boston Journal*, 26 May 1868.

41. M. W. Preston to WP, 7 Dec. [1874], box 62, W-PFP.

42. M. P. Brown to WP, [Dec. 1874], RWP to WP, 13 Dec. 1874, box 62, W-PFP.

43. RWP to WP, 16 July 1876, box 63, WP to M. W. Preston, 3 Oct. 1884, box 68, W-PFP.

44. R. Gibson to WPJ, [Sept. 1868], M-BC; M. W. Preston to RWP, 8 July [1870], 11 Aug. [1871], PJFP.

45. M. W. Preston to WP, 1 Aug. 1882, box 67, 5 Sept. 1878, box 64, 20 Sept. [1883], box 68, W-PFP; M. W. Preston to W. Lindsay, 15 July 1881, WPL.

46. E. Williams to WP, 13 April 1878, box 113, W-PFP; WP to S. Hepburn, 23 May 1878, 9 June [1886?], WP to M. P. Brown, 8 Jan. 1879, DC; WP to WPJ, 23 July 1876, M-BC; WP to RWP, 22 Jan. 1871, WPP.

47. Samuel D. Gross to WP, 14 Sept. 1878, box 113, W-PFP; Cassius M. Clay to Tilden, 28 June 1880, in Samuel J. Tilden, *Letters and Literary Memorials of Samuel J. Tilden*, ed. John Bigelow, 2 vols. (New York, 1908), 1: 601. See brochures collected in the 1880s from companies selling hearing aids, box 113, W-PFP.

48. WP to RWP, 22 Jan. 1871, WPP; RWP to S. Hepburn, telegram, 26 Sept. 1878, DC; Gross, *Autobiography of Samuel D. Gross*, 2: 35, 143.

49. RWP to S. Hepburn, 3, 10 June 1878, DC; M. W. Preston to RWP, [1872], 10 June 1878, WP to John M. Brown, 16 Aug. 1884, DC.

50. WP to Henry Watterson, 5 Nov. 1874, Papers of Henry Watterson, LC; WP to Andrew Buchanan, 27 June 1877, PJFP; WP to S. Hepburn, 23 Dec. 1881, DC; WP to

WPJ, 7 December 1886, M-BC.

51. John D. Wright, *Lexington: Heart of the Bluegrass* (Lexington, 1982), 107-8, 111, 118, 121; Tapp and Klotter, *Kentucky: Decades of Discord*, 63; M. W. Preston to W. Lindsay, 19 Jan. [1884], WLP; "Lexington Water Company," typed manuscript, 21 Nov. 1883, box 119, W-PFP; M. W. Preston to W. Lindsay, 13 May, 11 Dec. [1884], WLP.

52. Seymour V. Connor, *Texas: A History* (New York, 1971), 138; Hill, *Dallas*, xix; Hogan, *Texas Republic*, 11; Richardson, *Texas*, 191.

53. A. S. Johnston to WP, 27 Nov. 1841, box 44, W-PFP; Seymour V. Connor, *The Peters Colony of Texas: A History and Biographical Sketches* (Austin, Tex., 1959), 109.

54. WP, "Texas Association, Private Memorandum," handwritten manuscript, 1-7, 29, 37, John W. Buchanan, "Memorandum," 13 March 1883, box 137, W-PFP; *History and Statement of Mercer Colony Case* (Austin, Tex., 1882), 70-71.

55. WP to S. Hepburn, 23 Dec. 1881, box 65, "William Preston vs. Defendant," box 137, W-PFP; WP, "Texas Association," 65.

56. Untitled newspaper clipping, [March 1882], WP to Clarence A. McElroy, 2 March 1882, CHP; E. C. Dickinson to WP, 5 Dec. 1885, Claiborne and Wren to WP, 5 Dec. 1885, box 137, *Supreme Court of the United States. William C. Walsh* v. *William Preston*, box 139, W-PFP.

57. S. Hepburn to WP, 24 June, [Oct.] 1886, box 70, W-PFP; WP to S. Hepburn, 23 Dec. 1881, DC; Beauclerk obituary.

58. Susan Preston to WP, 24 Nov. 1884, box 68, S. Hepburn to WP, 24 Sept. 1886, invitation, 17 April 1886, box 70, W-PFP; WP, "Some Reflections on the Study of Greek Authors," 2 Nov. 1876, handwritten notes in Scapula, *Lexicon graeco-latinum*, WPA. See Preston's poor handwriting in WP to WPJ, 1 Aug. 1878, M-BC; WP to J. Davis, 20 Nov. 1870, WP to George M. Davie, 20 Oct. 1886, CHP.

59. WP to I. G. Walker, 2 Dec. 1866, DC; WP to J. C. Breckinridge, 6 Aug. 1867, William Preston Misc. Papers, FHS.

60. Ross A. Webb, *Kentucky in the Reconstruction Era* (Lexington, 1979), 12-16; Henry Watterson, *"Marse Henry": An Autobiography*, 2 vols. (New York, 1974), 1: 176; Smith, "Slavery and Antislavery," in *Our Kentucky*, 119.

61. Webb, "'The Past is Never Dead,'" 346; Tapp and Klotter, *Kentucky: Decades of Discord*, 11, 151; Singletary, *Negro Militia*, 27; Stickles, *Simon Bolivar Buckner*, 288, 318.

62. WP to S. Hepburn, 7 Jan. [1866], JC; WP to I. G. Walker, 2 Dec. 1866, DC.

63. John C. Noble to WP, 10 Dec. 1866, *Frankfort Yeoman*, clipping, [Dec. 1866?], box 57, W-PFP; WP to I. G. Walker, 2 Dec. 1866, DC; *Lexington Kentucky Gazette*, 23 Feb. 1867; Thomas L. Owen, "The Formative Years of Kentucky's Republican Party, 1864-1871" (Ph.D. diss., University of Kentucky, 1981), 64.

64. WP to RWP, 8 March 1868, WPP; Eric Foner, *Reconstruction: America's Unfinished Revolution, 1863-1877* (New York, 1988), 339-41; Stickles, *Simon Bolivar Buckner*, 298-99; *Lexington Kentucky Gazette*, 1 Aug. 1868.

65. WP to I. G. Walker, 2 Dec. 1866, DC; James B. Beck to WP, 19 April 1868, W. H. Seward to WP, 8 Dec. 1868, box 57, W-PFP.

66. *Lexington Kentucky Gazette*, 9, 12 Dec. 1868; WP to RWP, 16 Dec. 1868, PJFP; Tapp and Klotter, *Kentucky: Decades of Discord*, 26.

67. WP to J. C. Noble, 22 April 1869, in *Lexington Kentucky Gazette*, 8 May 1869; Tapp and Klotter, *Kentucky: Decades of Discord*, 54-56; M. W. Preston to RWP, 18 Dec. [1868], PJFP. See also *Lexington Kentucky Gazette*, 12 May 1869.

68. S. Tilden to WP, 22 Sept. 1878, box 113, W-PFP; WP to WPJ, 21 Nov. 1876, M-BC; Webb, *Kentucky in the Reconstruction Era*, 89.

69. Watterson, *"Marse Henry,"* 273; Joseph F. Wall, *Henry Watterson: Reconstructed Rebel* (New York, 1956), 146; H. Watterson to S. Tilden, telegram, 9 Nov. 1876, Tilden Papers; WP to WPJ, 21 Nov. 1876, M-BC.

70. Montgomery Blair to S. Tilden, 10 Dec. 1876, WP to S. Tilden, 11 Dec. 1876, Tilden Papers; *Louisville Courier-Journal*, 8 Jan., 25 Sept. 1877; Lenor C. Logan, "Henry Watterson, Border Nationalist, 1840-1877," (Ph.D. diss., Indiana University, 1942), 48, 444.

71. *Louisville Courier-Journal*, 18 Jan. 1877; Tapp and Klotter, *Kentucky: Decades of Discord*, 152; George M. Morgan to W. C. P. Breckinridge, 13 Jan. 1877, Tilden Papers; Foner, *Reconstruction*, 576-77; Watterson, *"Marse Henry,"* 274.

72. Isaac F. Marcosson, *"Marse Henry": A Biography of Henry Watterson* (New York, 1961), 131-32. Material on the negotiations between southern Democrats and Republicans on the Hayes-Tilden presidential contest are taken from C. Vann Woodward, *Reunion and Reaction: The Compromise of 1877 and the End of Reconstruction* (Boston, 1951); Foner, *Reconstruction*, 575-82; Kenneth M. Stampp, *The Era of Reconstruction, 1865-1877* (New York, 1965), 186, 210; John Hope Franklin, *Reconstruction after the Civil War* (Chicago, 1961), 212-17.

73. John Bigelow to H. Watterson, 13 Dec. 1905, Papers of Henry Watterson; Watterson, *"Marse Henry,"* 279; "The Hayes-Tilden Contest for the Presidency: The

Inside History of a Great Political Crisis," *Century Magazine* 86 (1913): 3-4.

74. WP to WPJ, 22 June 1877, M-BC; H. Watterson to WP, 7 Aug. 1876, box 63, W-PFP.

75. Thomas Scott to WP, 14 Jan. 1877, box 63, W-PFP.

76. WPJ to WP, 29 Jan. 1877, S. Tilden to WP, 28 Feb. 1878, box 63, W-PFP.

77. Lucius Q. C. Lamar to H. Watterson, 12 Dec. 1878, Papers of Henry Watterson; P. M. Henry to WP, 11 July 1877, J. C. S. Blackburn to WP, 15 Oct. 1877, box 63, W-PFP.

78. C. M. Clay to S. Tilden, 28 June 1880, in Tilden, *Memorials of Samuel J. Tilden*, 1: 601; *Harper's Weekly*, 31 July 1880.

79. J. W. Stevenson to WP, 28 March 1885, J. Stoddard Johnston to the President, [March 1885]; Attorney General of Kentucky to Grover Cleveland, 31 March 1885, W. C. P. Breckinridge to Thomas F. Bayard, [March 1885?], R. L. Wilson to WP, 11 March 1885, box 69, W-PFP.

80. Ranck, *History of Lexington, Kentucky*, 278; WP to "Dear Sir and Brothers," [1866], box 56, W-PFP; Reuben T. Durrett, "In Memoriam of William Preston," paper delivered in 1887 at the Filson Club, Louisville, Ky. For Preston's memberships, see invitations and programs in box 70, W-PFP.

81. Henry Watterson, *History of the Manhattan Club: A Narrative of the Activities of Half a Century* (New York, 1915), xx.

82. *History of the Ohio Falls Cities and Their Counties*, 1: 343; *Louisville Courier-Journal*, 22 July 1922; Briney, *Fond Recollections*, 93.

83. George A. Kinkaid to WP, 28 April 1877, box 63, S. Preston to WP, 3 Aug. 1883, box 68, W-PFP; *Lexington Daily Transcript*, 1 Aug. 1883; Schmidt, *Kentucky Illustrated*, 72; Tapp and Klotter, *Kentucky: Decades of Discord*, 100; Briney, *Fond Recollections*, 103.

84. *Lexington Kentucky Gazette*, 23 Sept. 1874; Hughes and Ware, *Theodore O'Hara*, 141; *Frankfort Tri-Weekly Kentucky Yeoman*, 19 June 1875; *Louisville Courier-Journal*, 18 June 1875; "Programme," 19 Aug. 1885, and [1886], box 69, W-PFP.

85. Durrett, "In Memoriam of William Preston"; Burial Records, Cave Hill Cemetery Company, in Welsh, *Medical Histories of Confederate Generals*, 176; WP to M. W. Preston, 23 June 1887, Notebook, 1887, box 71, W-PFP; unidentified newspaper clipping, 22 Sept. 1887, CHP.

86. WP, "Last Will and Testament," 13 Aug. 1887, box 71, W-PFP.

87. *Louisville Courier-Journal*, 23, 24, Sept. 1887.

88. M. P. W. Johnston, autobiographical statement. This marker gives the wrong birth dates for both William and Margaret W. Preston. He celebrated 16 Oct. (not 15 Oct.) as his birthday; see WP to M. W. Preston, 16 Oct. 1861, box 54, W-PFP. According to family papers, she was born on 24 March (not 25 March) 1819; Samuel W. Thomas, *Cave Hill: A Pictorial Guide and Its History* (Louisville, 1985), 19.

89. *Louisville Courier-Journal*, 22 Sept. 1887.

90. WP, "Some Reflections on the Study of Greek Authors"; Duke, *Reminiscences*, 196, 221.

Bibliography of Works Cited

Manuscript Collections

Alabama Department of Archives and History, Montgomery.
    Robert McKee Papers.

Archives du Ministère des Affaires Etrangères, Quai d'Orsay, Paris, France.
    Affaires Diverses Politiques.
    Correspondence Politique des Consuls, 1863-64.
    Correspondence Politique, Etats Unis, 1864.
    Correspondence Politique, Méxique, 1864.
    Mémoires et Documents, Etats Unis, 1848-65.

Archives Nationales, Paris, France.
    Dossiers du Méxique, Papiers des Tuileries.

Archivo del Ministerio de Asuntos Exteriores, Madrid, Spain.
    Correspondencia, Estados Unidos.
    Expedientes relativos a Preston, Wm.
    Política, Estados Unidos, 1856-1860.

Archivo Histórico Diplomático Mexicano, Mexico City.
    Legación de los Estados Unidos Mexicanos en Francia. Embajada de México, Paris.
    Legación de México en los Estados Unidos.

Christ Church Cathedral, Archives, Lexington, Kentucky.
    Parish records.
    [George Thomas] Chapman Record Book.

The Filson Historical Society, Louisville, Kentucky.
    Brown-Ewell Family Papers.
    Davie Collection. Preston Family Papers.
    John F. Dorman Manuscripts.
    Johnston Family Papers.
    Joyes Collection. Preston Family Papers.
    William Preston. Miscellaneous Papers.

Haus-, Hof- und Staatsarchiv, Vienna, Austria.
    Archiv Kaiser Maximilian von Mexiko.

Houghton Library, Harvard University, Cambridge, Massachusetts.
    Dudley M. Haydon Papers.

Howard-Tilton Library, Special Collections, Tulane University, New Orleans, Louisiana.
    Albert Sidney Johnston Papers.
    Mason-Barret Collection.

H. E. Huntington Library, San Marino, California.
    Simon Bolivar Buckner Collection.

Historical Society of Pennsylvania, Philadelphia.
    James Buchanan Papers.

Library of Congress, Manuscript Division, Washington, D.C.
    Benjamin Moran Diary.

Bibliography

Breckinridge Family Papers.
Lincoln Presidential Papers.
Papers of Henry Watterson.
Records of the Confederate States of America, 1861-1865 ("John T. Pickett Papers").

Margaret I. King Library, Division of Special Collections and Archives, University of Kentucky, Lexington.
Breckinridge Family Papers.
Charles Hay Papers.
Dicken-Troutman-Balke Papers.
Preston-Johnston Family Papers.
Wickliffe-Preston Family Papers.
William Preston, Account books, letter-books, letters, etc.
William Preston Letters.
William Preston Papers.

National Archives, Washington, D.C.
Compiled Service Records of Confederate Generals and Staff Officers and
Nonregimental Enlisted Men. Microfilm Publication. Microcopy 331.
Despatches of U.S. Ministers to Spain, 1792-1906. Microfilm Publication. Microcopy 31.
Diplomatic Instructions of the Department of State, 1801-1906.
Diplomatic Post Records.
U.S. Embassy, Spain. Preston, Wm., Department of State, Record Group 84.

New York Public Library, New York.
Samuel J. Tilden Papers.

Schweizerisches Bundesarchiv, Bern, Switzerland.
Consular Correspondence, Mexico.

Transylvania University Library, Special Collections and Archives, Lexington, Kentucky.
Jefferson Davis Papers.

University of Chicago Library, Chicago, Illinois.
Stephen A. Douglas Papers.

University of North Carolina Library, Chapel Hill.
John Hunt Morgan Papers. Southern Historical Collection.
Tucker Family Papers. Southern Historical Collection.

Published Works

Abernethy, Thomas P. *Three Virginia Frontiers*. Gloucester, Mass.: Peter Smith, 1962.
Adams, Ephraim D. *Great Britain and the American Civil War*. 2 vols. New York: Russell and Russell, 1925.
Allgeier, M.A. *Highland Neighborhood History*. Louisville: Highland Neighborhood Association. n.p., n.d. [1979].
Ambrose, Stephen E. *Citizen Soldiers: The U.S. Army from the Normandy Beaches to the Bulge to the Surrender of Germany, June 7, 1944-May 7, 1945*. New York: Simon and Schuster, 1997.
Aron, Stephen. *How the West Was Lost: The Transformation of Kentucky from Daniel Boone to Henry Clay*. Baltimore: Johns Hopkins University Press, 1996.
Auchampaugh, Philip G. *James Buchanan and his Cabinet on the Eve of Secession*. Lancaster, Penn.: Private Printing Co., 1926.
Bancroft, Frederic. *The Life of William H. Seward*. 2 vols. New York: Harper and Brothers, 1900.
Barker, Nancy N. *Distaff Diplomacy: The Empress Eugénie and the Foreign Policy of the Second Empire*. Austin: University of Texas Press, 1967.

Bibliography

_____. "France, Austria, and the Mexican Venture." *French Historical Studies* 3 (1963): 224-45.

_____. *The French Experience in Mexico, 1821-1861: A History of Constant Misunderstanding.* Chapel Hill: University of North Carolina Press, 1979.

Barry, Robert T. "William Preston." *Louisville Courier-Journal,* 22 July 1922.

Baxter, Maurice G. *Henry Clay and the American System.* Lexington: University Press of Kentucky, 1995.

_____. *One and Inseparable: Daniel Webster and the Union.* Cambridge, Mass.: Harvard University Press, 1984.

Bécker, Jerónimo. *Historia de las relaciones exteriores de España durante el siglo XIX.* 3 vols. Madrid: Jaime Ratés, 1924-26.

Bemis, Samuel F. *John Quincy Adams and the Union.* New York: Alfred A. Knopf, 1956.

Bentley, James R., ed. "Two Letters of Meriwether Lewis to Major William Preston." *Filson Club History Quarterly* 44 (1970): 170-75.

Berwanger, Eugene H. *The British Foreign Service and the American Civil War.* Lexington: University Press of Kentucky, 1994.

Bill, Alfred H. *Rehearsal for Conflict: The War with Mexico, 1846-1848.* New York: Alfred A. Knopf, 1947.

Binder, Frederick M. *James Buchanan and the American Empire.* Selinsgrove, Penn.: Susquehanna University Press, 1994.

Blasio, José Luis. *Maximiliano íntimo: El Emperador Maximiliano y su corte.* Mexico City: Libería de la Vda. de C. Bouret, 1905.

Blumberg, Arnold. *The Diplomacy of the Mexican Empire, 1863-1867.* Philadelphia: American Philosophical Society, 1971.

Blumenthal, Henry. "Confederate Diplomacy: Popular Notions and International Realities." *Journal of Southern History* 32 (1966): 151-71.

_____. *France and the United States: Their Diplomatic Relations, 1789-1914.* Chapel Hill: University of North Carolina Press, 1970.

_____. *A Reappraisal of Franco-American Relations, 1830-1871.* Chapel Hill: University of North Carolina Press, 1959.

Bodley, Temple. *History of Kentucky.* 4 vols. Chicago: S.J. Clarke Publishing Co., 1928.

Boles, John B. *Black Southerners, 1619-1869.* Lexington: University Press of Kentucky, 1983.

_____. *Religion in Antebellum Kentucky.* Lexington: University Press of Kentucky, 1976.

The Book of Common Prayer. . . . New York: Harper and Brothers, n.d.

Bowers, John. *Chickamauga and Chattanooga: The Battle that Doomed the Confederacy.* New York: Harper-Collins, 1994.

Brauer, Kinley. "Gabriel García y Tassara and the American Civil War." *Civil War History* 21 (1975): 5-27.

Briney, Melville O. *Fond Recollections: Sketches of Old Louisville.* Louisville: *Louisville Times,* 1955.

Brittan, Belle. *Belle Brittan on a Tour at Newport, and Here and There.* New York: Derby and Jackson, 1858.

Brown, Charles H. *Agents of Manifest Destiny: The Lives and Times of the Filibusters.* Chapel Hill: University of North Carolina Press, 1980.

Brown, John M. *Memoranda of the Preston Family.* Frankfort, Ky.: S.I.M. Major, 1870.

Brown, Kent M., ed. *The Civil War in Kentucky: Battle for the Bluegrass.* Mason City, Iowa: Savas Publishing Co., 2000.

Brown, Leonard E. "Fortress Rosecrans: A History, 1865-1900." *Tennessee Historical Quarterly* 50 (1991): 135-41.

Brown, Orlando. *Memoranda of the Preston Family.* Frankfort, Ky.: Hodges, Todd and Pruett, 1842.

Busch, Moritz. *Travels between the Hudson and the Mississippi, 1851-1852.* Translated by Norman H. Benzer. Lexington: University of Kentucky Press, 1971.

Bussey, Charles J. "James Guthrie: Kentucky Politican and Entrepreneur." In Klotter and Sehlinger, *Kentucky Profiles,* 57-71.

Butler, Pierce. *Judah P. Benjamin.* Philadelphia: G. W. Jacobs and Co., 1906.

Bibliography

Callahan, James Morton. *American Foreign Policy in Mexican Relations.* New York: Cooper Square, 1967.

_____. *The Diplomatic History of the Southern Confederacy.* 1901. Reprint, New York: Greenwood Press, 1968.

_____. *Evolution of Seward's Mexican Policy.* Morgantown: West Virginia University, 1909.

Callcott, Wilfrid H. *Santa Anna: The Story of the Enigma Who Once Was Mexico.* Hamden, Conn.: Archon Books, 1964.

Carlée, Roberta Baughman. *The Last Gladiator: Cassius M. Clay.* Berea: Kentucke Imprints, 1979.

Carr, Raymond. *Spain, 1808-1939.* Oxford, Eng.: Clarendon Press, 1966.

Carroll, Daniel B. "Henri Mercier and the American Civil War." In *Diplomacy in an Age of Nationalism: Essays in Honor of Lynn Marshall Case.* Edited by Nancy N. Barker and Marion L. Brown Jr., 109-23. The Hague: Martinus Nijhoff, 1971.

_____. *Henri Mercier and the American Civil War.* Princeton: Princeton University, 1971.

Cartlidge, Anna M. "Colonel John Floyd: Reluctant Adventurer." *Register of the Kentucky Historical Society* 66 (1968): 317-66.

Case, Lynn M. *French Opinion during the Second Empire.* New York: Appleton-Century, 1936.

_____. *French Opinion on the United States and Mexico, 1850-1867: Extracts from the Reports of the Procureurs Généraux.* New York: Appleton-Century, 1936.

Cashin, Joan E. *A Family Venture: Men and Women on the Southern Frontier.* New York: Oxford University Press, 1991.

Casseday, Ben. *The History of Louisville from Its Earliest Settlement till the Year 1852.* Louisville: Hull and Brothers, 1852.

Chadwick, French E. *The Relations of the United States and Spain: Diplomacy.* New York: Charles Scribner's Sons, 1909.

Chaffin, Tom. *Fatal Glory: Narciso López and the First Clandestine U.S. War against Cuba.* Charlottesville: University of Virginia, 1996.

Cheesebrough, David B. *Clergy Dissent in the Old South, 1830-1865.* Carbondale, Ill.: Southern Illinois University Press, 1996.

Cherry, Thomas C. *Kentucky: The Pioneer State of the West.* New York: D.C. Heath and Co., 1923.

Churchill, Winston. *Richard Carvel.* New York: Macmillan Co., 1899.

Cole, Arthur C. *The Whig Party in the South.* 1913. Reprint, Gloucester, Mass.: Peter Smith, 1962.

Coleman, J. Winston, Jr. *Famous Kentucky Duels: The Story of the Code of Honor in the Bluegrass State.* Frankfort: Roberts Printing Co., 1953.

_____. *Historic Kentucky.* Lexington: Henry Clay Press, 1967.

_____. *Lexington during the Civil War.* Lexington: Henry Clay Press, 1938.

_____. *Masonry in the Bluegrass.* Lexington: Transylvania Press, 1933.

_____. *Slavery Times in Kentucky.* Chapel Hill: University of North Carolina Press, 1940.

Collins, Richard H. *Historical Sketches of Kentucky: History of Kentucky.* 2 vols. Cincinnati: J.A. and U. P. James, 1847.

Connelly, Owen. *Blundering to Glory: Napoleon's Military Campaigns.* Wilmington, Del.: Scholarly Resources, 1987.

Connelly, Thomas L. *Army of the Heartland: The Army of Tennessee, 1861-1862.* Baton Rouge: Louisiana State University Press, 1967.

_____. *Autumn of Glory: The Army of Tennessee, 1862-1865.* Baton Rouge: Louisiana State University Press, 1971.

_____, and Archer Jones. *The Politics of Command: Factions and Ideas in Confederate Strategy.* Baton Rouge: Louisiana State University Press, 1973.

Connor, Seymour V. *The Peters Colony of Texas: A History and Biographical Sketches.* Austin: Texas State Historical Assoc., 1959.

_____. *Texas: A History.* New York: Thomas Y. Crowell Co., 1971.

_____, and Odie B. Faulk. *North America Divided: The Mexican War, 1846-1848.* New York: Oxford University Press, 1971.

Cooling, Benjamin F. *Fort Donelson's Legacy: War and Society in Kentucky and Tennessee, 1862-*

Bibliography

1863. Knoxville: University of Tennessee Press, 1997.

Cooper, Jacob. *William Preston Johnston: A Character Sketch*. New Haven, Conn.: Yale University Press, 1900.

Cooper, William J., Jr. *Liberty and Slavery: Southern Politics to 1860*. New York: Alfred A. Knopf, 1983.

_____. *The South and the Politics of Slavery, 1828-1856*. Baton Rouge: Louisiana State University Press, 1978.

Correspondencia de la Legación mexicana en Washington. Vol. 4. Mexico City: Imprenta del Gobierno del Palacio, 1871.

Cortada, James W. *Spain and the American Civil War: Relations at Mid-Century, 1855-1868. Transactions of the American Philosophical Society*. Vol. 70. Philadelphia: American Philosophical Society, 1980.

Corti, Egon C. *Maximilian and Charlotte of Mexico*. Translated from the German by Catherine A. Phillips. Hamden, Conn.: Archon Books, 1968.

Coulter, E. Merton. *The Civil War and Readjustment in Kentucky*. Chapel Hill: University of North Carolina Press, 1926.

_____. "The Downfall of the Whig Party in Kentucky." *Register of the Kentucky Historical Society* 23 (1925): 162-74.

Cozzens, Peter. *No Better Place to Die: The Battle of Stones River*. Urbana: University of Illinois Press, 1990.

_____. *This Terrible Sound: The Battle of Chickamauga*. Urbana: University of Illinois Press, 1992.

Craven, Avery O. *The Growth of Southern Nationalism, 1849-1861*. Vol. 6 of *A History of the South*. Edited by Wendell H. Stephens and E. Merton Coulter. Baton Rouge: Louisiana State University Press, 1953.

Crews, Clyde F. *An American Holy Land: A History of the Archdiocese of Louisville*. Wilmington, Del.: Michael Glazier, 1987.

_____. *Presence and Possibility: Louisville Catholicism and Its Cathedral*. N.p.: n.p., 1973.

_____. "Roots of a Renaissance: Cultural Visitors in Nineteenth- and Twentieth-Century Louisville." *Filson Club History Quarterly* 69 (1995): 275-92.

Crook, D. P. *Diplomacy during the American Civil War*. New York: John Wiley and Sons, 1975.

_____. *The North, the South, and the Powers, 1861-1865*. New York: John Wiley and Sons, 1974.

Curtis, George T. *Life of James Buchanan, Fifteenth President of the United States*. 2 vols. New York: Harper and Brothers, 1883.

Daniel, Larry J. *Shiloh: The Battle that Changed the Civil War*. New York: Simon and Schuster, 1997.

_____. *Soldiering in the Army of Tennessee: A Portrait of Life in a Confederate Army*. Chapel Hill: University of North Carolina Press, 1991.

Dantic, James I. "The Kentucky Volunteer Foot Soldier in the Mexican War." *Register of the Kentucky Historical Society* 95 (1997): 237-83.

Davenport, F. Garvin. *Ante-Bellum Kentucky: A Social History, 1800-1860*. 1943. Reprint, Westport, Conn.: Greenwood Press, 1983.

Davis, William C. *Breckinridge: Statesman, Soldier, Symbol*. Baton Rouge: Louisiana State University Press, 1974.

_____. *Diary of a Confederate Soldier: John S. Jackman of the Orphan Brigade*. Columbia: University of South Carolina Press, 1990.

_____. "John C. Breckinridge." *Register of the Kentucky Historical Society* 85 (1987): 197-212.

_____. *The Orphan Brigade: The Kentucky Confederates Who Couldn't Go Home*. Garden City, New York: Doubleday, 1980.

Degler, Carl N. *The Other South: Southern Dissidents in the Nineteenth Century*. New York: Harper and Row, 1974.

Dickens, Charles. *American Notes*. Greenwich, Conn.: Fawcett Publications, 1961.

Dictionary of National Biography. London: Oxford University Press, 1921-22.

Donald, David. *Charles Sumner and the Coming of the Civil War*. New York: Alfred A. Knopf,

Bibliography

1960.

Donaldson, Gary. "'Into Africa': Kirby Smith and Braxton Bragg's Invasion of Kentucky." *Filson Club History Quarterly* 61 (1987): 444-65.

Dorman, John Frederick. "General William Preston." *Filson Club History Quarterly* 43 (1969): 301-10.

———. *The Prestons of Smithfield and Greenfield in Virginia.* Louisville: Filson Club, 1982.

Duke, Basil W. *Reminiscences of General Basil Duke.* New York: Doubleday, 1911.

Dunn, C. Frank. *Old Houses of Lexington.* 2 vols in 3. Frankfort: Kentucky Historical Society, n.d. [ca. 1940s].

Durden, Robert F. *The Self-Inflicted Wound: Southern Politics in the Nineteenth Century.* Lexington: University Press of Kentucky, 1985.

Durrett, Reuben T. *The Centenary of Louisville.* Louisville: John P. Morton, 1893.

———. "The Early Bench and Bar of Louisville." In Johnston, *Memorial History of Louisville,* vol. 2, 1-10.

Eaton, Clement. *The Freedom-of-Thought Struggle in the Old South.* New York: Harper and Row, 1964.

———. *The Mind of the Old South.* Baton Rouge: Louisiana State University Press, 1967.

Eisenhower, John S. D. *Agent of Destiny: The Life and Times of General Winfield Scott.* New York: Free Press, 1997.

———. *So Far from God: The U.S. War with Mexico, 1846-1848.* New York: Doubleday, 1989.

Eisenschiml, Otto. *The Story of Shiloh.* Chicago: Civil War Round Table, 1946.

Elliott, Charles W. *Winfield Scott: The Soldier and the Man.* New York: Macmillan Co., 1937.

Engle, Stephen D. *Don Carlos Buell: Most Promising of All.* Chapel Hill: University of North Carolina Press, 1999.

Ettinger, Amos A. *The Mission to Spain of Pierre Soulé, 1853-1855.* New Haven, Conn.: Yale University Press, 1932.

Eubank, Damon R. "A Time for Heroes, A Time for Honor: Kentucky Soldiers in the Mexican War." *Filson Club History Quarterly* 72 (1998): 174-92.

———. "A Time of Enthusiasm: The Response of Kentucky to the Call for Troops in the Mexican War." *Register of the Kentucky Historical Society* 90 (1992): 323-44.

Evans, Eli N. *Judah P. Benjamin: The Jewish Confederate.* New York: Free Press, 1987.

Faust, Drew Gilpin. *The Ideology of Slavery: Proslavery Thought in the Antebellum South, 1830-1860.* Baton Rouge: Louisiana State University Press, 1981.

Ferris, Norman B. *Desperate Diplomacy: William H. Seward's Foreign Policy.* Knoxville: University of Tennessee Press, 1976.

Feuss, Claude M. *Carl Schurz: Reformer (1829-1906).* New York: Dodd, Mead and Co., 1932.

Finley, John. *The French in the Heart of America.* New York: Charles Scribner's Sons, 1915.

Foner, Eric. *Reconstruction: America's Unfinished Revolution, 1863-1877.* New York: Harper and Row, 1988.

Franklin, John Hope. *The Militant South, 1800-1861.* Boston: Beacon Press, 1956.

———. *Reconstruction after the Civil War.* Chicago: University of Chicago Press, 1961.

———, and Loren Schweninger. *Runaway Slaves: Rebels on the Plantation.* New York: Oxford University Press, 1999.

Freehling, William W. *Secessionists at Bay, 1776-1854.* Vol. 1 of *The Road to Disunion.* New York: Oxford University Press, 1990.

———. *The South vs. the South: How Anti-Confederate Southerners Shaped the Course of the Civil War.* New York: Oxford University Press, 2001.

Gavronsky, Serge. *The French Liberal Opposition and the American Civil War.* New York: Humanities Press, 1968.

Genovese, Eugene F. "'Our Family, White and Black': Family and Household in the Southern Slaveholders' World View." In *In Joy and in Sorrow: Women, Family, and Marriage in the Victorian South.* Edited by Carol Bleser, 69-87. New York: Oxford University Press, 1991.

———. *Roll, Jordan, Roll: The World the Slaves Made.* New York: Pantheon Books, 1972.

Goldin, Claudia D. *Urban Slavery in the American South, 1820-1860.* Chicago: University of Chicago Press, 1976.

Bibliography

Gooch, Brian D. *The Reign of Napoleon III*. Chicago: Rand McNally and Co., 1969.

Gooch, George P. *The Second Empire*. London: Longmans, Green and Co., 1960.

Graybar, Lloyd J. "The Buckners of Kentucky." *Filson Club History Quarterly* 58 (1984): 202-18.

Griffith, Paddy. *Battle Tactics of the Civil War*. New Haven, Conn.: Yale University Press, 1987.

Grimsley, Mark. *The Hard Hand of War: Union Military Policy Toward Southern Civilians, 1861-1865*. New York: Cambridge University Press, 1995.

Grimstead, David. *American Mobbing, 1828-1861: Toward Civil War*. New York: Oxford University Press, 1998.

Gross, Samuel D. *Autobiography of Samuel D. Gross, M.D., with Reminiscences of His Time and Contemporaries*. 2 vols. Philadelphia: George Barrie, Publisher, 1887.

Gwinn, Erna O. "The Liederkranz in Louisville, 1877-1959." *Filson Club History Quarterly* 55 (1981): 40-59.

Hagerman, Edward. *The American Civil War and the Origins of Modern War: Ideas, Organization, and Field Command*. Bloomington: Indiana University Press, 1988.

Hall, Margaret H. *The Artistic Journey: Being the Outspoken Letters of Mrs. Basil Hall Written during a Fourteen Months' Sojourn in America*. New York: G. P. Putnam's Sons, 1931.

Hamann, Brigitte, ed. *Mit Kaiser Max in Mexiko: Aus dem Tagebuch des Fürsten Carl Khevenhüller, 1864-1867*. Vienna: Amalthea Verlag, 1983.

Hamilton, Holman. *Zachary Taylor: Soldier of the Republic*. 1941. Reprint, Hamden, Conn.: Archon Books, 1966.

Hammon, Neal O. *Early Kentucky Land Records, 1773-1780*. Louisville: Filson Club, 1992.

_____. "The Fincastle Surveyors at the Falls of the Ohio." *Filson Club History Quarterly* 47 (1973): 14-28.

_____. "The Fincastle Surveyors in the Bluegrass, 1774." *Register of the Kentucky Historical Society* 70 (1972): 277-94.

_____, and James R. Harris, eds. "'In a Dangerous Situation': Letters of Col. John Floyd, 1774-1783." *Register of the Kentucky Historical Society* 83 (1985): 202-36.

Hanna, Alfred J., and Kathryn A. *Napoleon III and Mexico: American Triumph over Monarchy*. Chapel Hill: University of North Carolina Press, 1917.

Hanna, Kathryn A. "The Roles of the South in French Intervention in Mexico." *Journal of Southern History* 20 (1954): 3 21.

Harold, Stanley. *The Abolitionists and the South, 1831-1861*. Lexington: University Press of Kentucky, 1995.

Harrison, Lowell H. *The Anti-Slavery Movement in Kentucky*. Lexington: University Press of Kentucky, 1978.

_____. *The Civil War in Kentucky*. Lexington: University Press of Kentucky, 1975.

_____, and James C. Klotter. *A New History of Kentucky*. Lexington: University Press of Kentucky, 1997.

Harvard University. *Quinquennial Catalogue of the Law School of Harvard University, 1817-1834*. Cambridge, Mass.: The Law School, 1935.

Haslip, Joan. *The Crown of Mexico: Maximilian and His Empress Carlota*. New York: Holt, Rinehart and Winston, 1971.

Hattaway, Herman, and Archer Jones. *How the North Won: A Military History of the Civil War*. Urbana: University of Illinois Press, 1991.

Healy, Katharine G., comp. "Calendar of Early Jefferson County, Kentucky, Wills." *Filson Club History Quarterly* 6 (1932): 149-204.

Heck, Frank H. *Proud Kentuckian: John C. Breckinridge, 1821-1875*. Lexington: University Press of Kentucky, 1976.

Henderson, Gavin F. "Southern Designs on Cuba, 1854-1857, and Some Other European Opinions." *Journal of Southern History* 5 (1939): 371-85.

Hesseltine, William Best, and David L. Smiley. *The South in American History*. Englewood Cliffs, N.J.: Prentice-Hall, 1960.

Hill, Patricia E. *Dallas: The Making of a Modern City*. Austin: University of Texas Press, 1996.

Hogan, William R. *Texas Republic: A Social and Economic History*. Norman: University of Oklahoma Press, 1946.

Bibliography

Holland, Cecil F. *Morgan and His Raiders*. New York: Macmillan Co., 1942.

Hood, Fred J. *Kentucky: Its History and Heritage*. St. Louis: Forum Press, 1978.

Horn, Stanley F. *The Army of Tennessee*. Indianapolis: Bobbs-Merrill Co., 1953.

Howard, Victor B. *Black Liberation in Kentucky: Emancipation and Freedom, 1862-1884*. Lexington: University Press of Kentucky, 1983.

_____. *The Evangelical War against Slavery and Caste: The Life and Times of John G. Fee*. Selinsgrove, Penn.: Susquehanna University Press, 1996.

Hubbard, Charles M. *The Burden of Confederate Diplomacy*. Knoxville: University of Tennessee Press, 1998.

Hudson, Winthrop S. *Religion in America*. New York: Charles Scribner's Sons, 1965.

Hughes, Nathaniel C., Jr., and Thomas C. Ware. *Theodore O'Hara: Poet-Soldier of the Old South*. Knoxville: University of Tennessee Press, 1998.

Hughes, Sarah S. *Surveyors and Statesmen: Land Measuring in Colonial Virginia*. N.p. [Richmond, Va.]: Virginia Association of Surveyors, 1970.

Hutcheon, Wallace S., Jr. "The Louisville Riots of August 1855." In Hood, *Kentucky: Its History and Heritage*, 123-33.

Ikard, Robert W. "Lieutenant Thomas Reports on Chickamauga: A Comparison of Immediate and Historical Perspectives of the Battle." *Tennessee Historical Quarterly* 44 (1985): 417-38.

Johannsen, Robert W. *Stephen A. Douglas*. New York: Oxford University Press, 1973.

_____. *To the Halls of the Montezumas: The Mexican War in the American Imagination*. New York: Oxford University Press, 1985.

Johnson, E. Polk. *A History of Kentucky and Kentuckians*. 3 vols. Chicago: Lewis Publishing Co., 1912.

Johnson, Patricia Givens. *William Preston and the Allegheny Patriots*. N.p. [Pulaski, Va.]: n. p. [B.D. Smith], 1976.

Johnson, Timothy D. *Winfield Scott: The Quest for Military Glory*. Lawrence: University Press of Kansas, 1998.

Johnston, J. Stoddard. *Kentucky*. Vol. 9 of *Confederate Military History*. Edited by Clement A. Evans. 1899. Reprint, Secaucus, N.J.: n.p., ca. 1970s.

_____, ed. *Memorial History of Louisville from Its First Settlement to the Year 1896*. 2 vols. Chicago: Biographical Publishing Co., 1896.

Johnston, William Preston. "Albert Sidney Johnston and the Shiloh Campaign." *Century Illustrated Monthly Magazine* 29 (1885): 614-28.

_____. *The Johnstons of Salisbury*. New Orleans: Press of L. Graham and Sons, 1897.

_____. *The Life of General Albert Sidney Johnston*. New York: D. Appleton and Co., 1879.

Jones, Archer. *Civil War Command and Strategy*. New York: Maxwell Macmillan International, 1992.

_____. *Confederate Strategy from Shiloh to Vicksburg*. Baton Rouge: Louisiana State University Press, 1961.

_____. "Military Means, Political Ends: Strategy." In *Why the Confederacy Lost*. Edited by Gabor S. Boritt. New York: Oxford University Press, 1992.

Jones, Howard. "History and Mythology: The Crisis over British Intervention in the Civil War." In *The Union, the Confederacy, and the Atlantic Rim*. Edited by Robert E. May. West Lafayette, Ind.: Purdue University Press, 1995.

_____. *Mutiny on the Amistad: The Saga of a Slave Rebellion and its Impact on American Abolition, Law and Diplomacy*. New York: Oxford University Press, 1987.

Jones, Wilbur Devereux. *The American Problem in British Diplomacy, 1841-1861*. Athens: University of Georgia Press, 1974.

Kagan, Donald. *Fall of the Athenian Empire*. Ithaca, N.Y.: Cornell University Press, 1987.

Katz, Irving. *August Belmont: A Political Biography*. New York: Columbia University Press, 1968.

Kautz, Craig L. "Beneficial Politics: John Slidell and the Cuba Bill of 1859." *Louisiana Studies* 13 (1974): 124-32.

Kean, Robert G. H. *Inside the Confederate Government: The Diary of Robert Gatwick Hill Kean*. Edited by Edward Younger. New York: Oxford University Press, 1957.

Bibliography

Keating, L. Clark. *Audubon: The Kentucky Years*. Lexington: University Press of Kentucky, 1976.

Kendall, George Wilkins. *Dispatches from the Mexican War*. Edited by Lawrence D. Cress. Norman: University of Oklahoma Press, 1999.

Kerby, Robert L. *Kirby Smith's Confederacy: The Trans-Mississippi South, 1863-1865*. New York: Columbia University Press, 1972.

Kinkead, Ludie J., and Katharine G. Healy, eds. "The W. Preston dower Examd., 30 June 1824." In "Calendar of Division Book No. 1 Jefferson County Court, 1797-1850." *Filson Club History Quarterly* 8 (1934): 105-28.

Kirkham, Ralph W. *The Mexican War Journal and Letters of Ralph W. Kirkham*. Edited by Robert R. Miller. College Station, Tex.: Texas A&M Press, 1991.

Kleber, John E., ed. *The Encyclopedia of Louisville*. Lexington: University Press of Kentucky, 2001.

Klein, Philip S. *President James Buchanan: A Biography*. University Park: Pennsylvania State University Press, 1962.

Klotter, James C. *The Breckinridges of Kentucky, 1760-1981*. Lexington: University Press of Kentucky, 1986.

_____, and Peter J. Sehlinger, eds. *Kentucky Profiles: Biographical Essays in Honor of Holman Hamilton*. Frankfort: Kentucky Historical Society, 1982.

Klunder, Willard. *William Lewis Cass and the Politics of Moderation*. Kent, Ohio: Kent State University Press, 1996.

Kolchin, Peter. "In Defense of Servitude: American Proslavery and Russian Proserfdom Arguments, 1760-1860." *American Historical Review* 85 (1980): 809-27.

Komlos, John H. *Kossuth in America, 1851-1852*. Buffalo, N.Y.: Classic Printing Co., 1973.

Kramer, Carl E. "City with a Vision: Images of Louisville in the 1830s." *Filson Club History Quarterly* 60 (1986): 427-52.

Lancaster, Clay. *Antebellum Architecture of Kentucky*. Lexington: University Press of Kentucky, 1991.

_____. *Vestiges of the Venerable City: A Chronicle of Lexington, Kentucky*. Lexington: Lexington-Fayette County Historic Commission, 1978.

Lee, Elizabeth Blair. *Wartime Washington: The Civil War Letters of Elizabeth Blair Lee*. Urbana: University of Illinois Press, 1991.

Leonard, Ira M., and Robert D. Parmet. *American Nativism, 1830-1860*. New York: Van Nostrand Reinhold, 1971.

Levin, H., ed. *The Lawyers and Lawmakers of Kentucky*. 1897. Reprint, Easley, S.C.: Southern Historical Press, 1982.

Lincoln, Abraham. *Complete Works of Abraham Lincoln*. Edited by John Nicolay and John Hay. Vol. 8. New York: F. D. Tandy and Co., 1905.

Lincoln, Mary Todd. *Mary Todd Lincoln: Her Life and Letters*. Edited by Justin G. Turner and Linda Levitt Turner. New York: Alfred A. Knopf, 1972.

Linderman, Gerald F. *Embattled Courage: The Experience of Combat in the American Civil War*. New York: Free Press, 1987.

Little, Lucius P. *Ben Hardin: Times and Contemporaries*. Louisville: *Courier-Journal* Job Printing, 1887.

Longstreet, James. *From Manassas to Appomattox: Memoirs of the Civil War in America*. 1896. Reprint, New York: Mallard Press, 1991.

Lonn, Ella. *Foreigners in the Confederacy*. Gloucester, Mass.: Peter Smith, 1965.

_____. *Salt as a Factor in the Confederacy*. New York: W. Neale, 1933.

Lucas, Marion B. *A History of Blacks in Kentucky*. Vol. 1. *From Slavery to Segregation, 1760-1891*. Frankfort: Kentucky Historical Society, 1992.

_____. "Kentucky Blacks: The Transition from Slavery to Freedom." *Register of the Kentucky Historical Society* 91 (1993): 403-19.

Lucas, Scott J. "'Indignities, Wrongs, and Outrages': Military and Guerrilla Incursions on Kentucky's Civil War Homefront." *Filson Club History Quarterly* 73 (1999): 355-76.

Mahin, Dean B. *Olive Branch and Sword: The United States and Mexico, 1845-1848*. Jefferson,

Bibliography

N.C.: McFarland and Co., 1997.

Mallalieu, William. "The Origins of Louisville Culture." *Filson Club History Quarterly* 38 (1964): 149-56.

Mallory, William M., comp. *Treaties, Conventions, International Acts, Protocols and Agreements between the United States and Other Powers, 1776-1909.* Vol. 2. Washington, D.C.: n.p., 1910.

Mapp, Alf J., Jr. *Frock Coats and Epaulets: The Men Who Led the Confederacy.* Lanham, Md.: Madison Books, 1996.

Marcosson, Isaac F. *"Marse Henry": A Biography of Henry Watterson.* New York: Dodd, Mead and Company, 1961.

Marshall, Humphrey. *The History of Kentucky.* 2 vols. Frankfort: Geo. S. Robinson Printers, 1824.

Martin, Asa E. *The Anti-Slavery Movement in Kentucky Prior to 1850.* 1918. Reprint, New York: Negro Universities Press, 1970.

Mason, Virginia. *The Public Life and Diplomatic Correspondence of James M. Mason with Some Personal History by His Daughter.* Roanoke, Va.: Star Printing and Publishing Co., 1903.

May, Robert E. "James Buchanan, the Neutrality Laws, and American Invasion of Nicaragua." In *James Buchanan and the Political Crisis of the 1850s.* Edited by Michael J. Birkner, 123-45. Selinsgrove, Penn.: Susquehanna University Press, 1996.

_____. *John A. Quitman: Old Southern Crusader.* Baton Rouge: Louisiana State University Press, 1985.

_____. *Manifest Destiny's Underworld: Filibustering in Antebellum America.* Chapel Hill: University of North Carolina Press, 2002.

_____. *The Southern Dream of a Caribbean Empire, 1854-1861.* Baton Rouge: Louisiana State University Press, 1973.

_____, ed. *The Union, the Confederacy, and the Atlantic Rim.* West Lafayette, Ind.: Purdue University Press, 1995.

McCaffrey, James M. *Army of Manifest Destiny: The American Soldier in the Mexican War, 1846-1848.* New York: New York University Press, 1992.

McClendon, R. Earl. "The *Amistad* Claims: Inconsistencies of Policy." *Political Science Quarterly* 48 (1933): 386-412.

McDonough, James L. *Shiloh–in Hell before Night.* Knoxville: University of Tennessee Press, 1977.

_____. *Stones River: Bloody Winter in Tennessee.* Knoxville: University of Tennessee Press, 1980.

_____. *War in Kentucky: From Shiloh to Perryville.* Knoxville: University of Tennessee Press, 1994.

McDowell, Robert E. *City of Conflict: Louisville in the Civil War, 1861-1865.* Louisville: Louisville Civil War Round Table, 1962.

McGann, Sister Agnes Geraldine. *Nativism in Kentucky to 1860.* Washington, D.C.: Catholic University of America, 1944.

McMurry, Richard M. *Two Great Rebel Armies: An Essay in Confederate Military History.* Chapel Hill: University of North Carolina Press, 1989.

McPherson, James M. *Battle Cry of Freedom: The Civil War Era.* New York: Ballantine Books, 1988.

_____. *For Cause and Comrades: Why Men Fought in the Civil War.* New York: Oxford University Press, 1997.

_____. *What They Fought For, 1861-1865.* Baton Rouge: Louisiana State University Press, 1994.

McWhiney, Grady. *Braxton Bragg and the Confederate Defeat.* Vol. 1. *Field Command.* New York: Columbia University Press, 1969.

_____, and Perry D. Jamieson. *Attack and Die: Civil War Military Tactics and the Southern Heritage.* Tuscaloosa: University of Alabama Press, 1982.

Meade, Robert E. *Judah P. Benjamin: Confederate Statesman.* London: Oxford University Press, 1943.

_____. "The Relations between Judah P. Benjamin and Jefferson Davis." *Journal of Southern History* 5 (1939): 468-78.

Bibliography

Meffert, W.H. *History of Preston Lodge No. 281, F. and A.M., Held at Louisville, Kentucky, from January 19, 1854, up to January 19, 1904.* Louisville: Franklin Printing Co., 1903.

Mentelle, Charlotte. *A Short History of the Late Mrs. Mary O. T. Wickliffe.* Lexington: Kentucky Statesman Printing, 1850.

Miller, William L. *Arguing about Slavery: The Great Battle in the United States Congress.* New York: Alfred A. Knopf, 1996.

Mittlebeeler, Emmet V. "The Aftermath of Louisville's Bloody Monday Election Riot of 1855." *Filson Club History Quarterly* 66 (1992): 197-219.

Monaghan, Jay. *Diplomat in Carpet Slippers: Abraham Lincoln Deals with Foreign Affairs.* Indianapolis: Bobbs-Merrill Co., 1945.

Moore, John Bassett, ed. *The Works of James Buchanan.* 12 vols. 1908-11. Reprint, New York: Antiquarian Press, 1960.

Nagel, Paul G. *John Quincy Adams: A Public Life, a Private Life.* New York: Alfred A. Knopf, 1997.

Nevins, Allan. *The Emergence of Lincoln.* Vol. 1. *Douglas, Buchanan, and Party Chaos, 1857-1859.* New York: Scribner, 1950.

_____. *War for the Union.* 4 vols. New York: Scribner, 1959-71.

Newcomb, Rexford. *Old Kentucky Architecture: Colonial, Federal, Greek Revival, Gothic, and Other Types Erected Prior to the War Between the States.* New York: Bonanza Books, 1940.

Nichols, Roy F. *The Disruption of American Democracy.* New York: Macmillan Co., 1948.

Noe, Kenneth W. *Perryville: This Grand Havoc of Battle.* Lexington: University Press of Kentucky, 2001.

_____. *Southwest Virginia's Railroad: Modernization and the Sectional Crisis.* Urbana: University of Illinois Press, 1994.

Nolan, Alan. *Lee Considered: General Robert E. Lee and Civil War History.* Chapel Hill: University of North Carolina Press, 1991.

O'Connor, Richard. *Thomas: Rock of Chickamauga.* New York: Prentice Hall, 1948.

O'Toole, William G., and Charles E. Aebersold, trans. "Louisville's Bloody Monday Riots from a German Perspective." *Filson Club History Quarterly* 70 (1996): 419-25.

Oakes, James. *The Ruling Race: A History of American Slaveholders.* New York: Alfred A. Knopf, 1982.

Olliff, Donathon C. *Reforma Mexico and the United States: A Search for Alternatives to Annexation, 1854-1861.* Tuscaloosa: University of Alabama Press, 1981.

Opatrny, Josef. *U.S. Expansionism and Cuban Annexationism in the 1850s.* Prague: Charles University Press, 1990.

Ormsby, R. McKinley. *A History of the Whig Party, or Some of Its Main Features.* Boston: Crosby Nichols and Co., 1859.

Owens, William A. *A Black Mutiny: The Revolt on the Schooner Amistad.* Baltimore: Black Classics Books, 1953.

Owsley, Frank Lawrence. *King Cotton Diplomacy: Foreign Relations of the Confederate States of America.* 2nd ed. rev. Chicago: University of Chicago Press, 1959.

Parkman, Francis. *The Discovery of the Great West: La Salle.* 1869. Reprint, New York: Rinehart and Co., 1956.

Parks, Joseph H. *General Edmund Kirby Smith, CSA.* Baton Rouge: Louisiana State University Press, 1954.

Perkins, Dexter. *The Monroe Doctrine, 1826-1867.* Baltimore: Johns Hopkins Press, 1933.

Perrin, William H., ed. *History of Fayette County, Kentucky With an Outline Sketch of the Blue Grass Region by Robert Peter.* 1882. Reprint, Easley, S.C.: Southern Historical Press, 1979.

Pessen, Edward. *Jacksonian America: Society, Personality, and Politics.* 2nd ed. rev. Homewood, Ill.: Dorsey Press, 1978.

_____. "Society and Politics in the Jacksonian Era." *Register of the Kentucky Historical Society* 81 (1984): 1-27.

Peter, Frances D. *Window on the War: Frances Dallam Peter's Lexington Civil War Diary.* Edited by John David Smith and Wiliam Cooper Jr. Lexington: Lexington-Fayette County Historic Commission, 1976.

Peterson, Merrill D. *The Great Triumvirate: Webster, Clay, and Calhoun*. New York: Oxford University Press, 1987.

Poage, George R. *Henry Clay and the Whig Party*. 1936. Reprint, Gloucester, Mass.: Peter Smith, 1965.

Pollard, Edward A. *The Lost Cause: A New Southern History of the War of the Confederates*. New York: E. B. Treat and Co., 1866.

Potter, David M. *The Impending Crisis, 1848-1861*. New York: Harper and Row, 1976.

_____. *The South and the Sectional Conflict*. Baton Rouge: Louisiana State University Press, 1968.

Preston, William. *Remarks of Mr. Preston of Kentucky*. Washington: Congressional Globe Office, n.d. [1853].

_____. *The Slave Question*. N.p., n.d. [1854].

Price, Glenn W. *Origins of the War with Mexico: The Polk-Stockton Intrigue*. Austin: University of Texas Press, 1967.

Quisenberry, Anderson C. *Lopez's Expedition to Cuba, 1850-1851*. Louisville: Filson Club, 1906.

Ramage, Andrea S. "Love and Honor: The Robert Wickliffe Family of Antebellum Kentucky." *Register of the Kentucky Historical Society* 92 (1996): 115-33.

Ramage, James A. *Rebel Raider: The Life of General John Hunt Morgan*. Lexington: University Press of Kentucky, 1986.

Ranck, George W. *Guide to Lexington, Kentucky: With Notices Historical and Descriptive of Places and Objects of Interest, and a Summary of the Advantages and Resources of the City and Vicinity*. Lexington, Ky.: Transylvania Printing and Pub. Co., 1883.

_____. *History of Lexington, Kentucky: Its Early Annals and Recent Progress*. Cincinnati: R. Clarke and Co., 1872.

Randall, James G., and David Donald. *The Civil War and Reconstruction*. 2nd ed. Lexington, Mass.: D. C. Heath and Co., 1969.

Rankins, Walter H. *Augusta College, Augusta, Kentucky: First Established Methodist College, 1822-1849*. Frankfort: Roberts Print Co., 1957.

_____. *Historic Augusta and Augusta College*. Augusta, Ky.: n.p., 1985.

Reed, D.W. *The Battle of Shiloh and the Organizations Engaged*. Washington, D.C.: Government Printing Office, 1913.

Remini, Robert V. *Henry Clay: Statesman for the Union*. New York: W.W. Norton, 1991.

Report of the Debates and Proceedings of the Convention for the Revision of the Constitution of the State of Kentucky, 1849. Frankfort: A.G. Hodges and Co., 1849.

Rich, Joseph W. *The Battle of Shiloh*. Iowa City: State Historical Society of Iowa, 1911.

Richardson, H. Edward. *Cassius Marcellus Clay: Firebrand of Freedom*. Lexington: University Press of Kentucky, 1976.

Richardson, James D., ed. *A Compilation of the Messages and Papers of the Confederacy, Including the Diplomatic Correspondence, 1861-1865*. Vols. 1, 2. Nashville: United States Publishing Co., 1902, 1905.

Richardson, Rupert N. *Texas: The Lone Star State*. New York: Prentice-Hall, 1943.

Ridley, Jasper G. *Maximilian and Juárez*. New York: Ticknor and Fields, 1992.

Rister, Carl C. "Carlota, A Confederate Colony in Mexico." *Journal of Southern History* 11 (1945): 33-50.

Rivera Cambas, Manuel. *Historia de la intervención europea y norte-americana en México y del Imperio de Maximiliano de Habsburgo*. Vol. 2B. Mexico City: Editorial Academia Literaria, 1961.

Roeder, Ralph. *Juarez and His Mexico: A Biographical History*. New York: Viking Press, 1947.

Roland, Charles P. *Albert Sidney Johnston: Soldier of Three Republics*. Austin: University of Texas Press, 1964.

_____. *An American Iliad: The Story of the Civil War*. Lexington: University Press of Kentucky, 1991.

Rolle, Andrew F. *The Lost Cause: The Confederate Exodus to Mexico*. Norman: University of Oklahoma Press, 1965.

Bibliography

Romero, Matías. *Correspondencia de la Legación mexicana en Washington durante la intervención extranjera, 1850-1868.* Vol. 4. Mexico City: Imprenta del Gobierno del Palacio, 1871.

Ross, Fitzgerald. *A Visit to the Cities and Camps of the Confederate States.* In *A Confederate Reader.* Edited by Richard B. Harwell, 225-29. New York: Longmans, Green, 1957.

Rothenberg, Gunther E. *The Art of Warfare in the Age of Napoleon.* Bloomington: Indiana University Press, 1980.

Rush, Dorothy C. "Early Accounts of Travel to the Falls of the Ohio: A Bibliography with Selected Quotations." *Filson Club History Quarterly* 68 (1994): 232-66.

Scapula, Johann. *Lexicon graeco-latinum.* Oxford, Eng.: Clarendon Press, 1820.

Schlesinger, Arthur M., Jr. *The Age of Jackson.* New York: New American Library, 1958.

Schmidt, Martin F. *Kentucky Illustrated: The First Hundred Years.* Lexington: University Press of Kentucky, 1992.

Scholes, Walter V. *Mexican Politics during the Juárez Regime, 1855-1872.* Columbia: University of Missouri Press, 1957.

Schoonover, Thomas D. *Dollars over Dominion: The Triumph of Liberalism in Mexican-U.S. Relations, 1861-1867.* Baton Rouge: Louisiana State University Press, 1978.

_____, ed. and trans. *Mexican Lobby: Matías Romero in Washington, 1861-1867.* Lexington: University Press of Kentucky, 1986.

Schroeder, John H. *Mr. Polk's War: American Opposition and Dissent, 1846-1848.* Madison: University of Wisconsin Press, 1973.

Schurz, Carl. *Reminiscences, 1852-1863.* 2 vols. New York: McClure Co., 1907.

_____. *Speeches, Correspondence and Political Papers of Carl Schurz.* Edited by Frederick Bancroft. Vol. 1. New York: G. P. Putnam's Sons, 1913.

Sears, Louis M. "A Confederate Diplomat at the Court of Napoleon III." *American Historical Review* 26 (1921): 255-81.

_____. *A History of American Foreign Relations.* Rev. ed. New York: Thomas Y. Crowell, 1935.

_____. *John Slidell.* Durham: Duke University Press, 1925.

Sears, Richard D. *The Day of Small Things: Abolitionism in the Midst of Slavery, Berea, Kentucky, 1854-1864.* New York: University Press of America, 1986.

Sehlinger, Peter J. "General William Preston: Kentucky's Last Cavalier Fights for Southern Independence." *Register of the Kentucky Historical Society* 93 (1996): 257 85.

_____. "'At The Moment of Victory . . .': The Battle of Shiloh and General A. S. Johnston's Death as Recounted in William Preston's Diary." *Filson Club History Quarterly* 61 (1987): 315-45.

_____. "William Preston, Kentucky's Diplomat of Lost Causes." In Klotter and Sehlinger, *Kentucky Profiles,* 72-98.

Seitz, Don C. *Braxton Bragg: General of the Confederacy.* Columbia: University of South Carolina Press, 1924.

_____. *Famous American Duels.* New York: Thomas Y. Crowell Co., 1929.

Sellers, Charles G., Jr. "Who Were the Southern Whigs?" *American Historical Review* 59 (1954): 335-46.

Shackelford, George G. *George Wythe Randolph and the Confederate Elite.* Athens: University of Georgia Press, 1988.

Shalhope, Robert E. *Sterling Price: Portrait of a Southerner.* Columbia: University of Missouri Press, 1971.

Share, Allen J. *Cities in the Commonwealth: Two Centuries of Urban Life in Kentucky.* Lexington: University Press of Kentucky, 1981.

Shaw, Arthur. *William Preston Johnston: A Transitional Figure of the Confederacy.* Baton Rouge: Louisiana State University Press, 1943.

Simms, Henry H. *Emotion at High Tide: Abolition as a Controversial Factor.* Richmond, Va.: William Byrd Press, 1960.

Simpson, Elizabeth M. *Bluegrass Houses and Their Traditions.* Lexington, Ky.: Transylvania Press, 1932.

Singletary, Otis A. *The Mexican War.* Chicago: University of Chicago Press, 1960.

_____. *Negro Militia and Reconstruction.* Austin: University of Texas Press, 1957.

Bibliography

Slater, Lucy B. "Kentucky Biographical Notebook: William Burke Belknap, 1811-1889." *Filson Club History Quarterly* 66 (1992): 578-84.

Smiley, David L. *Lion of White Hall: The Life of Cassius M. Clay*. Madison: University of Wisconsin Press, 1962.

Smith, E. Kirby. *To Mexico with Scott: Letters of Captain E. Kirby Smith to His Wife*. Edited by Emma Jerome Blackwood. Cambridge, Mass.: Harvard University Press, 1917.

Smith, Elbert B. *Francis Preston Blair*. New York: Free Press, 1980.

_____. *The Presidency of James Buchanan*. Lawrence: University of Kansas, 1975.

Smith, John David. "Slavery and Antislavery." In *Our Kentucky: A Study of the Bluegrass State*. Edited by James C. Klotter, 105-21. Lexington: University Press of Kentucky, 1992.

Smith, William E. *The Francis Preston Blair Family in Politics*. 2 vols. New York: Macmillan Co., 1933.

Smith, Zachariah F. *The History of Kentucky*. Louisville: *Courier-Journal* Job Printing Co., 1886.

Speed, Thomas. *Records and Memorials of the Speed Family*. Louisville: *Courier-Journal* Job Printing Co., 1892.

Spencer, Donald S. *Louis Kossuth and Young America: A Study of Sectionalism and Foreign Policy*. Columbia: University of Missouri Press, 1977.

Sprague, Stuart Seely. "Slavery's Death Knell: Mourners and Revelers," *Filson Club History Quarterly* 65 (1991): 441-73.

Stampp, Kenneth M. *The Era of Reconstruction, 1865-1877*. New York: Vintage Books, 1965.

Stickles, Arndt M. *Simon Bolivar Buckner: Borderland Knight*. Chapel Hill: University of North Carolina Press, 1940.

Stillwell, Lucille. *John Cabell Breckinridge*. Caldwell, Idaho: Caxton Printers, 1936.

Stone, Richard G., Jr. *A Brittle Sword: The Kentucky Militia, 1776-1912*. Lexington: University Press of Kentucky, 1977.

_____. *Kentucky Fighting Men, 1861-1945*. Lexington: University Press of Kentucky, 1982.

Stowe, Steven M. *Intimacy and Power in the Old South: Ritual in the Lives of the Planters*. Baltimore: Johns Hopkins University Press, 1987.

Sutton, R., ed. *Report of the Debates and Proceedings of the Convention for the Revision of the Constitution of the State of Kentucky*. Frankfort: n.p., 1849.

Swinford, Frances Keller, and Rebecca Smith Lee. *The Great Elm Tree: Heritage of the Episcopal Diocese of Lexington*. Lexington, Ky.: Faith House Press, 1969.

Sword, Wiley. *Shiloh: Bloody April*. New York: William Morrow and Co., 1974.

Taney, Mary Florence. *Kentucky Pioneer Women: Columbian Poems and Prose*. Cincinnati: Press of Robert Clarke and Co., 1893.

Tapp, Hambleton. "The Battle of Perryville, 1862." *Filson Club History Quarterly* 9 (1935): 158-81.

_____. "Colonel John Floyd, Kentucky Pioneer." *Filson Club History Quarterly* 15 (1941): 1-24.

_____, and James C. Klotter. *Kentucky: Decades of Discord, 1865-1900*. Frankfort: Kentucky Historical Society, 1977.

Taylor, John M. *William Henry Seward: Lincoln's Right Hand*. New York: Harper Collins, 1991.

Thomas, Edison H. *John Hunt Morgan and His Raiders*. Lexington: University Press of Kentucky, 1975.

Thomas, Emory M. *The Confederate Nation: 1861-1865*. New York: Harper and Row, 1979.

Thomas, Samuel W. *Cave Hill: A Pictorial Guide and Its History*. Louisville: Cave Hill Cemetery Co., 1985.

Thompson, Edwin Porter. *History of the Orphan Brigade*. Louisville: Lewis N. Thompson, 1898.

Tilden, Samuel J. *Letters and Literary Memorials of Samuel J. Tilden*. Edited by John Bigelow. 2 vols. New York: Harper and Bros., 1908.

Tillson, Albert H., Jr. *Gentry and Common Folk: Political Culture on a Virginia Frontier, 1740-1789*. Lexington: University Press of Kentucky, 1991

Tise, Larry E. *Proslavery: A History of the Defense of Slavery in America, 1701-1840*. Athens: University of Georgia Press, 1987.

Tocqueville, Alexis de. *Journey to America*. Translated by George Lawrence. Garden City, N.Y.:

Bibliography

Doubleday and Co., 1971.

Townsend, William H. *Lincoln and the Bluegrass: Slavery and the Civil War in Kentucky*. Lexington: University of Kentucky Press, 1955.

_____. *Lincoln and His Wife's Home Town*. Indianapolis: Bobbs-Merrill Co., 1929.

Trollope, Frances. *Domestic Manners of the Americans*. 1839. Reprint, Barre, Mass.: Imprint Society, 1969.

Tucker, Glenn. *Chickamauga: Bloody Battle of the West*. Indianapolis: Bobbs-Merrill Co., 1961.

Tutorow, Norman E. *Texas Annexation and the Mexican War: A Political Study of the Old Northwest*. Palo Alto, Calif.: Chadwick House, 1978.

Tyler, Ronnie C. *Santiago Vidaurri and the Southern Confederacy*. N.p.: Texas State Historical Association, 1973.

Van der Heuvel, Gerry. *Crowns of Thorns and Glory: Mary Todd Lincoln and Varina Howell Davis: The Two First Ladies of the Civil War*. New York: E. P. Dutton, 1988.

Van Deusen, Glyndon. *William Henry Seward*. New York: Oxford University Press, 1967.

Varg, Paul A. *United States Foreign Relations, 1820-1860*. East Lansing: Michigan State University Press, 1979.

Wade, Richard C. *The Urban Frontier: The Rise of the Western Cities, 1790-1830*. Cambridge, Mass.: Harvard University Press, 1959.

Walker, Henry. "Power, Sex, and Gender Roles: The Transformation of an Alabama Planter Family during the Civil War." In *Southern Families at War: Loyalty and Conflict in the Civil War South*. Edited by Catherine Clinton. New York: Oxford University Press, 2000.

Wall, Joseph F. *Henry Watterson: Reconstructed Rebel*. New York: Oxford University Press, 1956.

War of the Rebellion: A Compilation of Official Records of the Union and Confederate Armies. 129 vols. Washington, D.C.: Government Printing Office, 1880-1901.

Watterson, Henry. "The Hayes-Tilden Contest for the Presidency: The Inside History of a Great Political Crisis." *Century Magazine* 86 (1913): 3-21.

_____. *History of the Manhattan Club: A Narrative of the Activities of Half a Century*. New York: n.p., 1915.

_____. *"Marse Henry": An Autobiography*. 2 vols. 1919. Reprint, New York: Beckman Publishers, 1974.

Webb, Ross A. *Kentucky in the Reconstruction Era*. Lexington: University Press of Kentucky, 1979.

_____. "'The Past is Never Dead; It's Not Even Past': Benjamin P. Runkle and the Freedmen's Bureau in Kentucky, 1866-1870." *Register of the Kentucky Historical Society* 84 (1986): 343-60.

Weems, John E. *To Conquer a Peace: The War between the United States and Mexico*. Garden City, N.Y.: Doubleday and Co., 1974.

Weigley, Russell F. *A Great Civil War: A Military and Political History, 1861-1865*. Bloomington: Indiana University Press, 2000.

Welsh, Jack D. *Medical Histories of Confederate Generals*. Kent, Ohio: Kent State University Press, 1995.

Wert, Jeffry D. *General James Longstreet: The Confederacy's Most Controversial Soldier*. New York: Simon and Schuster, 1993.

Wiley, Bell I. *Embattled Confederates: An Illustrated History of Southerners at War*. New York: Harper and Row, 1964.

Williams, T. Harry. "The Military Leadership of North and South." In *Why the North Won the Civil War*. Edited by David Donald, 33-54. Baton Rouge: Louisiana State University Press, 1960.

Winders, Richard B. *Mr. Polk's Army: The American Military Experience and the Mexican War*. College Station: Texas A&M University Press, 1997.

Wise, Stephen R. *Lifeline of the Confederacy: Blockade Running during the Civil War*. Columbia: University of South Carolina Press, 1988.

Woodward, C. Vann. *Reunion and Reaction: The Compromise of 1877 and the End of Reconstruc-*

Bibliography

tion. Boston: Little, Brown, 1951.

Woodworth, Steven E. *Jefferson Davis and his Generals: The Failure of Confederate Command in the West.* Lawrence: University of Kansas Press, 1990.

_____. *No Band of Brothers: Problems in the Rebel High Command.* Columbia: University of Missouri Press, 1999.

_____. *Six Armies in Tennessee: The Chickamauga and Chattanooga Campaigns.* Lincoln: University of Nebraska Press, 1998.

Worthington, Thomas. *Shiloh: Or the Tennessee Campaign of 1862.* Washington, D.C.: M'Gill and Witherow Printers, 1872.

Wright, George C. *Racial Violence in Kentucky, 1865-1940: Lynchings, Mob Rule, and "Legal Lynchings."* Baton Rouge: Louisiana State University Press, 1990.

Wright, John D. *Lexington: Heart of the Bluegrass.* Lexington: Lexington-Fayette County Historic Commission, 1982.

Wyatt-Brown, Bertram. *Southern Honor: Ethics and Behavior in the Old South.* New York: Oxford University Press, 1982.

Yáñez, Agustín. *Santa Anna: Espectro de una sociedad.* Mexico City: Ediciones Océano, S.A., 1985.

Yater, George H. *Two Hundred Years at the Falls of the Ohio: A History of Louisville and Jefferson County.* Louisville: Heritage Corp., 1979.

Young, Bennett H. *History of the Texts of the Three Constitutions of Kentucky.* Louisville: *Courier-Journal,* 1890.

Unpublished Works

Alexander, Ronald R. "Central Kentucky during the Civil War, 1861-1865." Ph.D. diss., University of Kentucky, 1976.

Bentley, James R. "Calendar of the Preston Papers-Joyes Collection." M.A. thesis, College of William and Mary, 1972.

Congleton, Betty. "George Prentice and his Educational Policy." Ph.D. diss., University of Kentucky, 1961.

Dugan, John Louis. "James Guthrie: His Interests in Internal Improvements in Kentucky 1820-1869." M.A. thesis, University of Florida, 1952. Typescript at Filson Historical Society.

Durrett, Reuben T. "In Memoriam of William Preston." Paper delivered in 1887 at the Filson Club, Louisville, Ky.

Fayette County. "Taxbook." 1869.

Fields, Carl R. "Making Kentucky's Third Constitution, 1830-1850." Ph.D. diss., University of Kentucky, 1951.

Hollingsworth, Randolph. "She Used Her Power Lightly: A Political History of Margaret Wickliffe Preston of Kentucky." Ph.D. diss., University of Kentucky, 1999.

Johnston, William Preston. "My Father's Family." Mason-Barret Collection, Howard-Tilton Library, Tulane University, New Orleans, La.

Kramer, Carl E. "The Origins of the Subdivision Process in Louisville, 1772-1932." In "An Introduction to the Louisville Region: Selected Essays." Edited by Don E. Bierman. Mimeographed. Louisville, 1980.

Liebert, Tracy McMahan. "The Germans in Louisville, Kentucky, in the 19th Century." M.S. thesis, Georgetown University, 1993.

Logan, Lenor C. "Henry Watterson, Border Nationalist, 1840-1877." Ph.D. diss., Indiana University, 1942.

Mathias, Frank F. "The Turbulent Years of Kentucky Politics, 1820-1850." Ph.D. diss., University of Kentucky, 1966.

Owen, Thomas L. "The Formative Years of Kentucky's Republican Party, 1864-1871." Ph.D. diss., University of Kentucky, 1981.

Paine, Christopher M. "'Kentucky Will Be the Last to Give Up the Union': Kentucky Politics, 1844-1861." Ph.D. diss., University of Kentucky, 1998.

Preston, William. "Journal in Mexico." 1848. Handwritten copy made by William Preston Johnston. Mason-Barret Collection, Howard-Tilton Library, Tulane University. Typescript,

Bibliography

made by Preston Brown, at Filson Historical Society. Manuscript was also privately printed as *Journal in Mexico*.

Ramage, Andrea S. "Bluegrass Patriarch: Robert Wickliffe and His Family in Antebellum Kentucky." M.A. thesis, University of Kentucky, 1993.

Sullivan, James P. "Civic and Business Advancements in Louisville's Rioting Decade 1850-1860." M.A. thesis, University of Louisville, 1958.

Terry, Gail S. "Family Empires: A Frontier Elite in Virginia and Kentucky, 1740-1815." Ph.D. diss., College of William and Mary, 1992.

Turner, Wallace. "Kentucky in a Decade of Change, 1850-1860." Ph.D. diss., University of Kentucky, 1954.

Watkins, Andrea S. "Patriarchical Politics: Robert Wickliffe and His Family in Antebellum Kentucky." Ph.D. diss., University of Kentucky, 1999.

Newspapers, Magazines, Journals, and Directories

La América (Madrid). Nov. 1858.

Boston Journal. May 1868.

Cincinnati Gazette. April 1865.

Congressional Globe. Washington, D.C. 32ᵈ Cong., 2ᵈ sess., 1852-53.

_____. 33ʳᵈ Cong., 1ˢᵗ sess., 1853-54.

_____. 35ᵗʰ Cong., 2ᵈ sess., 1858-59.

El Diario (Madrid). Jan. 1859.

Frankfort (Ky.) Tri-Weekly Kentucky Yeoman. June 1875.

Gazeta de Madrid. Jan.-June 1859, May 1861.

Harper's Weekly. July 1880.

Journal of the Congress of the Confederate States. Vol. 2. Washington, D.C., 1904.

Journal of the House of Representatives of the Commonwealth of Kentucky. Frankfort, 1850.

Lexington (Ky.) Daily Leader. Feb. 1898.

Lexington (Ky.) Daily Transcript. Aug. 1883.

Lexington Kentucky Gazette. Jan.-Dec. 1867, Jan.-Dec. 1868, Jan.-July 1869, Jan.-July 1870, Jan. 1871, Sept. 1874.

Lexington (Ky.) Leader. Sept. 1887, June 1914, June 1938.

Louisville Anzeiger. Nov. 1852, 1855.

Louisville Courier-Journal. June 1875, Sept.-Oct. 1887, Feb. 1888, Feb. 1898, July 1917, March 1922.

Louisville Daily Courier. Feb., May 1850, July-Dec. 1851, Jan.-Dec. 1852, July-Dec. 1853, Aug. 1855, July 1857, Jan.-June 1859.

Louisville Daily Democrat. July-Dec.1853, July-Aug. 1855, June-July 1857.

Louisville Daily Journal. July-Dec. 1850, Aug. 1855, July 1857.

Louisville Directory for the Year . . . (and various other titles) 1832, 1836, 1838-39, 1841, 1843-44, 1844, 1845-46, 1848, 1848-49, 1851-52, 1855-56, 1858-59, 1859-60, 1883.

Louisville Journal. March 1852, April 1855.

Louisville Morning Courier. Aug.-Nov. 1849, July-Dec. 1850.

Louisville Times. March 1940.

Mexican Times (Mexico City). Sept. 1865-June 1867.

La Nation (Paris). 1864.

National Police Gazette. 26 Dec. 1885.

New York Herald. Jan.-March 1861.

New York Times. Jan.-March 1859.

La Patrie (Paris). 1864.

El Público (Madrid). April 1861.

Revue de la Quinzaine de l'Estafette (Mexico City). July 1865.

Richmond (Va.) Enquirer. Jan.-June 1864.

Richmond (Va.) Sentinel. Oct. 1863

The Times (London). Dec.-Jan. 1858-59, Nov. 1863.

Trait d'Union (Mexico City). 1861, 1864.

Washington (D.C.) Constitution. June 1859.

Washington Union. Dec. 1858.

Index

Abingdon (Va.), 132, 147, 148, 156, 161
abolitionists, 36, 38-39, 54, 83, 85, 94, 100, 111, 129-30. *See also* emancipationists
Abraham Masonic Lodge No. 8, 78
Adams, John Quincy, 100, 111
Alexis, Grand Duke (of Russia), 221
Allen, Henry, 188
Allen, James L., x
Allen, R. T. P., 200
Altamonte, Juan Nepomuk, 171, 172, 174, 175, 179, 180, 184
Ambruster, William, 90
Ambruster Brewery, 89
La América (Madrid), 104
American Colonization Society, 38, 39
American Medical Association, 210
American party, 86-90, 95-97, 146, 191
American Revolution, 4, 7, 9, 11, 55, 56
La Amistad: abolitionists' defense of mutineers on, 111; Africans' mutiny on, 110-11; Republican opposition to settlement of claims for, 111, 113, 117; Spanish claims for, 111-13, 117
Anderson, Edward, 131
Anderson, Thomas L., 112
Anglin, Timothy, 196
antislavery. *See* abolitionists; emancipationists
Ariosto, 25
Army of Tennessee, 139, 141, 149, 152, 155, 156
Arrangoiz, F. de, 174, 178
Arthur, Chester A., 221
Arthur, Mrs. Chester A., 221
Augusta College, 19, 20
Augusta County (Va.), 2, 3
Austin (Tex.), 213
Aztec Club, 61-62, 220

Bahamas, 179, 188
Bancroft, George, 177
Bank of Kentucky, 11, 163
Bank of Louisville, 28, 44
Barbee, John, 87, 90
Bardstown (Ky.), xvi, 10, 19, 21, 52, 76, 140
Bar Harbor (Me.), 210
Baring Brothers Bank, 102
Barnum, P.T., 69

Bath County (Ky.), 159, 162, 164, 196, 206
Bayard, Thomas F., 220
Beauclerk, Charles. *See* Saint Alban, Duke of
Beauclerk, Laura. *See* Saint Alban, Duchess of
Beauclerk, Preston, 213
Beauclerk, Thomas Wentworth Sydney, 123, 127, 186, 200, 202, 213
Beauregard, A. M. Toutant, 181
Beauregard, Pierre Gustave Toutant, 135, 137, 138
Beck, James B., 215
Belknap, William B., 43, 45
Bell, John, 126
Belmont, August, 98, 101, 220
Benjamin, Judah P.: decides Britain will not recognize Confederacy, 178; decides France will not recognize Confederacy, 179; gives instructions to Preston, 175-76; and Mexican interests, 175; opposes Preston's diplomacy, 182, 184-85; overestimates importance of cotton, 185; qualifications of as diplomat, 185; mentioned, 98, 174, 180, 183, 190
Bennett, John A., 170
Benton, Elizabeth Preston McDowell (cousin), 12, 191
Benton, Thomas Hart, ix, 12, 191
Berea, 74
Bermuda, 179, 186, 190
Birney, James G., 39
Blackburn, J. C. S., 219
Blackburn, Joseph, 147
Blacksburg (Va.), 6
Blair, Francis Preston, Sr., 92, 93
Blair, Francis Preston, Jr., 215
Blair, Montgomery, 191
"Bloody Monday," 89-90, 96
Bob (Preston's slave), 61
Bocanegra, José María de, 62
Boonesborough, 3
Boston (Mass.), 28, 50, 208
Botetourt County (Va.), 3
Bourbon County (Ky.), 73
Bowling Green (Ky.), 131, 132, 133, 138
Boyle, Jeremiah T., 162
"Boy Peter." *See* Thompson, "Boy Peter"

www.ingramcontent.com/pod-product-compliance
Lightning Source LLC
Chambersburg PA
CBHW030531100426
42813CB00001B/218

* 9 7 8 0 9 1 6 9 6 8 3 3 5 *